THE ULTIMATE WINE COMPANION

THE COMPLETE GUIDE TO UNDERSTANDING WINE BY THE WORLD'S FOREMOST WINE AUTHORITIES

EDITED BY

KEVIN ZRALY

author of the best-selling *Windows on the World Complete Wine Course*

STERLING

New York / London

www.sterlingpublishing.com

To all writers, for taking readers to new heights—
and a special thank-you to all the wine and food writers
who have taken me on my path to wine wisdom.
You are all my teachers.

STERLING and the distinctive Sterling logo are registered trademarks of
Sterling Publishing Co., Inc.

Library of Congress Cataloging-in-Publication Data Available

2   4   6   8   10   9   7   5   3   1

Published by Sterling Publishing Co., Inc.
387 Park Avenue South, New York, NY 10016
© 2010 by Kevin Zraly
Map Illustrations by Jeffrey Ward
Distributed in Canada by Sterling Publishing
c/o Canadian Manda Group, 165 Dufferin Street
Toronto, Ontario, Canada M6K 3H6
Distributed in the United Kingdom by GMC Distribution Services
Castle Place, 166 High Street, Lewes, East Sussex, England BN7 1XU
Distributed in Australia by Capricorn Link (Australia) Pty. Ltd.
P.O. Box 704, Windsor, NSW 2756, Australia

Manufactured in the United States of America

BOOK DESIGN: RACHEL MALONEY

Sterling ISBN 978-1-4027-7666-3

For information about custom editions, special sales, premium and
corporate purchases, please contact Sterling Special Sales
Department at 800-805-5489 or specialsales@sterlingpublishing.com.

❧ CONTENTS ❧

⚜ INTRODUCTION ⚜

Kevin Zraly

I have read many books and articles over the forty years that I've been studying wine, and I've always found most to be informative and, for me, enjoyable reading. When I was approached by my publisher to edit a wine anthology I was thrilled with the idea. I grew up 30 miles north of New York City in a town called Pleasantville, which was the "home" of *Reader's Digest*. My grandmother worked there, which meant we would have copies of the magazine everywhere in our house. Even as a teenager it was quick and easy reading with valuable information. When I began to think about writing my first wine book, *Windows on the World Complete Wine Course,* I had the model of *Reader's Digest* in the back of my mind. That first book has gone on to become the best-selling wine book in the world with over 3 million copies sold. Its success was due in large part to the simplicity of presenting a difficult subject and making it easier to understand.

Every year I update the *Windows on the World* wine book and must read, as a research analyst, all the books, articles, and blogs to keep on top of the wine market. As a writer I know that sometimes you can find so much information just in the introduction of someone's book, and at other times some individual chapters stand out more than others.

For me, editing this book was great fun—a perfect opportunity to revisit the books and articles I read when I was a young man studying wine, and also catch up on the newest material that has recently been published.

It is with great pleasure to begin Part I of the book with three of the heavyweights in the wine world, Hugh Johnson, Robert M. Parker Jr., and Jancis Robinson.

One of the first books I ever read as a student of wine was by Hugh Johnson. In "The Power to Banish Care," from his book *The Story of Wine*, he explains the importance of wine/alcohol over the last 2,000 years and its relationship with food, its virtues, and why it is sometimes very expensive.

Robert M. Parker Jr., who told me recently that he tastes 7,500 wines a year (down from 10,000), gives us his definition of "what constitutes a great wine" from *Parker's Wine Buyer's Guide,* such as its ability to improve with age, to please the palate, and to offer a singular personality.

Jancis Robinson, along with Hugh Johnson, is one of the most prolific wine writers in the world. In "Capturing the Flavor" from the book *How to Taste: A Guide to Enjoying Wine,* she gives us a guide to enjoying wine by learning how to taste it, to finding your own wine language and vocabulary, and to such things as the difference between aroma and bouquet.

Frank Schoonmaker was one of the first and most vocal proponents of varietal labeling in the United States. "American

Names for American Wines" was written in 1941, seven years after the repeal of Prohibition, and it sets the tone for where California is today.

To understand wines from around the world, it is important to have a grasp of the flavors of all different grape varieties. In Oz Clarke's book *Let Me Tell You About Wine*, he gives us an informative guide to recognizing the great grapes of the world and where they are grown.

Gary Vaynerchuk is one of the new voices on wine. The excerpts from his first book, *Crush It!*, show his refreshing new approach to the business of wine.

In his piece on terroir from *Reflections of a Wine Merchant,* Neal I. Rosenthal takes on the difficult task of defining the word "terroir" and gives us his own view of old world wines versus new world wines.

In "Silent Revolution," by Gerald Asher, you will learn the pros and cons of being organic as well as biodynamic.

Joe DeLissio (Joey D, as his friends call him) developed a great wine program at the famous Brooklyn restaurant, The River Café. He describes the role of the "sommelier/ wine server" in this piece from *The River Café Wine Primer.*

I've added a short chapter in Part II on wine basics from *Windows on the World Complete Wine Course*, especially for anyone just starting out with wine. I felt it would be helpful in understanding some of the aspects of wine tasting.

I loved reading Lettie Teague's book, *Educating Peter*, which is filled with her wit, cynicism, and sense of fun. To help Peter understand wine better, she created a

tasting vocabulary for him. If you have ever wondered what the words "closed," "firm," "hot," and "mouth-feel" mean, I am sure you will enjoy Lettie's definitions.

What is it like to spend $25,000 on wine and food in a week? *Food & Wine* writer and hedonist Alan Richman tells us his tale of excess and expense while dining through some of the greatest restaurants in France.

What would it be like to taste old Burgundies? Ever wonder what a '46 Meursault Charmes would taste like? From *1846*? *New York Times* wine writer Eric Asimov did just that with the "venerable" producer and négociant Bouchard Père et Fils.

Blindfolded, would you be able to tell the difference between a red wine and a white wine? Humorist Calvin Trillin gives us the surprising answer.

One of my first teachers, Alexis Bespaloff, wrote a piece for *New York* magazine in 1977 about the still controversial subject of "does a wine improve with aeration?" What was his conclusion? You'll have fun reading about his experiment.

In Part III, Andrea Robinson's book *Great Wine Made Simple* sets the tone for understanding "foundation flavors" and "wine-loving foods." And I am sure that everyone will appreciate her wine, corn, and tomatoes discussion.

Evan Goldstein tackles the age-old question of what wine to pair with what foods in his new book *Daring Pairings*. This piece explains the five keys to recognizing how the major components of wine will affect the food you are eating.

Joshua Wesson and David Rosengarten provide a tasting that explains why some wines work better with certain foods in "The Great, the Bad, and the Average." Follow along to learn what flavors complement each other best.

Jay McInerney's piece from *A Hedonist in the Cellar* will take you on a chocolate high combined with Amarone, Port, and Late Harvest Zinfandel.

What is it like for a family to own and operate their own vineyard? In Molly Chappellet's piece from her book *A Vineyard Garden* you will feel the excitement, energy, and the great food and wine that come out of helping her family business.

For Part IV, in his piece from *Harvests of Joy*, Robert Mondavi tells about his early years, including lessons learned from his mother, and how he first learned to taste and appreciate wine.

Steven Kolpan, author and teacher, and Francis Ford Coppola, writer and director, are both passionate about wine. They tell the story of the purchase of the famous Inglenook Estate in Napa Valley in these pieces from *A Sense of Place*.

Baron Philippe de Rothschild (of Château Mouton-Rothschild) was one of the most important vineyard owners in the history of Bordeaux, and he takes us through his first season of the vine, month by month, in this piece from *Baron Philippe: The Very Candid Autobiography of Baron Philippe de Rothschild*.

"Harvest and Winemaking," from *A Cultivated Life* by Joy Sterling of Iron Horse Vineyards, gives a great introduction to the process of winemaking told in real terms, not technical, with Pinot Noir, Chardonnay, and sparkling wine production.

Starting off Part V, Michael Broadbent decided to write something original for his

contribution to this collection. In a few short pages, he is able to give you an overview of why Bordeaux is the greatest wine region in the world.

Alexis Lichine, in "Shall the Order Change? The Case for Reclassification," from *Alexis Lichine's Guide to the Wines and Vineyards of France*, questions the validity of the famous Bordeaux 1855 Classification, and replaces it with his own version.

If you are a Burgundy wine lover, Clive Coates's understanding of this region will take you on a quick, but complete, history of Burgundy with very interesting facts, anecdotes, and trivia, from his *Wines of Burgundy*.

Kermit Lynch is the ultimate storyteller, and the southern Rhône Valley comes to life with the soil, slopes, stones, and Grenache grape that create the great wine Châteauneuf-du-Pape. Through Henri Brunier, owner of Vieux Télégraphe, this story is told. You must have a glass of their wine when reading this chapter from *Adventures on the Wine Route*.

Ever wonder about the different styles of Champagne? Tom Stevenson explains all the different ways Champagne is produced in "Putting on the Style."

Vino Italiano, by Joseph Bastianich and David Lynch, is one of the best books written on Italian wine in recent years. In their chapter "Toscana: The Center of the Italian Wine Universe," you will learn how to catch a wild boar, the origins of the Sangiovese grape, the origin of Super Tuscans, the changing style of Chianti, the development of Brunello di Montalcino, and where Vino Nobile di Montelpulciano fits into the hierarchy of Tuscan wines.

Mary Ewing-Mulligan and Ed McCarthy are the authors of *Italian Wine for Dummies*. They are two well-known wine educators, and they have contributed a piece on Piedmont.

Understanding German wines can be daunting due to the hundreds of different villages and vineyards. German wine expert Peter Sichel helps to break down all of the intricacies you need to know without overwhelming you, with his edits to Frank Schoonmaker's original text.

In his piece, "Spanish Wine: A Brief History," John Radford takes us on a journey from the early history of Spanish wine to the "New" Spain.

Prepare to be immersed in the Duoro Valley in "Postcard from Porto." Mike DeSimone and Jeff Jenssen write about the history of the region, as well as describe what it's like to be entertained by the winemakers there. Get ready to stomp some grapes!

In Frank Prial's article that starts off Part VI, "The Day California Shook the World," you will learn the real story for the film *Bottle Shock* and the famous 1976 Judgment of Paris wine tasting.

From Karen MacNeil's *Wine Bible* you will understand why the residents of Napa Valley have an appetite for life and a hunger for success, all within a thirty-mile radius.

In Matt Kramer's *New California Wine*, he explains why it has taken Sonoma so long to catch up to its neighbor, Napa. It is both a lesson in sociology and winemaking. He puts a pulse on Sonoma through historical events.

Tony Aspler, the expert on Canadian wines, explores the process of making Ice Wine and why Canada is the largest producer in the world of this very special wine, from his book *Vintage Canada*.

Christopher Fielden gives us a history of winemaking in Argentina, from the mid-sixteenth century to the great Malbecs that are being produced today, from *The Wines of Argentina, Chile, and Latin America*.

"The Wines of Chile," by Peter Richards, describes the country of Chile through its landscape of mountains and oceans that Isabel Allende describes as "poetry in motion."

In "Climate," from *The Wine Atlas of Australia*, James Halliday writes about Australia's climate and weather, distinguishing the wine regions from each other.

Campbell Mattinson poses the question "Penfolds Grange: Australia's Best Wine?" and relays back his findings, while taking you through the close history of the famous wine.

"A Recent Overview of the South African Wine Industry" by Andrew Jefford and Michael Fridjhon will take you from apartheid to the new South Africa, and update you on all of the great wine being made there.

Within these pages, you will discover why wine has become my life's work and my life's passion. I hope that this collection will become your premier guide in learning to appreciate and love wine as much as I do.

Cheers,
Kevin

PART I

THOUGHTS ON WINE

THOUGHTS ON WINE

THERE'S A LOT TO KNOW ABOUT WINE. Actually there's too much to know! Last year I traveled to 15 countries, 400 wine regions, and tasted thousands of wines updating the 25th Anniversary Edition of *Windows on the World Complete Wine Course*.

The "good news" is that we are living in the Golden Age of Wine. We are at the zenith in the history of winemaking. When I started studying wines forty years ago it was all about French wines, and maybe a smidgeon about German wines. But that's all you studied.

The "bad news" is there is more to know than ever before. Walking into a retail store today with a 6,000-plus wine selection to choose from, how does the consumer decide? In order to understand the world of wine today I have to know Pinot Noirs from New Zealand, Pinotage from South Africa, Malbecs from Argentina, and then also revisit and reacquaint myself with the great wine regions of France, Italy, Spain, and Germany, as well as California, on a vintage basis.

More than 300 years worth of wine experience are summed up just by the writers in this section. They attempt to answer some of the most important questions about wine. These passionate and well-traveled people are guides in the very large world of wine. Their answers are based on their palates and experience. In the end, each of us will have to find out the answers for ourselves.

—*KZ*

THE POWER TO BANISH CARE

Hugh Johnson

It was not the subtle bouquet of wine, or a lingering aftertaste of violets and raspberries, that first caught the attention of our ancestors. It was, I'm afraid, its effect.

In a life that was "nasty, brutish, and short," those who first felt the effects of alcohol believed they were being given a preview of paradise. Their anxieties disappeared, their fears receded, ideas came more easily, lovers became more loving when they drank the magic juice. For a while they felt all-powerful, even felt themselves to be gods. Then they were sick, or passed out, and woke up with a horrible headache. But the feeling while it lasted was too good to resist another try—and the hangover, they found, was only a temporary disease. By drinking more slowly, you could enjoy the benefits without suffering the discomforts.

Wine provided the first experience of alcohol only for a privileged minority of the human race. For the great majority it was ale. Most of the earliest cities grew up in the grain- rather than grape-growing lands of the Near East: Mesopotamia and Egypt. Although ancient Egypt made strenuous efforts to grow good wine, only a minority had access to it.

But wine was always the choice of the privileged. Mesopotamia imported what it could not make itself. Why should this be? A simple and cynical answer is that wine is usually stronger than ale. It also kept longer, and (sometimes) improved with keeping. One can hardly state categorically that it always tasted better. All we can say for sure is that it was valued more highly.

Other foods and drinks had mind- (and body-) altering effects. Primitive people were acutely aware of poisons. But whatever spirit was in this drink, mysterious as the wind, was benevolent; was surely, indeed, divine. Wine, they found, had a power and value far greater than ale and quite unlike hallucinatory drugs. Its history pivots around this value.

It is only appropriate that this book begins with the world's best-selling wine writer. Hugh Johnson has been writing about wine since 1960 and wrote his first book, Wine, *in 1966 followed by* The World Atlas of Wine *in 1971. He has also been publishing* Hugh Johnson's Pocket Wine Guide *annually since 1977. Both of his first two books were instrumental in my early education of wine. Outside of wine he is a horticulturist and wrote a book called* The Principles of Gardening.

What is wine, and what are its effects? What has made men from the first recorded time distinguish between wines as they have done with no other food or drink? Why does wine have a history that involves drama and politics, religions and wars? And why, to the dismay of young men on first dates, do there have to be so many different kinds? Only history can explain.

The polite, conventional definition of wine is "the naturally fermented juice of fresh grapes." A more clinical one is an aqueous solution of ethanol with greater or lesser traces of sugars, acids, esters, acetates, lactates, and other substances occurring in grape juice or derived from it by fermentation. It is the ethanol that produces the obvious effect. What is ethanol? A form of alcohol produced by the action of yeasts on sugar—in this case, grape sugar.

Ethanol is clinically described as a depressant, a confusing term because depression is not in the least what you feel. What it depresses ("inhibits" makes it clearer) is the central nervous system. The effect is sedation, the lifting of inhibitions, the dulling of pain. The feeling of well-being it brings may be illusory, but it is not something you swallow with your wine: your wine simply allows your natural feelings to manifest themselves.

What is true of wine is true of other alcoholic drinks—up to a point. Ethanol is the principal active component in them all. Its effects, though, are significantly modified by other components—in other words, the differences between wine and beer, or wine and distilled spirits. Little that is conclusive about these differences has yet been discovered by scientific experiment. We are talking about tiny traces of substances whose precise effect is very difficult to monitor through the complexities of human responses. But much that is clearly indicative has accumulated over centuries of usage.

Wine has certain properties that mattered much more to our ancestors than they do to ourselves. For 2,000 years of medical and surgical history it was the universal and unique antiseptic. Wounds were bathed with it; water made safe to drink.

Medically, wine was indispensable until the later years of the nineteenth century. In the words of the Jewish Talmud, "Wherever wine is lacking, drugs become necessary." A contemporary (sixth century BC) Indian medical text describes wine as the "invigorator of mind and body, antidote to sleeplessness, sorrow and fatigue . . . producer of hunger, happiness and digestion." Enlightened medical opinion today uses very similar terms about its specific clinical virtues, particularly in relation to heart disease. Even Muslim physicians risked the wrath of Allah rather than do without their one sure help in treatment.

But wine had other virtues. Not only does the natural fermentation of the grape produce a drink that is about one-tenth to one-eighth alcohol, but its other constituents, acids and tannins in particular, also make it brisk and refreshing, with a satisfying "cut" as it enters your mouth, and a lingering clean flavor that invites you to drink again. In the volume of its flavor, and the natural size of a swallow (half the size of a swallow of ale), it makes the perfect drink with food, adding its own seasoning, cutting the richness of fat, making meat seem more tender,

4

and washing down dry pulses and unleavened bread without distending the belly.

Because wine lives so happily with food, and at the same time lowers inhibitions, it was recognized from earliest times as the sociable drink, able to turn a meal into a feast without stupefying (although stupefy it often did). But even stupefied feasters were ready for more the next day. Wine is the most repeatable of mild narcotics without ill effects—at least in the short or medium term. Modern medicine knows that wine helps the assimilation of nutrients (proteins especially) in our food. Moderate wine drinkers found themselves better nourished, more confident, and consequently often more capable than their fellows. It is no wonder that in many early societies the ruling classes decided that only they were worthy of such benefits and kept wine to themselves.

The catalogue of wine's virtues, and its value to developing civilization, does not end there. Bulky though it is, and often perishable, it made the almost perfect commodity for trade. It had immediate attraction (as soon as they felt its effects) for strangers who did not know it. The Greeks were able to trade wine for precious metals, the Romans for slaves, with a success that has a sinister echo in the activities of modern drug pushers—except that there is nothing remotely sinister about wine.

In this sense it is true to say that wine advanced the progress of civilization. It facilitated the contacts between distant cultures, providing the motive and means of trade, and bringing strangers together in high spirits and with open minds. Of course, it also carried the risk of abuse. Alcohol can be devastating to health. Yet if it had been widely and consistently abused it would not have been tolerated. Wine, unlike spirits, has long been considered the drink of moderation.

Even at its most primitive, wine is subject to enormous variations. Climate is the first determining factor; then weather. The competence of the winemaker comes next; then the selection of the grape. Underlying these variables is the composition of the soil and its situation. The key word is selection: of grape varieties, yes, but also of a "clone," a race of vines propagated from cuttings of the best plants in the vineyard. Then restraint in production: to produce only a moderate number of bunches, whose juice will have more flavor than the fruit of an overladen vine. In the ancient world such practices probably first developed in the sheltered economy of royal or priestly vineyards. But the principle has not changed. Selection of the best for each set of circumstances has given us the several thousand varieties of grape which are, or have been, grown in the course of history.

Taking this panoramic view, the discovery that must have done most to advance wine in the esteem of the rulers of the earth was the fact that it could improve with keeping—and not just improve, but at best turn into a substance with ethereal dimensions seeming to approach the sublime. Beaujolais Nouveau is all very well (and most ancient wine was something between this and vinegar), but once you have tasted an old vintage Burgundy you know the difference between tinsel and gold. To be able to store wine, the best wine, until maturity performed this alchemy was the privilege of pharaohs.

5

It was wonderful enough that grape juice should develop an apparent soul of its own. That it should be capable, in the right circumstances, of transmuting its vigorous spirit into something of immeasurably greater worth made it a god-like gift for kings. If wine has a prestige unique among drinks—unique, indeed, among natural products—it

stems from this fact and the connoisseurship it engenders.

How can a rare bottle of wine fetch the price of a great work of art? Can it, however perfect, smell more beautiful than a rose?

No, must surely be the honest answer. But what if, deep in the flushing velvet of its petals, the rose contained the power to banish care?

WHAT CONSTITUTES A GREAT WINE?

Robert M. Parker Jr.

What is a great wine? This is one of the most controversial subjects of the vinous world. Isn't greatness in wine, much like a profound expression of art or music, something very personal and subjective? As much as I agree that the appreciation and enjoyment of art, music, or wine is indeed personal, high quality in wine, as in art and music, does tend to be subject to widespread agreement. Except for the occasional contrarian, greatness in art, music, or wine, though difficult to define precisely, enjoys a broad consensus.

Many of the most legendary wines of this century—1945 Mouton-Rothschild, 1945 Haut-Brion, 1947 Cheval Blanc, 1947 Pétrus, 1961 Latour, 1982 Mouton-Rothschild, 1982 Le Pin, 1982 Léoville–Las Cases, 1989 Haut-Brion, 1990 Margaux, and 1990 Pétrus, to name some of the most renowned red Bordeaux—are profound and riveting wines,

even though an occasional discordant view about them may surface. Tasting is indeed subjective, but like most of the finest things

Robert Parker's wine interest started on a visit to France with his girlfriend (now his wife) in 1967. Bob created a consumer guide about wine in 1975 and three years later the guide became known as The Wine Advocate. Since then he has written fourteen books on wine and his wine review website www .erobertparker.com, is the number-one visited wine website in the world. The British publication Decanter *magazine named him the number-one most powerful wine person in the world in 2009. I have had the pleasure of working and tasting great wines with Bob over the last five years and working together on an educational project, "The Parker and Zraly Wine Certification Program," an online wine course.*

in life, though there is considerable agreement as to what represents high quality, no one should feel forced to feign fondness for a work of Picasso or Beethoven, much less a bottle of 1961 Latour.

One issue about the world's finest wines that is subject to little controversy relates to how such wines originate. Frankly, there are no secrets about the origin and production of the world's finest wines. Great wines emanate from well-placed vineyards with microclimates favorable to the specific types of grapes grown. Profound wines, whether from France, Italy, Spain, California, or Australia, are also the product of conservative viticultural practices that emphasize low yields and physiologically rather than analytically ripe fruit. After 24 years spent

tasting more than 200,000 wines, I have never tasted a superb wine that was made from underripe fruit. Does anyone enjoy the flavors present when biting into an underripe orange, peach, apricot, or cherry? Low yields and ripe fruit are essential for the production of extraordinary wines, yet it is amazing how many wineries seem not to understand this fundamental principle.

In addition to the commonsense approach of harvesting mature (ripe) fruit and discouraging, in a viticultural sense, the vine from overproducing, the philosophy employed by a winery in making wine is of paramount importance. Exceptional wines (whether red, white, or sparkling) emerge from a similar philosophy, which includes the following: 1) permit the vineyard's *terroir* (soil, microclimate, distinctiveness) to express itself; 2) allow the purity and characteristics of the grape variety or blend to be represented faithfully in the wine; and 3) follow an uncompromising, noninterventionalistic winemaking philosophy that eschews the food-processing, industrial mind-set of high-tech winemaking—in short, give the wine a chance to make itself naturally without the human element attempting to sculpt or alter the wine's intrinsic character, so that what is placed in the bottle represents as natural an expression of the vineyard, variety, and vintage as is possible. In keeping with this overall philosophy, winemakers who attempt to reduce traumatic clarification procedures such as fining and filtration, while also lowering sulfur levels (which can dry out a wine's fruit, bleach color from a wine, and exacerbate the tannin's sharpness) produce wines with far more aromatics and flavors, as well as more enthralling textures. These are wines that offer consumers their most compelling and rewarding drinking experiences.

Assuming there is a relatively broad consensus as to how the world's finest wines originate, what follows is my working definition of an exceptional wine. In short, what are the characteristics of a great wine?

THE ABILITY TO PLEASE BOTH THE PALATE AND THE INTELLECT Great wines offer satisfaction on a hedonistic level and also challenge and satiate the intellect. The world offers many delicious wines that appeal to the senses but are not complex. The ability to satisfy the intellect is a more subjective issue. Wines that experts call "complex" are those that offer multiple dimensions in both their aromatic and flavor profiles, and have more going for them than simply ripe fruit and a satisfying, pleasurable, yet one-dimensional quality.

THE ABILITY TO HOLD THE TASTER'S INTEREST I have often remarked that the greatest wines I've ever tasted could easily be recognized by bouquet alone. These profound wines could never be called monochromatic or simple. They hold the taster's interest, not only providing the initial tantalizing tease but possessing a magnetic attraction because of their aromatic intensity and nuance-filled layers of flavors.

THE ABILITY OF A WINE TO OFFER INTENSE AROMAS AND FLAVORS WITHOUT HEAVINESS An analogy can be made to eating in the finest restaurants. Extraordinary cooking is characterized by its purity,

intensity, balance, texture, and compelling aromas and flavors. What separates exceptional cuisine from merely good cooking, and great wines from good wines, is their ability to offer extraordinary intensity of flavor without heaviness. It has been easy in the New World (especially in Australia and California) to produce wines that are oversized, bold, big, rich, but heavy. Europe's finest wineries, with many centuries more experience, have mastered the ability to obtain intense flavors without heaviness. However, New World viticultural areas (particularly in California) are quickly catching up, as evidenced by the succession of remarkable wines produced in Napa, Sonoma, and elsewhere in the Golden State during the 1990s. Many of California's greatest wines of the 1990s have sacrificed none of their power and richness but no longer possess the rustic tannin and oafish feel on the palate that characterized so many of their predecessors of 10 and 20 years ago.

THE ABILITY OF A WINE TO TASTE BETTER WITH EACH SIP Most of the finest wines I have ever drunk were better with the last sip than the first, revealing more nuances and more complex aromas and flavors as the wine unfolded in the glass. Do readers ever wonder why the most interesting and satisfying glass of wine is often the last one in the bottle?

THE ABILITY OF A WINE TO IMPROVE WITH AGE This is, for better or worse, an indisputable characteristic of great wines. One of the unhealthy legacies of the European wine writers (who dominated wine writing until the last decade) is the belief that in order for a wine to be exceptional when mature, it had to be nasty when young. My experience has revealed just the opposite—wines that are acidic, astringent, and generally fruitless and charmless when young become even nastier and less drinkable when old. That being said, it is true that new vintages of top wines are often unformed and in need of 10 to 12 years of cellaring (for top California Cabernets, Bordeaux, and Rhônes), but those wines should always possess a certain accessibility so that even inexperienced wine tasters can tell the wine is—at minimum—made from very ripe fruit. If a wine does not exhibit ripeness and richness of fruit when young, it will not develop nuances with aging. Great wines unquestionably improve with age. I define "improvement" as the ability of a wine to become significantly more enjoyable and interesting in the bottle, offering more pleasure when old than when it was young. Many wineries (especially in the New World) produce wines they claim "will age," but this is nothing more than a public relations ploy. What they should really say is that they "will

survive." They can endure 10 to 20 years of bottle age, but they were more enjoyable in their exuberant youthfulness.

THE ABILITY OF A WINE TO OFFER A SINGULAR PERSONALITY Their singular personalities set the greatest wines apart from all others. It is the same with the greatest vintages. Descriptions such as "classic vintage" have become nothing more than a reference to what a viticultural region does in a typical (normal) year. Exceptional wines from exceptional vintages stand far above the norm, and they can always be defined by their singular qualities— both aromatically and in their flavors and textures. The opulent, sumptuous qualities of the 1982 and 1990 red Bordeaux; the rugged tannin and immense ageability of the 1986 red Bordeaux; the seamless, perfectly balanced 1994 Napa and Sonoma Cabernet Sauvignons and proprietary blends; and the plush, sweet fruit, high alcohol and glycerin of the 1990 Barolos and Barbarescos—all are examples of vintage individuality.

CAPTURING THE FLAVOR

Jancis Robinson

Wine's great attraction is that, more than any other drink, it is capable of an amazing range of flavors—particularly when one considers that there is only one raw ingredient. (Imagine smart societies devoted to tasting different vintages of fermented carrot juice, or specialist gourmet tours of potato warehouses.)

[…] Our taste buds are capable of receiving only the fairly crude messages that the liquid wine can transmit. The really interesting part, the wine's character that we call its flavor, is carried by the volatile elements— up through the nose when we sniff and up from the back of the mouth when we taste— to the olfactory center, the ultra-sensitive mechanism that deals with flavor. The vapor of the wine consists of the volatile molecules that form only a tiny but vital proportion of each wine's composition. It is the particular profile of these molecules that makes up each wine's flavor, and to experience this flavor fully it does, of course, make sense to get the vapor up to the olfactory center by consciously smelling or "nosing" the wine.

THE WORDS TO SAY IT

Now for the problem: how to describe wine flavor. "Mmm, delicious," or even "Urggh" will do perfectly well—if you never want to communicate with anyone else about wine, if you see no need to remember anything about specific wines, or if you choose not to enjoy the pleasures of comparison and monitoring that wine can offer. [You], however, will already have decided that you are interested in tasting wine properly, in order to assess it and to enjoy it more—possibly even with a view to blind tasting. What you will find is how frustrating it is to be confronted by a wide and thrilling range of sensations for which there is no cut-and-dried notation or vocabulary.

Like many of us, including myself, it was a great Burgundy that changed Jancis Robinson's life. She has been writing about wine since 1975 and achieved her Master of Wine title in 1984. Jancis has won every prestigious wine award in the world and continues to be a great presence through her excellent speaking skills, and to date she has written more than twenty books on wine including her monumental book of over 800 pages, The Oxford Companion to Wine.

Music lovers know perfectly well what is meant by middle C and *fortissimo*. Connoisseurs of the visual arts agree on what is meant by square and (more or less) scarlet. For wine tasters, however, there is no objective vocabulary or measurement of something as simple and distinctive as the flavor of the Gamay grape, say; let alone for the nuances from the various other factors that paint the "palate picture," such as the soil the grapes were grown in, the weather that led up to the harvest, and the way the wine was made and stored.

FINDING PARALLELS

An accepted vocabulary would clearly be very useful for wine tasters, and considerable efforts are being made to agree on one. Each nation has their accepted tasting terms, but there is no way of extracting and comparing the sensory impression each of us associates with a given word because the business of tasting is so essentially hidden and subjective. (We each have slightly different tasting equipment and sensitivities.)

Some work has been done by an enterprising Burgundian, Jean Lenoir, to come up with definitive essences representing in a very concrete and indisputable way exactly what each term "smells" like. The Burgundian

has even marketed a little box of vials under the brand name "Le Nez du Vin" so that, as you taste a wine, you can smartly refer to the essence bank to see whether you are right to describe it as "woody" or as "violets." But there are curious disparities between different nationalities and which flavors they associate with wine. In South Africa, for example, "guava" is a common tasting note. Californians are more likely to spot "bell pepper." The more traditional French tasters go in for long lists of scents, such as "acacia," "toast," "honey," and "chocolate"; while Australians are more likely to dissect a wine into component chemicals, such as aldehydes and sulfides. As most of these examples suggest, choosing words to describe wine is largely a matter of making comparisons with things that are not wine. [There are] suggested terms such as "medium dry," "full-bodied," and "soft," which are fairly widely accepted conventions for describing some of wine's more obvious dimensions, the sorts of things that can be detected in the mouth rather than by the nose. When it comes to something as subtle as the wine's flavor, however, finding suitable descriptions is more difficult. It's a bit like the difference between describing someone's physical attributes (height, complexion, and so on) and their character. Tasters tend to look for similarities to other flavors they've experienced or can imagine. Sometimes accepted tasting terms bear only the loosest of similarities to the flavors whose names they carry. The distinctive smell of the Gewürztraminer grape is commonly called by wine professionals "spicy." This is not because Gewürz smells like any particular spice, but because Gewürz is German for "spiced" and the tasting term "spicy" has become a convenient and accepted shorthand, or "trigger word," for the smell of Gewürz.

WHAT WORKS FOR YOU

You can evolve your own wine-tasting vocabulary. If a wine smells like clean sheets or tennis balls to you, then register the connection. It may help you to identify flavors and wines later on. All you need is a term that leads you from a sniff of the wine to recognition or a judgment of it. We all have our own trigger words for various flavors [. . .] It will be useful, but not essential, if your vocabulary is like that of other people. Non-professionals can make up their own rules for the game of wine tasting—though people in the wine trade who attempt its stiffest test, the Master of Wine examinations, are expected to use commonly accepted terms. [. . .] At this early stage it is useful to distinguish between the words "aroma" and "bouquet." The relatively simple smell of a young wine is described as an aroma, but as it ages in the bottle and develops a more complex set of smells, this combination is known as its bouquet.

COMMON WINE AROMAS

Microbiological	Mineral	Earthy	Fruity		Vegetal
Lactic	Flint	Undergrowth	Lemon	Blackcurrant	Grassy
Buttery	Wet stones	Mold	Lime	Gooseberry	Nettles
Yeasty	Petrol/kerosene	Dirty dishcloth	Grapefruit	Grape	Green pepper
			Orange	Raisin	Eucalyptus
Spicy	Animal	Sweet	Pineapple	Prune	Mint
Spicy	Cat's pee	Biscuit	Melon	Fig	Geranium leaves
Licorice	Mousey	Honey	Banana		Currant leaves
Black pepper	Meaty	Barleysugar	Lychee		Canned asparagus
Vanilla	Game	Caramel	Peach		Boiled cabbage
	Bacon fat	Molasses	Apricot		Tobacco
Woody	Leather	Chocolate	Apple		Straw
Wet wood			Pear		Tea
Oaky			Black cherry		
Cigar box	Burnt	Nutty	Mulberry		Floral
Pencil shavings	Smoky	Almond	Blackberry		Violet
Pine	Burning rubber	Marzipan	Raspberry		Elderflower
	Coffee	Coconut	Strawberry		Rose
	Burnt toast	Chestnut			Orange blossom
	Toasted bread	Hazelnuts			

Source: http://www.jancisrobinson.com

AMERICAN NAMES FOR AMERICAN WINES

Frank Schoonmaker

When the New Year came in with a hurrah (and confetti) and a huzzah (with horns), the average American wine producer was not out celebrating. He probably heaved a sigh of relief as we shut the door on 1940—his seventh lean year was over and done with, and it looked as if a few fat years—perhaps seven, certainly two or three—were on their way. Wine consumption, at long last, is on its way up in the United States, and people as a whole are beginning to show a genuine interest in American wine.

Seven years ago, at the time of Repeal, American wine producers had a chance such as few ever get: this country had no drinking habits worthy of the name, people were favorably disposed toward wine, ready to try anything, and, after the Prohibition years, to accept anything good.

American vintners proceeded to muff the chance, miss the boat. This was largely their fault, but as we look back on December 1933 across the intervening years, we can see pretty clearly why the muff was made, why it was more or less inevitable, and why the United States did not become overnight (as a good many people rashly predicted it would) at least as much of a wine-drinking country as Argentina or Chile.

First, there were, in 1933, scarcely a dozen fine vineyards in North America. Plenty of raisin grapes, plenty of table grapes, but a pitifully few thousand acres of wine grapes. A good many California producers had torn up their superior vines during Prohibition and planted in their place the tough, common, heavy-bearing varieties then in demand as "juice grapes" for the home winemaker. A certain number of good vineyards had been simply abandoned.

Second, at the time of Repeal there was only an infinitesimal amount of good,

I have been very fortunate to meet and taste wine with some of the best wine writers in the world. Unfortunately I never had the opportunity to meet Frank Schoonmaker. The first book I ever read on wine as a nineteen-year-old waiter, soon to be bartender, was Frank Schoonmaker's Encyclopedia of Wine. *It was loaned to me by the owner of the restaurant where I first worked, but I never gave it back to him and it is still in my possession today. I decided then that wine would be my profession and I began to memorize everything in his book!*

properly aged American wine on hand. But most American producers, underfinanced if not in actual financial straits, had to sell what they had available, good or bad, mature or fresh from the fermenting vat. And they did.

Third, instead of explaining, to a public then definitely sympathetic, their problems and plans and hopes, American vintners, with a few notable exceptions, decided to brazen the thing out. They announced that their wines were quite as good as the better vintages of Germany and France and Spain— but any beginner with a couple of dollars in his pocket could buy two bottles and find out that this was not by any means true.

Fourth, American vintners insisted on selling their wines under European names to which these wines had no moral and precious little commercial right—St.-Julien, Château d'Yquem, Pommard, Chablis. The government finally stepped in and stopped the worst of these abuses; meanwhile American growers had, by inference, admitted that their wines were imitations and invited the public to compare the imitation with the original. The public did, and for the next two or three years almost all of the American wines sold were sold on a price basis.

Fifth, and this is not the fault of the vintners, there appeared, with Repeal, a collection of self-styled connoisseurs, most of them quite as ignorant as the public they pretended to instruct, who published, generally with the imprimatur of some wine merchant, enormously complicated vintage and service charts which baffled and embarrassed the average housewife—anyone was a barbarian to serve a '24 claret after a '29; an average Sunday dinner required three wines, none of which, in the majority of cases, the local liquor store carried; good wine should not be served to those who smoked, when all of one's friends smoked.

Faced with all this, after one or two unfortunate experiences with widely advertised domestic wines, the American housewife decided to concentrate on Martinis or Manhattans and highballs, and I can only praise her good sense.

American wine will never take the place which it deserves on America's dinner tables until it is honestly presented to the American public, and by "honestly" I mean under American names. California and New York and Ohio have now, after seven years, the vineyards to produce good wine, and considerable and fairly adequate stocks of good wine laid by. In justice to the wine and to ourselves, this ought to be sold for what it is. Let us look into this subject.

What is a French Chablis or a French Sauternes? And what is a California "Chablis" or a California "Sauternes"? Well, a French Chablis (unless shipped by a downright thief) is a wine made from Pinot Chardonnay grapes, incidentally one of the four or five best white-wine grapes in the world, either in the township of Chablis itself or in one of nineteen adjoining townships which enjoy the same climatic conditions and have pretty much the same type of soil. A French Sauternes is a wine produced in a delimited district about one-fourth as big as a California county, from Sauvignon, Sémillon, and Muscat grapes. Well, what is a California "Chablis"? Legally, it is any white California wine which the producer (who has probably never tasted a good French Chablis in his life) thinks tastes like Chablis. It can be made from Pinot Chardonnay grapes or from culls thrown out by raisin pickers, in the best viticultural district of California or the worst. A California "Sauternes" can be made anywhere in a state nearly as large as the wine-producing area of France, and it can be made of any kind of grape that the winemaker happens to have or cares to buy, including Tokays, Muscats, and Concords. Actually, I do not believe there are five thousand acres of true Sauternes grapes in California, and I am certain there are not three hundred acres of Pinot Chardonnays.

The trouble, therefore, with European names for California wines is not primarily that they are wrong or dishonest: It is simply that they mean absolutely nothing, that they give the consumer no idea what he is buying, no guarantee, and no information; that they give the producer of superior grapes and the owner of superior vineyards no advantage and no higher prices; that to the merchant they mean endless complaints and explanations. No two American "Sauternes" taste exactly alike.

Despite this lack of standards, these foreign type names, as Harold J. Grossman says, in his excellent *Guide to Wines, Beers, and Spirits*, "are more appropriate when applied to California wines than to American wines, as they do bear some resemblance to the originals, which is not true of the Eastern types."

Wine, it is important to remember, is not a manufactured article but a farm product, and its excellence or mediocrity is primarily the result of the soil on which the grapes were grown and of the grape variety which the producer chose to plant. Thus, in all of the great wine-producing countries of the world the local wines take their names from the factors which make them what they are—the place from which they come, the grapes from which they are made. We have our full share of pleasant and picturesque place-names in this country, and there is no reason why we should be unwilling or reluctant to use them. A few progressive winegrowers have already started using them, and the public response has been overwhelmingly favorable.

Away, then, with California "Moselle," New York State "Burgundy," and the whole crew of hyphenated Americans. The fine vineyard districts of the United States are these: the Napa Valley, the Sonoma Valley, the Livermore Valley, and the foothills of the Santa Cruz Mountains in Santa Clara County, California; the Lake Erie Islands off Sandusky, Ohio; the Finger Lakes district of New York State, especially the shores of Lake Canandaigua and Lake Keuka. Other districts will, no doubt, soon come into production, and some of them may prove every bit as good as those already known.

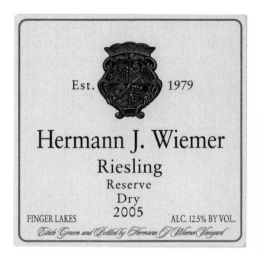

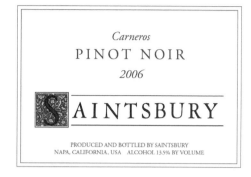

The fine-wine grapes grown in this country are, in California, the Pinot (from Burgundy), the Cabernet (from Bordeaux), the Gamay (from the Beaujolais), the Riesling, Sylvaner, and Traminer (from the Rhine and Alsace), the Folle Blanche (from the Cognac country), the Sauvignon and Sémillon (from the Graves and Sauternes districts). In the East the grapes are native grapes, and the best of them, all of which yield white wine, are the Delaware, the Elvira, Moore's Diamond, the Catawba, the Diana, the Dutchess.

These, then, are the names one should look for on American wines, the names of the American districts in which the wines were made and the names of the grapes from which they came.

17

DISCOVER GRAPE VARIETIES

Oz Clarke

The simplest way to become familiar with wine flavors is through grape variety. Each grape variety has its own hallmark flavors, so two wines with different names made in places thousands of miles apart will have a fair amount in common if they are made from the same variety.

Not all wines are made from a single grape variety. Red Bordeaux, for example, usually contains at least three, and one of Australia's classic wine styles is a blend of two famous varieties: Cabernet Sauvignon and Shiraz. But once you know the taste of different grapes you'll have a good idea of what to expect from a blend.

RED WINE GRAPES

I'm going to start with red grapes—some people call them black, but they're deep purple or bluish in reality, so I reckon it's easier to link them to the type of wine they generally make. There's more to red wine than sturdiness, power and "good with red meats and cheese." Delicacy, freshness and intriguing perfumes are all within the scope of the world's red grape varieties. It all depends on where you grow the grapes and what style of wine the winemaker wants to achieve. In general, red grapes grown in warm places will give richer, riper styles, and you'll get more delicacy, perfume, and restraint from grapes grown in cool places.

Cabernet Sauvignon

The epitome of the intense, blackcurrant style of red wine, Cabernet Sauvignon is never among the lightest of reds and it always has some degree of tannic backbone. The best mature slowly to balance sweet blackcurrant flavors with a scent of cedar, cigar boxes, and lead pencil shavings. It is often blended with Merlot for a richer flavor.

I think Oz Clarke is one of the most important personalities in wine today. I think that we have a lot in common: all of his books are written to be easily understood and his notes are accessible to all, especially a new wine drinker. I have been lucky enough to hear Oz speak at many different wine events and he is arguably the best speaker on wine in the world, and we finally got to "break bread" in June 2010.

WHERE IT GROWS Almost every country where wine is made has a fair bit of Cabernet in its vineyards. Bordeaux is its homeland, but you'll find it in the south of France as well. Italy has some top-class versions; good Spanish ones come mostly from Navarra or Penedès; and it produces inexpensive wine over large tracts of Eastern Europe, notably in Bulgaria.

New World examples are vibrantly fruity, with rich texture, soft tannins, and sometimes a touch of mint or eucalyptus. California and Australia have world-class examples; Chile's have piercing fruit and are excellent value; South Africa's are dry and blackcurranty; and New Zealand goes for a style closer to Bordeaux.

KEEP IT OR DRINK IT? Lots of people think of Cabernet Sauvignon as being a wine that needs to age in bottle after you buy it, but that's only because the best red Bordeaux and top California and Australian Cabernets need age. Most New World Cabernets, and most less expensive red Bordeaux, can be drunk straight away.

SPLASHING OUT Wine from Bordeaux villages like Margaux, Saint-Julien or Pauillac, from Coonawarra and Margaret River in Australia and Napa Valley in California.

BEST VALUE Chile and southern France are the places for tasty bargains. Bulgaria is, well, cheap.

CABERNET WITH FOOD Modern Cabernet is an all-purpose red, but it's best with simply cooked red meats.

NOT TO BE CONFUSED WITH Cabernet Franc, a related variety, or the white grape Sauvignon Blanc.

VASSE FELIX

2005

Cabernet Sauvignon

MARGARET RIVER

14.5% Vol   WINE OF AUSTRALIA 750mL

Merlot

Juicy, fruity wine that is lower in tannic bitterness and higher in alcohol than Cabernet Sauvignon, with which it is often blended. Blackcurrant, black cherry, and mint are the hallmark flavors.

WHERE IT GROWS Merlot started out as Cabernet Sauvignon's support act in Bordeaux, but has risen to worldwide popularity because of its softness. The great wines of Pomerol and Saint-Émilion in Bordeaux are based on Merlot, with Cabernet in the blend. These wines show Merlot at its sturdiest and most intense, but they're still fruitier and juicier than Bordeaux's top Cabernet-based wines.

Chile is Merlot heaven, at best producing gorgeous garnet-red wines of unbelievably crunchy fruit richness that just beg to be drunk. California and Washington State have more serious aspirations for the grape, but the soft, juicy quality still shines

19

through. Australia and South Africa are only just catching on, but Merlot already makes some of New Zealand's best reds.

Italy uses Merlot to produce a light quaffing wine in the Veneto region, and offers more flavorsome examples from Friuli, Alto Adige, and Tuscany. Hungary and Bulgaria are making rapid progress with the grape. In the hot South of France Merlot tends to lack distinctive character but produces a fair bit of gently juicy red.

KEEP IT OR DRINK IT? In general, drink it young, especially Chilean and Eastern European examples. Top Bordeaux Merlots, however, can last for up to 20 years.

SPLASHING OUT Château Pétrus and Château le Pin from the Pomerol region of Bordeaux are the two most expensive wines in the world. Other Pomerols and Saint-Émilions are less expensive lush mouthfuls.

BEST VALUE When it's good, you can't beat young Merlot from Chile.

MERLOT WITH FOOD Merlot is a great all-rounder—barbecue red, casserole red, picnic red—but savory foods with a hint of sweetness, such as honey-roasted ham, particularly suit the soft fruitiness.

Pinot Noir

At its best Pinot Noir is hauntingly beautiful with a seductive silky texture; at worst it is heavy and jammy or insipid and thin. Good young Pinot has a sweet summer-fruit fragrance and taste. The best mature to achieve unlikely and complex aromas of truffles, game, and decaying leaves—and fruit, of course.

WHERE IT GROWS Pretty widely these days, since winemakers tend to fall in love with it. Its home is in Burgundy, and the aim of all those acolytes worldwide is to make a wine that tastes like great red Burgundies such as Volnay or Vosne-Romanée. Outside Burgundy the most successful Pinots are from regions that have developed their own style—like Carneros and Sonoma Coast in California, and Wairarapa, Marlborough, and Central Otago in New Zealand. Not very obliging, it obstinately refuses to taste as it should unless you treat it precisely as it likes. The best wines from California, Oregon, and New Zealand show that wine-makers there have cracked it and there are some good ones from Victoria and Tasmania in Australia and Overberg in South Africa. Chile's cooler vineyards can produce lovely delicate styles. Northern Italy produces an attractive, fragrant style and Germany more serious stuff. Other versions can be less convincing.

KEEP IT OR DRINK IT? Drink it, on the whole. Only the best ones repay keeping—and then not for as long as you'd keep the equivalent quality of Cabernet Sauvignon.

SPLASHING OUT Grand Cru Burgundies in the Côte d'Or are the pinnacle of Pinot Noir. Premier Cru Burgundy should still seduce you, but for a fraction of the price.

BEST VALUE Chile makes some reasonably priced examples, as does Marlborough in New Zealand. For a taste of true Burgundy, try a basic Bourgogne Rouge from a leading Burgundy grower.

PINOT WITH FOOD This is food-friendly wine. It suits both plain and complex meat and poultry dishes. It also goes well with substantial fish, such as fresh salmon.

ALSO KNOWN AS Spätburgunder in Germany, Pinot Nero in Italy, and Blauburgunder in Austria.

NOT TO BE CONFUSED WITH the white grapes Pinot Blanc and Pinot Gris, or the related red grape Pinot Meunier.

FIZZ FACT Pinot Noir is a major component in much white Champagne, even though it is a red grape.

Syrah/Shiraz

Intense is the word for Syrah/Shiraz wines. Intensely rich, intensely spicy, intensely ripe-fruited, or even all three at once. The most powerful begin life dark, dense, and tannic but mature to combine sweet blackberry and raspberry flavors with a velvety texture. Others are gorgeous right from the word go.

WHERE IT GROWS Most famously in France's Rhône Valley and Australia—and unusually, the two styles are running neck and neck in terms of quality. French Syrah is more smoky, herby, and austere; Australian Shiraz is richer, softer, more chocolaty, sometimes with a leathery quality. But Australia is a big place, and styles vary across the country. Victoria Shiraz can be scented and peppery, Barossa Valley Shiraz leathery and chocolaty. Old vines Shiraz, wherever it's from, should be gratifyingly intense.

There's some Shiraz in South Africa, a bit in Italy and Switzerland. California, New Zealand, and Chile are now making some good stuff in their cooler regions.

KEEP IT OR DRINK IT? All Syrah/Shiraz needs a year or two's aging to hit its stride. Top wines will last over ten years, and a great Hermitage might peak at 15.

SPLASHING OUT Hermitage or Côte-Rôtie from the northern Rhône; Grange from Australia (it's no coincidence that this wine was known for years as Grange Hermitage).

21

BEST VALUE Gluggers from southern France or Chile.

SYRAH/SHIRAZ WITH FOOD This is a wine that can stand up to powerful flavors. I love it with peppered salami and tangy cheese.

WHY TWO NAMES? It's Syrah in France; Shiraz in Australia. Other regions use either name.

NOT TO BE CONFUSED WITH Petite Sirah, a grape grown in California and Mexico.

Other Red Wine Grapes

BARBERA

This is a high-quality, characterful grape, yet without a single world-famous wine style to its name. Its base is in northwest Italy, in Piedmont, where it makes wines so Italian-tasting that you find yourself instantly craving a plate of pasta. It's that herby, sour-cherries bite that does it: Barbera is the epitome of mouthwatering, sweet-sour style [...]. But that rasping acidity is matched by plum and raising fruit, and it's low in gum-puckering tannin.

It appears in umpteen guises all over Piedmont, but Barbera d'Alba and Barbera d'Asti are the best versions to go for. California uses Barbera for its simplest wines, but there's good stuff from Argentina.

Not to be confused with Barbaresco, a tough, tannic wine from the same region of northwest Italy.

CABERNET FRANC

A relative of Cabernet Sauvignon which makes earthy, blackcurranty wines. Used in red Bordeaux blends and on its own in the Loire Valley and northeast Italy. Now starting to make its mark in places like Chile, Australia, Virginia, New York State, and Ontario.

CARMENÈRE

Red grape from Chile making delicious spicy wines. It was originally a Bordeaux grape thought to be extinct. It reappeared in Chile under the umbrella title of Merlot and is now proudly labeled under its own name. Makes marvelously rich, spicy, savory reds. Some of the Cabernet in northeast Italy is now reckoned to be Carmenère.

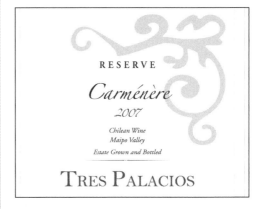

RESERVE

Carménère

2007

Chilean Wine
Maipo Valley
Estate Grown and Bottled

TRES PALACIOS

GAMAY

Gamay, for all intents and purposes, equals Beaujolais. It's one of those freaks of wine that this grape happens to flourish on an expanse of granite hills in the south of Burgundy, and effectively nowhere else. The Ardèche region of southern France has some, as does the Loire Valley in the west. But that's about it.

Gamay is never a grape to take too seriously. It makes refreshing light wines with sharp, candy-like cherry and raspberry flavors, perfect for drinking lightly chilled on hot summer days.

GRENACHE

The most widely planted red grape in the world. Most of its plantings are in Spain and the south of France where it makes wines high in alcohol with sweet and peppery flavors. It's most often used in blends—mainly with the more scented and powerful Syrah/Shiraz, the pallid Cinsaut, or the rough and ready Mourvèdre. If you ever come across a heady, juicy rosé, there's a good chance that it's made from 100 percent Grenache.

It's actually a Spanish grape, and its original name is Garnacha Tinta. It beefs up the blend of some red Riojas, makes juicy, herby reds in Campo de Borja and Calatayud, makes Rioja and Navarra *rosado* (the Spanish for rosé) in increasingly good light styles, and produces extremely concentrated, usually expensive, rich, full-bodied reds in Priorat and Monsant. Old vine Grenache makes some gorgeous sexy fruit bombs in South Australia, often from century-old vines. Morocco uses it for reds and pinks.

But Grenache is, as I said, at its best in good company, and it finds it in France, in the southern Rhône Valley. Grenache features among no fewer than 13 permitted grape varieties in this region's most famous wine, Châteauneuf-du-Pape—a complex, sweet-fruited, super-rich red splashed with the scent of hillside herbs. The raspberry/strawberry character of this grape shines alongside a hint of hot, dusty earth in the softest Côtes du Rhône and Côtes du Rhône-Villages. Vin de pays Grenache from the neighboring Ardèche region is light, fruity, and good value. A lot of the juiciest, headiest rosés and rosados around the Mediterranean come from Grenache.

Also known as Garnacha in Spain and Cannonau in Sardinia.

MALBEC

The best red grape in Argentina, making smooth, rich reds at all price levels. It's also the major grape of Cahors in southwest France, which can be juicy and plummy at best. Chile, Australia, New Zealand, California, and South Africa also have some Malbec. Expect to hear more of this variety as Argentina's reds become more famous.

Also known as Côt or Auxerrois.

NEBBIOLO

If you taste it too young, Nebbiolo could well be the most fiercely aggressive red you will ever encounter. It takes a few years for the staggering levels of tannin and acid to relax their grip and release the remarkable flavors of tar and roses, backed up by chocolate, cherries, raisins, and prunes, and an austere perfume of tobacco and herbs. It's the severest incarnation of the sweet-sour style of Italian reds, always at its best with sturdy food.

Nebbiolo is virtually exclusive to the Piedmont region of northwest Italy. The classic wines are the forbidding Nebbiolos from Barolo and Barbaresco. Modern styles mature in five years rather than the traditional twenty, which is a relief for today's wine drinkers. Softer, plummier wines come from elsewhere in Piedmont—Nebbiolo d'Alba, Langhe, Gattinara, Ghemme, and Carema.

A few committed Italophiles in California are pretty much the only other producers, though a few Australians are starting to look at it seriously and Argentina has some.

Also known as Spanna.

SANGIOVESE

The name of the grape might not be familiar, but it's the principal variety behind Chianti,

Italy's most famous red wine. It's responsible for Chianti's tea-like bitter twist and cherry-and-plum fruit. So it's one of those mouth-watering sweet-sour grapes, Italian down to its toes.

And it's not just grown for Chianti. You'll find wines made from Sangiovese in most of Italy, though not the very north, and some will be a bit dilute and thin and acidic, but a lot will be light, attractive everyday reds with herby fruit and a rasping finish—just the thing with the lunchtime pasta.

In the best parts of Tuscany, however, it is taken very seriously indeed. Big, heavy-weight wines like Brunello di Montalcino and Vino Nobile di Montepulciano are made entirely from Sangiovese. These are world-class wines that need aging, as do the best Chiantis, but most Sangiovese is best drunk young and fresh.

You'll find some Sangiovese in California, Australia, and Argentina, as well, and they're starting to do interesting things with it; but for the moment there is nothing to equal the best Italian wines. *Also known as* Brunello *and Prugnalo.*

TEMPRANILLO

Spain's maid-of-all-work crops up all over the country, producing wines of all shapes and sizes. There are grand, prestigious wines in Ribera del Duero, mellow but ageworthy reds in Rioja and Catalunya, powerful beasts in Toro, and young, juicy, unoaked styles in Valdepeñas, La Macha, Somontano, and many other regions. Its flavor is good but not always instantly recognizable the way that Cabernet Sauvignon or Pinot Noir is: Tempranillo's most distinctive feature is its good whack of strawberry fruit, but in the biggest, weightiest wines this tends to go plummy and blackber-ryish and spicy, overlaid with vanilla oak. Only the finest wines need aging—and the simplest really must be drunk young and fresh.

In northern Portugal Tempranillo is called Tinta Roriz and it is an important grape for port, the classic fortified wine, as well as appearing in reds from both Dão and Douro. Under the alias Aragonez it's respon-sible for some juicy numbers from Alentejo in the south.

Argentina grows it for its vivacious fruiti-ness and Australia, California, Oregon and the south of France are experimenting with it.

Also known as Ready for this? Cencibel, Tinto del País, Tinto del Toro, Tinto Fino, Tinto de Madrid, or Ull de Llebre in Spain; Tinta Roriz or Aragonez in Portugal. And that's the abbreviated list.

BRUNELLO DI
MONTALCINO
DENOMINAZIONE DI ORIGINE CONTROLLATA E GARANTITA
RED WINE

2004

IL POGGIONE

ESTATE BOTTLED BY
FRANCESCHI s.s.
MONTALCINO - ITALIA

750 ML - PRODUCT OF ITALY - ALC.14% BY VOL

ZINFANDEL

California's specialty grape can be all things to all people. The best Zinfandel and the type I'm interested in is spicy, heart-warming, dry red wine. Other styles range from off-white, sweetish, and insipid "blush" wines to high-intensity sweet port-style reds. All red California Zinfandel shares a ripe-berries fruitiness, but the intensity varies dramatically from light to blockbustingly powerful.

Cheap examples are usually lightweight, juicy, fruity reds. The top-quality Zinfandels are at the sturdier end of the scale and they're expensive. Mendocino County produces strapping Zin full of blackberry fruit, spice, and tannin. It's rich, ripe, dark, and chunky in Napa; rounder and spicier in Sonoma; and wild and wonderful from old vineyards in the Sierra foothills. The full-throated, brawny flavors of these big Zins will wash down anything from barbecued ribs to the richest Pacific Rim cooking.

Zinfandel from regions outside the U.S., which place a lower value on the grape, are an economical alternative. It's grown in one or two outposts in Australia, South Africa, Brazil, and Chile, and not much money will buy you a sumptuous, rich, almost overripe mouthful.

Researchers have shown that Zinfandel is the same variety as the southern Italian grape Primitivo, and if you're looking for good value, Primitivo gives you the most bang for your bucks. Some Primitivo is even being labeled as Zinfandel to make it seem more fashionable.

Also known as Primitivo in Italy and it's probably the same as Croatia's Crljenak Kastelanski, too.

RAVENS WOOD

2005

NAPA VALLEY

ZINFANDEL

25

WHITE WINE GRAPES

Green, yellow, pinkish, or even brown on the vine, these are the grapes that promise refreshment. But that's not all: white wines range from the breathtakingly sharp to the most luscious and exotic flavors you will ever encounter.

Chardonnay

The world's most famous white grape variety can make anyone fall in love with wine, because it's so generous with its easy-to-relish buttery, lemony flavors. Chardonnay has an affinity for oak-aging and styles divide into unoaked which is lean, minerally, and restrained; lightly oaked, when it can be nutty and oatmealy; and heavily oaked, which is where butteriness, tropical fruits, and butterscotch come in.

WHERE IT GROWS Chardonnay is grown everywhere. I'd be hard pushed to name a wine-producing country that doesn't grow it. It originates from the French region of Burgundy, where it produces stylish, succulent wines with a nutty richness from time spent in oak barrels yet still with bone-dry clarity. However, in the north of Burgundy is Chablis, where Chardonnay has a sharp, minerally acidity that may or may not be countered by the richness of oak—I prefer it all in its naked, unoaked glory.

The modern style has its origins in Australia and California: upfront, pineappley, oaky, and sumptuous, but nowadays becoming a little more restrained. New Zealand versions are either fruity or surprisingly nutty. Chilean versions are on the fruity side. South African ones are mixed in styles, but very good at their best. In Europe, modern styles come from southern France, Italy, Portugal, Greece, and Spain.

KEEP IT OR DRINK IT? Most Chardonnay is ready the moment you buy it, but top wines from France, Australia, and California will improve for five years or so.

SPLASHING OUT Of all Burgundy's mercilessly expensive Grands Crus, Le Montrachet is finest of the fine. Top Californian Chardonnays sell at almost the same price.

BEST VALUE Chilean, Australian, or southern French.

CHARDONNAY WITH FOOD The whole point of modern Chardonnay is that it will

go pretty well with almost anything. It is wonderful with all fish, whether lightly grilled or drowned in rich, buttery sauce. The richer the sauce, the oakier the wine can be.

Riesling

It's not the grape that everyone takes an instant liking to, Riesling, but it has undeniable finesse. Piercing acidity is the most startling and recognizable feature in styles ranging from thrillingly dry to richly sweet, with flavors that range from apple and lime zing to pebbles and slate to peaches and honey.

Dispel any confusion lurking in your mind between Riesling and Liebfraumilch, that simple, sweetish, first step in wine drinking invented in Germany which rarely contains any Riesling at all.

WHERE IT GROWS Riesling is the grape of Germany's greatest wines. In the Mosel region it produces mostly light, floral wines with a slaty edge. Rheingau Rieslings are generally richer, fruitier, and spicy. Both are surprisingly low in alcohol. They need a few years to mature before the flavors are at their best.

Just across the border into France, Alsace makes a more alcoholic dry, spicy Riesling. In Austria it's dry and minerally with a good, weighty, slap of alcohol. Australian Riesling is different again—with an invigorating lime aroma that goes toasty with age. Other countries, including New Zealand, South Africa, and the U.S., have some decent Riesling, but Germany, Alsace, and Australia have defines key styles.

KEEP IT OR DRINK IT? Some German Rieslings can age almost indefinitely, but the simpler everyday ones can be drunk at 1–2 years old. As Riesling ages it often develops a petrolly aroma (nicer than it sounds). Top Australian wines will keep for 10 years or more.

SPLASHING OUT The great sweet German Rieslings. Alsace, Austria, and Australia make superb dry versions.

BEST VALUE Mosel and Rhein Kabinetts from Germany and surprisingly good, big-brand Australians.

RIESLING WITH FOOD Good dry Rieslings, such as those from Austria and Australia, are excellent with spicy cuisine. Sweet Rieslings are best enjoyed for their own lusciousness but can also partner light, fruit desserts.

ALSO KNOWN AS Johannisberger Riesling, Rhine Riesling, or White Riesling—and Riesling Renano in Italy.

NOT TO BE CONFUSED WITH Laski Rizling, Olasz Rizling, Riesling Italico, or Welschriesling.

Sauvignon Blanc

This is the epitome of the green, tangy style: an unrestrained wine with aromas and flavors of green leaves, nettles, gooseberries, and lime zest.

WHERE IT GROWS New Zealand, particularly the Marlborough region, produces what has become the classic style, all pungent gooseberries and nettles. Australia seldom matches New Zealand for lean pungency. Chile delivers lean, fairly punchy flavors from cooler regions such as Casablanca and Leyda. South Africa is becoming increasingly exciting for Sauvignon Blanc, particularly from the cold west coast. California is a little warm for Sauvignon, but is now producing some good lean examples as well as fuller styles aged in oak barrels.

The grape's European home is in France's Loire Valley. The wines are milder and less pungent than New Zealand versions. Sancerre and Pouilly-Fumé are the Loire's

27

famous wines; Menetou-Salon and Sauvignon de Touraine offer more green flavor for less money.

Sauvignon is also an important grape in Bordeaux, and elsewhere in Europe there are full-flavored Sauvignons in Spain, especially in Rueda; neutral ones in the north of Italy; and light ones in Austria. Eastern European versions vary, but tend to lack pungency, except in Hungary and Slovenia.

KEEP IT OR DRINK IT? Apart from a few top wines, Sauvignon Blanc is for drinking as soon as you can get the bottle home and the cork out.

SPLASHING OUT Cloudy Bay from New Zealand is a cult wine that sells out as soon as it hits the shops. Its Marlborough neighbors are just as good at around half the price.

BEST VALUE Entre-Deux-Mers in Bordeaux—and Bordeaux Blanc in general—is pumping out bargains with a good tangy flavor.

SAUVIGNON WITH FOOD New World Sauvignon is a favorite match for the sweet-sour, hot-cool, spicy flavors of Chinese and Southeast Asian foods; it goes well with some Indian cuisine and with tomato-based dishes in general. It's also fine to drink on its own.

ALSO KNOWN AS Fumé Blanc in California and Australia.

NOT TO BE CONFUSED WITH Cabernet Sauvignon, the famous red grape.

Other White Wine Grapes
CHENIN BLANC

What an extraordinary flavor—a striking contrast of rich honey, guava, and quince with steely, minerally flavors and whiplash acidity. Chenin can produce gum-numbing dry wines, sparkling wines, medium-sweet styles, or super-sweet wonders from noble rot–affected grapes. That's Chenin in France's Loire Valley. Chenin in South Africa might taste as pale as water. Let's deal with France first.

Chenin accounts for the white wines from the Loire's heartland—Vouvray, Savennières, Saumur, and others. It can have a problem ripening here but global warming has recently provided a series of excellent vintages. Simple dry Chenin has a flavor of apple peel and honey but a good Vouvray has a streak of minerally flavor. The best sweet Loire Chenin comes from Bonnezeaux, Quarts de Chaume, and Coteaux du Layon. These wines need to mature for years to attain their full quince and honey richness.

Chenin is South Africa's most widely planted grape. It generally makes rather hollow stuff but an increasing number of winemakers realize it could make South Africa's best whites if treated seriously. New Zealand and Australia produce small amounts of good fruity Chenin. California and Argentina use it for unmemorable gluggers.

GEWÜRZTRAMINER

A fragrant blast of lychee and rose petals followed up by a luxurious, honeyed, oil-thick texture, a whiff of Nivea hand cream, a twist of fresh black pepper—dry or sweet, it's the most intensely aromatic wine in the world. "Gewürz" translates as spice, although it's difficult to think of a single spice that exactly resembles Gewürztraminer. Still, if you're searching for a wine to match spicy Asian food, look no further. It's also wonderful to sip by itself.

Alsace is the place to go for Gewurztraminer (they take the accent off the "u" here). Even the most basic wines have a swirl of aromatic spice, while great vintages can produce super-intense wines in styles from dry to richly sweet.

You have to keep your nerve to make Gewürz (its short nickname) work. If you don't like its perfume, why grow it? But the rise in popularity of Asian cuisine has seen producers become more confident. Germany, northern Italy (where the grape originates), and New Zealand all now produce a few deliciously indulgent examples.

Also known as Traminer.

MUSCAT

The only grape to make delicious wine that actually smells of the grape itself comes in a multitude of styles. Rich, sweet, and fortified, floral and dry or exuberantly frothy, Muscat wines all share a seductive grapy aroma. Intensely sweet Muscats often add an orange-peel fragrance.

To start with the darkest and sweetest, Rutherglen in northeastern Victoria, Australia, is a sticky heaven for those who crave its raisiny, perfumed, fortified Muscats. Golden, sweet Muscats, again fortified, come from the south of France (from Beaumes-de-Venise, Frontignan,

Rivesaltes, and other villages) and Portugal, and have lighter, but sensuous, delicate orange-and-grape aromas with a touch of rose petals. Spain's Moscatel de Valencia is cheaper, more foursquare, but a good rich mouthful all the same.

Alsace is the place for dry Muscat—heavenly scented, thrillingly dry—though Italy, Spain, Portugal, and Australia all have a go. And if you're in a bubbly sort of mood, Muscat makes delightful grape and blossom-scented sparklers in Italy (Asti is the most famous) and Brazil.

Also known as Muscat Blanc à Petits Grains (its full name), Muscat de Frontignan or, in Australia, Brown Muscat. The Italians call it Moscato. The less thrilling Muscat of Alexandria (Spain's Moscatel) and Muscat Ottonel are related grapes. Orange Muscat does smell of oranges, and the rare pink Muscat (Moscato Rosa) does make divine wine smelling of tea roses. Black Muscat—well, I like it; we used to grow it in a greenhouse when I was little.

Not to be confused with Muscadet, the bone-dry white wine from the Loire Valley in France.

PINOT GRIS

Intensity is a key issue with Pinot Gris. Whether you like your white wine bone dry and neutral or rich and spicy, or anything in between, the right Pinot Gris for you is out there somewhere. A hint of honey (sometimes admittedly very faint) is the linking theme that connects the grape's different incarnations.

Rich, smoky, and honeyed dry whites from Alsace in France show Pinot Gris at its most pungent and impressive. The U.S. has had success with lighter, crisper,

spicy versions from Oregon, while New Zealand is producing a fair number of soft, pear-scented examples. Eastern Europe produces outstanding dry or off-dry and spicy wines.

Germany takes the grape into sweet-wine territory and sometimes called it Ruländer. Dry German Grauburgunders aged in oak are fat and smokily honeyed. Fairly neutral wines, and plenty of them, labeled as Pinot Grigio, come from Italy. But really good Italian Pinot Grigio is floral and honeyed.

Also known as Pinot Grigio in Italy, Ruländer (usually sweet) or Grauburgunder (usually dry) in Germany, Malvoisie in Switzerland.

Not to be confused with the other Pinots: Pinot Noir, Pinot Blanc, and Pinot Meunier (one of the official Champagne grapes).

SEMILLON

Semillon comes into its own in two key areas, France's Bordeaux and Australia, and it comes in two totally different styles: dry and sweet. By the way, the French put an accent on the "é." Either way, it can produce wonderful quality.

It pops up in various parts of Australia for dry wine, but Hunter Valley Semillon is the most famous. The traditional style here is unoaked. When young, unoaked Hunter Semillon tastes neutral, even raw, with just a bit of lemony fruit. But unoaked Hunter Semillon should not be drunk young. It needs up to a decade in bottle—and then it will amaze you with its waxy, lanoliny, custardy fruit. Oaked Australian Semillon, often from the Barossa or Clare Valleys, is different. Dry, toasty, waxy, and lemony, it's good young but the best can age for a few years, too. Riverina makes light, waxy Semillon, much of which is blended with Chardonnay.

In Bordeaux Sémillon is usually blended with Sauvignon Blanc, which adds a refreshing streak of sharp acidity. The best dry versions come from Graves and Pessac-Léognan: oaked with flavors of cream and nectarines, they improve for several years in bottle.

Sweet wines are another story. Here Sauternes is the star: this Bordeaux appellation produces extraordinarily concentrated wines from grapes affected by noble rot, with flavors of barley sugar and peaches. This golden, sweet style is imitated, in small amounts, in California, Australia, and New Zealand. Hand-picking the noble-rotted grapes, sometimes berry by berry, means these wines can never be cheap; but the flavor is so special it's worth the money.

VIOGNIER

Heady, hedonistic, with a rich scent of apricots and breeze-blown spring flowers, Viognier is an aromatic dry wine so luxurious that it seems almost sweet.

It used to be confined to a few small areas of the northern Rhône Valley in France, but fashion is a powerful force. Suddenly Viognier is appearing all over the south of France—never in large quantities, to be sure, but at prices that give a taste of the grape to those of us who can't fork out the premium-plus rates for classic top-quality Condrieu and Château-Grillet from the northern Rhône.

California, Australia, and South America are trying their hands at it, too. Results vary, but are distinctly promising to very good. Viognier should be drunk young and fresh—the ravishing scent fades rapidly after a year or two.

VIOGNIER
OAK KNOLL DISTRICT OF NAPA VALLEY

EXCERPTS FROM *CRUSH IT!*

Gary Vaynerchuk

LEARNING THE TRADE

To go from self-made baseball card king of Hunterdon County, rolling in the dough, to grunt bagging ice for two bucks an hour was a hard fall. It wasn't until I turned sixteen that I was even allowed up on the floor and became a cashier. Not too exciting, but it beat hours of shoveling ice and dusting shelves. I couldn't drink anything we sold (my parents were strict about that), but I was good at regurgitating data, so when business was slow I'd flip through trade magazines to pass the time and then use what I'd learn to help customers. One of those magazines was *Wine Spectator*. Now, the store was called Shopper's Discount Liquors for a reason. Most of our business came from selling the hard stuff. Beer, too, was a big seller— the beer cooler took up about 33 percent of the entire store. But I learned two things from my time behind the cash register. First, thanks to *Wine Spectator*, I learned that there

was a whole cultural cachet to drinking wine and that people collected it the same way I collected baseball cards, *Star Wars* toys, and comic books. That was interesting to me. I also started noticing a pattern: people would come in to buy their Absolut or their Johnnie Walker and I knew that I or any staff could talk until we were blue in the face about the other brands, they were still walking out with their Absolut or their Johnnie Walker. Those brands were just too established. The wine buyer, though, would often walk in looking a little lost and spend ten minutes tentatively peering at labels as though hoping a bottle would jump out and spare them from making a decision. I knew from my experience with the baseball card business that people want to be told what's good and valuable, and that they enjoy feeling like they've been turned on to something not everyone can appreciate.

The wine buyers, unlike the liquor customers, were open to any suggestions I had, and I realized that they represented

---

I met Gary Vaynerchuk for the first time in 2009. Of course, I knew who he was from watching his Wine Library Web TV shows. Although some of his shows are wacky, in person he is a very sincere, humble, intelligent young man whose future is very bright. I was happy to hear that Gary signed a major book deal, and recently published his book Crush It! *which has great advice to entrepreneurs and small businesses. Go Jets!*

opportunity. Spotting that social trend was enough to turn what started out as a casual interest in wine into an obsession. I had started out at Shopper's Discount Liquors hating every second of my time there, but now I was determined to turn the place into the number one wine shop in America.

CHANGING THE WINE WORLD

No one had any illusions that I was a great scholar as I started my senior year of high school, so it made sense to me that my plan should be to eke out the grades to graduate and start working full-time at the liquor store. Some time in February . . . yes, February (sorry, Mom, you know it's true) . . . my mother asked me what college I was planning to attend. College? As luck would have it, a postcard from Mount Ida College in Newton, Massachusetts, showed up in the mail a few days later. I filled it out, and Mount Ida became my home in the fall. By then, though, my life was the store, and I'd come home almost every weekend to work there.

In September 1995, I was hanging out in a friend's dorm room when he turned on his computer and introduced me to this thing called the Internet. I let my friends bumble around chat rooms trying to meet girls for a little while, then kicked them off and spent the next nine hours hunting down baseball card trading forums and figuring out how I was going to use this thing to grow the store. There was no doubt in my mind this was going to be the future of business. It would take me another year to get the courage to approach my dad about selling wine online.

What can I say, my dad was a scary guy. At first he resisted. But he believed in me, and as soon as he relented I was off to the races.

Winelibrary.com launched in June 1997 (the store itself wouldn't take on the name Wine Library until 1999). The store brought in about 2 or 3 million per year in 1994. I came onboard full time after graduating in 1998 and grew the business from about 4 million to 10 million in a year with 0 percent of that in online sales. By 2001, we were doing about 20 million. Not bad. Not bad at all. Life was good and business was booming. Most guys my age would have thought they had it made.

Then, on my thirtieth birthday, November 14, 2005, I was driving along the New Jersey Turnpike on my way to work thinking about my day, and I realized that as perfect as life seemed, I wasn't entirely happy. I knew deep in my soul that there was no way I was ever going to buy the Jets if I stayed on the retail path. It was time to go big.

We had a computer department at Wine Library by now, and I had seen Erik Kastner and John Kassimatis spending their lunch breaks spitting food all over themselves from laughing at these things called video blogs (the two ones at the time were Rocketboom and the show with zefrank). I had been trying to figure out how to leverage this new medium to show people that there was more to drink out there than Yellowtail. I'd also noticed that sites like MySpace and Flickr and YouTube were becoming popular, sites that had nothing to do with commerce and everything to do with being social and sharing stories and meeting people, and that was something I was good at. It was there, on the New Jersey Turnpike, that I had my *aha* moment. I wasn't going to use video blogs to sell wine; I was going to use video blogs to build a whole new world for wine, and for myself. I waited to get the store through the holiday season, and then launched Wine Library TV in February 2006, three months later.

OPPORTUNITY LIES IN TRANSPARENCY

Consumers want you to tell them the truth, Sure, they want quality and service and value and entertainment, but above all they want to know that the person they're dealing with is being honest. Entrepreneurs don't really have a choice—the lines between the private and the public are becoming increasingly blurred, and with people able to share their experiences and thoughts and photographs on video by spraying them all over the Internet within minutes after they happen, the days of being able to con the consumer without repercussions are pretty much over. So no matter how you shape and color your personal brand, honesty has got to be your core.

I come online five days a week to taste and review wines. Some wines are tremendous, some taste like horse crap. Do the makers of the wines I pan like me? Probably not. Do I care? Nope. Do I sell some of the ones that I think taste bad? You bet I do, because you might totally disagree with me (someone at the winery who made them sure did). All I'm doing on my blog is being myself and voicing my opinion loud and clear. When you launch your videos, blogs, or podcasts, you're going to do the same. That goes for

everyone, including those of you who are used to keeping information close to the vest, or you will lose, one way or another.

Let's say you're in real estate and you love it. Part of the real-estate game is learning to put some serious spin on a loser property, right? You pitch it as a "charming fixer-upper" or a gem "just waiting for some TLC." Even the appealing properties get the rose-colored treatment. But what if you sat down in front of a camera and posted a series of video blogs telling people what you really thought of the homes or commercial sites or lots you were selling? What if you said something like, "I have got one ugly house to sell. Seriously, folks, you've got to see this one if only to take in one of the last surviving examples of red shag carpeting matched with faux-deer-antler, woodland-creature chandeliers. The sellers are supernice and I would love to get them the $360K they originally wanted, but I've talked to them about it and they understand that they need to set their sights lower because this sucker needs some serious renovations. I'm thinking you should take a look at it if you've got about $275K to spend, plus some extra bucks for a contractor. And bring your imagination. Lots of it."

Now, I know there are laws in real estate that might make it hard to execute this idea. Clearly, I was pushing the limits in the last paragraph. But would that kind of transparency hurt your business? Maybe at first you'd have a hard time getting sellers to list with you. But imagine what kind of coin you'd earn if you became the most trusted real-estate agent in town because no one would ever doubt that you'd try to sell them a house you didn't think was worth every dime for which you were asking? Your listings would go up because sellers would be confident their properties weren't going to gather dust on the market, your sales would go up because buyers would know they weren't going to have to deal with any BS. On top of that, you'd have the satisfaction of doing something you loved entirely your way. And on top of *that*, you'd have built a solid personal brand—the no-BS real-estate agent—that you can now carry with you wherever you go and use as leverage to find bigger and better professional opportunities, including book-writing gigs, television appearances, and a variety of other media appearances.

Do it. Do it right now.

Trust Your Own Palate

When you're thinking about your personal brand, don't worry that it will have to look anything like mine in order for you to crush it. You'll crush it as long as you concentrate on being yourself. Besides, you can't be like me. I like wines that you don't. I like White Castle and the New York Knicks, and you probably don't. I'd rather drink a V8 than any fruit juice, and I hoover my veggies. All of those quirks and preferences have shaped my brand. Your brand will be unique and interesting because you are unique and interesting. Don't put on an act to try to imitate me or anyone else who's had some success with social marketing. You

will lose because people can sniff out a poser from a mile away. I had to wait a long time to find a platform that allowed me to create and share an authentic personal brand. Before I launched Wine Library TV, I saw that blogs were on the rise and I knew there was an opportunity there and was desperate to get in on it. But I looked in the mirror and asked, "Can you write? No . . . Damn!" Now, I could have hired someone to write elegant blog posts for me and pretended they were mine (note to some celebrities I won't name: I love you but cut that out, we know you're not writing those tweets on Twitter yourself), but I knew that if I was going to get people interested in me, everything was going to have to come straight from me, unfiltered and unpolished. Creating and disseminating my content would be the only thing that I absolutely could not and would not delegate. Besides, if I was going to spend the time building a gazillion-dollar business so that I could buy the Jets, I had to do it in a way that was authentically me and that I couldn't wait to do every day. So I waited until I found a medium that spoke to my DNA—video blogs—jumped on it, and never looked back.

Embrace your DNA, be yourself, put out awesome content, and people will be interested in what you have to say. Believe me, if you're that good, people are going to find you, and they're going to follow you, and they're going to talk. And getting people to talk is the whole point.

TERROIR

Neal I. Rosenthal

I admit to a firmly held prejudice. I have a distinct preference for the traditional wines of western Europe and a matching skepticism about most of the wines produced in the New World as well as for those wines made in the Old World that seek to imitate the characteristics of their New World brethren. My perspective, once so common in the wine trade, is now shared by a small, probably aging, minority of wine merchants. Nevertheless, I am content with my choices.

When I first stumbled into the wine business in late 1977, learning about wine was essentially a series of geography lessons. The market for wine, small as it was at that time in the United States, consisted almost exclusively of the wines of western Europe, with a smattering of wines, mostly of rank commercial quality, from a few other grape-growing regions such as the vast central valley of California, where volume rather than quality was paramount. It was a given that the finest of wines came from the Moselle and the Rhine in Germany; from Bordeaux, Burgundy, and the Loire and Rhône valleys of France; from Piedmont and Tuscany in Italy; and on the Iberian peninsula, from the Rioja in Spain and the Porto district in Portugal. There were hints of possible worthy competitors elsewhere, but the game was to be played on the European fields.

The romance of European wine was, for me, like the experience of map reading in which the names of far-off places stimulated the imagination. The seemingly infinite series of villages, little communities that gave their names to the wines produced there, whether in Italy or France or Germany or Spain or Portugal, created a library of potential stories. And, as I dug into the reference works and scanned the labels on the bottles of wine and engaged in an endless series of tastings, it became clear to me that a wine was

My wine students often ask me the best way to choose a wine, especially with so many wines that are available to the consumer. One way is to know who the best importers are. A Neal Rosenthal selection on the label is a guarantee that you will be getting the finest quality wine from grape growers and winemakers who are passionate about their wine. Over the last twenty years, Neal and his partner Kerry Madigan have grown their portfolio to over seventy-five different producers from France, Italy, and California.

a creature of its geographical origin; for if it were not, then there would never have been any reason for this memory-straining list of appellations and subsets of appellations, all providing with greater and greater specificity the details of a wine's birthplace.

In many ways, that era was a simpler time. There were perhaps a handful or two of American importers of the finest wines; harvest time occurred from mid-September through early autumn, sometimes extending into November or perhaps December for the curious eisweins of Germany; everyone knew the names of the great growths of Bordeaux and the group of powerful family firms in Burgundy or the Rhône or Tuscany that controlled much of the production in those regions; and there was usually a retailer or two in each major American city who had branched out beyond the sale of spirits to embrace the snobbish trade in fine wines. This was the world of wine in the States at the moment of my almost inexplicable immersion in the commerce of wine.

Much has changed since the late 1970s. There has been, in the intervening years, an explosion of interest in both the making and the consumption of wine. Vineyards have proliferated in places where the grapevine never existed before or where European influence may have placed only an occasional grapevine to maintain a cultural habit. There are vast tracts covered with the vine throughout the west coast of the United States, from Washington State through Oregon and on through much of California. The valleys of Chile produce massive quantities of wine, as do the plains of Australia. There are vineyards to be found almost

everywhere now, including China and India. We are awash in wine and there are, as a result, armies of wine merchants plying this new-growth industry. Harvest now occurs in February and March in the southern hemisphere, and six to eight months later in the north. Our understanding of vintage quality is a more difficult feat to master. The wine market is a veritable souk with a different set of rules—or perhaps with no rules at all.

To simplify this jumble of wines and places and traders, initiates now more often start by reading about, or hearing, the litany of grape varieties. The list is a short one, certainly when compared to the large number of wine appellations that have been recognized and authorized. This approach makes comparable, and comprehensible as well, an Australian Chardonnay, a Chardonnay from Meursault in Burgundy, and a Chardonnay vinted in Sonoma County, California. The geography of wine, the standard with which I grew up, becomes submerged in, and perhaps even obliterated by, this simplified approach to wine.

This is more than unfortunate; it is blasphemy. Learning of Chardonnay, Pinot Noir, Syrah, and the other grape varieties is an exercise in botany. It is interesting, but it doesn't become compelling until the vine is married to the place where it can flourish. More important, it is a list that, for me, lacks the drama and the history of the rules of geography upon which I built my love of wine. To contemplate the reasons why a wine made from the chardonnay grape planted on a particular hillside in the Côte d'Or of Burgundy differs so markedly not only from its kin harvested on a slope in Australia thousands of miles and a hemisphere away but also from its sister wine made from grapes harvested by the same grower just meters away is to begin to grasp the logic of the phenomenon known as *terroir*. The concept that the particulars of a zone—the combination of soil, climate, grape type, and, perhaps, human history—are responsible for producing very special characteristics that are unique to a quite specific spot turns the consumption and the study of wine, as well as the commerce in it, into more fascinating and ultimately more satisfying activities. It also reveals the truth about wine and anchors us to a respect for the natural world that is fundamental to our well-being. The most satisfying of wines reveal their characters slurp by slurp as they speak of their origins and their traditions. The best of wines always proudly tell you from where they come.

There are isolated voices in the wine trade that decry the existence of terroir, yet, by and large, the wine community not only believes in the concept but considers it fundamental. That is why, for example, in those areas where growing grapes for the purpose of making wine is relatively new, there is an ongoing search to define places that appear to produce wine of special character. Regard, for example, the decades-long and still incomplete process of delineating territories in northern California, first sepa-

rating Sonoma as an appellation from Napa and further refining Napa to carve out the Stag's Leap and Mayacamas Mountains and Rutherford Bench areas, just to name a few. All of this is based upon the rational European ideal that finds its most complex expression in the rigorous appellation laws that not only define special geographical areas known after centuries of farming to be the source of special vinous habitat but also control what grapes get planted where and often even in what proportions. Despite the modern notion that man can create miracles given enough money and time and expertise, and despite the extravagant praise thrown at wines that appear on the scene without a scintilla of heritage, to truly understand the hierarchy of wine we must reference the trinity of soil, climate, and grape that is canonized in rules established by the Europeans.

It is that set of standards that has disciplined my efforts over a thirty-year career as a wine merchant. My selections as a wine merchant are grounded entirely on my understanding of those rules, and I marry that discipline to my personal tastes to assemble a portfolio of wines to present to the public. I am comfortable within this world of wine. My tastes have been honed by wines bearing allegiance to these concepts, which explain the prejudice that informs what I do.

SILENT REVOLUTION

Gerald Asher

How good are organic wines? For a start, there are far more of them out there than you might suspect. They're not in some fringe niche either: They include, for instance, Château Margaux, the Médoc first

growth; the wines of the Domaine Leroy in Burgundy; those of Robert Sinskey Vineyards in Napa Valley; and certain bottlings from the Penfolds vineyards in South Australia's Clare Valley.

The question, then, would seem to answer itself, but there's a catch: Wines like these rarely display the word "organic." Sometimes it's to avoid having the wine perceived as funky, or bought for what the grower believes is the wrong reason. Robert Sinskey says he doesn't want people to think first about the way he cultivates his grapes and then about the quality of the wine. "We want the customer to buy our wine because it's good. The way we nurture the vines is simply part of our effort to make it that way."

Robert Gross of Cooper Mountain Vineyards in Oregon also insists that quality is the point of the wine and that organic cultivation

Gerald Asher has written many books, but reading his articles in Gourmet *magazine for the last thirty years was something that I looked forward to in every issue. They were always international, detailed, interesting, and written in such perfect "British English." Among his many awards, he received the order of the Mérite Agricole, France's oldest civil award, and was inducted into California's Vintners Hall of Fame.*

is simply a technique. Gross does use the words "organically grown" on his label because he knows there are people looking for it. "But it can also be a turnoff," he said. "Some wine drinkers see it and think we're being preachy."

Many producers of wine from organically grown grapes keep mum on the subject to leave their options open in the vineyard. Organizations that certify organic compliance sometimes impose parameters based on philosophically wholesome principles rather than on the practical needs of viticulture. In an extreme emergency, growers might be faced with the choice of spraying, as innocuously as possible, or losing a crop. They argue that it's better not to carry an "organic" statement at all—even when the vineyard is certified—rather than find themselves obliged to explain, in such a situation, why it had to be dropped. And then there are the many grape growers of California who ignored the chemical revolution of the 1950s and continue to do what they have always done. As bemused as Monsieur Jourdain—the character in Molière's *Le Bourgeois Gentilhomme* who discovered he'd been speaking prose all his life—they now learn that they have long been practicing organic viticulture without having once given it a thought. "They just don't make a big deal of it," Bob Blue, winemaker for the Bonterra organic wines of Fetzer Vineyards, told me. "They don't even bother to sell their grapes as 'organically grown.' But that's probably because they'd have to get involved with the maze of certifying organizations and state regulators to do it. And the fees can be heavy for a small producer."

Aside from those who had never grown grapes in any other way, the return to organic practices, both in California and in Europe, began in the early 1980s. I remember my surprise, sometime about then, when I found Ulysses Lolonis of Redwood Valley

in Mendocino County dumping buckets of predator ladybugs among the vines in his family's vineyard. He says he started because of concern about the pesticides being proposed to him. "Eventually we found we didn't need them at all," he told me recently. "If we left enough grass between the rows of vines to serve as bug territory, it soon had a mixed population of insects keeping themselves busy devouring each other without bothering us.

"We've come a long way since then. Now, rather than grass, we grow a nitrogen-rich cover crop to feed the soil when we plow it under. The bugs are just as happy, and we can do without pesticides, herbicides, and fertilizers. Do these organic methods enhance the flavor or quality of our wine? Well, they don't seem to take anything away from it." (In fact, Lolonis's Zinfandel is one of the best in California.)

John Williams of Frog's Leap Winery in Napa Valley is more forthright. He is convinced that organic cultivation does make a difference to wine quality. "The first vineyard we purchased in 1987," he said, "had been farmed by an old-timer on what we would now call organic principles. Wanting to do things right, we retained a firm to test the vines and the soil and make recommendations to us. They found many things wrong, but fortunately were able to supply us with all the chemical supplements they said we needed. The effort was grandly expensive and soon led to a general decline in the vineyard, the quality of its fruit, and the wine we made from it.

"I was urged to talk to an organic-farming consultant. Amigo Bob [Cantisano] certainly looked the part—ponytail, shorts, and tie-dyed T-shirt. What he said made sense, and we decided to give it a try in a couple of test areas. We now have nine growers in Napa Valley producing organically grown grapes for us.

"We found that a soil rich in organic matter absorbs and holds moisture better— so we were able to go back to dry farming, the old way of growing grapes in California, instead of relying on irrigation. We discovered that plants fed by compost and cover crops, rather than chemical fertilizers, draw in nutrients in a measured way that helps control growth. Our vines are therefore strong and healthy and give balanced fruit. We've learned to think about the causes of problems rather than react with a quick fix to each one as it comes up. It's made us better farmers. In doing all this, I'm not trying to save the world. I just want to make good wine."

There are others who farm organically simply because they don't like the idea of using industrial products in the vineyard. Jean-Pierre Margan of Château La Canorgue in the Côtes de Luberon (Peter Mayle country) told me he was taught in his viticulture courses which synthetic fertilizers to use and what and when to spray. "I never liked the idea," he said. "My father and grand-father had made good wine in the traditional way, and when my wife and I started to revive her family's dormant vineyard, I decided to do the same. It wasn't an act of defiance.

"But confronting nature directly means you have to be vigilant. You must look ahead—mistakes are difficult to correct organically. You become more efficient because you have to stay on top of every detail of every vine—and perhaps that's why the wine is better.

"Though the 'organic' aspect of the vineyard is simply the way we work, I put it on the label to allow those who want wine from organically grown grapes to find us. But there should be no need for me to say anything.

41

Organic cultivation is and should be the norm. It's those who use chemicals that should have to identify themselves.

"I'm not alone in the way I work. There has been a tremendous awakening among winegrowers in France. Usually it starts with the growers getting involved with a program of reduced reliance on synthetic sprays and fertilizers and the reintroduction of more benign techniques—but they soon see the difference in their vineyards and move increasingly toward the freedom that organic cultivation allows."

That awakening has been greatly accelerated by the work of Claude Bourguignon, whose highly influential book, *Le sol, la terre et les champs* (*The Soil, the Land and the Fields*), is now in its third edition. Almost every French winegrower I've talked to in the past several years has at some point introduced Bourguignon's name into our conversation. Now he's one of the leading French experts in soil analysis—his client list includes Domaine de la Romanée-Conti and Château Latour and reads, in fact, like an honor roll of French viticulture. Much of what he has to say comes down to the essential role of microorganic life in the soil. He expresses regret, in the introduction to his book, that the issues involved have become noisily politicized.

In the second edition of his book *Burgundy*, Anthony Hanson describes a visit to Bourguignon's laboratory, north of Dijon. Having collected a random sample of earth from a flower bed, Bourguignon shook it with water, added a coloring agent, then put it under his microscope for Hanson to look at. "I shall never forget the sight," Hanson

writes. "Tiny specks of solid particles (clays and other inanimate matter) were bathed in liquid which teemed with swimming, turning, thrashing, pulsing little organisms—bacteria, yeasts, microbes of all sorts."

In an ounce or two of healthy soil, Bourguignon will tell you, there are billions of such microorganisms. They transform mineral elements in the soil to make them available to plants that could not otherwise assimilate them. They attach iron to acetic acid, for example, forming the iron acetate that a plant can absorb. This symbiotic relationship allows a plant to function properly, to capture the energy in sunlight. That's where the energy-into-matter-and-matter-into-energy food chain starts. Soil bacteria need no human presence to flourish and do their work. It's sobering to be reminded that our lives depend on them.

Biodynamic farming takes organic cultivation one step further by paying special attention to soil bacteria and to harnessing the rest of the energy in the cosmos in ways that strengthen the vine. It has developed from theories expounded by Rudolph Steiner, the Austrian social philosopher, in the 1920s. Those who practice it are used to the skepticism, even the mockery, of others—there's an air of both New Age mysticism and Old Age witchcraft about it. But it works.

Robert Sinskey, who is heading toward biodynamic certification for all his vineyards, got interested because of a specific problem with one vineyard in particular. "The soil was as hard as rock," he told me. "It was dead. It was planted with Chardonnay, and the wine from those vines was always green and lean. We put in a cover crop and began using biodynamic sprays to encourage the development of microorganisms in the soil. Gradually we brought that vineyard around, and the wine is now so appealing and distinctive that we will soon be bottling it with a special designation."

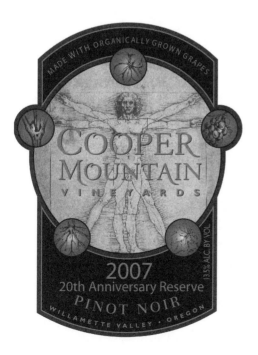

Robert Gross, a physician whose interests include alternative medicine, is also moving toward biodynamic certification for his vineyards at Cooper Mountain. "It brings the vines into harmony with their environment," he told me.

Two of the biodynamic sprays—500, a very dilute solution of cow manure that has been aged in a cow horn placed underground through the winter and then stirred into blood-warm water with a motion calculated to maximize its effect; and 501, a similarly dilute solution of powdered silica—are basic to the system. Other sprays, mostly homeopathic teas of herbs and flowers, are used by some and not by others. Working in accordance with phases of the moon and reserving certain days for spraying, pruning, or planting to take advantage of propitious movements of the planets are ideas that some accept and others reserve judgment on.

Farming with due provision for the gravitational pull of the moon is ancient wisdom. Jim Fetzer—who started the program of wines made from organic grapes at Fetzer and is now owner of the Ceago Vinegarden, a fully accredited biodynamic vineyard estate in Mendocino County—said he never has to explain any of this to his Mexican workers. "They're used to the idea that various aspects of agricultural work should coincide with the phases of the moon," he said. "It makes sense: If the changes in atmospheric pressure associated with the moon's waxing and waning can affect the rise and fall of oceans, you can be sure it affects the position of the sap in the vines." As for the special days, Alan York, Ceago Vinegarden's biodynamics consultant (and consultant to Joseph Phelps and Benziger, among others), put it to me this way: "We don't know why or how the plant responds to the changing positions of the planets. It's like surfing. There's this force and you try to ride it."

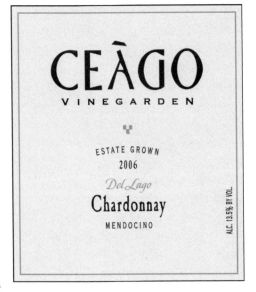

There is much more to biodynamics than homeopathy and "root" days. A key element is the systematic introduction of other plants among the principal crop. There is a rich diversity of them growing among the vines at Ceago Vinegarden, including olive trees, lavender, and buckwheat—habitat to tiny wasps that lay their eggs inside the eggs of leafhoppers and stop that problem before it starts. When I was young, I took it for granted that most vines in Italy and France had peach trees and even a line or two of corn planted among them. I thought it was to make full use of the land, but now I know better.

"Biodynamics is neither a recipe nor even a specific technique," says Nicolas Joly,

owner of Coulée de Serrant, the white-wine jewel of Loire Valley vineyards. "It can't be applied mechanically. It demands a complete understanding of what is happening in the life cycle of a plant and the formation of its fruit so that the functions can be enhanced."

Joly, an articulate advocate and proselytizer, condemns completely what he sees as the sins of modern viticulture. "Herbicides and pesticides annihilate the microbial life peculiar to any particular soil, and synthetic fertilizers then standardize the vines' nourishment and thus the character of the fruit. What is the point of talking about *terroir* in such circumstances?"

There is a wide gap between biodynamics and conventional viticulture, and a considerable one even between standard and organic practices. Part of that difference is cost. The abuse of pesticides, herbicides, and synthetic fertilizers can create an imbalance ever more expensive to address. But the considerable handwork involved in organic viticulture is also costly—and justified economically only if higher quality attracts a better price for the wine.

In the detailed report on its experiment of organically cultivating roughly 125 acres of vineyard on its Clare Valley estate over the past ten or twenty years, Penfolds (owned by Southcorp Wines) shows that the cost of cultivating those blocks of vines was as much as 50 percent higher than that of cultivating similar neighboring blocks by conventional methods. Australia has high labor costs, and that accounts to some extent for this startling difference; but, when expressed as cost per ton because of the smaller yields when compared with conventional viticulture, the cost of Penfolds's organically grown grapes becomes 100 percent higher.

In the face of such numbers, we can't ignore the fact that whatever satisfaction growers may get from the quality of their products and from their stewardship of the land, they accept the risk inherent in growing a crop as fragile as grapes in order to make a fair return.

In most parts of the winemaking world, particularly in California, there are programs designed and supported by growers' associations to help members wean themselves from dependence on synthetic chemical treatments and to combine organic farming principles with a sound and limited use of environmentally safe products in a cost-effective manner. The program run by the Lodi-Woodbridge Winegrape Commission, financed by an assessment on grape production voted by the growers themselves, includes a step-by-step workbook that encourages growers to meet regularly in small groups for mutual support and the exchange of information and to constantly survey every aspect of their work. They evaluate their progress in sowing cover crops, for example, and installing nesting boxes near their vineyards for predator barn owls. There are similar programs organized by the Central Coast Vineyard Team, and still more are being developed on a smaller scale in Amador and Lake counties.

These programs encourage growers to check their vines closely and, by thinking ahead, to discover new options for dealing with problems. They lead them to a system of fully sustainable agriculture—or beyond— and at the same time help them steadily improve the quality of their wines.

Paul Pontallier, manager of Château Margaux—where herbicides, pesticides, and synthetic fertilizers are rarely used— commented to me recently that there's much to be said for organic farming and for biodynamic viticulture, whatever the circumstance, so long as the approach is always practical. "The danger comes," he said, "when some particular way of doing things is turned into an ideology."

THE SOMMELIER/WINE SERVER

Joseph DeLissio

The sight of an approaching sommelier has been known to provide more than a passing moment of anxiety to many a diner. Is he friend or foe? Will she know that I don't know much about wine? Please, don't let me be embarrassed in front of my client! I hope he doesn't recommend too expensive a wine. Or, Here we go, one more tip!

How did the sommelier develop such an intimidating reputation? Any diner who has ever had a bad experience with an unqualified sommelier can tell you that, for the most part, the sommelier's poor reputation was earned when he acted in an intimidating and self-serving manner. This doesn't mean that qualified and caring sommeliers do not exist, because they do. Like good chefs, however, they are rare. Part of the problem is different perceptions of the position itself. There is a big difference, for example, between a traditional European and the American sommelier. Top restaurants in Europe consider the sommelier's to be a position of prestige, one that requires an extremely high level of training and experience. The sommelier can be one of the great assets of a fine restaurant. His competence and integrity can often make the difference in a customer's choice (especially a repeat customer's) of where to dine. In short, the sommelier's position is both noble and highly respected. With the acknowledgment by both management and ownership of his importance, it is not unusual for a talented sommelier to work at a single establishment for many years—even decades. And long-term employment is key in the development of a great wine program.

Joseph DeLissio, or as all of his friends call him, "Joey D," has been part of my family for over thirty years. Joey was one of my wine students at the Windows on the World Wine School when he started to run the wine program at The River Café restaurant in Brooklyn. As a teacher, one of the most gratifying experiences you can have is when your student becomes a teacher and an author. Outside of our wine affiliation, Joey, writer and retailer Josh Wesson, importer Michael Skurnik, New York Times wine critic Bryan Miller, and our wine friend Richard Regner formed the "famous" rock 'n' roll band "The Winettes" in the late eighties. We were actually hired to play around the country, and in many cases gave seminars during the day about wine education. Get ready for our reunion concert tour!

In the United States sommeliers are often viewed quite differently. Here too many restaurateurs view the sommelier as just another salary. Many do not seem to understand the importance of having a person on staff who is dedicated to the development of a wine program. I have always found that odd, as the wine and beverage program usually represents the most profitable area in any restaurant. Odder still is that the same ownership thinks nothing of employing a full-time coat check person, parking valet, or telephone receptionist. This type of nonsupport by ownership leads to job insecurity, which reduces this important position to little more than that of a transient worker. And while transient workers are not usually driven to be dedicated or caring to management or the consumer, they *are* driven by money. It does not take long to figure out that the more they sell, the more money they will make. With this dangerous mentality in place, the sommelier often recommends expensive wines and may overpour the wine so that a second—or even third—bottle will be needed.

Just one such sommelier can provoke disrespect, contempt, and total distrust from an entire group of diners. This type of employee will never be an asset to the restaurant, because he is seldom employed by one establishment long enough for a true wine program to be developed. It is sad to think that such a noble position, one that has endured for centuries, can be brought low so quickly by so few. The good news is that many of today's top restaurants are beginning to realize the importance of employing someone to be in charge of their wine program. The bad news is that change takes time, and until attitudes shift, wine and wine service in the American restaurant may never reach their true potential.

With that said, let's discuss the role of the sommelier. Above all, remember that the sommelier is there to help you. He should do this by gently and skillfully guiding you in choosing a wine to accommodate your tastes, menu selections, and budget. He should happily—and without intimidation—answer any questions you may have, regardless of how simple or silly those questions may seem. And as wine is meant to be consumed with food, the sommelier should have a good working knowledge of the menu as well as an understanding of food and wine pairings.

Qualities of a Good Sommelier/ Wine Server

➤ Will not be intimidating
➤ Will answer all questions
➤ Should work within your pricing parameters, and if smart, will help you find the proper wine for less
➤ Will always ask the host before opening any additional wine bottles
➤ Should be able to offer more than one wine recommendation
➤ Should offer his expertise without insisting on it
➤ Should never embarrass or strongly correct the person ordering the wine
➤ Will know how to serve wine properly—will not overpour
➤ Will suggest decanting before doing it
➤ Will inform the table of any vintage, vineyard, or price change before opening the wine

47

➤ Understands when a wine is bad and has the ability to explain why a wine is not

➤ Should offer the same professional service regardless of the wine's price

➤ Offers half bottles or wine by the glass when appropriate

➤ Has a good knowledge of the menu

➤ Should understand that sometimes the best recommendation is no wine at all (certain salads, artichokes, asparagus, very salty foods)

➤ Provides clean glassware

➤ Lets the table relax and enjoy themselves

ORDERING WINE WITH THE SOMMELIER/WINE SERVER

There are two basic scenarios that you can experience with a wine sommelier, and the first requires blind faith. While relinquishing control is difficult for most people (myself included), doing so in the gentle hands of a qualified and experienced sommelier can result in the most rewarding experience possible, for who better to match the food and wine than someone whose job is to do exactly that, someone with a working knowledge of the wine cellar as well as a very current awareness of what is going on in the kitchen? A qualified wine sommelier might just be the single most important connection between the restaurant itself and the diner. This type of sommelier is rare, but when you do find one, you will quickly understand his value. True to the laws of yin and yang, this same blind faith does have its dark side, as giving an inex-

perienced sommelier carte blanche can be disastrous as well as expensive.

The second, much safer scenario requires some input from you. Yes, you will actually talk with the sommelier, and after your first brave attempts, you will look forward to this exchange. It is important—as well as rewarding—that you set parameters. Following is a list of information that will help the sommelier select a wine for you:

➤ Wine type. Are you looking for a red, a white, or a sparkling wine?

➤ Taste preference. Do you want a dry or a sweet wine? Do you want it to be fruity? Woody? Tannic? Light? Medium-bodied?

➤ Wine grape type. Chardonnay, Merlot, Syrah, Cabernet Sauvignon, Riesling?

➤ Region. California, Oregon, France, Germany, Spain, Italy, Chile?

➤ Vintage year. Do you have a preference?

➤ The table's menu selection.

➤ Price range.

➤ Bottle size. If this is not discussed, it will be assumed you are looking for a full .750-liter bottle.

Sequence of Ordering Wine in a Restaurant

1. Presentation of wine list and menu
2. Ordering of selection
3. Presentation of unopened bottle by the sommelier/wine server
4. Approval and opening of bottle
5. Presentation of cork
6. The sampling
7. The approval
8. Pouring of the wine

TALKING TO THE SOMMELIER/ WINE SERVER

Let's say that you're looking for a white wine to go with your grilled chicken and your guest's tuna. You tell the sommelier that you would like a wine that's very dry, medium-bodied with some oak, preferably something French made from the Chardonnay grape, and in the $25 to $35 price range. Armed with this much information, any wine sommelier or server should be able to recommend an appropriate wine for your table. You will most likely discover that the sommelier very much appreciates your input and direction. If he doesn't, be careful.

When the sommelier returns, he will present the unopened bottle to you for your inspection and approval. If there is any discrepancy with the vintage, producer, or price, it is the sommelier's job to inform you. Once you give a sign of approval (usually a simple nod of the head), the wine will be opened. It is tradition that when the wine server removes the cork, he places it by the person who has ordered the wine. At this point you may inspect the cork by sniffing for any off odors and by gently squeezing the cork for elasticity. It is important to know that any concerns you may have with the wine due to the condition of the cork must be reconfirmed by sniffing and tasting the wine, since a bad cork alone is not a valid reason for returning a bottle of wine. (I have had some wonderful wines with horrible corks.)

The server will now pour a small sampling (a half ounce) in your glass for you to taste and approve. I strongly recommend that before you taste the wine you take a small sip of water or a bite of bread to neutralize any strong flavors—salad dressing or salt, for example—that may be lingering on your palate. This is because strong flavors can interfere with your assessment of the wine. It is at this stage that any faults or displeasures with the wine should be brought to the server's attention. If you are not certain whether the wine is correct, you should mention it to the server and request a few additional minutes to see if the off odor or bad taste dissipates, as it often does.

Once you have decided that the wine is correct, tell or signal your approval to the server. The server will now pour everyone at the table a proper-size portion (a third to a half glass) of wine. Proper wine service dictates that ladies be poured first, followed by gentlemen, and finally the person who ordered the wine. However, this rule is not etched in stone.

FREQUENTLY ASKED QUESTIONS ABOUT TIPPING, AND THE LIKE

Should all restaurants have a wine sommelier?
Although many top restaurants have sommeliers, most restaurants do not. At The River Café, for example, there is no wine sommelier; however, the maître d' and all the captains are trained to handle the wine service. While all restaurants do not need a wine sommelier, they do need a staff that is adequately trained in the handling of wine and wine service.

Should you tip the sommelier, and if so, how much?

It is important to remember that the sommelier is there to serve and properly guide you. A gratuity should not be considered automatic and should be earned by the sommelier. The amount given, of course, is up to you. Tips can be calculated on a percentage of the bottle cost or can be a set sum. Some customers prefer tipping a fixed amount per bottle. If you feel that no extra attention has been given, you may decide that a tip is not necessary.

Does the standard [20] percent tip for food apply to wines on the check as well?

There is much debate on this question, as most restaurant staff believe that wine costs are to be treated as part of the check. In France a standard [20] percent gratuity is added automatically to the entire check, including all wines. In America, however, a gratuity is not added automatically to the check, and many diners feel wine—to some degree—has a different tipping standard. Does a wine server give a greater amount of attention when he opens a bottle of Dom Pérignon Champagne [at $250 a bottle] than he does when he opens a bottle of Veuve Cliquot Gold Label nonvintage Champagne [at $100 a bottle]? Again, the amount of the tip is up to you, and while the staff may feel that if you can afford the wine, you can afford the tip, it is your decision. Personally, unless I have had bad service, I tip on the wine as well.

How do you approach tipping in one of the many bring-your-own-wine restaurants?

In this type of restaurant the staff is not involved with wine choice but is very much involved with wine service. Usually a fixed tip per bottle is considered fair. The amount per bottle may be dictated by the cost of the wine or the amount of wine service required—decanting, for example. The staff in restaurants in larger cities seem to expect larger tips.

What do you do if the sommelier/wine server makes you feel uncomfortable?

Although it may seem a little impolite, either tell him how you feel or ask the maître d' or captain to handle your wine needs. If enough people do this, you can be sure the sommelier will either adjust his attitude or risk being out of work.

What is the silver cup that sommeliers wear around their necks?

The silver cup usually worn around the neck of the wine sommelier is called a *taste-vin*. Traditionally, upon opening a bottle of wine, a sommelier would pour a little wine into his cup and taste it for soundness. The idea behind this custom was that the customer should not have to taste a bad wine. While this ritual is seldom performed today, the tradition of wearing a taste-vin has remained a symbol of the sommelier.

PART II

ON TASTING WINE

ON TASTING WINE

THERE ARE NO RIGHT OR WRONG ANSWERS WHEN it comes to wine tasting. It's everyone's subjective opinion. There never has been and there never will be an absolute and infallible wine expert. The average person has 10,000 taste buds. Some people have more. Some people have less. Some people are considered to be "super tasters" and others are "non-tasters." Women are actually considered to be better tasters than men since they can discern more flavors and nuance than their male counterparts. Age also plays a part. Our acuity of smell decreases as our age increases.

There are hundreds of variables that can affect how and what you taste when you drink a glass of wine. Medications can affect you. Who you're with, the environment, the glass you're drinking from, the food you're having with it—these all can change the whole experience of what we taste in a wine.

I did something for a well-known travel magazine many years ago. We ran a little experiment to see if space and conditions affected how wines tasted. We tasted sixty wines in an office in New York City. We then took the same wines, and boarded a plane and set up camp in the first class cabin on a 747 flight bound from New York to Los Angeles. We then tasted each of the wines again. Many of the wines tasted differently. There were so many factors in our experience. The stress of travel was a major factor. Other factors included dehydration, the change in time, claustrophobia, fatigue, etc. The result was that wines with high tannins didn't have the same balance of fruit and tannins as they did in the New York City office. Because of the dehydration induced by the air system, the tannins became more pronounced. Big Cabernet Sauvignons can be brutally tannic without balance. When you're on a flight, especially long distances, look for a light Beaujolais or Pinot Noir, a fruity German Riesling, or a crisp Sauvignon Blanc.

You can rely on wine publications, critics, blogs, and books to learn about tasting wine. They can help you start on your journey but they don't have all the answers. The real judge is going to be you and your own tastes. Trust yourself.

—KZ

THE BASICS

Kevin Zraly

You're in a wine shop looking for that "special" wine to serve at a dinner party. Before you walked in, you had at least an idea of what you wanted, but now, as you scan the shelves, you're overwhelmed. "There are so many wines," you think, "and so many prices." You take a deep breath, boldly pick up a bottle that looks impressive, and buy it. Then you hope your guests will like your selection.

Does this sound a little farfetched? For some of you, yes. Yet the truth is, this is a very common occurrence for the wine beginner, and even someone with intermediate wine knowledge, but it doesn't have to be that way. Wine should be an enjoyable experience. This section should help you to be able to buy with confidence from a retailer or even look in the eyes of a wine steward and ask with no hesitation for the selection of your choice. But first let's start with the basics—the foundation of your wine knowledge.

What's fermentation?

Wine is the fermented juice of grapes. Fermentation is the process by which the grape juice turns into wine.

The simple formula for fermentation is:
$$\text{Sugar} + \text{Yeast} = \text{Alcohol} + \text{Carbon Dioxide} \ (CO_2)$$

The fermentation process begins when the grapes are crushed and ends when all of the sugar has been converted to alcohol or the alcohol level has reached around 15 percent, the point at which the alcohol kills off the yeast. Sugar is naturally present in the ripe grape through photosynthesis. Yeast also occurs naturally as the white bloom on the grape skin. However, this natural yeast is not always used in today's winemaking. Laboratory strains of pure yeast have been isolated and may be used in many situations, each strain contributing something unique to the style of the wine. The carbon dioxide dissipates into the air, except in Champagne and other sparkling wines, in which this gas is retained through a special process.

Why do the world's fine wines come only from certain areas?

A combination of factors is at work. The areas with a reputation for fine wines have the right soil and favorable weather conditions, of course. In addition, these areas look at winemaking as an important part of their history and culture.

Is all wine made from the same kind of grape?

No. The major wine grapes come from the species *Vitis vinifera*, including both red and white. However, other grapes are used for winemaking. The most important native grape species in America is *Vitis labrusca*, which is grown widely in New York State as well as other East Coast and Midwest states. Hybrids, also used in modern winemaking are a cross between *Vitis vinifera* and native American grape species.

⁓ THERE ARE THREE ⁓ MAJOR TYPES OF WINE

Table wine Approximately 8 to 15 percent alcohol

Sparkling wine Approximately 8 to 12 percent alcohol + CO_2

Fortified wine 17 to 22 percent alcohol

Does it matter where grapes are planted?

Yes, it does. Grapes are agricultural products that require specific growing conditions. Just as you wouldn't try to grow oranges in Maine, you wouldn't try to grow grapes at the North Pole. There are limitations on where vines can be grown. Some of these limitations are: growing season, number of days of sunlight, angle of the sun, average

temperature, and rainfall. Soil is of primary concern, and adequate drainage is a requisite. The right amount of sun ripens the grapes properly to give them the sugar/acid balance that makes the difference between fair, good, and great wine.

Where are the best locations to plant grapes?

Many grape varieties produce better wines when planted in certain locations. For example, most red grapes need a longer growing season than do white grapes, so red grapes are usually planted in warmer locations. In colder northern regions—in Germany and northern France, for instance—most vineyards are planted with white grapes. In the warmer regions of Italy, Spain, and Portugal, and in California's Napa Valley, the red grape thrives.

When is the harvest?

Grapes are picked when they reach the proper sugar/acid ratio for the style of wine the vintner wants to produce. Go to a vineyard in June and taste one of the small green grapes. Your mouth will pucker because the grape is so tart and acidic. Return to the same vineyard—even to that same vine—in September or October, and the grapes will taste sweet. All those months of sun have given sugar to the grape.

What effect does weather have on the grapes?

Weather can interfere with the quality of the harvest, as well as its quantity. In the spring, as vines emerge from dormancy, a sudden frost may stop the flowering, thereby reducing the yields. Even a strong windstorm can affect the grapes adversely at this crucial time. Not enough rain, too much rain, or rain at the wrong time can also wreak havoc.

Rain just before the harvest will swell the grapes with water, diluting the juice and making thin, watery wines. Lack of rain will affect the wine's balance by creating a more powerful and concentrated wine, but will result in a smaller crop. A severe drop in temperature may affect the vines even outside the growing season. In New York State the winter of 2003–04 was one of the coldest in fifty years. The result was a major decrease in wine production, with some vineyards losing more than 50 percent of their crop for the 2004 vintage.

What is phylloxera?

Phylloxera, a grape louse, is one of the grapevine's worst enemies because it eventually kills the entire plant. An epidemic infestation in the 1870s came close to destroying all the vineyards of Europe. Luckily, the roots of native American vines are immune to this louse. After this was discovered, all the European vines were pulled up and grafted onto phylloxera-resistant American rootstocks.

Can white wine be made from red grapes?

Yes. The color of wine comes entirely from the grape skins. By removing the skins immediately after picking, no color is imparted to the wine, and it will be white. In the Champagne region of France, a large percentage of the grapes grown are red, yet most of the resulting wine is white. Cali-

fornia's White Zinfandel is made from red Zinfandel grapes.

What is tannin, and is it desirable in wine?

Tannin is a natural preservative and is one of the many components that gives wine its longevity. It comes from skins, pits, and stems of the grapes. Another source of tannin is wood, such as the oak barrels in which some wines are aged or fermented. Generally, red wines have a higher level of tannin than whites because red grapes are usually left to ferment with their skins. A word used to describe the sensation of tannins is "astringent." Especially in young wines, tannin can be very astringent and make the wine taste bitter. Tannin is not a taste, however—it's a tactile sensation.

Tannin is also found in strong tea. And what can you add to tea to make is less astringent? Milk—the fat and the proteins in milk soften the tannin. And so it is with a highly tannic wine. If you take another milk by-product, such as cheese, and have it with wine, it softens the tannin and makes the wine more appealing. Enjoy a beef entrée or one served with a cream sauce and a good bottle of red wine to experience it for yourself.

Is acidity desirable in wine?

All wine will have a certain amount of acidity. Generally, white wines have more perceived acidity than reds, though winemakers try to have a balance of fruit and acid. An overly acidic wine is also described as tart or sour. Acidity is a very important component in the aging of wines.

What is meant by "vintage"? Why is one year considered better than another?

A vintage indicates the year the grapes were harvested, so every year is a vintage year. A vintage chart reflects the weather conditions for various years. Better weather usually results in a better rating for the vintage, and therefore a higher likelihood that the wine will age well.

Are all wines meant to be aged?

No. It's a common misconception that all wines improve with age. In fact, more than 90 percent of all the wines made in the world should be consumed within one year since purchase, and less than 1 percent of the world's wines should be aged for more than five years. Wines change with age. Some get better, but most do not. The good news is that the 1 percent represents more than 350 million bottles of wine every vintage.

What makes a wine last more than five years?

THE COLOR AND THE GRAPE Red wines, because of their tannin content, will generally age longer than whites. And certain red grapes, such as Cabernet Sauvignon, tend to have more tannin than, say, Pinot Noir.

THE VINTAGE The better the weather conditions in one year, the more likely the wines from that vintage will have a better balance of fruits, acids, and tannins, and therefore have the potential to age longer.

WHERE THE WINE COMES FROM Certain vineyards have optimum conditions for growing grapes, including such factors as soil, weather, drainage, and slope of the

land. All of this contributes to producing a great wine that will need time to age.

HOW THE WINE WAS MADE (VINIFI-CATION) The longer the wine remains in contact with its skins during fermentation (maceration), and if it is fermented and/or aged in oak, the more of the tannin it will have, which can help it age longer. These are just two examples of how winemaking can affect the aging of wine.

WINE STORAGE CONDITIONS Even the best-made wines in the world will not age well if they are improperly stored.

ON TASTING WINE

You can read all the books (and there are plenty) written on wine to become more knowledgeable on the subject, but the best way to truly enhance your understanding of wine is to taste as many wines as possible. Reading covers the more academic side of wine, while tasting is more enjoyable and practical. A little of each will do you the most good. The following are the necessary steps for tasting wine. You may wish to follow them with a glass of wine in hand. Wine tasting can be broken down into five basic steps: Color, Swirl, Smell, Taste, and Savor.

Color

The best way to get an idea of a wine's color is to get a white background—a napkin or tablecloth—and hold the glass of wine on an angle in front of it. The range of colors that you may see depends, of course, on whether you're tasting a white or red wine. Color tells you a lot about the wine. Since we start with the white wines, let's consider three reasons why a white wine may have more color:

1. It's older.
2. Different grape varieties give different color. For example, Chardonnay usually gives off a deeper color than does Sauvignon Blanc.
3. The wine was aged in wood. In class, I always begin by asking my students what color the wine is. It's not unusual to hear that some believe that the wine is pale yellow-green, while others say it's gold. Everyone begins with the same wine, but color perceptions vary. There are no right or wrong answers, because perception is subjective. So you can imagine what happens when we actually taste the wine!

Swirl

Why do we swirl wine? To allow oxygen to get into the wine. Swirling releases the esters, ethers, and aldehydes that combine with oxygen to yield a wine's bouquet. In other words, swirling aerates the wine and releases more of the bouquet and aroma.

Smell

This is the most important part of wine tasting. You can perceive just four tastes—sweet, sour, bitter, and salty—but the average person can identify more than two thousand different scents, and wine has more than two hundred of its own. Now that you've swirled the wine and released the bouquet, I want you to smell the wine at least three times. You may find that the third smell will give you more information than the first smell did. What does the wine smell like? What type of nose does it have? Smell is the most important step in the tasting process and most people simply don't spend enough time on it. Pinpointing the nose of the wine helps you to identify certain characteristics. The problem here is that many people in class want me to tell them what the wine smells like. Since I prefer not to use subjective words, I may say that the wine smells like a French white Burgundy. Still, I find that this doesn't satisfy the majority of the class. They want to know more. I ask these people to describe what steak and onions smell like. They answer, "Like steak and onions." See what I mean?

The best way to learn what your own preferences are for styles of wine is to "memorize" the smell of the individual grape varieties. For white, just try to memorize the three major grape varieties: Chardonnay, Sauvignon Blanc, and Riesling. Keep smelling them, and smelling them, and smelling them until you can identify the differences, one from the other. For the reds it's a little more difficult, but you still can take three major grape varieties: Pinot Noir, Merlot, and Cabernet Sauvignon. Try to memorize those smells without using flowery words, and you'll understand what I'm talking about.

For those in the Wine School who remain unconvinced, I hand out a list of five hundred different words commonly used to describe wine. Here is a small excerpt:

acetic	aftertaste	aroma
astringent	austere	baked-burnt
balanced	big-full-heavy	bitter
body	bouquet	bright
character	corky	delicate
developed	earthy	finish
flat	fresh	grapy
green	hard	hot
legs	light	maderized
mature	metallic	moldy
nose	nutty	off
oxidized	pétillant	rich
seductive	short	soft
stalky	sulfury	tart
thin	tired	vanilla
woody	yeasty	young

You're also more likely to recognize some of the defects of a wine through your sense of smell. If you're smelling vinegar there's probably too much acetic acid in the wine. If you smell something that reminds you of sherry then there's probably oxidation. If it smells dank, wet, or like a moldy cellar then the wine has probably absorbed the taste of a defective cork (referred to as "corked wine"). If you smell sulfur (such as burnt matches) then there's most likely too much sulfur dioxide.

Taste

To many people, tasting wine means taking a sip and swallowing immediately. To me,

this isn't tasting. Tasting is something you do with your taste buds. You have taste buds all over your mouth—on both sides of the tongue, underneath, on the tip, and extending to the back of your throat. If you do what many people do, you take a gulp of wine and bypass all of those important taste buds. When I taste wine I leave it in my mouth for three to five seconds before swallowing. The wine warms up, sending signals about the bouquet and aroma up through the nasal passage then on to the olfactory bulb, and then to the limbic system of the brain. Remember, 90 percent of taste is smell.

What should you think about when tasting wine?

Be aware of the most important sensations of taste and your own personal thresholds of those tastes. Also, pay attention to where they occur on your tongue and in your mouth. As I mentioned earlier, you can perceive just four tastes: sweet, sour, bitter, and salty (but there's no salt in wine, so we're down to three). Bitterness in wine is usually created by high alcohol and high tannin. Sweetness occurs only in wines that have some residual sugar left over after fermentation. Sour (sometimes called "tart") indicates the acidity in wine.

SWEETNESS The highest threshold is on the tip of the tongue. If there's any sweetness in a wine whatsoever, you'll get it right away.

ACIDITY Found at the sides of the tongue, the cheek area, and the back of the throat. White wines and some lighter-style red wines usually contain a higher degree of acidity.

BITTERNESS Tasted on the back of the tongue.

TANNIN The sensation of tannin begins in the middle of the tongue. Tannin frequently exists in red wines or white wines aged in wood. When the wines are too young, tannin dries the palate to excess. If there's a lot of tannin in the wine, it can actually coat your whole mouth, blocking the fruit. Remember, tannin is not a taste: It is a tactile sensation.

FRUIT AND VARIETAL CHARACTERISTICS These are not tastes, but smells. The weight of the fruit (the "body") will be felt in the middle of the tongue.

AFTERTASTE The overall taste and balance of the components of the wine that lingers in your mouth. How long does the balance last? Usually a sign of a high-quality wine is a long, pleasing aftertaste. The taste of many of the great wines lasts anywhere from one to three minutes, with all their components in harmony.

Savor

After you've had a chance to taste the wine, sit back for a few moments and savor it. Think about what you just experienced, and ask yourself the following questions to help focus your impressions.

- ➤ Was the wine light-, medium-, or full-bodied?
- ➤ For a white wine: How was the acidity? Very little, just right, or too much?
- ➤ For a red wine: Is the tannin in the wine too strong or astringent? Does it blend with the fruit or overpower it?
- ➤ What is the strongest component (residual sugar, fruit, acid, tannin)?
- ➤ How long did the balance of the components last (ten seconds, sixty seconds, etc.)?

- ➤ Is the wine ready to drink? Or does it need more time to age? Or is it past its prime?
- ➤ What kind of food would you enjoy with the wine?
- ➤ To your taste, is the wine worth the price?
- ➤ This brings us to the most important point. The first thing you should consider after you've tasted a wine is whether or not you like it. Is it your style?

You can compare tasting wine to browsing in an art gallery. You wander from room to room looking at the paintings. Your first impression tells whether or not you like something. Once you decide you like a piece of art, you want to know more: Who was the artist? What is the history behind the work? How was it done? And so it is with wine. Usually, once oenophiles (wine aficionados) discover a wine that they like, they want to learn everything about it: the winemaker; the grapes; exactly where the vines were planted; the blend, if any; and the history behind the wine.

How do you know if a wine is good or not?

The definition of a good wine is one that you enjoy. I cannot emphasize this enough. Trust your own palate and do not let others dictate taste to you!

When is a wine ready to drink?

This is one of the most frequently asked questions in my Wine School. The answer is very simple: when all components of the wine are in balance to your particular taste.

59

WHITE GRAPES OF THE WORLD

Now that you know the basics of how wine is made and how to taste it, let me answer the question most frequently asked by my wine students on what will help them most in learning about wine. The main thing is to understand the major grape varieties and where they are grown in the world.

My choice is not to overwhelm you with information about every grape under the sun. My job as a wine educator is to try to narrow down this overabundance of data. So let's start off with the three major grapes you need to know to understand white wine. More than 90 percent of all quality white wine is made from these three grapes. In order from the lightest style to the fullest, they are: Riesling, Sauvignon Blanc, and Chardonnay.

This is not to say that world-class white wine comes from only these grapes, but knowing these three is a good start.

One of the first things I show my students is a list indicating where these three grape varieties grow best:

RIESLING Germany; Alsace, France; New York State; Washington State

SAUVIGNON BLANC Bordeaux, France; Loire Valley, France; New Zealand; California (Fumé Blanc)

CHARDONNAY Burgundy, France; Champagne, France; California; Australia

There are world-class Rieslings, Sauvignon Blancs, and Chardonnays made in other countries, but in general the above regions specialize in wines made from these grapes.

DOMAINE LENOIR

MACON-VILLAGES
APPELLATION MACON-VILLAGES CONTROLEE
WHITE BURGUNDY WINE
MIS EN BOUTEILLE PAR
LES VINS GEORGES DUBŒUF
71570 ROMANÈCHE-THORINS FRANCE
PRODUCED AND BOTTLED IN FRANCE

ALC. 12.5% BY VOL.   750 ML
SELECTED AND BOTTLED FOR CALVERT WOODLEY
IMPORTED BY : W.J. DEUSTCH & SONS LTD., HARRISON, NY.

MARKHAM
VINEYARDS®

SAUVIGNON BLANC
NAPA VALLEY

With vineyards located in Napa Valley's best growing regions, Markham has been crafting exceptional wines for more than 125 years.

ESTABLISHED
18 M 79

COMMON AROMAS

Riesling	Sauvignon Blanc	Chardonnay
Fruity	Grapefruit	Green apple, Butter, Citrus
Lychee nut	Grass, Herbs, Grapefruit	Melon, Oak
Sweet	Cat pee	Pineapple, Toast, Vanilla

RED GRAPES OF THE WORLD

I usually like to start with a list of what I consider to be the major red-wine grapes, ranked from lightest to fullest-bodied style, along with the region or country in which the grape grows best. By looking at the chart, not only will you get an idea of the style of the wine, but also a feeling for gradations of weight, color, tannin, and ageability.

61

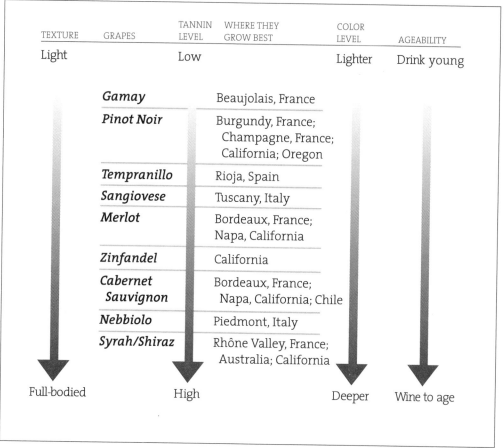

TEXTURE	GRAPES	TANNIN LEVEL	WHERE THEY GROW BEST	COLOR LEVEL	AGEABILITY
Light		Low		Lighter	Drink young
	Gamay		Beaujolais, France		
	Pinot Noir		Burgundy, France; Champagne, France; California; Oregon		
	Tempranillo		Rioja, Spain		
	Sangiovese		Tuscany, Italy		
	Merlot		Bordeaux, France; Napa, California		
	Zinfandel		California		
	Cabernet Sauvignon		Bordeaux, France; Napa, California; Chile		
	Nebbiolo		Piedmont, Italy		
	Syrah/Shiraz		Rhône Valley, France; Australia; California		
Full-bodied		High		Deeper	Wine to age

⌐ THE 60-SECOND WINE EXPERT ⌐

Over the last few years I have insisted that my students spend one minute in silence after they swallow the wine. I use a "60-second wine expert" tasting sheet in my classes for students to record their impressions. The minute is divided into four sections: 0 to 15 seconds, 15 to 30 seconds, 30 to 45 seconds, and the final 45 to 60 seconds. Try this with your next glass of wine. Please note that the first taste of wine is a shock to your taste buds. This is due to the alcohol content, acidity, and sometimes the tannin. The higher the alcohol or acidity, the more of a shock. For the first wine in any tasting, it is probably best to take a sip and swirl it around in your mouth, but don't evaluate it. Wait another thirty seconds, try it again, and then begin the 60-second wine expert tasting.

0 to 15 seconds If there is any residual sugar/sweetness in the wine, I will experience it now. If there is no sweetness in the wine, the acidity is usually at its strongest sensation in the first fifteen seconds. I am also looking for the fruit level of the wine and its balance with the acidity or sweetness.

15 to 30 seconds After the sweetness or acidity, I am looking for great fruit sensation. After all, that is what I am paying for! By the time I reach thirty seconds, I am hoping for balance of all the components. By this time, I can identify the weight of the wine. Is it light, medium, or full-bodied? I am now starting to think about what kind of food I can pair with this wine.

30 to 45 seconds At this point I am beginning to formulate my opinion of the wine, whether I like it or not. Not all wines need sixty seconds of thought. Lighter-style wines, such as Rieslings, will usually show their best at this point. The fruit, acid, and sweetness of a great German Riesling should be in perfect harmony from this point on. For quality red and white wines, acidity—which is a very strong component, especially in the first thirty seconds—should now be in balance with the fruit of the wine.

45 to 60 seconds Very often wine writers use the term "length" to describe how long the components, balance, and flavor continue in the mouth. I concentrate on the length of the wine in these last fifteen seconds. In big, full-bodied red wines from Bordeaux and the Rhône Valley, Cabernets from California, Barolos and Barbarescos from Italy, and even some full-bodied Chardonnays, I am concentrating on the level of tannin in the wine. Just as the acidity and fruit balance are my major concerns in the first thirty seconds, it is now the tannin and fruit balance I am looking for in the last thirty seconds. If the fruit, tannin, and acid are all in balance at sixty seconds, then I feel that the wine is probably ready to drink. Does the tannin overpower the fruit? If it does at the sixty-second mark, I will then begin to question whether I should drink the wine now or put it away for more aging.

It is extremely important to me that if you want to learn the true taste of the wine, you take at least one minute to concentrate on all of its components. In my classes it is amazing to see more than a hundred students silently taking one minute to analyze a wine. Some close their eyes, some bow their heads in deep thought, others write notes.

One final point: Sixty seconds, to me, is the minimum time to wait before making a decision about a wine. Many great wines continue to show balance well past 120 seconds. The best wine I ever tasted lasted more than three minutes—that's three minutes of perfect balance of all components!

TASTING WORKSHEET

60-Second Wine Expert:
Identify the major component in each time slot.

0–15 seconds _____

15–30 seconds _____

30–45 seconds _____

45–60 seconds _____

Color:
_____

Aroma/Bouquet:
_____

_____

_____

	Low	Medium	High
Residual sugar			
Fruit			
Acid			
Tannin			

Light-bodied _____ Medium-bodied _____ Full-bodied _____

Ageability: Ready to drink? _____ Needs more time? _____ Past its prime? _____

Personal rating/Comments _____

PETER'S TASTING VOCABULARY

Lettie Teague

To truly understand a subject as complex as wine, one must acquire a vocabulary or at least learn a few key words and tasting terms. Peter, for example, had a lot of good instincts and some interesting ideas, but lacked the right words to properly describe (to himself and others) what he found in a wine. He needed to develop a wine vocabulary. (For example, the word *ouch* is not considered a valid tasting term—although it was one of Peter's favorites and seemed to sum up his feelings about certain wines.)

Aroma—*Aroma* and *bouquet* are often used interchangeably to describe the nose of a wine, but in fact only a young wine has an aroma—that is, scents of primary fruit and oak—whereas a bouquet develops over time as the wine develops secondary aromas such as truffles and mushrooms and earth. "That's fascinating," remarked Peter. "I might have to obsess over that for a while."

Barrique—These are small, fashionable French oak barrels used by producers all over the world. You'll see them mentioned on the back labels of many expensive wines. The tighter-grained French barriques impart a much more subtle flavor than most (wider-grained) American oak barrels.

Beefy—A beefy wine has lots of everything—tannin, fruit, structure—in an unsubtle way.

Body—Wines with body are wines of substance, of fullness and generosity in the mouth. A wine with a "good body" is as much to be admired as a person similarly endowed.

Breathe—When people open a bottle and say, "I want the wine to breathe," they forget that they're just giving the wine a one-inch-diameter bit of air. To truly enable a wine to "breathe," it's best to decant it. This softens the tannins of a young, tight wine and also helps to open up its aromas.

Over the last twelve years, Lettie Teague has been the wine columnist for Food & Wine *magazine, and now her columns appear in the* Wall Street Journal. *This chapter is from her book* Educating Peter. *She has won many awards for her writing skills. If you ever get a chance to meet Lettie, her writing style (witty, opinionated, and humorous) parallels her personality.*

Chewy—A chewy wine has lots of texture and fairly strong, though not necessarily astringent, tannins.

Claret—This is a British term for Bordeaux, though more and more California winemakers are making wines they call Claret, which are mostly Cabernet-dominant blends. Francis Ford Coppola was one of the first in Napa to call his Cabernet-based wine Claret.

Closed—A wine that has no aroma is often referred to as closed. This is usually because the wine is still quite young. "I think I've had a lot of closed wines," Peter remarked. I didn't have the heart to tell him that the $7 wines he was drinking probably weren't closed as much as they were just . . . cheap and lacking in aroma—and a whole lot else besides.

Corked—If a wine is infected with something called TCA and smells like wet newspapers or a wet basement, it is said to be "corked." Or if a wine is lightly corked it can simply have no flavor at all.

Ester—"My favorite word!" Peter says. These are the compounds that contribute to the aroma of a wine.

Extracted—This word is (now commonly) used to describe a big, concentrated wine. It is what is left when all the possible solubles are removed in the making of a wine, reducing it to its core, "extracted" element: wine in its most concentrated form.

Finish—This is the way that a wine lingers on your tongue. Some tasters even time the length of a finish, but I didn't want to get Peter started with a stopwatch. A notebook was all he could handle right now.

Firm—A wine that has lots of structure and tannin, such as Cabernet Sauvignon or Syrah, is often described as "firm."

Flabby—This word describes a wine that lacks acidity and lacks a refreshing quality. Just as no person would want to be described thus, no winemaker would be proud of having produced a flabby wine.

Fresh—*Fresh* is just as it sounds: a wine that is bright and invigorating.

Fruity—People too often equate fruitiness with sweetness. A fruity wine is simply a wine with a lot of exuberant, primary fruit character.

Green—A green wine is often made from underripe, or "green," fruit.

Hard—The tannins are excessive and obtrusive in a hard wine.

Hollow—A hollow wine simply has nothing in the middle; it may have a beginning, or "attack," as Peter liked to say, and an end or "finish," but there's nothing in between.

Hot—A hot wine has an excess of alcohol. "It's interesting that *hot* should mean too alcoholic," Peter observed. "It sounds like a positive thing. Or something Paris Hilton would say, like 'This wine is so hot!'"

Length—This refers to the length of time that a wine lingers in your mouth. "Is that always going to be a big fat wine like Chardonnay?" Peter asked. Not necessarily, I said. A wine with good length can also be something as streamlined as a Riesling or Sauvignon Blanc.

Middle palate—A great wine always has a good beginning, middle, and end. When wine tasters talk about a wine's "midpalate," they mean the collective sensations that tie the start and the finish of a wine together.

Mouth feel—A high-quality wine has a good "mouth feel," that is, its texture is pleasurable, and its elements—fruit, tannin, and acidity—are in balance.

Nose—This word serves as both a noun and a verb in the world of wine tasting. This was good news for Peter, who liked nothing better than talk about noses and "nosing."

Oxidized—A wine that has been exposed to excessive amounts of oxygen and frequently smells like a bottle of Sherry that's been left open on the sideboard for a long time. "I've been in houses where people have bottles like that," remarked Peter.

Rich—This means pretty much what it sounds like—a rich wine has lots of intensity, in both body and flavor.

Round—This is a pretty self-explanatory term, used to describe a wine that is pleasant, easy to drink.

Soft—This can be a good thing, i.e., the wine is not overly tannic, or too much of a good thing, that is, the wine lacks definition, but it depends on whether the wine has enough balancing acidity. If a wine is soft in a bad way, it lacks acidity.

Tears—These are the drops of wine that stream down the inside of the glass after the wine has been poured; they are alternately referred to as tears or legs. A wine that is big and rich, aka more viscous, will always have longer tears. Many people believe (incorrectly) that tears indicate a high-quality wine, but it has more to do with the type of wine than anything else. For example, a full-bodied Chardonnay will have longer, and longer-lasting, tears than a lighter, leaner Riesling.

Texture—The texture of a wine is the way that it feels in the mouth (aka its mouth feel). Words commonly used to describe wine texture include *smooth, creamy, thin,* or *coarse.*

Tight—A tight wine is generally one that is young and therefore inaccessible, i.e., its tannins or acidity are more pronounced, often masking its fruit. When a tight wine (more often red wines are described as tight than white) begins to open up and to reveal itself (either through time or exposure to air), it is said to "unwind."

SOME FREQUENTLY ENCOUNTERED WINE TERMS

Appellation—The French were the first to create an appellation system (Appellation d'Origine Contrôlée) for their wines, in 1935, as a means of identifying a wine of a particular grape or grapes, made in a particular place. The French appellation system has served as a model for wine classification systems all over the world, including the United States. The French model, however, remains the most rigorous (and detractors would say "rigid") of all. There are more than five hundred appellations in France, although only 15 percent of French wines are actually AOC-designated wines.

Château—This is simply the name given to an estate where wine is made, most famously in Bordeaux.

Commune—A commune is a recognizable subregion of a more important region. For example, Pauillac is a commune of Bordeaux.

Cru—This term is used in both Bordeaux and Burgundy to recognize the most important

châteaux (Bordeaux) and vineyards (Burgundy), which are ranked either "premier" or "grand" cru.

Growth—This term was first used in Bordeaux in the Médoc classification of 1855 to recognize that region's most important wines. In that classification system, the wines were ranked first through fifth "classified growths."

Négociant—A négociant is a broker, one who sells wine or grapes, as opposed to one who owns vineyards. (Although négociants such as Drouhin may own vineyards as well.)

$25,000 WINE WEEK:
A Tale of Excess

Alan Richman

I have friends who regularly travel to Europe on wine-drinking pilgrimages, excursions into decadence that leave me gasping with envy. After hearing their stories, I find myself delusively imagining I'm one of them. I see myself picking up a wine list at a magnificent restaurant such as Monaco's Louis XV and ordering a grand cru white Burgundy with a rim as golden hued as the Limoges china. There I am, gazing upward, as the bouquet of my perfumed Corton-Charlemagne soars toward the nymphs and angels gamboling on the 25-foot ceiling.

This past January, I gathered up my courage and my bankroll and informed my friends that I would be joining them on their upcoming trip to Europe. The itinerary included La Beaugravière in Provence, a restaurant that is unstarred by the Michelin guide but has an enthusiastic following among wine drinkers; as well as four of the most esteemed establishments in Europe, all with three-star ratings: Le Louis XV; Trois-gros, in Roanne; Paul Bocuse, outside Lyon; and Guy Savoy, in Paris.

My fantasy was not just to be with wine connoisseurs but also to be one of them, and it was at the distressingly appointed La Beaugravière, which looks as though it was transplanted intact from Guadala-jara, that I thought I would succeed. I'd spotted a treasure on the wine list, an old-vines Châteauneuf-du-Pape from a fabulous vintage. I expected my companions to carry me to the dinner table on their shoulders. I gulped my gougère and tried to get their attention.

Everybody was sitting around perusing wine lists, a predinner ritual of ours. The man I'll call Sommelier No. 1 was asking the man I'll call Wine Merchant No. 1, in a wine-weary sort of way, "Do you like Clape's wines?" Auguste Clape is a renowned producer of Cornas. To the group of connoisseurs I was with, however, Cornas is just a simple, heat-soaked Syrah of little consequence.

I have had the pleasure of knowing Alan Richman for over twenty years. We once had a show on the Food Network called Wine A to Z (A – Alan and Z – Zraly). His knowledge of wine and food, his professionalism, and his sense of humor made for a great show. He holds the record for the most James Beard journalism awards (fourteen) and has taken the top prize, the M.F.K. Fisher Distinguished Writing Award, twice.

Excitedly, I interrupted: "Look, the 1989 Domaine de la Janasse Vieilles Vignes, only $120!"

Nobody looked up. The merchant turned to the sommelier. He replied, "I find them rustic, never really appealing."

I was beginning to understand my place as a noncollector. The sounds I made were as insignificant as those of a distant train or a small forest animal rustling leaves. That evening we did not drink my wine discovery. It did not even rate consideration. I was among my betters, as far as selecting wine was concerned.

I spent a week dining with these men, all of whom I still call my friends, which demonstrates my forgiving nature. Of the five restaurants we visited, three—Louis XV, Troisgros, and Beaugravière—had extraordinary wine lists, both in scope and value. The wine service was perfect at Louis XV, Troisgros, and Guy Savoy. Great wine service in France is unrivaled, because it encompasses discreet attention, appropriate glassware, and formidable knowledge. I anticipated exquisite service, even though we were American tourists, and for the most part we got it. French restaurateurs, like all restaurateurs, are very polite to customers who spend $3,000 to $4,000 per night on wine. (Prices have been rounded off to one euro equaling $1.10.) I felt the sommelier at Beaugravière could have been more congenial and the glasses at Bocuse washed with more care.

Our meals typically lasted five hours, including the time we spent studying wine lists, often in cushy anterooms with complimentary hors d'oeuvres. On the single occasion when one of my friends knocked over a glass of wine, the sort of accident one might expect, the person soaked from neck to waist was me. I told these men I would protect their identities, describing them only by their professions or hobbies, and it was Wine Collector No. 1 who marinated my Giorgio Armani Collezioni shirt ($175, on sale) in 1990 Beaucastel Hommage à Jacques Perrin Châteauneuf-du-Pape ($710, in magnum).

I can only demonstrate so much restraint. Thanks a lot, Alan Belzer.

The group included two wine directors from top New York City restaurants, two principals in one of the most prestigious wine shops in Manhattan, and two wine collectors. Five of the six characterize themselves as bargain hunters. The sixth, Wine Merchant No. 2, says he refuses to spend excessively but is mostly interested in finding once-in-a-lifetime rarities. To them, seeking out well-priced wines means paying less for a bottle on a list in France than they would pay for it in a shop in America. For the most part, that meant drinking cult wines by Coche-Dury (white Burgundies), Henri Jayer (red Burgundies), Guigal (single-vineyard Côte-Rôties), and, to a lesser extent, Jaboulet (Hermitage).

I've always believed that rational persons should not consume magnificent wines in high-priced restaurants, because of excessive markups. That proves I've spent too much time dining in New York. At Alain Ducasse's Louis XV, a soaring restaurant with gilded 18th-century accoutrements, the 1992 Coche-Dury Corton-Charlemagne, a mineral-laced bombshell of a white, cost $400. Wine Merchant No. 2 said, "Any time you see Coche for $400, you should drink it for breakfast, lunch, and dinner. This bottle is about $1,000 below the retail price in New York."

At Troisgros, we paid $825 for the 1990 Jayer Cros Parantoux, a stunning (although youthful) red Burgundy. On the generally well-priced wine list of Washington Park restaurant in Manhattan, the same bottle is $3,750. None of these men, no matter what they already had in their cellars, was able to resist a bargain, much as a woman with a dozen pairs of $800 Manolo Blahnik shoes in her closet cannot stop herself when she sees another pair on sale for $400. To them, Henri Jayer is the Manolo Blahnik of wine.

They almost always drink Burgundies and red wines from the Rhône, and they seldom, if ever, believe Bordeaux is worth the price it commands on wine lists. Even though the three greatest reds I've ever tasted—1953 Margaux, 1961 Trotanoy, and 1975 Pétrus—were all Bordeaux from their personal collections, we did not drink a single Bordeaux on this trip. Explained Wine Merchant No. 1, "None of us particularly enjoy young Bordeaux, and the ones that are ready to drink, the pre-1982s, are always too expensive."

Almost every wine we ordered came from a memorable vintage, although we did have 1991 Comte de Vogüé Musigny ($620, in magnum) at Louis XV because my friends knew that the estate had produced a long, sweet, beautifully colored Burgundy in that difficult year. They know years the way rabbis know the Ten Commandments, the way Roman Catholic priests know the Stations of the Cross. They know when hail fell in the Côte de Nuits (most famously in 1983) and when labor shortages caused difficulties with the harvest in Germany (most infamously in 1945). On impulse, we sent a glass of the 1991 Musigny to a man dining alone, and he sent back a charming note wishing us luck and thanking us for making him feel a part of such a fortunate group. "Doing something like that makes me feel like a god," said Wine Merchant No. 2, an unintentionally perceptive remark, because wine collectors, I've found, often see themselves that way.

Their weakness where wine is concerned is a disinclination to experiment. At Louis XV, I spotted a bottle of 1982 Cotnari Grasa

Sélection de Grains Nobles in the La Moldavie section of the list, a sweet wine none of us had ever heard of, selling for $70. (1982 was a famous year in Bordeaux, and perhaps in Moldavia, too.) Although I am not, nor have I ever been, a member of the Communist Party, I could not have resisted the call of an authentic Marxist-Leninist wine produced in Romania during the dictatorship of Nicolae Ceaușescu. My friends refused to order it. Wine Collector No. 2 said, "We seek out opportunities we will remember for the rest of our lives. We are not here to rough it."

Only once did they drink a wine of my choosing, and that was because I arrived before they did at Guy Savoy—they took taxis, I rode the Métro. I selected a 2000 Ostertag Pinot Gris (overpriced at $140, but these connoisseurs would have sneered at something inexpensive), and the sommelier agreed to serve it blind.

They guessed the grape. I never said they weren't good.

Wine collectors are not like stamp collectors. They are not passive or diffident, and they do not hoard. They are aggressively social, and their labels are their calling cards. They come accompanied by Baron Rothschild of Bordeaux and René Dauvissat of Chablis. They do not serve their wines; they trumpet them. When a half dozen wine collectors of equal stature get together, not one will entirely agree with another man's choice. They want to drink what they like. They are type A-plus, one and all, correctly perceiving themselves as winners in the wine world. The three words you will never hear one wine collector say to another are these: "You know best."

My friends frequently argued over who was getting to pick the wines and who was being ignored, but these discussions always took place at lunch, when the wine was not too serious—a modest vertical of $200 J. L. Chave Hermitages, for example. Dinners were amiable, no matter how much wine was consumed; the men all seemed to become more mellow the more they drank, as though the wines passed along their harmonious qualities.

Wine collectors are seldom aware of their shortcomings, because they are rarely pointed out. They always assume they will be admired wherever they go, and the fact that they arrive with their wines makes it so. They are certain their ability to drink well and converse articulately about what is in their glasses makes them desirable companions. So self-assured are they that they believe people in less fortunate wine circumstances are pleased to have them around. Generally speaking, they are correct.

I have sat spellbound, listening to their tales of excess. A few years back the two merchants and the two collectors lunched at Alain Chapel and noticed a 1929 DRC Romanée-Conti on the list, although without a price. They inquired, and thought they heard the sommelier say 14,000 francs (just over $2,000). When the bill came, the price was 40,000 francs. Even after paying just under $7,000, they reveled in their good luck. The wine was that wonderful. It is probably unnecessary to add that these gentlemen are willing to spend fortunes on wine but nothing on French lessons.

So it was on this trip when the connoisseur of rarities noticed a 1929 Jaboulet

Hermitage La Chapelle on the list at La Beaugravière for $1,300. By reputation, this is a wine of majesty, produced in a region beloved by Thomas Jefferson and the Russian imperial court. The owner of Beaugravière announced that it was the last of a full case of 12 bottles that had been topped off and recorked at the winery in the 1990s. Knowing something is the last of anything makes my friends want it all the more.

A bottle that old is not a guarantee of pleasure but a venture into high-stakes poker. If it is as magnificent as the Romanée-Conti they drank at Alain Chapel, the experience can be existential. If not, it is merely expensive.

Sommelier No. 2 accepted the responsibility of tasting the '29 Hermitage.

Merchant No. 1 whispered to me, "I wouldn't order it, because I don't want to take on the responsibility."

Sommelier No. 1 disagreed. "It's worth having so we don't regret not having it for the rest of our lives," he said.

The cork came out, perhaps too easily. The wine burbled into the glass. The designated taster sniffed, then breathed deeply. I looked at his face, and I did not see rapture. I saw $1,300 worth of perplexity. I saw costly indecision. He chewed. He stared. His eyes went down. The table hushed. He spoke the three words I would soon learn to loathe.

He said, "Tastes like wine."

I felt as though I had opened the door to greet my mail-order bride and the best I could utter was, "Well, it's a woman." (Did I mention the testosterone level of wine collectors?)

He tasted again and added, "Wine's been cooped up a long time. A slight Madeira and chocolate to it."

Madeira and chocolate are not a $1,300 food-and-wine pairing. To those notes, I'd add tea. We had a $1,300 bottle of Lipton's. La Beaugravière's owner tasted and pronounced it fine, one of the best bottles from the case. Added La Beaugravière's sommelier, "Very good." I felt these were not disinterested opinions.

We drank it in silence, and silence is a bad thing at dinner, particularly the silence of despair.

In the course of our trip, we sent back just one bottle, a 1989 La Mouline from Guigal that was indisputably corked, and

we accepted many that I would have sent back had I any influence with the group. I wondered why they accepted so many flawed bottles and decided they were so proud of their ability to make excellent selections they were ashamed to admit they had erred. Most of the wines I thought unacceptable were either tired from age, technically flawed, or had low fills (the wine barely reaching the neck of the bottle). The attitude of the group seemed to be that if it was still a wine, they were obligated to pay for it. Their most charitable act, in my opinion, was accepting a bottle of 1967 Beaucastel Châteauneuf-du-Pape that cost $380 at La Beaugravière.

It came to the table with such a low fill that I would immediately have said *non*, had I spoken French. As the bottle was being opened, the glass collar that holds the cork, in essence the entire tip of the bottle, snapped off. To me, this constitutes defective goods, since I'm the kind of picky fellow who doesn't like drinking beverages containing shards of glass. The wine was accepted and it was surprisingly good, with a lovely, complex nose and fast-fading, dark berry flavors, more Burgundian than Rhône-like. Nevertheless, drinking it gave me the willies.

The worst bottle we accepted was at Paul Bocuse, the gaudy shrine to the most famous chef in the world. (The napkins there are awesome, only slightly smaller than the tablecloths.) For sentimental reasons, Sommelier No. 1 wanted to have 1976 Guigal La Mouline ($770). He told us he was working as a waiter in 1983 when he bought this wine in a shop for $30. It convinced him that he wanted to spend the rest of his life in the wine business.

Although the wine was still full of fruit, it was also cloudy and murky, so dark and ugly that it could be studied only by someone wearing a miner's hat. The Paul Bocuse sommelier insisted it had been stored impeccably, but we decided the only way it could have looked the way it did was if the waiter assigned to bring it up from the cellar had tripped on the steps and shaken up the sediment. I found it entirely without

pleasure and left almost all of my share in the glass.

If the finest white wine (and possibly the best value) of the trip was the 1992 Domaine Jean-François Coche-Dury Corton-Charlemagne at Louis XV, the two best red wines came from the cellars of Troisgros, a restaurant of unparalleled finesse, where everything is impressive except the attire of the male customers, who all appear to be regular visitors to the church thrift shop.

Unrivaled was the 1971 Romanée-Saint-Vivant Marey-Monge ($700), a profoundly rich, impeccably aged Burgundy with a hint of pleasing gaminess. The moment I tasted it, I said, "This is it." Almost as impressive was the 1985 La Turque ($820). The release of this celebrated wine in the late '80s caused a stampede among collectors, but since then it has largely been ignored. I tried it young and thought it was good. This bottle was magnificent. It had hints of smoke and licorice, and the structure was unusually elegant for a Rhône.

Finally, my time came. Weary of my complaints, my friends at last announced that I could select all the wines at Guy Savoy, a small, austere establishment down the street from the Arc de Triomphe. I went to the restaurant early. I grabbed a wine list. A kindly captain served me slivers of foie gras while I made my choices. My budget was $3,000.

By now, I knew what everybody liked, and I was sure I could come through. The Ostertag Pinot Gris served blind to begin the meal was just a tease. I planned to follow it with 1995 Gagnard Bâtard-Montrachet in

73

magnum, several 1985 Domaine de Montille Pommards, and a magnum of 1985 Dujac Clos de la Roche. If they wanted to go for the jackpot, I would suggest 1947 Gaunoux Pommard Rugiens ($1,470).

I announced my selections, and praise came showering down upon me. I was declared a man of perception, taste, and thoughtfulness.

Then they picked up their wine lists, chatted with the sommelier and changed everything. They didn't order a single bottle I wanted. When I requested an explanation, Wine Collector No. 2 said, "I have to say we didn't find the wines we really wanted until the professionals got here." By "the professionals," I believe he primarily meant himself.

Later, I asked my friends what I had done wrong. One told me I hadn't spoken loudly or authoritatively enough. Another said I had lost confidence in my own selections. I was about to protest, but then I remembered something.

It would do me no good to complain. Wine collectors never admit they're wrong.

ANCIENT MESSAGES, HIDDEN IN A DUSTY BOTTLE FROM LONG AGO

Eric Asimov

The lineup of wines to be served with dinner was extraordinary, including a Montrachet from 1939 and a Volnay Caillerets from 1929. Still, the wine I couldn't wait to try was the '46 Meursault Charmes.

That would be the 1846.

The dinner was in honor of Bouchard Père & Fils, the venerable Burgundy producer and négociant, which was celebrating its 275th anniversary with a tasting of some very, very old wines. It was held at the historic Château de Beaune, a 15th-century fortress here that has been the producer's ceremonial and corporate home since 1810. In addition to the 1846, Bouchard was to pour a relative youngster, the 1865 Beaune Grèves Vigne de L'Enfant Jésus.

Both of these ancient vintages had spent their long lives in the bowels of the château, where thick walls keep the cellars cool and

the bottles can rest undisturbed. As rare as it is to taste wines this old, it's even more unusual to taste bottles with such an unimpeachable provenance.

Scientists know that the gradual interaction between a fine wine and small amounts of oxygen results in what we call aging. Firm tannins soften and aggressive aromas of fruit mellow and evolve into complex new

As the chief wine critic for the New York Times, Eric Asimov is one of the most powerful wine writers. He has been involved in many aspects of the New York Times as the editor of the Living section and Styles of the Times. He created the "$25 and Under" restaurant review column. In my opinion, Eric's understanding of food and restaurants adds more dimension to his wine reviews. I have been lucky enough to participate in his tasting panels, which almost always include food writer Florence Fabricant and two other judges in the wine field. I look forward to many more years of Eric's articles and future books.

75

characteristics. A wine becomes harmonious and shows new dimensions.

That's the ideal, anyway. How the wine is stored and handled and a host of other factors can be the difference between a sublime old bottle and an expired soup. What no one has been able to do is predict when a wine will be at its peak or exactly how it will fare in its descent. What happens after a few decades along the aging trail is a mystery. But wine as old as these bottles borders on the mystical.

"No producer makes a wine to be drunk after 80 years," said François Audouze, a retired French steel executive who now arranges dinners centered on old wines and who was at this dinner. "When a wine is older than that, it is generally not the result of a will but of an accident."

The evening had begun in a nondescript industrial area outside this handsome little city, which has been the center of the Burgundy wine trade for 300 years or more. First, we toured Bouchard's new winery with its great steel tanks, catwalks, lots of oak barrels, the smell of fermented grape juice, even—gasp—a bottling apparatus. Then there was a tasting of Bouchard's 2005 lineup; 2005 was an excellent year in Burgundy, and Bouchard's wines are elegant and pure.

But the luminaries on the tour this soggy late fall evening—including Clive Coates, the British writer; Serena Sutcliffe, the head of Sotheby's international wine department; Allen Meadows of burghound.com, a leading Burgundy critic; and the French writers Thierry Desseauve and Jacky Rigaux —hadn't come to Bouchard

to sample unreleased wines. So it was with a discernible eagerness that we dispatched the initial tasting and headed to the chateau. After a Champagne reception (magnums of 1988 Cuvée des Enchanteleurs from Henriot, a corporate sibling of Bouchard), the 49 guests trooped expectantly to the dining tables, where the six wines would accompany six courses.

What's in an ancient bottle almost matters less than the vivid historical images conjured up by the year on the label. An 1865? By the first hint of green on the vines that mid-April, Lincoln was dead, "Hush'd Be the Camps Today," as Walt Whitman wrote that year.

The 1846? Not quite as resonant with me, although the French might have thought of Louis-Philippe, the last king to rule France, who was teetering on the throne before being unseated in 1848. The 1929 brought up the stock market crash and the start of the Great Depression, though I couldn't help thinking of my father, who was born in 1929 at the height of the summer.

Yet none of the wines summoned visions as searing as the 1939 Montrachet. As New Yorkers were enjoying their World's Fair, the French army had just been mobilized with France's entry into World War II. The harvest that fall stretched from days to weeks, Mr. Meadows recounted, as the women and children who were left behind picked grapes when they could, resulting in uneven degrees of ripeness.

Perhaps that explained why the '39 Montrachet, the second wine served after a well-balanced 1992 Chevalier-Montrachet, seemed so odd. It was a dark amber gold, with flavors of sherry and caramel, as if it were slightly oxidized. It smelled sweet yet tasted dry, and truthfully it was slightly disappointing. At first, at least. But an hour later, around the time I might have thought exposure to air would have dried out an older wine, the '39 Montrachet was just coming alive, with a beautiful, brilliant minerality. It was lesson No. 1 of this meal: never give up on a wine.

Lesson No. 2 came from Mr. Meadows, who has made it his business to taste wines from every vintage of the 20th century and before, if he can find them. "Pay attention to the texture," he advised, alluding to the fact that the two 19th-century wines predated the phylloxera epidemic, which devastated European vineyards in the late 1800's. The 1846 and '65 would be those rare Burgundies grown on their own rootstock instead of on grafted American roots, the only protection against phylloxera.

The moment of truth came. The 1846 was poured carefully but generously by the wine stewards, who had opened five bottles. The labels looked almost new, no surprise there. The humidity in a good wine cellar will rot paper, so wineries rarely label bottles until they are ready for shipping. The corks looked fresh, too. With its older bottles, Bouchard replaces the cork every 25 to 30 years, sacrificing one bottle to top off the others, which keeps air from aging the wine more rapidly.

What can one say about a wine 160 years old? It was amber, browner than the 1939, but with wonderfully fresh aromas of lime, grapefruit, chalk, and earth, and the

slightest overlay of caramel. In the mouth it was vibrant with acidity that was remarkable in a wine this old.

Tasting it blind, I would have guessed it to be 100 years younger—no, make that 130 years younger. And Mr. Meadows was right about texture: this wine was alive and joyous, almost thrusting itself out of the glass. I thought of horse carts, canals, and steam engines. *Pas mal*, as the French say—not a bad little Chardonnay. And it got even better over time. What was it served with? I seem to remember chicken in cream sauce. It didn't much matter.

Reds were next, beginning with an appetite-whetter, Le Corton 1990, young and dark with wild berry aromas. Then, with the lamb, the 1929 Volnay Caillerets, Ancienne Cuvée Carnot, was poured. The '29 and '90 vintages were both exceptional in Burgundy, and the '29 was almost as dark as the '90, yet with a sedate sweet fruit aroma balanced by minerals. With time in the glass it developed a smell of truffles.

Finally, the last wine of the evening was poured, the 1865 Beaune Grèves Vigne de L'Enfant Jésus, from a vineyard entirely owned by Bouchard. Like the 1846, it too had the lively texture of youth. Its color was still vibrant, pale ruby with touches of orange around the edges. The fruit was gentle yet striking, reminiscent of the 1929 and even the '90, like a family resemblance seen over generations.

Where I was simply dazzled by the 1846, the 1865 conjured up a feeling of respect and awe. We were tasting a legacy, transmitted long after its makers had died and conveying emotions that might have been inconceivable back then. At a moment like that, I had no doubt that winemaking can rise to the level of an art.

I thought of those bottles deep in the cellar. They had survived the Franco-Prussian War, World War I, and World War II, when Bouchard had constructed false walls in the cellars to conceal their older bottles from the Nazis. This year, Bouchard will no doubt put away a few bottles of those promising 2005's. May their passage be somewhat easier.

THE RED AND THE WHITE:
Is It Possible That Wine Connoisseurs Can't Tell Them Apart?

Calvin Trillin

Before we get onto the question of whether experienced wine drinkers can actually tell the difference between red wine and white, I should probably tell you a little something about my background in the field. I have never denied that when I'm trying to select a bottle of wine in a liquor store I'm strongly influenced by the picture on the label. (I like a nice mountain, preferably in the middle distance.) When I was growing up, in Kansas City, Missouri, I didn't know about people drinking wine at meals that were not being eaten in celebration of a major anniversary. I assume that my neighbors would have been as startled as I to hear about such carryings on. Years later, after I'd moved to New York, a newspaperman in my hometown did me a great favor, and when I wondered aloud what I could get for him, a friend in New York—a sophisticated friend, who considered himself something of a gourmet, now that I think of it—said

that a case of wine was always appreciated. I phoned the newspaperman's son-in-law in Kansas City to ask if he could find out, discreetly, what sort of wine was particularly fancied in his in-laws' house, and the son-in-law got back to me with a question of his own: "Does Wild Turkey count?" These days, I do drink wine, although if I'm at a meal at which drink orders are being given by the glass, I am likely to say to the waiter, "What sort of fancy beer do you have on tap?"

I have spent a certain amount of time in the company of wine cognoscenti, but I wouldn't claim that I have distinguished myself on those occasions. Many years ago, for instance, a winemaker I know was kind enough to invite me to the "barrel tasting" of California wines which used to be held annually at the Four Seasons restaurant, in New York—an event that was considered a very hot ticket in the wine game. At the table, many glasses of wine were put in front of us.

A prolific writer, Calvin Trillin combines family, travel, and food as themes in his works. such as American Fried, Alice, *and* Let's Eat. *I am sure he would never remember me, but as a sommelier during the early days of Windows on the World, I took care of his wine selection. I have always loved reading his books and articles that relate to wine and food, since he has a different perspective of the subject through a consumer's eyes.*

Then someone who had his mouth very close to the microphone talked about each wine in what I believe scholars would call excruciating detail—the type of vines that had been grafted together to produce it, for instance, and how long it had been in stainless-steel vats or oak barrels. Displaying manners that I thought would have made my mother proud, I drank what was placed before me—not noticing, as I glanced around to see whether more food was ever going to appear, that everyone else was just sipping. I have since heard two or three versions of what transpired that evening, but they do not differ in whether or not I fell asleep at the table. Particularly considering my performance at the Four Seasons that evening, it's perfectly possible that some people asked to sum up my knowledge of and attitude toward wine might respond "ignorance, tempered slightly by philistinism."

On the other hand, I have, in a manner of speaking, worked in the wine industry for a number of years. An old friend named Bruce Neyers makes wine in the Napa Valley. I think it would be too much to say that I'm an adviser to Bruce in his business, unless suggesting that he put a mountain on his label counts. Thanks to the miracle of the fax machine, though, I act as a sort of volunteer copy editor of the announcements that he sends out to his regular customers—what people in the trade would call his "offering letters." Bruce, a wry man who grew up in Wilmington, Delaware, and assumed through college that he would spend his life as a research chemist for DuPont, tends to discuss wine in straightforward terms even when he's addressing the sort of wine fiends who do close readings of offering letters. Still, I can't claim that I know precisely what he means when he writes, say, "The malolactic fermentation went to completion." What I bring to my editing task is not expertise in viticulture but a long experience in such matters as comma placement.

If Bruce shows up at my house during a business trip to New York, he is usually carrying some wine, a custom that reflects both his natural generosity and his concern about what he otherwise might be forced to drink. He has never considered my scenery-selection strategy a completely satisfactory way to build a cellar. He has particularly grim memories of a Chardonnay that attracted me with a view of mountains that are apparently near enough to the grape-growing region of the Hungarian Danube to be depicted in the middle distance. He doesn't ask in advance if I'd prefer red or white—presumably because he knows that the question would give me the opportunity to say, "But can anybody really tell the difference?"

Why? Because, as best I can remember, it was from Bruce or one of his acquaintances in the Napa Valley that I first heard about the color test given at the University of California at Davis, whose Department of Viticulture and Enology is renowned in the wine world. I got the impression that the Test was often given to visitors from the wine industry, but since this was about twenty years ago, such details are hazy. I was definitely told, though, that the folks at Davis poured wine that was at room temperature into black glasses—thus removing the temperature and color cues that are a large part of what people assume is taste—and that the tasters often couldn't tell red wine from white. After Bruce returned from a short course at Davis in the mid-seventies, he had someone at the Joseph Phelps winery, where he then worked, set up a red-white test with black glasses. Bruce got three out of five.

I suppose I am programmed to expect that sort of result. I was raised by a man who, although he had never tasted coffee in his life, once told me that blindfolded I couldn't tell the difference between coffee with milk and coffee without milk. It has never occurred to me that the software drummers who are in the habit of saying to the bartender "J. & B. on the rocks" or "Ketel One with a twist" might actually be able to recognize their favorite booze in a blind tasting. Many years ago, when a friend in England began raising chickens and boasting of the gloriously distinctive taste of their eggs, I secretly replaced the freshly gathered eggs in his larder with eggs from a London supermarket, and I try to remind him at least semi-annually that he raved about the next omelette to come out of the kitchen. In temperament and genes as well as in geographic origin, I'm from the Show Me state.

For years, I was likely to mention the Davis test whenever the subject of wine connoisseurship came up, even if I happened to be drinking a glass of beer at the time. A couple of years ago, for instance, a pleasant young man who was showing us around a winery owned by an acquaintance of mine in New York State mentioned that, as part of his final year at the Culinary Institute of America, he had gone to Davis for a six-week wine course. Naturally, I asked him how he did on the Test. He changed the subject. But

at the end of the tour, after we'd all downed a friendly glass of wine or two and become better acquainted, he suddenly turned to me and said, quietly, "I got three out of seven."

I know what you're thinking: Is it possible that a self-confessed beer-swilling ignoramus got interested in the Davis test simply as a way of debunking wine connoisseurship? As another wine-business friend likes to point out, wine is way beyond any other subject in inspiring in the American layman an urge to refute the notion of expertise. (Modern art must come in second.) I'd like to think that I'm above that sort of thing. I took it for granted that experts could explain not only why certain red wines and certain white wines would be difficult for even a connoisseur to tell apart but also why that did not call into question the legitimacy of wine expertise—and could do so, if necessary, in excruciating detail.

Also, it's not as if wine connoisseurship lacks informed criticism from people who are not beer-swilling ignoramuses. Marc Dornan, of the Beverage Testing Institute, for instance, says to anyone who asks him that rating wines on a hundred-point scale, which is now common practice, is "utterly pseudoscientific." Tim Hanni, a Master of Wine, believes that most commentary about wines fails to take into account the biological individuality of consumers; he claims that he can predict what sort of wine appeals to you according to such factors as how heavily you salt your food and whether your mother suffered a lot from morning sickness while carrying you. Hanni has said for years that the matching of a particular wine with a particular food is a scam, there being "absolutely

81

no premise historically, culturally, or biologically for drinking red wine with meat." As a way of illustrating the role played by anticipation in taste, Frédéric Brochet, who is a researcher with the enology faculty of the University of Bordeaux, recently asked some experts to describe two wines that appeared by their labels to be a distinguished grand-cru classe and a cheap table wine—actually, Brochet had refilled both bottles with a third, mid-level wine—and found his subjects mightily impressed by the supposed grand cru and dismissive of the same wine when it was in the vin ordinaire bottle.

An urge to refute the notion of expertise certainly seemed to be reflected in the headline of an article from the *Times* of London about the research Brochet has been carrying on—"CHEEKY LITTLE TEST EXPOSES WINE 'EXPERTS' AS WEAK AND FLAT." The headline caught the tone of the article, by Adam Sage, which began, "Drinkers have long suspected it, but now French researchers have finally proved it: wine 'experts' know no more than the rest of us." The test of Brochet's that caught my eye consisted partly of asking wine drinkers to describe what appeared to be a white wine and a red wine. They were in fact two glasses of the same white wine, one of which had been colored red with flavorless and odorless dye. The comments about the "red" wine used what people in the trade call red-wine descriptors. "It is a well known psychological phenomenon—you taste what you're expecting to taste," Brochet said in the *Times*. "They were expecting to taste a red wine and so they did. . . . About two or three percent of people detect the white wine flavor, but invariably they have little experi-

ence of wine culture. Connoisseurs tend to fail to do so. The more training they have, the more mistakes they make because they are influenced by the color of the wine."

Reading about Brochet's color experiment revived my interest in the Davis test. I was curious, for one thing, about whether there was a way to compare his results with the results the Davis people had collected over the years—although, as I understood it, the Davis testers, working in the straightforward tradition of the American West, told a subject that he was choosing between red and white rather than trying to sneak a bottle of adulterated white past him. I decided it might be time to visit Davis and collect some statistics on what the Test actually showed. I got the Department of Viticulture and Enology on the telephone and explained my interest to a friendly woman there who is employed to field inquiries from people like me. She told me that as far as she knew Davis had never conducted such a test.

"Imagine that!" Bruce Neyers said, when I told him of my chat with the folks at Davis. He found it unsurprising that an institution with an interest in the distinctions among wines would have difficulty recalling evidence that the most elementary distinction can often not be made. Like a lot of wine people I've spoken to about the Test over the years, Bruce thinks it would be easy enough to pick out some unusual wines that might muddy the difference between the taste of red and white; that is presumably what was done in the test he'd taken years ago at Phelps. But even a loaded test might be pounced on as evidence that the judgments of wine experts are, as Adam Sage put it in his *Times* of London piece, "little more than self-delusion." When I asked Bruce if he could round up some Napa Valley wine people to take the red-white test, assuming I couldn't track it down at Davis, he said they might want to remain anonymous, since there were probably better ways to begin a wine-industry résumé than "Although I can't distinguish red wine from white wine . . ."

If anybody at Davis knew about a red-white test, I'd been told, it would probably be Ann Noble, who, at the time I dropped in to see her, was just winding up a twenty-eight-year teaching career in the Department of Viticulture and Enology. Professor Noble's field is taste and smell, particularly smell. She has noted that as children we are taught to label colors but not smells. In an effort to correct that oversight, she not only conducted in her courses what she calls "a kindergarten of the nose" but also invented the Wine Aroma Wheel, which permits someone to describe the aroma of a wine in specific terms and to identify varietals by their smell. Someone with an aroma wheel knows, for instance, that a Pinot Noir can be distinguished from a Zinfandel because it has the smell of berry, berry jam (strawberry), vanilla, butter, and spiciness rather than the smell of berry, black pepper, raisin, soy, butter, and vanilla.

Professor Noble told me that the test I'd heard about sounded like an urban myth. She regularly tested her students at the end of the semester by asking them to identify wine in black glasses, she said. But what they were trying to name was the varietal, not the color. For a couple of years, she kept track of wrong answers, and she found that perhaps five to ten percent of them were

not simply the wrong varietal but a wrong varietal that was also the wrong color. Conceivably, it occurred to me, that test could have been embellished over the years to become the Davis test I'd heard about, although five or ten percent amounted to a lot fewer wrong answers than I would have expected. Then Professor Noble told me that in the tests she gave her students they were, of course, reaching their conclusions by smell alone.

"Smell alone?" I said.

"This is only by smell," she said. "The minute you put it in your mouth, it's game over. The difference is night and day."

She could imagine some wines that would be less obvious—Beaujolais, for instance, has less tannin than most red wines—but basically she thought that the astringency of red wine would be a give-away if you were allowed to taste as well as smell. She offered to demonstrate this on the spot, and after ducking across the hall into her lab she returned with two wines in black glasses for me to taste. I tried both of them, and then I said, "The first one was red and the second one was white."

Professor Noble seemed taken aback. "It was the other way around," she said.

She was kind enough to come up with some mitigating circumstances. "It could have been test anxiety," she said. Then she tasted the wines and added, "I should have gotten a different red wine. This is not as astringent as I thought." Then she said that the red was, in fact, a weird wine, from Georgia. She didn't mean Georgia as in Tbilisi, where wine consumption is among the highest in the world; she meant Georgia as in Waycross. Then she mentioned that I hadn't had a warmup taste.

I tried to help her think of other excuses. I told her the sun was in my eyes. I thought I'd reserve my other standard excuse—the ball hit a pebble—just in case she suggested that we do the Test again.

Professor Noble said she'd ask around among other faculty members whose concerns were most likely to have included a red-white test, but by the weekend of the test that Bruce Neyers had agreed to set up she had e-mailed me that no one at Davis seemed to know about such a test. (Neither, it later turned out, did the people in charge of the Culinary Institute of America's six-week California course that our winery guide had apparently been referring to.) By chance, both of my sons-in-law, Brian and Alex, were in San Francisco that weekend, and they were willing to act as tasters. Both of them have some interest in wine. My daughters, neither of whom drinks much wine, opted out; when we discussed the test over dinner in San Francisco the night before we were to drive up to Bruce's house, someone suggested that the sort of wine descriptors my younger daughter would use if asked to taste two wines might be "yucky" and "yuckier." Both of my sons-in-law seemed pretty free of test anxiety. "I'm not worried about failing," Alex said, partway through dinner. "I'm worried about failing and Brian passing."

Rather than repeat the sort of test he'd taken years before, Bruce had avoided wines he considered particularly likely to fool the tasters; he had gathered eight French wines that he thought of as typical products of the grapes they'd been made from.

Not wanting to skew the results, I didn't mention what Ann Noble had told me about the way to increase your odds—take about three sips instead of one, building up the astringency of the tannin if it's red wine to produce a drying sensation in your mouth which would be hard to miss. As Bruce stood where he couldn't be observed and poured the wine into black glasses, he said that a couple of visiting wine retailers from Springfield, Missouri, sometimes known as the Gateway to the Ozarks, had dropped in just before we arrived and identified eight out of eight wines. Although he insisted he was telling the truth, I figured he was trying to make Brian and Alex nervous with some sort of Napa Valley version of trash talk, and I tried to keep them calm. "I want you to know that I'm totally evenhanded on this," I said to them. "Either one of you guys can be humiliated. I don't care which one it is."

As it turned out, they both did pretty well. Each person, wearing sunglasses as an added security measure, was asked to go through the wines twice—once trying to identify the color by smell, and then by taste. Alex got seven out of eight both times. Brian got only four by taste, but he got six by smell. By taste, both of them misidentified as white a Sancerre Rouge made from Pinot Noir grapes in the Loire Valley. That was also one of two wines misidentified when tasted by another guest, Larry Bain, a San Francisco restaurant proprietor considered by Bruce to be knowledgeable in enological matters— which means that if your brother-in-law is particularly arrogant about the sophistication of his palate you might consider keeping a bottle of Reverdy Sancerre Rouge on hand, along with a black glass and a pair of sunglasses.

And what other information did the test at Bruce's provide? Taking an average of the three participants I witnessed— if Bruce's earlier guests really were from Missouri, they will understand that I can't count anything I didn't see with my own eyes—I concluded that experienced wine drinkers can tell red from white by taste about seventy percent of the time, as long as the test is being administered by someone who isn't interested in trying to fool them. That made me wonder whether there were similar statistics somewhere in a file drawer in Davis. If the Test never existed, after all, what test was that young man who showed us around the New York State winery taking when he got three out of seven? What test did I keep hearing about in California all those years? I sometimes ponder these questions when I listen to wine talk while sipping the amber microbrew the waiter brought when I asked him if he had any fancy beers on tap. At least, I think it's an amber microbrew.

A CORKING NEW WINE THEORY

Alexis Bespaloff

Many people are confused and discouraged by the number of rules associated with the proper serving of a bottle of wine. Choosing the right wines to complement particular dishes, serving wines at the correct temperature and in the appropriate glasses—these concerns and many others have certainly done their share to annoy people who would just like to enjoy wine, without fuss.

One rule, however, seems fairly fixed in the minds of even occasional wine drinkers: Red wines should be uncorked half an hour or an hour before they are served, so that the wine can "breathe." The theory is that when a red wine is allowed to breathe—that is, to react with oxygen—the bouquet of the wine develops, and the tannic astringency present in many young red wines is somewhat softened as well.

As far as most wine drinkers are concerned, letting a red wine breathe simply means remembering to open the bottle sometime before dinner. In restaurants, helpful waiters often make a point of bringing a red wine to the table as soon as it's ordered and uncorking it so that it can breathe while the first course is eaten. And I don't think I've ever been to a red-wine tasting at which someone did not ask and then note down how long the wines had been uncorked.

Well, not long ago I was talking to Professor Emile Peynaud, one of the most respected enologists of Bordeaux, and he told me he had conducted experiments which indicated that when a bottle of red wine is uncorked, so little wine is exposed to air in the neck of the bottle that he could detect no changes whatsoever, even when the bottle had been opened for several hours.

Alexis Bespaloff was one of my earliest mentors and friends in the wine business. As a twenty-year-old student of wine I read his Signet Book of Wine, *which made wine easier to understand with his common sense approach. His second book,* The Fireside Book of Wine, *was one of the inspirations for this collection and was full of great stories, anecdotes, quotes, and much more. From 1972–1996 he was the wine columnist for* New York *magazine. I was lucky enough to be invited to his many wine tastings at his Upper East Side New York City apartment, and honored at the age of twenty-six to be one of the tasters for this article that appeared in 1977.*

I decided to test for myself the theory that red wines should be uncorked in advance. I arranged several tastings in which four bottles of the same wine would be treated in four different ways and then served blind. The first bottle would be decanted—that is, simply poured into a carafe—an hour before being served; the second bottle would be uncorked for an hour (which is, of course, the conventional approach); the third would be decanted just before serving; the fourth would be uncorked and immediately poured. The first bottle would not only be fully aerated by being poured into a carafe, but would also breathe for an hour. At the other extreme, the wine in the fourth bottle would not have breathed at all. (At the tastings, the bottles were served in random order without the participants' knowing which was which.)

I thought it would be more interesting if I could get some winemakers to taste their own wines, so the first tasting I arranged was with Paul Draper, winemaker at Ridge Vineyards. The wine we tasted was his Geyserville Zinfandel 1974, a young, full-bodied wine with the intense, spicy fruit of the Zinfandel grape. He preferred the wine that had just been opened and poured, followed by the one just decanted and poured. He found that the bottle uncorked for an hour was the least attractive, with musty odors, and the one decanted for an hour showed a slight lack of fruit, suggesting that certain young wines are diminished by too much aeration.

Naturally, a wine will develop in the glass during the course of a dinner party, so we retasted the wines twenty minutes after they were poured. The wine just decanted

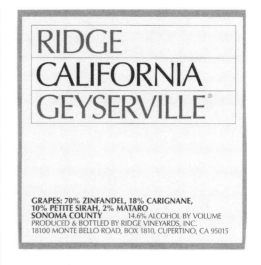

and served was still very good, but the wine simply opened and poured was still preferred. The one uncorked for an hour showed the most improvement, suggesting that all the development took place in the glass and that opening the bottle early had no useful effect.

For my next tasting, I invited Robert Mondavi and Alexis Lichine to taste their own and each other's wines—four bottles each of Mondavi's Cabernet Sauvignon 1973 and Lichine's Château Prieuré-Lichine 1967. We began with the 1973 Cabernet, a young tannic wine not yet ready to drink.

Both agreed that the wines in two of the four glasses stood out for their powerful bouquet and well-defined character. As it turned out, the two preferred wines were those that had just been opened, and, as in the case of Ridge Zinfandel, the wine that had simply been opened and poured was the favorite of the four. Twenty minutes later, this bottle was still preferred and the bottle uncorked an hour before serving was the least attractive through out the tasting.

These comments about the effect of breathing apply to young red wines, of course. White wines don't have to breathe because the bouquet comes up right away, and too much aeration would just oxidize them and dull their appeal. (Sometimes a cheap white wine contains an excess of sulfur and must be swirled in the glass for a few minutes before this smell disappears.) Old red wines present quite a different problem, since they usually throw a deposit after eight or ten years and must therefore be decanted so that the sediment stays in the bottle rather than ending up in the glass. As red wines get older, they often get more fragile, and most people prefer to decant older reds immediately before they are to be served. Nothing is sadder to a wine drinker than to discover that a wine decanted an hour before dinner has lost whatever bouquet and flavor it had while sitting on the sideboard.

Getting back to the four glasses of Prieuré-Lichine 1967: We discovered that one of them (which turned out to be the one decanted for an hour) was corked— that is, the wine tasted of cork rather than of wine. Of the other three glasses, the one just opened and poured was preferred by

Lichine for its finesse, the one decanted and poured was preferred by Mondavi for its deeper bouquet. The wine uncorked for an hour before serving did not "come together" and was the least liked by far. After twenty minutes in the glass, the wine decanted and poured had evolved nicely, but the bottle that had simply been opened and poured was preferred by both men.

I arranged one more tasting, and this time I invited two people who are particularly concerned, with the proper service of wine: Kevin Zraly, cellar master at Windows on the World; and John Sheldon, wine consultant at Tavern on the Green and Maxwell's Plum. We first tasted two bottles of a popular Valpolicella, and agreed that the one opened and poured had slightly more fruit and intensity that the one decanted an hour before. Light-bodied wines such as Valpolicella and

Beaujolais are likely to taste better if they are simply poured than if any effort is made to aerate them, which may reduce the freshness and fruit, which is their most appealing characteristic.

We then tried four bottles of a 1972 Burgundy, Beaune Clos de la Féguine of Jacques Prieur, an elegant and drinkable wine. The bottle uncorked for an hour was the least interesting throughout the tasting; the one opened and poured, firmer than the others, was very good, and retained its character throughout the tasting. The surprise came with the two bottles that had been decanted, since the one decanted and poured was softer and more evolved than the one that had been decanted for an hour. Our experience suggests that aerating a good Burgundy by decanting it may soften it and decrease its intensity, but it may be just as well simply to open and pour the wine, letting it develop in the glass.

We then compared four bottles of a young Bordeaux, Château Pichon-Lalande 1973. We all agreed that the bottle opened and decanted for an hour was the softest and most evolved, yet we preferred the bottle that had just been opened and poured. The bottle that had been decanted and poured was also good, but the one uncorked for an hour was the least liked.

Is there any conclusion to be drawn from these informal experiments with experienced tasters? According to Peynaud, uncorking a bottle an hour before dinner has no effect whatsoever on the wine, yet in most cases the bottle so treated was actually the least attractive, suggesting that this traditional approach to letting a wine breathe may even have a negative effect. If you do want to let a wine breathe, it certainly makes more sense to pour it into a carafe or to let it stand a few minutes in large glasses (which are, of course, filled no more than halfway). It's also pretty clear that the most effective way to let a wine breathe in a restaurant is to have it poured at the start of the meal, so that the wine has time to develop in the glass. That a wine can breathe in a wineglass is a concept which apparently never occurred to a waiter I once encountered. When I asked him to pour the wine to accompany my steak, he replied, "I can't serve it yet. It hasn't breathed enough."

Although just pulling the cork from a bottle is obviously the least effective way to let a wine breathe, the tastings I arranged also raise another question: Is any breathing necessary? After all, in every case the bottle that had just been opened and poured was the one preferred by the tasters. I called Vernon Singleton, a professor of enology at the University of California at Davis whose particular specialty is the aging of wine and the evolution of tannins, the component that gives young red wines their puckerish quality. He told me that my informal tastings confirmed his own laboratory experiments analyzing the effects of oxygen on red wines. He feels certain that even several hours of aeration does not soften tannins, which are so slow to react that they can't oxidize fast enough to have any effect on an open wine during the course of an evening. He also feels that the only positive effect of breathing is to dissipate any off odors—notably sulfur dioxide or hydrogen sulfide—that may occasionally be present in a wine. Otherwise, the effect of air on wine is to diminish its bouquet and flavor more or less rapidly, depending on the wine. What we imagine to be the improvement of a wine as we drink it through a meal is really a change in our perception. Professor Singleton opens and pours a wine only when he is ready to drink it.

The next day I received a letter from Professor Peynaud, in answer to some further questions I had posed. In his opinion, the tradition of uncorking a wine some hours before serving dates way back to a time when much less was known about winemaking: Wines might sometimes re-ferment in the bottle and uncorking them would enable the trapped gas to escape. Professor Peynaud decants only older wines that have thrown a deposit, and then only at the last minute. He never decants Burgundies, which are more fragile, but always pours them directly from the bottle. As to younger red wines, Professor Peynaud has never observed any improvement in quality from aeration of any kind: He always opens his red wines just before sitting down to a meal.

This is rather incredible news for those of us who have spent hours of our lives waiting for wines to breathe or have anxiously signaled waiters to open the red wine as soon as possible. You can easily test the effects of aeration for yourself at home the next time you plan to open two bottles of the same red wine for dinner. Try the two extremes: Decant one bottle an hour in advance, and then open the second bottle a few minutes before the start of dinner. I recently had occasion to try this experiment myself at two dinners—once with two bottles of Château Figeac 1967, once with

two bottles of Château Latour 1967. In each case, the four other wine drinkers present discovered, to their astonishment, that the bottle just opened and poured had more flavor and a bigger bouquet than the one decanted an hour before, which had already started to fade. If you get the same results, you may also conclude that you no longer have to go to any extra trouble—except to decant old wines that have sediment.

Of course, not everyone is prepared to accept the nonbreathing theory. When I described the results of my tastings and discussions to a friend who always scrupulously uncorks his wine an hour before dinner, he thought over for a few moments and then said seriously, "I think you're forgetting the placebo theory. I think wines taste better if they're opened in advance, and so I plan to continue to let them breathe." Okay, but if you want to make at least one aspect of wine service easier for yourself, don't bother.

PART III

WINE AND FOOD

WINE AND FOOD

IN 1976 I WAS HIRED AS THE CELLAR MASTER at Windows on the World atop One World Trade Center by the legendary restaurateur Joe Baum. The main dining room in the restaurant seated over three hundred customers. Joe knew he would always be able to put out good food, but with those numbers it could never be a four-star restaurant. So he created a restaurant-within-a-restaurant called Cellar in the Sky, an intimate, thirty-two-seat enclosed wine cellar that featured a seven-course menu matched with five extraordinary wines. To make it more interesting for the consumer, and make it more of a challenge to the chef and myself, the menu changed every two weeks. This was the ultimate education for the next seventeen years of my life—at least twenty-five times a year, I had to sit with all the chefs of Windows on the World and find the right wine to go with the right food. Happily, most of the time the pairings worked.

One of my real secrets when pairing food with wine, which I try to tell everyone, is: When in doubt, order or prepare roast chicken. Roast chicken is like a blank canvas for almost any wine style. Whether you or your guests like light-, medium-, or full-bodied wines, white or red, roasted chicken will show off any wine you pair with it. I've used this method many times to great success.

Many wine lovers fret over how to pair wine with food. You do not have to be a wine expert to make these choices if you just use what you already know. Everyone is a food expert! Since the time you were teething you've been tasting and sampling a multitude of flavors, aromas, and textures. All you need is a basic understanding of wine and food styles to pick combinations that will please you and others.

When you are pairing wine and food, you're looking for balance and harmony. When you are eating food you will always feel the firmness or texture of the meal itself. Like your meal, the wine also has textures and nuances of flavor. Every time you drink a glass of wine, the flavors and textures help you determine for yourself whether the wine was outstanding, acceptable, or forgettable. Your palate will immediately recognize mouth-filling, bold, rich flavors. However, these wines don't always pair well with all food. With more delicate fare they can clash or outright overpower your experience. Conversely, some bigger, spicier, and more flavorful dishes can completely subjugate a lighter, more subtle wine.

So I have come up with a general rule: The sturdier or fuller in flavor the food, the more full-bodied the wine should be. For foods that are milder the best wines to use would be medium- or light-bodied.

WHITE WINES

LIGHT-BODIED WHITES	MEDIUM-BODIED WHITES	FULL-BODIED WHITES
Alsace Pinot Blanc	Pouilly-Fumé	Chardonnay*
Alsace Riesling	Sancerre	Chablis Grand Cru
Chablis	White Graves	Meursault
Muscadet	Chablis Premier Cru	Chassagne-
German Kabinett	Mâcon-Villages	Montrachet
and Spätlese	Pouilly-Fuissé	Puligny-Montrachet
Sauvignon Blanc*	Saint-Véran	Viognier
Orvieto	Montagny	
Soave	Sauvignon Blanc*/	
Verdicchio	Fumé Blanc	
Frascati	Chardonnay*	
Pinot Grigio	Gavi	
Pinot Gris	Gewürztraminer	
	Gruner Veltliner	

MATCHING FOODS

Sole	Snapper	Salmon
Flounder	Bass	Tuna
Clams	Shrimp	Swordfish
Oysters	Scallops	Lobster
	Veal paillard	Duck
		Roast chicken
		Sirloin steak

*Note that starred wines are listed more than once. That's because they can be vinified in a range of styles from light to full texture, depending on the producer. When buying these, if you don't know the style of the particular winery, it's a good idea to ask the restaurant server or wine merchant for help.

RED WINES

Light-Bodied Reds	**Medium-Bodied Reds**	**Full-Bodied Reds**
Bardolino	Cru Beaujolais	Barbaresco
Valpolicella	Côtes du Rhône	Barolo
Chianti	Crozes-Hermitage	Bordeaux (great châteaux)
Rioja-Crianza	Burgundy Premiers	Châteauneuf-du-Pape
Beaujolais	and Grands Crus	Hermitage
Beaujolais-Villages	Bordeaux (Crus Bourgeois)	Cabernet Sauvignon*
Burgundy (Village)	Cabernet Sauvignon*	Merlot*
Bordeaux (proprietary)	Merlot*	Zinfandel*
Pinot Noir*	Zinfandel*	Syrah/Shiraz*
	Chianti Classico Riserva	Malbec*
	Dolcetto	
	Barbera	
	Rioja Reserva and Gran Reserva	
	Syrah/Shiraz*	
	Pinot Noir*	
	Malbec*	

Matching Foods

Salmon	Game birds	Lamb chops
Tuna	Veal chops	Leg of lamb
Swordfish	Pork chops	Beefsteak (sirloin)
Duck		Game meats
Roast chicken		

—KZ

THE FLAVOR OF "FRESH" IS SWEET

Andrea Robinson

My first wine and food epiphany, though humble, endures as one of the most powerful taste lessons I ever learned. It started with a bag of microwave popcorn. I was earning $15,000 per annum—*in New York City*—at my first real wine job at a wine school. This called for budget lunches. But between glamorous activities like cleaning spittoons and mailing out course brochures, I was learning every second from the owner Mary Ewing Mulligan, a Master of Wine, who is one of the greatest teachers and tasters I've ever met. "Taste this," she said one day, interrupting me midmunch in my lunch "with the popcorn." In that one sip, I got it: buttery Chardonnay (at last I knew what "buttery" wine meant!), but more important, I really sensed, for the first time, the dramatic interplay between the wine and the food. In this case, it was the seamless affinity of buttery-toasty-rich flavors in both the wine and the popcorn, plus a subtle impression of sweetness shared by two players as diverse as Chardonnay and corn. I've gone back to that lesson time and again, to deliciously match wine with everything from tamales to succotash to a clambake.

And now, when I teach about wine and food, I start out with a blank canvas (OK, a flipchart), and ask my students to help me illustrate it with answers to the question, "What do you like about food?" Among my students at the French Culinary Institute, there's always the glib answer, "Having someone *else* do the cooking!" (With the Wall Streeters it's "Having someone else pick up the check!") But in answer to the real question, "What are the flavors and textures

Andrea Robinson and I worked together at Windows on the World, where she began as the coordinator for the Windows on the World Wine School and then became the first female sommelier at Windows. She was at the restaurant in February 1993 for the first bombing of the World Trade Center and led all the customers down 107 flights to safety. Windows was closed for three years from 1993 to 1996, but when we reopened Andrea came back, not only to run the wine department but all beverages. She is an extremely hard-working and energetic person with a tremendous amount of talent, one of which is writing. Andrea is one of only sixteen women in the world to pass the very rigorous master sommelier test. After that Andrea went on to writing many best-selling books, beginning with Great Wine Made Simple. *Today she is the wine consultant for Delta Air Lines.*

that make you come back for more?," there's virtual unanimity on the food tastes to which most every eater, from indifferent fueler to inveterate foodie, ultimately responds: "Sweetness!" "Meatiness!" "Fat!" The answers come flying fast and loud—often from the folks in the crowd who look as if they can consume any of them to their hearts' desire and never battle the bulge. Heads nod. Intuitively, we all know they're *so* right.

Sweetness, meatiness, and fattiness are what I call *foundation flavors*. They're the anchors of eating, in the sense that every recipe, dish, and menu must be mindful of balancing them to have appeal beyond a single bite. For example, a slice of chocolate cake is seductive, a plate full of chocolate frosting is not—there's just too much sweetness and too much fat to enjoy more than a forkful straight (that's why it's the icing on the cake, not the other way around). As a practical matter, I group all the food foundation flavors—sweet, meaty, fatty—under the general category of *richness*, from delicate to intense. [...] Wine's foundation is richness, too—of fruit flavor and concentration, courtesy of Mother Nature, and of style and structure owed to the winemaking techniques used.

Whether consciously or not, the pairing instincts of every skilled waiter and sommelier are keyed to the foundation flavors in wine and food, because they make the task as simple and sure as this: put the partners on equal footing in terms of richness, and you'll have a good match virtually every time. And what about a great match? As in baseball, hitting a home run means finding and connecting with the "sweet spot." For

so many, the sweet spot between wine and food seems mysterious and untouchable. But the truth is that all the while you've been agonizing over wine and food matches, that sweet spot's been hiding in plain sight. It is wine-loving food.

What exactly do I mean? Wine-loving food is my terminology for anything edible that really flatters wine. Wine-loving foods are everywhere, and can be as real-world and easy to pull off as that bag of microwave popcorn, or as rarefied as white truffle risotto. What binds wine-loving foods is their emphasis on the foundation flavors I've described—sweetness, meatiness, and fattiness. While not every food accentuates these qualities, all the foods that most flatter wines have one or more of them. As such, they definitely form the foundation for *my* eating repertoire. And for anyone who wants more everyday enjoyment from wine and food, dialing into them is where it all begins.

SWEETNESS, NOT SUGARINESS

We'll explore each of the foundation flavors, and their interplay with wine, beginning with sweetness. By sweetness, I mean not the *sugariness* of dessert, but rather a more essential sweetness that's owed to either nature, or nurture, and sometimes both.

The "Peak" Sweetness of Fresh Foods—Nature's Gift to Wine Lovers

Nature gives us what I call "peak-condition" sweetness. Think about it: from lettuce to lobster and carrots to cod, most quality food-stuffs from the soil and the sea possess, at peak freshness, a very real and delicious underlying sweetness to their taste.

I have come to believe that very sweetness was the seed for, and remains the life-blood of, modern American cooking. In the world of American food, we trace our gastronomic evolution away from postwar processed food—whose message was American industrial might—to Alice Waters and her Berkeley, California, restaurant Chez Panisse. Her emphasis on purity and authenticity of flavor and form was the equivalent of a culinary earthquake, with aftershocks that spread to every part of the country, spawning a new regional American cuisine that spotlights the vibrance of local ingredients, at their freshness peak.

But in addition to inspiring an awareness of, and emphasis on, regional cuisines, peak-fresh sweetness in food is a perfect match-point for wine. As I discovered in working with some of the great American chefs and in my own culinary training, these flavors have a vinous counterpart—namely, wine styles emphasizing fresh, vibrant fruit flavor. To find them, focus on the following:

YOUNG WINES Young wines in good condition have the best fruit flavor. Wine follows the same path as food from tired, to stale, to bad-tasting as it gets too old. I think this confuses many, because we've developed the impression that wine is supposed to be "cellared" before we drink it. But the truth is that wine is like cheese—yes, a tiny percentage can improve with age, but the rest are meant to be consumed young and fresh. Just as you wouldn't "age" your deli Swiss or your American singles (at least not intentionally!), most wines on the market are meant for current consumption. Therefore, buy and drink young, keeping in mind that most whites in the marketplace hold well for one to two years from the vintage on the label, reds from two to three years.

NEW WORLD WINES By New World, I mean the Americas, plus the rest of the major southern hemisphere wine countries—specifically the United States, Chile, Argentina, Australia, and New Zealand. While it's true that all those countries model their wine styles on Old World classics (from France, Italy, Spain, Germany, and Portugal), they do so with a New World riff. In my first book, *Great Wine Made Simple*, I describe what I call the "New World wine style" as fruit-forward, in contrast to the Old World's subtler, more restrained, and sometimes earthier taste profile. Many readers, both wine pro and amateur, have told me that after doing the comparative tasting lessons I use in the book to teach those styles, they really understood the differences.

Of course there are some exceptions to the Old World/New World dichotomy, but they're minor. By contrast, the value of the matching principle:

Peak-Sweet Foods + Vibrant-Fruit Wines

97

is major, both in terms of flavor affinity and because many of these New World wines are some of the most popular, readily available, and affordable wines on the market. With this principle in mind, we'll explore matching wine to the peak-sweetness in popular and delicious foods, starting literally from the ground up.

WINE AND THE FLAVORS OF PEAK-FRESH VEGETABLES

Pick your produce, select your season: whether spring peas, summer tomatoes, or autumn squashes; baby carrots, sweet corn, or new potatoes: when they're freshly

---

⁓ FROM MATCHES TO MENUS ⁓

Wine and Tomatoes "Tasting Menu"

Pig out on this whole menu when tomatoes are at their peak of summer succulence, or just pick one of the courses. I've paired both a red and white with the starter and the main course, and given two different sparkling choices with the last course.

Heirloom tomatoes and fresh goat cheese (with a grind of black pepper if you like, but taste before salting because some goat cheeses are quite salty)

> *Geyser Peak Sauvignon Blanc or BV Coastal red Zinfandel*

Hot pasta and cold tomato toss—I like orecchiette or shells to catch the juice. but any shape is fine. Cut tomato chunks the same size as the pasta, toss with salt, pepper, and a drizzle of olive oil. If you want to add meat, chunks of chicken, or cooked and crumbled bacon or sweet Italian sausage, are nice.

> *Kendall-Jackson Vintner's Reserve Chardonnay or Rosemount Diamond Label Shiraz*

Fresh tomato and strawberry "gazpacho" —Whirl equal parts peeled, fresh tomatoes and sweet, fresh strawberries in a blender with balsamic vinegar (½ teaspoon per cup of purée) and sugar or honey to taste. Serve with spoons in teacups garnished with a dollop of mascarpone or crème fraiche, and fresh mint if desired. This can also be served as a "salsa" on grilled fish or shrimp, or with biscuit layers like shortcake.

> *Moscato, Famiglia di Robert Mondavi (soft bubble, lightly sweet)*
>
> *Iron Horse Brut Rosé (sparkling)*

harvested, they're hauntingly sweet. Mature garlic is, well, garlicky, but when plucked early as garlic shoots, it's as sweet as a baby's breath. My grandpa used to pick his garden-grown plump tomatoes and eat them out of hand, still sun-warm, like apples. At age seven, I was skeptical—raw tomatoes. But he tempted me, I yielded, and my idea of fresh flavor has never been the same. (You have seen kids afflicted with the utterly summer phenomenon known as "watermelon-shirt"? Well, I had "tomato-shirt" that not even Tide could tame.)

THE *BEST* TOMATOES: THE ULTIMATE WINE-LOVING FOOD

Another twenty years would pass before I learned of the tomato's extraordinary wine worthiness—twenty years of the agony and ecstasy extremes that every tomato-lover knows. Because while tomatoes are every-where, shirt-soakers are about as rare as rainbows in the desert. When you do luck into them, grab the wine, and I guarantee that, impossible as it may seem, they will taste even better. You don't even have to worry about which wine. I'll never forget the day I made that discovery. It was at a picnic smack in the middle of the Napa Valley, where some sommeliers had gath-ered to taste New World wines of every stripe and color—sparkling, white, red, pink, every grape you can think of. A local chef had brought a literal rainbow of heir-loom tomatoes, ranging from deepest eggplant-purple to poppy-red to sage-green, even striped ones. We were popping them by the fistful into our mouths, and tasting the wines. Someone said the combination was like speed for the tastebuds. I had been thinking maybe hallucinogens, because the new flavor sensations seemed to burst forth kaleidoscopically and then morph into other captivating flavors that were almost unspeakably delicious.

To be sure, tomatoes are a treat for the foodie and wine-lover, but also a trial. That's because the typical grocery-store tomatoes taste not like the juicy jewels I call shirt-soakers, but rather more like the shirt: sodden and squishy. Consequently, wine-matching tomatoes is an opportu-nistic exercise, depending on how bold and true their flavor is. For example, fried green tomatoes and tomatillos populate the tangy end of the tomato flavor spectrum [...].The middling tomatoes that populate our markets for the most part do not merit eating *au natural*, and much of classic and ethnic cooking acknowledges this. From the salsas of Mexico to France's concassé to Italy's marinara, traditional tomato cookery is engineered to concentrate their flavor, and often casts tomatoes as a medium for other flavors—for example, the piquancy of chilis in the salsa, the earthy-sweetness of shallots in concassé, or the creamy complexity of cheese atop marinara. [...] Then there are the top tomatoes, the genuine sugar-sweet shirt-soakers, which in my opinion rank among the greatest wine-loving foods in the world—especially with wines of equally vibrant ripeness. Only one food, corn, has comparable inherent wine worthiness.

A Wine Lover's Ode to Corn

As wine-loving foods go, corn deserves special attention (which in my world amounts to worship but I realize others may not feel quite the same). I find it a great irony that one of the most wine-loving foods *in the entire world* is native to one of the least wine-loving cultures of the world—America. This disconnect is even more ironic given the fact that the great wine affinity of corn, in every form from popped to posole to polenta, is America's ultimate favorite: Chardonnay, and notably the big-style Californian and Australian ones. When you reflect on the star power of corn in virtually all American foods, both north and south of the equator, from fritters to flautas, it's tantalizing to imagine the tsunami of pleasure that would sweep the country if more Americans discovered the glorious flavor affinity of Chardonnay and corn. Now you're blazing the trail.

As a start, I strongly encourage you to do the Chardonnay and popcorn tasting that was such an eye-opener for me. You can buy it popped or pop it yourself, and choose a "buttery" Chardonnay to taste alongside. If you make or buy buttery popcorn, the wine's butteriness will burst through in the pairing; naked air-popped corn will emphasize the wine's toastiness from oak. But you needn't stop with Chardonnay, either, because popcorn is the perfect, easy pairing to illustrate corn's amazing affinity with a huge range of different wine styles. Try brut sparkling wine (this pairing is a delicious must), German Riesling Kabinett, Italian Pinot Grigio, and New Zealand Sauvignon Blanc for whites. For reds, try French

⟶ OUR DAILY RED ⟵

All right, it's not really that Americans don't love wine, it's just not yet in our culture to think of drinking it routinely with dinner the way Europeans do. That might seem surprising, considering so many of us share European roots. But Puritanism and Prohibition wrought havoc on the custom of wine-with-meals; and fast-food pretty much finished it off for anyone who frequents drive-throughs. (No, eating in the car does *not* count as mealtime, as you'd certainly not be drinking wine there.) My hope is that [I] will inspire readers to alter this perception, and change the concept of wine from "special occasion" to "every occasion."

CLOUDY BAY

SAUVIGNON BLANC 2008

Beaujolais-Villages, French Côtes du Rhône, Italian Chianti, American red Zinfandel, and Australian Shiraz. Every pairing will show how the popcorn brings up the prominence of the wine's fruit, and may also bring forth new tastes that you didn't notice when you tasted it by itself. And you may never go to the movies again unless and until they start serving wine by the glass.

Based on what we've already learned about balancing richness and body in wine and food, it's easy to articulate the basic pairing logic, and then extrapolate from there to specific dishes, as follows:

- ➤ Corn is a fundamental wine-loving food. I have yet to find a wine that it *doesn't* flatter.
- ➤ Corn's vibrant sweetness and textural richness, ranging from tender to chewy to creamy, particularly complements the vibrant ripeness and rich texture of the full-bodied, oaky Chardonnays

～ UMAMI ～

Some wine experts are gaga over what a group of Japanese flavor researchers have identified as possibly the fifth taste—joining sweet, sour, bitter, and salt. They have named that taste umami, which translates roughly as "deliciousness"—and they say that tomatoes are bursting with it. Does that explain their wine affinity? I'm not so sure—many of the other foods I consider to be drop-dead delicious, and very wine-friendly, apparently are not loaded with umami. So I have to be honest and say that the umami discovery hasn't yet helped me in my food-matching research, and thus I don't really know what to say about it here except that, if it's as good as it sounds. I wish you a lifetime of umami abundance. For the purposes of fun cocktail-party chitchat, the pronunciation is ooh-MOM-me.

101

for which California and Australia are famous.

- ➤ As you enrich the flavor and texture of the corn dish or recipe (by layering on more peak-flavor sweetness, or fattiness or meatiness), you can enrich the wine in proportion, with delicious results.

CREATING PAIRINGS THAT WORK

Evan Goldstein

To many people, learning about pairing food and wine is like mastering a foreign language. Both require a little study. Both become easier with practice. And with both, you reach a point when your knowledge becomes reflexive.

I feel fortunate enough to be able to speak fluent French. For years I studied it in school, diligently memorizing verb tenses, vocabulary, and grammar. Then, on arriving in Paris to work, I realized that despite all that study, I was far from being able to communicate, much less speak fluently. Nobody I worked with spoke English, and had it not been for the patience and diligence of the chef with whom I worked on the line (who is still my best friend), I would have been sunk. He taught me *argot* (slang) and, more important, spoke with me, patiently and without judgment, for months as I listened, translated, thought about what I wanted to say, translated it back into French, and spoke the words to him. Five steps, every time. Then one day he said something, and I replied automatically, without translating and retranslating. I had finally begun to think in French. Since then it's been easy.

Learning that "language" of food and wine may feel similarly forced and awkward at first. You may feel as if you are getting things right and wrong without knowing why, and frustrated by the randomness of it all. Trust me, over time it will turn from five steps (reading the recipe or looking at the menu, thinking about your wine selection, tasting the dish, tasting the wine, and deciding whether the pairing works) to two steps (picking a wine that you're confident will pair well with the food and then enjoying the match).

First and foremost Evan Goldstein is one of the "good guys" in the wine business and we have been friends for over twenty-five years. He is one of the top wine and food educators in the world and we have shared the stage at many wine symposiums. Evan is a Master Sommelier and has worked in restaurants in Paris, Napa Valley (Auberge du Soleil), and Berkeley (Chez Panisse) before joining his mother, chef and author Joyce Goldstein, in their restaurant Square One in San Francisco. His expertise in food, wine, and hospitality has made his books must-reads for restaurant owners, chefs, and sommeliers in understanding the "perfect pairings" for wine and food.

It would be self-serving for me to say that the best way to approach wine and food pairing is to read my previous book, *Perfect Pairings*. That said, those of you who have read the book and understand my thinking on pairing will find the process simpler this time around as we explore new grapes, wines, and [foods]. For new readers, I summarize my approach below and adapt it to the grapes, wines, and [foods] that follow.

Pairing wine and food is a lot like falling in love. In true love, we may be blind to color, race, religion, and gender, and we find genuine happiness with a lover based on shared values, experiences, interests, and innate attraction. Wine and food come together when the character traits of the wine mesh with the food's personality. The wine doesn't care what the dish is or is not, or where it originates. The food couldn't care less if it's flouting time-honored expectations. For example, an Argentine Malbec isn't a significantly better match with an *asado* (Argentine barbecue) than similar-styled wines from other wine-producing grapes, regions, or countries; nor does that delicious Argentinean slow-roasted beef require that the wine come from the same country or even that it be red. What heresy, you say—a white wine with red meat? Depends on the wine: read on.

The bulk of the baggage we bring to wine and food tends to be psychological. As we remove the pressures of emotions and environment (friends, location, and so on), the rationale for most wine and food pairings comes down to your skill at picking out a given wine's identifiable and measurable characteristics and matching them with what you are eating. These wine characteristics are often referred to as primary tastes.

In talking about wine, we need to distinguish between *flavors*, which are subjective and descriptive associations, and *tastes*, which are objective and quantifiable. Although it's wonderful to be able to identify flavors in wine and food, they are not the main basis for successful pairings. After all, what an avocado tastes like to you may not be exactly what it tastes like to me. For some people the flavor nuances of peach versus nectarine can be very difficult to distinguish, and they are certainly not empirically measurable. We can't rate how *porky* a pork chop is or the intensity of orange flavor in an orange. By contrast, there are four classic tastes—sweet, sour, salty, and bitter—and a fifth, recently identified one, *umami*. They are pure and primal and can be measured on a scale from nonexistent to high. On this scale, we can express the sourness of a lime, the sweetness of honey, the bitterness of eggplant, the savor of tomato and mushroom, or the saltiness of a good old American hot dog. The role of these tastes and how they work in creating pairings with food follow shortly.

Ultimately, you have to choose whether the food or the wine will be the star of your pairing: only one of the two can take center stage. A "Swiss" or neutral route is possible, with neither one dominating, but if your goal is to highlight a special bottle of wine, the accompanying food should play second fiddle. If you want to showcase a recipe you've fallen in love with, select a less assertive wine.

Whatever your perception of a wine's flavor and personality when you taste it on its own, the wine will taste different when it

103

accompanies a meal. I was always impressed with the short-lived *The Wine and Food Companion* newsletter written in the 1990s by David Rosengarten and Joshua Wesson, the authors of *Red Wine with Fish* (1989), still one of the most innovative works on wine and food pairing. When they rated wines, they gave two scores. The first was a numeric score for the intrinsic qualities of the wine, much like those assigned by *Wine Spectator, Wine & Spirits,* and *The Wine Advocate,* among other publications. But their second score rated the wine's ability to be paired with food, from very good (A) through terrible (F). The findings were always interesting and at times surprising. Many highly rated wines showed gorgeously as soloists but failed when paired with food. Learning how to choose between a 94D and an 85A was an eye-opening experience for many sommeliers.

It's accepted today that some wine and food pairings are based on the attraction of opposites. This is why a crisp glass of Pinot Blanc goes sublimely with a basket of deep-fried clams. A squeeze of lemon cuts through the salty, somewhat oily taste and feel of the bivalves. The wine acts the same way by countering the seasoning and preparation of the clams and refreshing the palate.

For me, however, the most obvious and successful wine and food pairings are grounded in shared rather than contrasting characteristics. An off-dry Chenin Blanc served alongside pork medallions with sautéed apples clearly illustrates this type of pairing: the sweetness of the apples complements the slight sweetness of the wine.

At the root of this thinking is the principle that wines and foods share certain basic tastes. Tastes, as I explained earlier, are not flavors. They are omnipresent in food, with most dishes exhibiting various combinations of them. For example, some recipes are founded on plays of salt and sweet, such as crisply fried Vietnamese spring rolls served with an accompanying sipping sauce of sugar, fish sauce, lemon juice, garlic, and chili. Chinese sweet and sour pork is an example of the sweet/sour contrast. The new classic dessert, freshly baked bittersweet chocolate cake with a molten center, is an example of the bitter/sweet encounter. In wine, salt is not an element, but the remaining three classic tastes (sweet, sour, and bitter) are the building blocks that define a wine's profile and help us decide how (and with what) it is best served. As I explained in *Perfect Pairings*, this interplay of tastes holds what I call the keys to wine and food matching. There are five keys for wine [. . .]

THE KEYS TO UNDERSTANDING WINE

Key 1: Acidity

Understanding the wine's acidity is the single most important factor in pairing wine with food. There are several ways in which acidity—the sourness or tartness factor—figures in wine.

ACIDITY IS THE COUNTERPOINT TO AN ARRAY OF DISHES If you are seeking to "cut" a dish that is rich, salty, oily, fatty, or mildly spicy, serving it alongside a tart-tasting wine will be effective and refreshing. Think of what I call the "lemon wedge rule": just as a squeeze of lemon will accent or cut a rich or salty dish (tempering the brininess of seafood, for example), an acidic wine will do the same. Foods served with cream- or butter-based sauces, oily or strong-tasting fish or shellfish, mildly piquant dishes, and virtually all deep-fried foods are prime candidates.

ACIDIC WINES ARE THE BEST WINES TO PAIR WITH TART FOODS Tart dishes, such as a green salad dressed with vinaigrette, and sharp ingredients, such as capers, leeks, and tomatoes, harmonize best with wines of similar sharpness. A wine that is less tart than the dish it is accompanying will be thinned out and may taste quite unpleasant. When serving wine with a sharp dish or ingredients, you would be hard-pressed to find a wine that is too tart! Example of wines that can be too puckery on their own but sing with food include Assyrtiko, Txacolu, and some Pinot Blancs.

ACIDIC WINES LESSEN THE PERCEPTION OF SALT Again, whites and sparkling wines, as a rule, are inherently sharper and therefore fare better with salty dishes than most red wines do. For example, the zesty bite of acidity from a glass of young Vermentino is a refreshing foil to a deep-fried Italian fritto misto or shrimp tempura.

ACIDITY BRINGS OUT THE INTEGRITY OF GOOD, SIMPLE INGREDIENTS I like to think of the acidity in wine as the gastronomic equivalent of the yellow highlighter pen. A quick swoosh of the highlighter makes words stand out on a page. A wine's acidity can do the same with food by bringing out the essence of an ingredient. The summer's first sweet corn or vine-ripened heirloom tomatoes, freshly cracked boiled crab or lobster, and farm-fresh mozzarella cheese all take on another dimension when paired simply with a sharp, uncomplicated wine to make their vibrant and delicious flavor "pop."

A tart wine that may seem too sharp for sipping on its own may work perfectly in conjunction with food. Sometimes an initially sour, unpleasant bottle can turn into liquid magic at the table.

Counterintuitively, perhaps, low-acid wines are more difficult to match with food. It's best to serve them with milder ingredients that contain a touch of sharpness (such as just a squeeze of lime or lemon). A flat Trebbiano or Marsanne may perk up if paired with an otherwise mild fish terrine served with a wedge of lemon and a tangy celery-root remoulade. With some experimentation and exploration, the role and importance of acidity will become clear to you.

105

Key 2: Sweetness

Wines can be sweet in varying degrees. Dessert wines aside (I address those case by case), wines can be dry (absent of any noticeable sugar), off-dry (a little sweet), or semidry (medium sweet). We often find a little sweetness in Prosecco, Chenin Blanc, lighter-style Muscats, and some styles of Torrontés.

SWEETNESS IS A GREAT COUNTERBALANCE TO MODERATE LEVELS OF SPICY HEAT Fiery Asian preparations, such as Malaysian curry or the archetypal Chinese hot and spicy chicken, need not be paired exclusively with beer! Moderate amounts of sweetness in the wine provide a nice foil for the heat and tame its ferocity, even alleviating the burning sensation caused by peppers.

SWEETNESS IN THE WINE CAN COMPLEMENT A SLIGHT SWEETNESS IN FOOD Offering an off-dry Chenin Blanc with a fillet of grouper and a fresh mango salsa is a good example of this observation. Others include pairing sweet wines with dishes accompanied by chutney or sauces made with fresh or reconstituted dried fruit (such as raisins, apricots, and cherries). The fruit flavors resonate well with most off-dry wines.

SWEETNESS CAN BE AN EFFECTIVE CONTRAST TO SALT From Reese's Peanut Butter Cups to Ben and Jerry's Chocolate Chip Cookie Dough ice cream, Americans love salt and sugar juxtaposed. This is the same rationale behind the long-established matches of sweet French Sauternes with salty Roquefort (and other similar blue cheeses) and port with English Stilton. Most

successful with Latin and Asian cuisines, this genre of wine and food pairing nevertheless requires some experimenting, as not all of these marriages are happy ones.

SWEETNESS CAN TAKE THE EDGE OFF FOODS THAT ARE TOO TART This type of contrast requires precise balance, or the food can make the wine come across as sour. Many Asian appetizers with vinaigrettes that are at once tart and sweet pair seamlessly with off-dry wines. Green papaya salad, found in the cuisines of Thailand, Vietnam, and Myanmar, is a classic example.

DESSERT-STYLE OR EXTREMELY SWEET WINES MUST BE SWEETER THAN THE DESSERT ITSELF The wisdom of this rule is evident to anybody who has ever attended a wedding and experienced the unfortunate pairing of expensive dry brut Champagne with cake covered in gloppy white buttercream frosting. Your expensive Dom Pérignon suddenly tastes like lemony seltzer water. At a minimum, the levels of sweetness in the wine and the dessert should match, though it's always safer to have the wine's sweetness exceed that of the dessert. With wedding cake, serving a sweeter bubbly (such as the seemingly misnamed, but actually sweeter, extra-dry or demi-sec styles) would be a much better call, as the sweetness of the wine and the cake are better matched. Fruit-based desserts are more compatible table-mates for dessert wines; avoid thick, sweet buttercream and ganache with bubblies!

Key 3: Tannin

In wine, tannin can be associated with a bitter taste and a somewhat gritty texture. This is the same astringency (from tannic acid) encountered in black tea that has been steeped too long. If you have ever forgotten to cut an overly strong cup of black tea with milk, cream, or lemon, you have experienced firsthand the taste and mouthfeel of a high level of tannic acid. Tannins in wine come from two sources: fruit tannins generated from the skins of grapes, especially in big, generous red wines; and wood tannins from the oak barrels in which the wine is aged. Longer maceration of wine with its skins amplifies fruit tannins, whereas extended barrel aging, especially in newer barrels, accentuates the wood tannins.

Some thoughts on pairing wine's tannin with food:

SERVE BITTER FOODS WITH TANNIC WINES Foods that have been grilled, charred, or blackened are excellent vehicles for showing off bitter-edged wines. Ingredients that are inherently bitter, like arugula, endive, and sautéed broccoli rabe, are great, too. And there's nothing like a charcoal-grilled steak with a full-bodied, tannic Cabernet Sauvignon.

COUNTERBALANCE TANNINS WITH FAT AND PROTEIN This is the fancy way of saying drink red wine with red meat. Those hard and astringent tannins are tamed by pairing rare to medium-rare red meat (with ample fat and protein) and many cheeses (also chock-full of both). If the wine is too tannic, however, the tannins can still dominate. Also, certain hard, sharp, or pungent cheeses—such as aged Parmesan or Romano, French goat cheese, aged Spanish Manchego, aged dry English or Vermont cheddar, or Dutch Gouda—can give the tannic red wines a metallic character, while many of the soft, "stinky" cheeses bring out an unpleasant ammonia flavor in a big-tannin wine. Finally, if you serve a very tannic wine alongside a dish containing little or no protein (a vegetarian entrée, for example), the tannins can react chemically with the available protein (you'll notice it on your tongue and the inside of your mouth) and may well come across as even more tannic.

TANNINS CAN ACCENTUATE THE PERCEPTION OF SALT Tannin is an important

107

consideration when serving a salty dish. Particularly when you're serving a rich red wine, tannin will often accentuate the salt in the food, resulting in a match with as much charm as sucking on a salt lick.

TANNIN AND FISH OIL USUALLY AREN'T HAPPY TOGETHER This lesson requires no subtle training of the palate. Generally, all it takes is one bite of fish (or strong shellfish) alongside a rich, tannic wine to provoke the unpleasant "sucking on a penny" reaction between fish oil and tannin. Red wines with less tannin (Gamay is a prime example) fare far better in this challenging pairing of wine and food.

Key 4: Oak

Although plenty of wines are not aged in wood barrels, many winemakers claim it's nearly impossible to create a fine wine without oak. The vanilla and coconut that you may enjoy in Chardonnay as well as some Roussannes and Marsannes, and the smoke and chocolate identifiable in Cabernet Sauvignon, Touriga Nacional, and expensive Malbec don't come from the grapes: the flavors are often due to the extended time spent in oak.

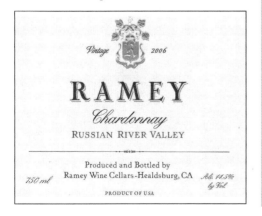

OAK FLAVORS ARE ACCENTUATED BY FOOD Food amplifies the oak in wine, making it stand out as a distinct flavor component. Try any extremely oaky wine with virtually any entrée, and lo and behold, you'll have wine, food, and a lumberyard!

OAKY WINES NEED VERY SPECIFIC FOOD TO SHOW THEM AT THEIR BEST This is not to say that you can't enjoy oak-aged wines with food; you simply need to choose carefully. In addition to its distinctive flavors, most oak imparts tannins (bitterness) that can easily dominate food and need to be balanced. If you want to show off an oaky wine (a youthful Petite Sirah or Nebbiolo, for example), match the flavors in the wine (toast, char or smoke, caramel, and so on) by using cooking techniques, or ingredients cooked with those techniques, that also impart those flavor: grilling, blackening, smoking, caramelizing, and so on.

LIGHTLY OAKED OR EVEN UNOAKED WINES ARE THE EASIEST TO PAIR WITH FOOD Most of the time, I prefer to serve wines that are low in oak, well balanced, or unoaked (that is, made and aged in stainless-steel tanks or in very old wooden barrels that impart little or no flavor). Minimizing oak creates a level playing field, allowing you more flexibility in matching your wine with different foods and methods of preparation. An unoaked Pinot Blanc can work with foods ranging from simply sautéed fillet of sole almandine to lamb vindaloo to chicken cacciatore, whereas an oakier version would pair well only with sole.

OAK ADDS SMOOTHNESS AND ROUNDNESS OF TEXTURE TO WINES Wines that spend little or no time in oak are often austere in texture, whereas wines aged in oak are more mouth-filling and voluptuous. You can play off this added texture by complementing, for example, a silky Rousanne with a dish accompanied by a cream sauce or compound butter. A smooth Grenache can be sublime when served with a slow-cooked beef stew or other slow-braised dishes.

Key 5: Alcohol

A wine's level of alcohol is its primary determinant of body and weight. As a rough guide, the higher the alcohol content, the fuller-bodied the wine seems. As with fat content in dairy products, an increase in alcohol content increases the perception of density and texture. A milder wine (7 to 10 percent alcohol) is significantly less weighty and textured on the palate that one of 14 to 15 percent.

MATCH WINES AND FOODS OF EQUAL WEIGHT The principle is somewhat intuitive. You shouldn't crush a gentle Dolcetto with a stick-to-the-ribs lamb stew. Nor should you match a light, simple fillet of trout with an amply textured Marsanne-Roussanne blend, which might obliterate the fish. For example, a medium-bodied red wine such as a Barbera or Pinotage is successful served with a medium-weight dish such as roast chicken. A rich wine like a barrel-aged Sémillon pairs well with a full flavored lasagna. As the wine's alcohol content increases, the food-pairing options decrease, and vice versa.

ALCOHOL IS ACCENTUATED BY SALT AND PEPPER An abundance of salt in food will make wines seem "hotter" (more alcoholic) than they actually are. This is extremely important to know, because you want the wine to harmonize with the dish, not come across like a shot of vodka. Similarly, if a very powerful wine is paired with spicy dishes, you may feel as though someone poured gasoline on the fire! High levels of spice and heat (from jalapeno, cayenne, and so on) make wine come across quite hot also. Drinking any full-bodied wine with Texas five-alarm chili almost always leads to heartburn! In general terms, wines with medium alcohol content (11 to 13 percent) and lighter wines are easier to work with at the table.

Armed with the five wine keys, we can begin to define profiles for wines that are more food-friendly than others. Sparkling, white, rosé, red, and dessert wines that pair well with food have the profiles described in the table on the next page.

109

Wines that don't fit these profiles aren't necessarily out of bounds or incompatible with food. They do, however, require more effort to pair, and matching options are more limited. A wine with excessive oak or alcohol mandates more careful matching with a dish, and an overly tannic red requires more thought than one with balanced tannins.

FOOD-FRIENDLY WINES

	SPARKLING	WHITE	ROSÉ	RED	DESSERT
ACIDITY	High	Balanced to high	Moderately high	Balanced plus	High
SWEETNESS	Dry to balanced off-dry	Dry to balanced off-dry	Dry to balanced off-dry	Dry (ripe fruit okay, but no actual sweetness)	Balanced with the acid
OAK	None	None to balanced	None	Balanced	None to balanced
TANNIN	None	None	None to very low	Balanced	None
ALCOHOL	Low to balanced	Low to balanced	Low to balanced	Balanced	Low to balanced

When I taste any wine, and in all of my teaching, I use a technique called mapping. Each wine has its own personality, defined by its unique combination of acid, sugar, oak, tannin, and alcohol. When I taste a wine I ask myself how it rates according to each of these keys. Once I have described a wine's unique fingerprint, I have a better idea of how it will pair up, and then I can choose dishes that will complement it, either from a restaurant menu or in my own kitchen. But, as with a new language, once you gain a little confidence, you'll be on the way to new and exciting discoveries.

THE GREAT, THE BAD, AND THE AVERAGE

Joshua Wesson and David Rosengarten

What makes a great food-and-wine match? It's surprising how seldom that question gets asked. There's no dearth of advice from "experts" on what cheese goes with what red wine, on what fish goes with what white wine, on what dessert goes with what dessert wine. But there are precious few words that attempt to explain *why* any of these things are so, *why* these matches are considered to be great.

You're told, for example, that soup is best with sherry. After you try ten soups with ten sherries—and every combination is vastly different—you'll still wonder what the experts are getting at. *Why* is soup best with sherry? What are we looking for?

What bells will announce that gastronomic compatibility has been reached?

The first order of business, we feel, is to establish our criteria for great wine-and-food matches. We could spend six volumes telling you that this match is great, or that match is great—but if you don't have a sense of what we mean by "great," it will be an empty exercise.

Toward this end, this [. . .] is a food-with-wine tasting that you conduct along with us. There are fifteen different "tastes" in this tasting, and by going through them with us you'll learn exactly what we mean by great matches, average matches, and bad matches.

I have known Josh Wesson and David Rosengarten for over thirty years. Josh has great wit and sense of humor, and utilizes a practical approach when writing about wine and food. In his early days, he worked as a sommelier and went on to open his own wine store called Best Cellars. In 2007, he merged Best Cellars with the Great Atlantic & Pacific Tea Company (A&P)—the company whose wine, beer, and spirits division he now leads. On a personal note, he and I cofounded the "famous" rock 'n' roll band of the '80s, the Winettes.

Over the years, David has contributed to many publications, including Gourmet *magazine, the* New York Times, *and* Newsday. *After writing the book* Red Wine with Fish: The New Art of Matching Food with Wine *with Josh, he moved onto the Food Network and has done over 2,500 television episodes on wine and food. In 2001, he created the* Rosengarten Report, *a subscription-only newsletter, one of the best out there today.*

Here's what you'll find:

FIVE FOOD ITEMS All are inexpensive, and easy to buy or prepare.

THREE WINE POSSIBILITIES FOR EACH FOOD ITEM The first is a wine that goes splendidly with the food; the second is a wine that complements the food in a humdrum, ordinary sort of way; and the third wine is downright awful. Taste through these matches so that you might get an idea of what others think of as great, ordinary, and bad wine-food matches.

A DISCUSSION OF WHY EACH MATCH MIGHT BE CONSIDERED GREAT, AVERAGE, OR BAD This is an excellent opportunity for you to compare tasting notes with us, and to perhaps develop a new perspective on matching wine and food. What you think is obviously the most important thing, but you might find your thinking changing, maturing, focusing, after you match your opinions against ours.

A GREAT, AVERAGE, OR BAD MATCH

THE WINE The wine that turned out to be great (or average or bad) with the food item under consideration.

LOOK FOR The details that you need to know in selecting the wine for this experiment. If we suggest a red Bordeaux, for example, you'll need to know what *kind* of red Bordeaux was used. Was it from the Médoc or from Pomerol? Was it from a vineyard that makes rich wine or light wine? Complex wine or simple wine? Was it old or young? All of these factors come into play in

choosing wine for food, and [. . .]we'll guide you toward the best wines for the experiment. Make your own selection—or show the section to a trusted merchant, and have him guide you to the appropriate wine.

THE MATCH A careful analysis of what went right—or wrong—in each particular match-up. Remember, if you read these notes without simultaneously experiencing the match, you're missing a wonderful opportunity to bring words and wine closer together.

Even with these precautions, it's still quite possible that your response to a specific match will be quite different from the printed response. Good. This would be true if we were standing in the same room tasting these matches, and there's nothing wrong with that. Be skeptical as you work your way through these matches. Be positively ornery. Don't accept anything at face value. You must be an active participant in order to derive benefits from this exercise. These are not writ-in-stone-tablet prescriptions meant to endure for eternity; these are matches designed to get a dialogue rolling, and provoke thought.

[Y]ou will learn to sharpen your perceptions and to approach the subject differently, but you probably won't learn exactly what wine to serve with what food. [. . .]Remember that the best matchers of wine and food do not have lists memorized. What they do have is lots of tasting experience backed by lots of reflection, and a developed intuition as to why certain things might reasonably be expected to go well together.

How you work through this [. . .] is of prime importance. It would not be a good idea, for example, to tackle all fifteen matches at one sitting. You'll find that palate fatigue sets in very quickly; most tasters experience a dulling of their senses after about six to eight wines.

We recommend planning a party or a dinner around these matches. We have found events like these to be a great deal of fun for people at all levels of wine knowledge—seasoned experts as well as first-time curiosity-seekers. In addition, by including more people—and asking each to bring a bottle—you ensure that a merry evening will have an extremely reasonable price tag.

Here's one way to go about things. Select two food items [. . .]. Line up three glasses for each taster. Pour the three wines from the first food match. Taste them one by one, so that everyone can become familiar with the wines before the serious work begins. Group discussion always helps to focus your impressions. Then serve the first food item. Taste it, then try it with the wine designated as making a bad match. Move on to the average match. Conclude with the great match. See if there's a consensus. Follow the notes [. . .] and disagree violently if you want to—but keep thinking.

Rinse the glasses—and repeat the process with the second food item. For an extra thrill, include a wine with each food item—a fourth wine—that you've selected. See if the group can come to a conclusion as to whether the fourth wine is great, average, or bad with the food.

If the crowd is a dedicated one, you may move on to a third, a fourth, or even a fifth food item.

When you've finished, you'll probably have some wine left over. Great! Now it's time to serve dinner. Use the leftover experiment wines to accompany the food you serve to your guests,

As you progress through the experiments [. . .], you'll no doubt discover that there are recurring ways in which wine and food can be good, bad, or ordinary together. Watch for the following patterns:

1. **SYNERGISM** This is the most dynamic action of wine and food together. It doesn't happen often, but when it does it usually makes a match either great or bad. In a synergistic action, the wine and the food combine to create a total effect that is different from the effects of the two taken individually. Most often this takes the form of a third flavor that is not found in either the food or the wine. For example—as you'll see later—Port and Roquefort together usually create an impression of butterscotch or vanilla in the mouth. Where did it come from? No one knows, but it makes the match lovely. Conversely, some wines and foods together, like tannic, low-fruit reds with oily fish, create a completely unpleasant third flavor that renders the match a disaster. Always be on the alert for synergistic action.

2. **REFRESHMENT** This is obviously a very simple way wine and food are good together. Cold white wines as well as red wines are often refreshing with food. Occasionally, a wine is so refreshing with a food that the match is elevated into the great category; more often, the refreshment is one of the elements in a match that is average—pleasant, but nothing special.

3. **NEUTRALITY** This doesn't sound very attractive, but it's a great improvement

113

over the plethora of matches that produce unpleasant additional tastes. In a match characterized by neutrality, nothing turns more acidic, or more harsh, or more bitter, or more sweet, or more anything; the wine and the food go their own ways, inflicting minimal damage on each other. Neutrality is found in matches described as average.

4. **THE TRANSFORMATION OF WINE OR FOOD** Sometimes a match features an enormous change in either the wine or the food; one element holds its ground, while the other appears completely different. As you'll see, this is the case in the bad match of artichoke hearts and red Bordeaux; the artichokes taste pretty much the same with the wine, but the wine is merely a ghost of its former self when drunk with the artichokes. Sometimes a transformation works for the better; a wine or a food can be improved by its marriage to a partner, e.g., an acidic wine with salad; its acidity is canceled out. Matches in which this phenomenon takes place can be characterized as great, average, or bad depending on the circumstances.

One last note before we begin: It's difficult indeed to write about the experience of tasting wine. Much of the literature on the subject is either too scientific (and therefore hard to understand), or too impressionistic to mean anything. We have tried to strike a balance. Our descriptions of the following matches are meant to be a faithful record—in specific but everyday language—of the sensations we experienced in tasting these wines and foods together.

The descriptions are scientific insofar as we have tried to be objective, accurate, and complete—but it's hard to avoid emotion completely in a subject such as this. In any event, do not be put off by the welter of detail that you're about to see; all of these words merely represent an attempt to put down on paper what's in the matches. Try writing a few precise descriptions yourself, and you'll soon discover that we're all speaking exactly the same language.

Food Item 1: Oysters

LOOK FOR fresh, raw oysters—still in their tightly closed shells. Shuck them yourself, and eat them as soon after shucking as possible. It is important that no strong-tasting sauces interfere with the oyster flavor in this experiment; a squeeze of fresh lemon juice will have to suffice.

A GREAT MATCH

THE WINE Three-year-old Chablis (village level)

LOOK FOR a French Chablis with a village appellation. Wines from specially designated vineyards in the village of Chablis—Premier Cru Chablis and Grand Cru Chablis—are better wines, but not necessary for this match. It is important that you *do not use* the California wine known as Chablis as this is usually among the worst of California wines, and bears no relation to its French namesake. California Chablis is fruity and slightly sweet; French Chablis is dry, acidic, and steely.

THE MATCH An all-time great. One of those rare matches in which the wine works equally well as a vital partner to the food and as an exquisite refreshment. An oyster is a living pump, taking in and belching forth as much as one hundred gallons of water a day. To the oyster, this may be hard work or great refreshment but no matter—to us, it is how the oyster picks up its subtle taste of minerals. And therein lies the key to the match: The ground beneath the grapevines in the village of Chablis is also rich in minerals. You can smell it in the wine. The bouquet of Chablis is often called steely or flinty; these are hard qualities to identify, but if you smell a white wine grown on the calcium-rich limestone slopes of Chablis and then smell a wine made from the same grape—Chardonnay— but grown on different soil, you will certainly discern a trace of minerals in the Chablis.

In any case, make short work of the oyster—then swirl and sniff the wine. The flavor compatibility already announces itself. Taste the wine, and the mineral aspects of the two items rush together—the oyster taste predominates, then the Chablis taste, then they're indistinguishable, then the oyster reemerges, then the Chablis . . . and so on through an exhilarating aftertaste. Further-more, the acidity of the Chablis cuts unerringly through the brininess of the oyster. You would not have thought that such quiet and simple items could create such furious energy. Not everything's dynamic, however; the marriage of similar textures—unctuous Chablis and slippery oyster— is the quiet anchor of the match, no less thrilling for its stillness.

AN AVERAGE MATCH
THE WINE One-year-old Vinho Verde

LOOK FOR the youngest Vinho Verde from Portugal that you can find; this is an exceptionally light, crisp, and neutral white wine that loses its charm within a year or two.

Beyond the question of youth: Try to find a Vinho Verde that has a good deal of sparkle in it—some Vinho Verdes are practically still, but some are like sparkling wine. Try to find one that's very dry; many prepared for the American market have some sweetness. Also make sure that the acid level is high; some of these wines are a bit flabbier and less lively than others. Ask your wine merchant for help in selecting a dry, acidic wine.

THE MATCH The Chablis is hard to top, but were it not for the existence of Chablis, Vinho Verde might be the finest solution available. The wine's acid cuts the fishiness. Its light body creates an attractive texture contrast. Its bubbles dance around the slow-moving oyster. There is a long aftertaste that heightens the oyster flavor, but the Vinho Verde itself is not improved. It's only a light refreshment, and that's exactly what's wrong with the match. It's all oyster. Lovely, but it's always more fun to watch *two* good musicians in a duet.

A BAD MATCH
THE WINE Ten-year-old red Rioja (Reserva)

LOOK FOR a light-bodied red Rioja, designated Reserva, from a good vintage, with ten years of age. Experiments showed that red wines with heavier body and younger fruit work better with oysters than red wines—like this one—with considerable delicacy. Do not buy one of the most expensive Riojas from a good vintage; this is likely to have too much body for this experiment. A low-to-medium cost wine, just at or past its peak, is perfect.

THE MATCH This is a classic demon-stration of the origins of the white wine with fish principle: The aftertaste of this Rioja-Oyster match is characterized by an intense, lingering fishiness that is most unattractive. This is exactly why you are always advised to steer clear of red wine with fish. In actuality, the fishy aftertaste does not materialize in all marriages between red wine and fish; in this experiment, many fruity, non-woody reds blended rather nicely with the raw oysters. But Rioja is a washout.

Food Item 2: Pizza

LOOK FOR a fresh-baked, store-bought pizza with plenty of spicy tomato sauce. The sauce is important here, because it offers the wine its greatest challenge. The dough and the cheese are relatively simple to match appropriately, but the tomato-based melange of herbs, acid, and sugar poses a few problems. To keep the experiment pure, do not get creative with toppings; plain pizza works best.

A GREAT MATCH

THE WINE Two-year-old Dolcetto d'Alba

LOOK FOR a Dolcetto from the Piedmont region in the northwest corner of Italy. The wine's name implies sweetness but, like a Beaujolais, it's really a dry red wine that sometimes creates an impression of sweetness through its buoyant fruitiness. It's also much richer than most Beaujolais. Try to find a Dolcetto from a rich Piedmont vintage, and try to find a wine from a producer noted for rich Dolcettos—like Vietti, Valentino, Ratti, Luciano Sandrone, or Aldo Conterno.

THE MATCH It's not as easy as you might imagine to match pizza perfectly. Many wines are turned harsh or sour by the sauce, many are turned insipid by the cheese, many are turned thin by the richness. The Dolcetto has safeguards against all of these problems.

To begin with, the Dolcetto is not without a good dose of its own acid, and one taste tells you that the acid of the tomato sauce is not going to be a problem: usually, two acids tend to smooth each other out. Tasting further, you find that the rich fruitiness of the wine handles the rich oiliness of the pizza very nicely. And the blend of flavors is superb; what was a whisper of spiciness in the Dolcetto before it met the pizza now becomes a statement.

AN AVERAGE MATCH

THE WINE Four-year-old Napa Valley Merlot

LOOK FOR a Napa Merlot with lively flavors, good body, and, at least, moderate tannin. A number of Napa Merlots would be perfect for this experiment (Newton, Duckhorn, Rutherford Hill, Stag's Leap). The Merlots being produced in the Santa Ynez Valley near Santa Barbara are very attractive as well. Avoid vintages known for lighter, thinner wines; medium richness helps in this match-up.

THE MATCH This is a quite pleasant match spoiled only by the fact that the Merlot is somewhat diminished by the pizza; it would do even better alongside a less busy dish. You'll be able to see this if you taste the wine first, then taste the pizza, then go back to the wine: nice, but diminished.

In any event, notice the fine blending of flavors between the food and wine: The herbal character of the Merlot is a lovely complement to the Italian tomato sauce. Notice the long finish after you've tasted the food and wine together; the flavors reverberate with neither the food nor the wine predominating. And there's very little development of bitterness or harshness. Though the Merlot is thinned out by the pizza, it makes a surprisingly appropriate and refreshing partner.

A BAD MATCH

THE WINE One-year-old Muscat de Beaumes de Venise

LOOK FOR a Muscat de Beaumes de Venise that's vintage-dated; not all of them are. If you buy a nonvintage one, it may be past its youth of minty, melony, honeyed flavors.

THE MATCH This is a silly match—the worst idea since Hawaiian Pizza (pizza with a pineapple topping). Beaumes de Venise is loaded with sweet apricot flavor, and if you try it with pizza you might feel as if you're at your fourth birthday party—guzzling sweet drinks with everything, appropriate or not. The situation is worsened by the fact that the "vin doux naturel" contains a light fortification—it's about 15 percent alcohol—and the wine's additional heat doesn't like the pizza any more than the sugar does. The cold wine is not even refreshing with the hot pizza—just cloying. Together, they produce a sweet aftertaste that seems to get sweeter and sweeter.

Food Item 3: Marinated Artichoke Hearts

LOOK FOR artichoke hearts—the ones that come in little glass jars— marinated in oil, herbs, and garlic. Not much to choose from here; there are a number of suitable brands that are widely available.

A GREAT MATCH

THE WINE Nondosage Champagne, nonvintage

LOOK FOR a French Champagne that is dry as a bone—with no dosage, or sweetening agent, added. One such is Laurent-Perrier Ultra Brut, and another is Piper Heidsieck Brut Sauvage; either is what you want for this experiment. Artichokes are notoriously difficult to match with wine—in fact, the classic rule is to serve *no* wine with artichokes— because of a naturally occurring chemical that makes everything you taste after you've tasted an artichoke taste sweeter. This is obviously not desirable if you're drinking wines of great subtlety.

117

However, if you think of the wine that accompanies the artichoke as a good refreshment—if you sacrifice the wine to the artichoke, essentially—you will enjoy this match a great deal. And, if you choose an extremely dry nondosage Champagne, the sweet aftertaste may even seem like an improvement.

THE MATCH Taste an artichoke heart, then swirl and sniff the wine. There is no hint of a problem here; the yeastiness of the Champagne is a most appealing aroma next to the subtle but unmistakable flavor of artichoke. Taste the sparkling wine, and remember to drink freely and fast; the key to appreciating this match is as much in the cool sensation of bubbles running over viscous artichoke hearts as in any flavor impressions. The two are lovely together; there's a nice play back and forth in the subtle flavors, and a splendid marriage of textures.

But is the wine ruined—turned to artificially sweetened syrup? The nondosage Champagne is not; its high acid content has staved off, to a great extent, the offending chemical. Drink freely again—this is not a match designed for small sips and close scrutiny—and observe the smooth finish which features aftertastes of wine and artichoke in roughly equal proportions. The winner is neither the wine nor food—it is, by a knockout, the match.

AN AVERAGE MATCH

THE WINE Four-year-old red Châteauneuf-du-Pape

LOOK FOR a rich and concentrated Chateauneuf-du-Pape—still in its youth—from a moderate vintage.

There has been a great change in recent years in the style of Châteauneuf-du-Pape;

only a handful of makers still produce the rich and vigorous wine of old. Many producers today are making a "modern" Châteauneuf-du-Pape: lighter, fruitier, more suitable for early consumption. Look for the former style here, from such wineries as Château de Beaucastel, Domaine de Chante Perdrix, Clos des Papes, and Domaine du Vieux Télégraphe. It is best that you choose a Châteauneuf-du-Pape of this ilk because thinner wines will get buried by the artichokes.

THE MATCH It is immediately apparent that this is a good flavor match-up; the spicy, peppery character of Châteauneuf-du-Pape marries well with the Provençal herbs and garlic of the artichokes. Some nice things also happen in the "feel" of the match. The wine is rich and the artichokes are oily; they feel right together.

The big problem, of course—as always with artichokes—is the sweetening of the food. It seems that the tannin and coarseness of the wine fend off the sweetening factor to some extent; the wine is certainly changed in an unnatural way by the artichokes—made a bit sweeter—but it's not at all unpleasant. And the wine is not complex or subtle enough to make us mourn excessively over the change.

A BAD MATCH

THE WINE Ten-year-old red Bordeaux from the Margaux appellation

LOOK FOR a Margaux from a château of moderate quality and from a vintage of moderate pedigree. There's no need to waste money on a great Bordeaux from a great year to see how bad this match can be; of course, the more you spend on the Bordeaux the more unpleasant this match becomes. But a nice wine from a nice château in a nice vintage—with 5–10 years of age—will make the point well.

THE MATCH Wine and food don't have to be positively awful together to make a bad match; it's enough, to our way of thinking, that either the wine or the food is completely ruined by the marriage.

This poor Bordeaux never had a chance. Taste it before you taste the artichokes; wines from the Margaux appellation are among the most delicate of red Bordeaux. You can feel in your mouth that there's not a great deal of weight—certainly not compared to a Cabernet Sauvignon from California—and yet the wine manages to be rich in flavor. Now try an artichoke. Go back to the wine. The beautiful balance that some vigneron struggled a whole summer to achieve is wiped away. The wine tastes thin, acidic, and sweet. It's not repulsive as a thirst-quencher after the artichokes, but it's a great waste of a lovely achievement.

Food Item 4: Roquefort

LOOK FOR a ripe piece of French Roquefort—creamy and well-veined with blue; avoid Roquefort that is very white, very waxy, and very salty. Other kinds of blue cheese won't work as well for these experiments, which are all based on true Roquefort.

A GREAT MATCH

THE WINE Twenty-year-old Vintage Port

LOOK FOR a rich Port past the unattractive hardness and vigor of youth. Vintage Port from a great house such as Warre's or Graham's will supply the greatest thrills, but

you can substitute less expensive wines—such as:

1. Late Bottled Vintage Port These can be drunk younger; Quinta do Noval made a good, moderately priced one in the 1975 vintage.

2. Tawny Port with an Indication of Age These lovely, nutty wines say "ten-year-old," "twenty-year-old," etc., depending on their age. The Taylor thirty-year-old is fabulous.

THE MATCH One of the very best examples of synergistic action. Ports at all quality levels love Roquefort, and produce with the wine a third flavor that might strike you as butter, butterscotch, caramel, or vanilla. The wine's tannin (if you're using Vintage Port) counteracts the powerful salt and flavors of the cheese, taming it, making it gentle, increasing its appeal. The same can be said of the cheese's effect on the wine. A jigsaw puzzle match if there ever was one.

AN AVERAGE MATCH

THE WINE Two-year-old California Zinfandel

LOOK FOR a forceful young buck of a wine—loaded with alcohol and fruit. Zinfandel is produced in many styles in California; they include a fruity Beaujolais-style wine, and a more complex claret-style wine. Neither of these is called for here. What works best is a Zin of larger proportions—spicy, briary, peppery, and rich. The wine should have medium to full body, and at least 13 percent alcohol. Try to find a wine that is meant to be aged for several years, but drink it young for this experiment. A two-year-old wine that has three years to go until its peak would be perfect. Dry Creek Valley in Sonoma produces many Zins that would be appropriate for this experiment, as does Amador County.

THE MATCH We feel that red wine with cheese has an inflated reputation. Cheese—especially strong cheese—tends to mask the tannin of wine, and to make most reds seem pleasant but bland. The one style of red wine that works reasonably well with cheese, we believe, is young, alcoholic, and very flavorful.

Zinfandel can fit this bill perfectly. The taste of the cheese brings out a lively grapiness in the bouquet of the wine. In the mouth, one senses a heightening of the wine's alcohol and acid—not at all to the detriment of the match. It's a titanic struggle that—unlike some titanic struggles—is most interesting to watch. As always with red wine and cheese, some of the tannins of the Zinfandel get reduced—but there's enough going on in this match so that the tannin reduction does not spell out insipidity. We prefer the Port, of course—and Sauternes—but Zin is a reasonable alternative.

A BAD MATCH

THE WINE One-year-old Muscadet

LOOK FOR a fruity young Muscadet—which also will undoubtedly be light and fairly acidic.

THE MATCH Taste the cheese. Problems start with the wine's bouquet; what seemed pleasant before the cheese (apple-buttery hints reminiscent of a very light Chardonnay), now seems like a mere insipid jug wine.

The taste is worse. Any Muscadet flavor is removed by the overpowering flavor of the

cheese; all that remains is a bitter harshness brought about by the response of the wine's alcohol to the cheese. (It's possible that the alcohol is emphasized because the wine has nothing else strong enough to stand up to the Roquefort.) What's especially remarkable is the obliteration—in one's perception—of the Muscadet's tremendously refreshing acidity.

Food Item 5: Roasted Almonds

LOOK FOR lightly roasted, moderately salty almonds. Even better, buy plain blanched almonds and roast them according to the following simple recipe.

Roasted Almonds

⅓ pound blanched almonds
1 teaspoon peanut oil
1½ teaspoon coarse salt

Preheat oven to 300 degrees F. Spread almonds in one layer in a roasting pan, and roast in oven for 22 minutes. Remove, mix with oil, then mix with salt. Spread on a towel to cool, 15–20 minutes. These are best when eaten within a few hours.

Serves six as an appetizer

NOTE: Following this recipe assures a better experiment, and an even better bowl of almonds.

A GREAT MATCH

THE WINE Bual Madeira (nonvintage)

LOOK FOR a medium-rich, medium-sweet, type of Madeira known as Bual, with great acidity. Malmsey (even sweeter) could also work in this combination—as could the drier Madeiras (Sercial and Verdelho)—but

Bual works best of all. There's no need to buy an expensive Vintage Madeira to conduct this experiment.

THE MATCH Madeira's cachet in the world of wine is that it's baked as it's being prepared for bottling—a practice that pays enormous dividends when the wine is drunk with roasted nuts. The roasted flavor of the wine reinforces the roasted flavor of the nuts, and the almond flavors bring out a nutty dimension in the wine. This action is most apparent in the long finish, where wine and food take turns in registering impressions; a third flavor seems always on the point of emergence. The Bual works better than other Madeira types because it has enough sweetness to override the potential bitterness in the almonds, but also has enough acid to cut their richness.

AN AVERAGE MATCH
THE WINE One-year-old White Zinfandel

LOOK FOR a fresh, young White Zinfandel with a pale orange or salmon color. (Though the wine is called white, it's actually a kind of rosé.) What's most important here is the wine's value as a refresher; it should be light, just slightly sweet, and with enough zingy acid to bring the package alive. This is a wine that goes downhill rapidly, so make sure that the bottle you buy is from this or last year's vintage.

THE MATCH The almonds are quite salty, and the first thing you notice is the cool relief offered by the White Zinfandel. It's a fairly neutral wine, but a subtle, new flavor dimension in the wine—a touch of nuttiness?—is created by the food and wine together. Noticeably absent, at any rate, are distasteful flavor clashes. Finally, the wine's acid cuts

through the storehouse of fat, rendering the nuts a little less cloying than usual. This is not a dynamic match, but it's easy to imagine mindlessly eating and drinking more than you should if these items were served together on a summer afternoon.

A BAD MATCH
THE WINE White Retsina (nonvintage)

LOOK FOR a white Greek Retsina. Many of the Retsinas available in the American market are similar: light, dry, and with the unmistakable taste of pine resin—which in fact has been added to the wine. It's a fabulous taste with Greek food, but it's a taste that's not always appropriate.

THE MATCH Though refreshing, the match features a distasteful synergistic action. The pine resin coaxes a very powerful bitterness out of the nuts, a sensation that grows in intensity for several seconds after you've swallowed the wine.

If you have carried out these experiments along with us, you now have a first-hand understanding of what we mean by "great," "average," and "bad" matches.

121

WHAT TO DRINK WITH CHOCOLATE

Jay McInerney

Not far from the spot where Romeo secretly married Juliet, in the Valpolicella hills overlooking Verona, I discovered a more fortunate and successful match. I had just finished lunch with Stefano Cesari, the dapper proprietor of Brigaldara, in the kitchen of his fourteenth-century farmhouse, and I was trying to decide if it would be incredibly uncouth to ask who made the beautiful heather-toned tweed jacket he was wearing, when he put some dark chocolates from Perugia in front of me and opened a bottle of his 1997 Recioto della Valpolicella. One hesitates to describe any marriage as perfect, but I was deeply impressed with the compatibility of his semisweet, raisiny red and the bittersweet chocolates. Cesari later took me up to the loft of the big barn and showed me the hanging trays where Corvina and Rondinella grapes are dried for several months after harvest, which concentrates the grape sugars and ultimately results in an intense, viscous wine that, like Tawny Port, Brachetto, and a few other vinous oddities, enhances the already heady and inevitably romantic experience of eating chocolate.

The Cabernet, Merlot, or Shiraz you drank with your steak may get along well with a simple chocolate dessert, especially if the wine is young and the fruit is really ripe, but real chocoholics should check out the dried-grape wines, many of which are fortified—that is, dosed with brandy, in the manner of Port, a process that stops fermentation and leaves residual sugar. "Fortification seems helpful in terms of matching chocolate," says Robert Bohr, the wine director at Cru, in Greenwich Village, which has one of the best wine lists in the country, if not the world. Bohr likes Tawny Port with many chocolate desserts, finding Vintage Port too fruity. (McInerney does too, and advises that

I have never had the pleasure of meeting Jay McInerney, but know of him through his non-wine novels, Bright Lights, Big City *and* Ransom, *and also his essays that he wrote and published in* Bacchus & Me *and* A Hedonist in the Cellar. *He also has a bi-monthly wine column in the* Wall Street Journal. *One of the biggest questions I get from my wine students is what to pair with Amarone, Port, and late harvest Zinfandel, to avoid overpowering the wine while still having a pleasant experience. I am not sure chocolate is the answer, but it is certainly a place to begin! You need to have chocolate and one of these wines when you read his chapter.*

some of the best Tawnies come from Australia's Barossa Valley.) But most of all Bohr likes Madeira.

If you were to order the Hacienda Concepción chocolate parfait at Cru, Bohr would direct you to a vintage Madeira like the 1968 d'Oliveiras Boal. Madeira has become so unfashionable in the past century that many putative wine lovers have never tasted it, but I'm sensing the stirrings of a cult revival spearheaded by supergeeks like Bohr. The sweeter Malmsey style seems to be best suited to chocolate desserts. And by chocolate, I mean, of course, dark chocolate. Milk chocolate should be consumed only by day, if at all, and accompanied by milk.

The cough-syrupy Umbrian *passito* wine is made in the same fashion as Recioto from the mysterious and sappy Sagrantino grape. These powerful, sweet reds seem to have originated as sacramental wines, and they continue to inspire reverence among a small cult of hedonists, myself among them. This practice of drying grapes goes back thousands of years; there are references to drying wine grapes prior to fermentation in Homer and Hesiod. ("When Orion and Sirius come into mid-heaven," Hesiod advises in *Works and*

Days, "cut off all the grape clusters and bring them home. Show them to the sun for ten days and ten nights.") I like to imagine that these dried-grape wines resemble those that were drunk at Plato's symposium or Caligula's bashes—although chocolate wouldn't appear in Europe until the sixteenth century, Columbus having stumbled upon a stash of cacao beans on his fourth and last voyage to the New World.

Two of the finest wines for chocolate, Maury and Banyuls, come from remote Roussillon in France's deep southeast. These so-called *vins doux naturels* are made (mostly) from late-picked Grenache grown on steep, terraced, wind-scoured hillsides near the Spanish border. The standard-bearing Banyuls estate is Domaine du Mas Blanc, one of the world's most famous obscure domaines. I first tasted this wine at JoJo, Jean-Georges Vongerichten's pioneering New York bistro, alongside the warm Valrhona chocolate cake, a nearly erotic experience that I try to re-create at least once a year. (And I'm a guy who doesn't usually even bother with dessert.)

Banyuls's neighboring appellation Maury also produces a chocolate-loving *vin doux*. The village cooperative makes the classic example; I recently had, alongside Le Bernardin's warm chocolate tart, a 1929 that was spectacular, with lots of caramel, date, coffee, and vanilla flavors, plus an oxidized Sherry note, which the French and Spanish call *rancio*. The finest estate in Maury is Mas Amiel (which once traded hands in a card game), producers of several cuvées of heady Maury, including one raised in the traditional manner of the region, spending a year outdoors in huge glass demijohns, exposed to

123

the extremes of the Roussillon climate. The demand for these labor-intensive wines, like that for most sweet wines, has been static in the past few decades (Mas Amiel is increasingly focusing on the production of dry table wines), and prices remain modest when compared with Vintage Port or Sauternes.

America's answer to Banyuls and Recioto is late-harvest Zinfandel—a fairly rare, sweet style of Zin that is eminently delicious with chocolate, the darker and more bitter the better. This is a good general rule:

chocolate with a high cocoa content and a lower milk and sugar content is the most complex, intense, and wine-friendly. As for the desserts, the more complicated they get, the harder they will be to match. Chocolate already has some five hundred flavor compounds—how many more do you need? A chocolate soufflé is a beautiful thing, but it's hard to improve upon a simple piece of Valrhona, Bernachon, or Scharffen Berger dark chocolate, unless of course you pour a Madeira or a Maury alongside it.

VINEYARD ENTERTAINING

Molly Chappellet

WORKING FOR THE DIVINE

If we were just selling our grapes, we might prune and feed and water to produce a larger crop. However, since our concern is not with tonnage but with producing the most intensely flavorful grape, our viticultural practices and choice of soil, mountainside, rootstock, and fruiting wood are critical.

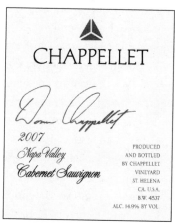

From the time of budbreak to the moment of harvest, every aspect of the weather—heat, rain, wind, fog—affects that vintage. This is why no two vintages are exactly alike. Two extreme examples come to mind—1976 and 1982.

Nineteen seventy-six was a drought year. The grapevines were feeling stressed from lack of water and produced only a small crop. The summer ripening weather was ideal— long, even temperatures of warm days and cool nights from verasion (the period when the berries soften a bit and start to sugar up and when the red grapes begin to turn color) to harvest. The Cabernet grapes were particularly intense in flavor and produced a big wine that matured slowly.

In direct contrast to 1976 was 1982, when an extraordinary amount of rain fell, producing lush growth and heavy crops. That year the Cabernet was lighter and ready to

One of the early pioneers of Napa Valley was the Chappellet family, who started their winery in 1967. I have vivid memories of my first visit to Pritchard Hill and the magnificent winery overlooking the valley. To me, Molly Chappellet was one of the first to combine wine, art, entertainment, photography, and gardening design all together. Maybe the best way to describe her is as the Martha Stewart of Napa Valley. Last year at Auction Napa Valley, there was Molly, royalty of Napa, as breathtaking as ever, strolling through the masses helping to raise money for those in need.

drink earlier than our previous Cabernets. Same vines, same care; very different wines.

As farmers, we can never forget the weather. One of the reasons so many people come here to make wine is that the Napa Valley offers very special climatic conditions required by *Vitis vinifera*, the wine grape. During the summer heat, the coastal fogs come into the Napa Valley at night and lower the temperature as much as forty degrees. On our hill, we even have a climate slightly different from the one on the valley floor. While we benefit from the cooling effect and moisture of the fog, at seventeen hundred feet we're often above the fog, and our grapes ripen a bit earlier. Nineteen seventy-five illustrates the climatic differences between the valley floor and the hillside vineyards. All summer, the fog settled in the valley and prevented the ripening of grapes. Then the rains came and many unripened grapes rotted on the vine. Sitting in sunshine above the fog, our grapes ripened nicely to produce one of our best vintages.

In the Napa Valley, everybody celebrates the end of harvest. The parties we have are ways to express joy, to mark the finale of a year's work, and to thank all who have participated in the harvest, including the powers that be. At our vineyard, we used to cook up a storm and throw a big party for the workers who had helped us all year long. But one fall, I got sick during the harvest. To my delight, the workers got together, cooked a marvelous Mexican feast, and treated us to a party. We've continued the tradition—we fund the party and the workers do the cooking. We decorate the crushing area with piñatas, bright banners, and four-foot balloons for the children. We all

enjoy good food, music, and great wine; and we begin thinking about the year ahead.

Seeing the result of an entire year's work come to fruition isn't just a phrase; where we live, it's what keeps us working day in and day out. Our 1969 Cabernet, which for eight years held the world's record for the highest price paid for a single bottle of American wine, was the realization of [my husband] Donn's dream. Not because it was a "high-priced pour" (although that was certainly nice), but because it was a memorable expression of the vintner's art.

Winemaking represents a collaboration of farmer, artist, and scientist, sometimes all inhabiting one body. In our vineyard, we're fortunate to have three talented individuals—a viticulturist, an enologist, and Donn, the artist—to round out the team.

There is, as Hugh Johnson points out, something quite "divine" about wine, perhaps because it comes from a process of natural fermentation or because its clean flavor and crisp acidity provide such a perfect counterpoint to food. When used in cooking, wine does magical things. Just as herbs and spices bring out the flavor of certain foods, so it is with wine. In cooking, the alcohol in wine virtually disappears, leaving only the unparalleled essence of aged grape juice to enhance the dish. Once you start experimenting with using wine in cooking, you want to put it in every dish, and I do—except hot cereal and waffles. All you need is an adventuresome spirit and a fairly good wine. Remember that the better the wine, the better the dish.

Wine seems, as an accompaniment to food, to cut the richness of fat and helps us assimilate nutrients in food, not to mention making even the most ordinary meal a feast. Some ordinary dishes that wine has turned into feasts for us are mussels with Chenin Blanc, spinach and pine nuts with Chardonnay, lamb and basmati rice or aged Jack cheese with Cabernet, a salad of smoked chicken, persimmon, and sunflower seeds with Riesling, and Donn's favorite, tuna sandwiches with Riesling. The excitement of discovering new combinations that make both the wine and the food seem more interesting is what it's all about. Sometimes it's finding wines that have components similar to the food's; other times, it's enjoying contrasting components. But at its most poetic, wine represents a product that truly transcends time, place, material, and, of course, human effort.[. . .]

BEYOND SURVIVAL

One day, visiting my friend Maggie Wetzel in Alexander Valley, I suddenly saw what scale and imagination could do to a garden. Her vegetable garden, with its graceful curves, trellised vegetables, and well-defined paths, was more spectacular and imaginative than most flower gardens. I immediately contacted her landscape architect, Leland Noel, to ask for his counsel. After spending some time on Pritchard Hill, he presented us with a handsome plan, which I liked but which seemed quite impossible to execute. He had placed the vegetables on the southwest side of the house for sun and proximity to the kitchen: a sound enough concept, but that particular plot of land was literally on top of a rock quarry.

It was [my daughter] Lygia and her friends who overcame the obstacles of cost and labor when they began clearing rocks for the vegetable garden. Then we brought in a few truckloads of redwood mulch. This, along with our own piles of horse manure, compost heaps, and rotted oak leaves, which Donn and I shoveled from the ditch at the edge of the long driveway, made a good base with which to begin our garden. Moving all these piles and working them into the soil was not a simple job. Although each of the older children took his or her turn at the wheelbarrow, digging, or turning soil, we barely made a dent. When my friend Maggie heard we were preparing the whole area by hand, she sent her son down in a big van with their small tractor inside. That was friendship, pure and simple. With so much goodwill, and so much practical help, the garden had to be a success.

Those first few summers after the vegetable garden was planted, dinner hour came around later and later. In midsummer, the last ray of light wouldn't disappear until 9:15, at which time I would finally surrender and head back to the house. While I was becoming a better gardener, in self-defense Donn was becoming a better cook.

I had found that a garden laid out with harmony and rhythm and a variety of plant combinations added a whole new dimension to growing vegetables. It became a thing of beauty and a source of surprise. Every day felt like Christmas. I could hardly wait to run outside in the early light to see what the plants had done. Work truly became play, as I began weeding, watering, and clipping in the fresh cool air.

CHENIN BLANC SORBET

[My daughter] Sequoia makes her simplified version of this sorbet by simply freezing a bunch of Chenin Blanc grapes and eating them just as they thaw.

2½ pounds green grapes (preferably Chenin Blanc)
1 cup Chappellet (dry) Chenin Blanc
⅓ cup sugar
Fresh grape leaves
Small clusters of green grapes, with leaves, for garnish

Chop grapes in a food processor in batches, using 10 on/off turns. Push pulp through a strainer into a measuring cup until you have 3 cups of grape juice. Set aside. Heat wine and sugar in a small saucepan over low heat, swirling pan occasionally, until sugar dissolves. Increase heat and bring just to a boil, then remove from heat and cool to room temperature.

Combine reserved grape juice and cooled syrup in a bowl, then freeze in an ice-cream maker. Serve immediately, or place in freezer for several hours to mellow flavors. Spoon into goblets and garnish with grape clusters.

THE PLEASURES OF PLANTING

I adore every single part of gardening. Unlike kitchen cleanup, the garden cleanup chores of weeding and raking are ones that I actually enjoy. I can't muster much enthusiasm for a sponge, no matter how beautiful or practical it might be. But garden tools—now, that's a different story. It makes a tremendous difference how a trowel, a shovel, or clippers feel in your hand. I especially like the way tools feel when they've been used for a long while; the soft, satiny feel of wood that's been worn down by daily contact with the gardener's hand. I have an antique wooden rake that I regularly use and cherish along with a trowel my son Cyril made me in wood shop, one that has a strong metal blade and a wooden handle crafted just for my hand. Thanks to Smith & Hawken and a handful of other companies, you can now buy wonderful English tools here in America. I give one of their beautiful, pewter-like trowels to every young bride and groom I know. I hope the couple will have a garden one day, of course—but even if they don't, the trowel makes a perfectly fine flour or sugar scoop.

When all elements used in gardening are of natural materials, every stage of cultivating is an aesthetic pleasure. I use redwood stakes and natural twine to lay out the garden, wooden roof shingles to protect new plants from too much sun, small branches from pruned tree limbs for staking, and hand-split grapevine stakes for trellising.

Growing vegetables provides pleasure to all the senses. Taste, of course, is first and foremost, but smell, texture, and sound are important. However, I must confess to being most seduced by the sight of vegetables; after all, they are the most colorful part of the meal.

Perhaps it has to do with being raised in the city—I don't know—but seeing vegetables growing as ornaments in the garden is still a sight I don't take for granted. There's an intangible pleasure, a delight to seeing something we are accustomed to eating dotting the greenery like ornaments throughout the garden. Think about light filtering through translucent green lettuce leaves, or jewel-like purple eggplant hanging among unusually shaped gray-green leaves, or shiny orange peppers gleaming out from bright green leaves.

Besides companion planting for pest control and growth, think about planting for contrasts of color and texture and size. Vegetables can make a more spectacular border than flowers, if attention is paid to texture, rhythm, form, and color. Instead of putting curly parsley next to peas, beans, or peppers, try it next to broad-leaf escarole. Greens that go toward the reddish (red leaf chard) or purple (purple cabbage) also look wonderful next to light greens. One combination I've found particularly pleasing is large-leaf gray-green cabbage next to tall, two-year-old purple salvia.

⟶ DONN'S LAYERED VEGETABLES ⟵

Yellow zucchini are easy to grow, beautiful as a centerpiece, fun for children to pick, and most tasty in Donn's triple-layer treat.

1 teaspoon olive oil
2 cloves garlic, crushed
2 large sweet onions, sliced ½ inch thick
1 slightly overgrown zucchini or summer squash, sliced ½ inch thick
2 large tomatoes, sliced ½ inch thick
Dried oregano
Cheddar, Jack, or Italian Fontina cheese

In a large skillet, heat olive oil and sauté garlic until tender. Layer bottom of the pan with slices of onion. On top of onions, place a layer of sliced squash. Compose the top layer of slices of tomatoes and a large handful of crushed dried oregano, or two handfuls of fresh oregano and some freshly ground pepper.

Turn heat to medium low, cover, and cook until fork tender—about 20 minutes. Then sprinkle with grated cheese to taste. Put lid back on skillet until cheese is melted.

PART IV

ON MAKING WINE

ON MAKING WINE

I have always been interested in farming. I have vivid memories of my grandfather's farm in Columbia County, New York. As soon as I got involved in wine, my first thought was to plant grapes. But alas, I was a broke college student.

But I was able to convince a resort in New Paltz, the Mohonk Mountain House, to lend me some of their six thousand acres of land for an experimental vineyard.

I was also able to convince Cornell's agricultural extension to give me experimental grapevines. They wanted to test their viability in the Hudson Valley. Unfortunately, my first venture in growing grapes ended in failure. Still, inspired by Thomas Jefferson, who also had many failures growing grapes in his home state of Virginia, I pushed ahead. I am now on my fourth go-around and have recently planted Chardonnay, Pinot Noir, Cabernet Franc, and Riesling.

In my forty years in wine, I have also had the opportunity to make wine. I was actually better at that than growing the grapes. I still have in my personal cellar some of the wines I made in the mideighties.

All of this has helped me understand and appreciate the trials and tribulations of viticulture and winemaking while at the same time giving me a sense of place, growth, and a new appreciation of the cycle of life.

My dream is to retire and have my house surrounded by a small vineyard that I can tend to every day, making as much wine as possible.

—KZ

TASTE

Robert Mondavi

What does it take to make a truly great wine?

ROBERT MONDAVI WINERY

2 0 0 5

NAPA VALLEY

CABERNET SAUVIGNON

RESERVE

ALC. 15.0% BY VOL.

Climate, soil, wonderful vineyards, superb grapes, research, innovation, state-of-the-art equipment—all these are vital. But they only provide part of the foundation. People are key as well. No one makes wine alone; you need dedicated specialists in the vineyards and throughout the entire process of harvest, crush, fermentation, aging, bottling, and corking. These people, too, are vital parts of the foundation. But in themselves, all these people and ingredients are not enough to turn humble grapes into the elegance and grandeur of a Romanée-Conti or a Château Mouton-Rothschild. In the art of making fine wine, the quest for greatness always comes down to this: the artist and his gifts. The wine maker and his skill, his passion, character, sensibility, vision, and, above all else, his powers of taste.

Taste. Some people are born with it. Some people learn to develop it. The best

Robert Mondavi was a mentor to me and thousands of others in the wine business around the world. He was one of the true pioneers of California wines. Anyone involved in wine knows the name Mondavi. The winery has always been able to produce inexpensive, everyday table wines, as well as some the best wines in the world. I dedicated my twenty-fifth anniversary edition of Windows on the World Complete Wine Course *to Robert Mondavi with the following words: "His energy, passion, commitment, and foresight, not only in winemaking but in combining wine with food, music, and art, paved the way for Americans to enjoy wine."*

ROBERT MONDAVI WINERY

2007

FUMÉ BLANC

Napa Valley

wine makers spend their lives trying to master it. In my view, it takes almost a lifetime of experience and dedication for a wine maker to master all the elements and subtleties of the art of tasting. And he or she had better start early! In my case, I did start early, very early, and I had marvelous teachers: my mother and father.

I have such wonderful memories of my mother. In stature, she was a small woman, but she was very powerful. Momma Rosa is what everyone called her and, believe me, you didn't cross her. Her manner was almost always warm and gentle, but in her domain she was the boss—and everyone knew it. I remember one episode that proved to me what a tough lady she was. This was when I was a little boy in Virginia, Minnesota, during the days of Prohibition. Because families were allowed to have a limited amount of wine for their own consumption, our cellar was full of wine barrels—not just for us; each boarder had his own supply. Well, word got around town. People said, "The Mondavis have all sorts of wine in their cellar." The local authori-

ties heard about it, and one day they showed up at our door, axes in hand. They went down to the cellar and they were just about to swing their axes into all those barrels when Mother appeared on the scene.

"Now you wait just a minute!" she cried. "We have every right to have this wine. It isn't all for us; we have boarders here and we're just housing most of this wine for them!"

The officers, axes in hand, told her to back away, but Mother stood her ground. I remember there was all sorts of yelling and screaming, so loud that I could hear it upstairs, where I had been ordered to go and stay put. I don't know exactly how she managed it, but somehow Mother convinced those men to stop. She then convinced them that we did, in fact, have boarders and that we had every right to have that quantity of wine. To our great relief, the officers soon left, with their tails between their legs. And all those wine barrels were spared the ax, thanks to Momma Rosa.

Also thanks to her, every day of my childhood was an education in taste. We always had at least five or six boarders in our house in Minnesota, and on weekends Mother would cook for fifteen or sixteen people, most of them hungry miners. She'd be up at four or five o'clock in the morning to get started. My sisters would help in the kitchen, and Peter and I would sometimes pitch in, too. Just watching and helping Mother work, we learned about cooking and nutrition and about the care, patience, artistry, and sheer hard work that go into a fine meal. Mother always cooked from scratch and according to the seasons, using what was fresh in the garden or in the market. She was also careful to prepare meals that went well with the weather—both in terms of taste and nutrition.

In those brutally cold Minnesota winters, for instance, when we needed all the strength we could muster to stand up to the subzero temperatures, Mother would prepare huge winter meals. In the morning, for the kids and her boarders going off to the mines, Mother would prepare huge pots of oatmeal or polenta reheated from the night before, and she'd serve them with hot stewed tomatoes. To prepare for lunch, she'd start in the early morning and put a couple of whole chickens in the kettle to make stock. Then with eggs and flour she'd make fresh noodles. From the stock and the noodles would come our first course at lunch or dinner: chicken noodle soup. Then would come one of my favorites: fresh pasta with her special game sauce, made from tomatoes, garlic, herbs, and either robins or some kind of game. Her brother, Nazzareno, whom we called Uncle Neno, was an avid hunter. He'd kill anything and everything, in and out of season, and the game he brought back always found its way onto our table or into a fresh sauce for pasta. As a main course, Mother often made roasts of pork, veal, or beef, or a marvelous roast chicken stuffed with her special dressing.

To go with her roasts, she often made polenta, a favorite among the kids. Making polenta was always a major operation, filled with merriment. We had a big wooden table in the center of the kitchen, and Mother would spread the polenta over the entire table; then we would all gather around and grind the meal and get it ready for cooking. We'd chatter like birds, sing songs, and just bask in the warmth of the kitchen and our mother's love. Mother made her own Italian desserts as well. One of my favorites as a boy was *ciambelle*, a breadlike dough she would fry and then top with honey or powdered sugar. Simple, yet so delicious.

Wine was part of my experience as early as I can remember. At lunch and dinner, my mother or father would routinely flavor my water with a dollop of wine. I didn't like water alone, but I loved it that way. So I grew up thinking of wine as liquid food. It tasted good and everyone thought even then that it was healthy—good for the circulation and a general tonic for the system. When I got a little older, along with the huge breakfasts we had on those cold winter mornings, I'd get a special treat. Mother would prepare for me a milder version of the peasant jump starter she made for the miners: strong coffee, a bit of sugar to taste, and a jigger of red wine. It's a peculiar taste, but I developed a lifelong love for this in the morning, whether it's cold or not!

Our family had a very reliable supplier of wine: my father. Every autumn he would bring grapes home and make wine in our basement. I loved to help him. The process we used was simple but effective. First, we'd put the grapes in little tubs, made from barrels cut in half. Then we'd put rubber boots on and stomp the grapes. Some peasant families stomped the grapes barefoot, but we always wore those rubber boots. Almost all the wine Dad made was red wine. The grapes he used most were Zinfandel, but sometimes he also used Carignane, Alicante Bouschet, and Muscat—the same varieties he later bought and shipped when we moved to Lodi. Dad made his wine as pure as possible. He didn't add yeast or anything else, he just let the grape

135

juice ferment naturally, right in the barrels, skins and all. He would make three or four barrels and that would last the family all year long. And he'd make wine for the boarders. So when we finished, we had a cellar well stocked for winter and the year ahead. Were the wines any good? Well, we thought so at the time. They always came out robust and tasting as pure and fruity as the grapes themselves. What they lacked in refinement they made up for in authenticity and richness of character. Just like my father.

After we moved to Lodi and the family began to prosper, Dad still made his own wine. Occasionally he would also buy bottled wines, and so I began learning about different wines and comparing their tastes. I also began to understand the impact of temperature on the taste of wine. Dad liked his wine very cold and I preferred mine at room temperature; I thought it had more flavor. So before mealtimes, I'd go down to the cellar and bring up two bottles. I'd keep his bottle cold and I'd set mine out so it could warm up to room temperature and the wine would properly open. My father not being much of a talker (I talked enough for the whole family, even back then), we rarely discussed wine; we just drank it and enjoyed it. I didn't fully realize it at the time, but by a daily process of osmosis, I was absorbing the basics and the subtleties of food, wine, and the art of tasting.

Watching Mother cook and Dad make wine, I was also absorbing a set of values that would later become the chrysalis of my own philosophy of making fine wine: Use only the best natural ingredients. Don't tamper with nature. Stay away from chemicals, additives, and anything that weakens or

masks the natural flavors. In cooking and in wine making, there are always gimmicks and shortcuts; for true artists, though, purity and simplicity are always the cardinal virtues.

From watching Mother in the kitchen, I also learned something deeper. Cooking to her was hard work, sure, but it was also a joy, a way of expressing the pride she took in her work and the love she had for her family. Her food brought the family together, first in the kitchen and then around the table. As I got older, I came to understand that for Mother, cooking was not work, it was a joy. It was a way for her to bathe us in the warmth of her spirit. Now just imagine if you could distill Mother's values, virtues, love, and generosity into a single bottle—that was exactly the wine I dreamed of making!

Growing up so steeped in the Italian way of life and wine, I didn't fully realize that many American families at that time looked askance at wine. In some quarters, the word wine usually signified cheap wine, and it was almost synonymous with winos and derelicts. Sure, some Americans enjoyed Champagne on holidays and birthdays, and in big cities some people would order French or Italian wines when they went out for dinner, but few young people had any exposure to wine or any appreciation of its origins and noble tradition. When this really hit me was when I got to Stanford. What a shock I had. We'd go out on what we called beer busts—drinking parties—and what did people bring? They'd bring beer, scotch, bourbon—no wine. And I'd say that over 30 percent of the people, maybe even 40 percent, would get absolutely plastered—and wind up with terrible headaches. I'd say to myself, "My god, I thought

Stanford was civilized! These people don't even know how to drink!" Really, I was dumbfounded. They'd get drunk, have headaches the next morning, and still go out and do crazy things like that almost every weekend. Wine was just as fun and so much healthier!

At Sunny St. Helena, I set out in earnest to master the art of tasting. And right away I noticed something funny. In the mornings at the winery, I would often do what my mother had done for me as a child: put a little wine in my morning coffee. But the mixture always seemed weak to me and I found myself putting in more and more of our Sunny St. Helena wine, as I tried to match the taste of what I had at home. Curious about this, I began tasting the wines we were making in the winery against the wines my father made at home, completely naturally. The difference was stark: our Sunny St. Helena wines just didn't have the same body and natural substance as the wines we made at home. Something vital had been stripped out. Because we were making bulk wines in such large quantities, we filtered it and added sulfur to help prevent spoilage. This was common practice; indeed, European wine makers have used sulfur dioxide for centuries to inhibit the growth of bacteria and molds. But while we gained in the cleanliness of our wines, we lost important elements of character and vitality. So right away I learned that wine making was often a tradeoff and a delicate balance; the finer the wine you wanted to make, the more delicate the balance.

At Sunny St. Helena I began a ritual that has been my standard operating procedure ever since: I'd ask myself, "OK, who makes the best wines?" Then I'd go buy those wines

and taste them carefully in order to discern how they were made and how they compared to our own wines. I'd buy wines from Beaulieu, Inglenook, Beringer Brothers, Larkmead, Wente—I tasted all the best. I didn't get any special budget for this from Jack Riorda—he was too old-fashioned for that—but I just felt that if I was going to learn to make good wines, I had to taste good wines and learn, right in my own mouth, what went into them. As the French would say, I had to "develop my nose" and "educate my palate." But no matter what fancy words you use, I knew that you don't learn the art of tasting from books; you learn it from drinking quality wines. Equally important, you learn it from tasting different foods along with fine wines to see how the flavors marry and harmonize. So in the evening I'd always come home with a new wine to try at dinner. Marge would often taste with me at dinner, though she never drank much at that time, and then I'd take the rest out to my lab in the tank house for a more thorough evaluation and analysis.

The results were often very surprising. I'd buy wines that had the best of reputations, then I'd taste the wines and find they were awful. I'd say, "Now wait a minute: this is for the birds! We're making better wines than that!" In this I learned a lesson that

137

would serve me well later on: always taste the wine, not the label! My regular tastings also led to important changes in our wine-making procedures. For instance, in some of the highly reputed wines I was tasting, and in some of our wines, I often picked up off flavors. One common cause I ferreted out: oxidation. After we ferment and the wine is moved to the storage tanks, if not topped constantly, the wine would become oxidized and show off flavors. The wine loses its vitality. To prevent that, I started insisting that our tanks be regularly "topped up" with more wine to keep the tanks full and keep out excess oxygen. This prevented oxidation—and helped us produce healthy, clean, lively, properly balanced wines.

When I moved over to Krug, I expanded my system of regular tastings. First of all, I invited in people outside our little wine-making circle. I wanted everyone working for us to better understand wine and what we were trying to accomplish. I also expanded the range of wines we were tasting. We no longer tasted just the best wines from California; we branched out and began tasting wines from Bordeaux and Burgundy. I would sit down with Peter; our cellar master, Joe Maganini; our assistant wine maker, Bill Bonetti; Frank Gould, editor of our newsletter *Bottles and Bins*; and some other people involved in wine making, and we would taste those wines and compare them to our own. André Tchelistcheff would also join us. This helped clarify what we needed to do to advance the quality of our wines. It also helped us size up the competition. This I did constantly, and still do today.

The more tastings I did, the more I came to understand the importance of climate and proper soil content and drainage. I found that the cooler the climate, the more flavor and character you get in the grapes; this is true with almost every fruit. So I came up with an axiom to guide us: The cooler the climate—but still warm enough to bring the grapes to full maturity—the finer the grapes. And the finer the grapes, the finer the wine. In our tastings, we studied how we could best match different grape varietals to the different microclimates and soil types on our properties and those of the Napa Valley growers who supplied us.

As useful as these regular tastings were at Krug, they took my education only so far. So in 1962, [...] I went to Europe and visited the great wineries of France, Italy, and Germany. During that seminal experience, I tasted wines I'd never find in the United States, and I saw firsthand the European way of making fine wines and aging them in oak barrels. I became fascinated by the art of the barrel, and I learned the different qualities that barrels can impart to wine.

I also came to see the role of the wine maker in a much fuller light. Up to then, my focus in wine making had been predominantly on the science side, worrying first and foremost about how to avoid or suppress the negative, such as mold, bacteria, off characters, spoilage, and the like. The approach of the very top European wine maker in many ways was just the opposite: He was trying to find ways to accentuate the positive. He was probing deep into the qualities of his soil and his *terroir*, and then asking himself, "What can I do to bring these innate qualities forth so that they can fully express themselves through the medium of wine?" The approach was [. . .]: "How do I bring forth the intrinsic goodness and flavors of a given meat, fish, or vegetable? What can I do to make those natural flavors burst forth with grace and harmony and create a symphony in the mouth?" Passion, character, individuality, temperament, and attention to detail—great painters and actors embrace these traits, make them part of their own artistic palette and creations. So do great chefs. And, as I came to understand in Europe, so do great wine makers.

So when I set out to make world-class wines at the Robert Mondavi Winery, I had no intention of trying to copy or imitate the great wines of France, Italy, Germany, Spain, or Portugal. No, I felt strongly that our California wines should have their own style and character; they should reflect our climate, our soil, our grapes, and—yes—our own unique American character and spirit. Our wines would be different from the Europeans', but I hoped that in terms of quality everyone would agree they belonged in the company of the great wines of the world.

With this lofty goal in mind, our tastings in Oakville became more serious and sophisticated. Our tasting room became a blend of science and art. On the one hand,

we would have before us a microanalysis of the chemical properties of a given wine in the making. We knew, for instance, that a certain sugar-acid ratio often yielded the flavor we desired. And we'd check our microanalysis: Was this wine within that norm? Then we'd taste—and check our own sensory findings against the scientific findings. This made for very thorough and detailed taste analyses—and passionate discussions! During harvest and crushing, our winemaking team would be tasting constantly, every day, to monitor the progress of our grapes and wines in the making. Later in our cycle, I'd sit down with Michael and later Tim for a crucial step: a progress tasting.

How do these tastings work? We would gather around the table in our makeshift tasting room, with spit buckets at our side. Let's say, for instance, that we were tasting Cabernet Sauvignon wines. Before us on the table might be fifteen or twenty bottles of fine Cabernets, some from California, others from Bordeaux and farther afield. We would definitely include samples of our own best finished Cabernets from earlier years to use as guides and reference points in our search for ever-higher quality. Next to these finished wines, we'd have several samples of our own Cabernets going into production, each carefully labeled and with its own microanalysis. These might include one barrel sample from To Kalon made from older vines. A second sample might also be from To Kalon, but made from grapes from younger vines. Another sample might be of a Cabernet made from grapes we bought from one of our growers in a different part of the valley.

139

How do we proceed? Each taster has his or her own idiosyncrasies, but as a general rule we'd take a given sample and pour it into a clean wineglass, stopping at just under half full. In tasting a wine, what we learn comes to us via our senses: the sight, smell, taste, touch, and temperature of the wine. I always begin with sight and examine the way the wine looks in the glass. I look for clarity: Is there any sign of cloudiness, impurity, or residue? I look at hue: Is there any browning or off coloring that would indicate problems in the wine making? Then depth of color: Does a given sample from To Kalon, say, have that deep ruby-red quality I like to see in our Cabernets? What is the depth of the color? If I tip the wine up to the rim of the glass, what does the color tell me? Does it show richness, or is the wine too thin? And when I twirl the wine in the glass, with a rhythmic roll of the wrist, what can I see in the color of the wine that coats the side of the glass? The eye brings us clear indications of a wine's body, texture, strength, and longevity. Part of wine tasting is subjective, of course, but this visual intake does give an experienced taster vital and objective information about the quality of the wine.

Now the nose. Some of the finest tasters do not even have to put wine in their mouth; their noses are so sensitive and discerning that they actually "taste" the wine in depth. In fact, we all smell tastes more than we realize. The mouth is very good at picking up the basics—sweet, sour, salt, and bitter—but the wider range of tastes that emerge from a Cabernet, for instance, are registered by sensing nerves located in the upper nasal cavity and even higher in the head and deeper in the brain. Some tasters make a distinction between a wine's aroma and its bouquet. Aroma pertains to odors coming from the grapes; bouquet refers to odors coming from winemaking practices, such as fermentation, processing, aging, and even bottling and corking. Either way, with nose deep in a glass, a discerning wine maker can determine grape quality, levels of grape maturation, sugar and acid levels, styles of crushing and fermentation, fermentation time, and temperatures—and these are just for starters. With the nose, the taster can also discern flaws such as over-oaking, poor storage or corking, the improper use of sulfites, and the presence of mold or bacteria in the vats or barrels.

Finally, the mouth. Serious tasters don't drink the wine; many don't even take a single swallow. Instead, the taster draws some into the mouth and holds it there for analysis. The warmth of the mouth helps vaporize the wine, exploding its flavors around the palate and up into the nasal cavity. Holding the wine in the mouth, the taster then gently sucks in air between the lips. This, too, helps the flavors blossom forth in the mouth, enabling the taster to better decipher the wine's component flavors and nuances.

How do we communicate to each other the many characteristics we discern in the tasting process? Ah, here's a rub: Wine Speak. As many of you know, wine has inspired a vocabulary all its own. The words vary from country to country, winery to winery, and taster to taster. Some Wine Speak expressions, of course, are pretentious and easy to parody and belittle. But such communication is vital; how else can I convey to my wine makers what I like in any given wine? So we taste the same wines, talk about them, and search for words we both understand to describe the same tastes and sensations. Here, too, though, there is a problem: taste is such an individual matter. What is salty or bitter, for instance, to some people is not to others. So what to do? Work closely with your fellow tasters, understand their palate, talk extensively, and have the patience of Job.

I also like to get opinions from people outside our winemaking staff; their tastes often keep us from veering too far away from our consumers. I also feel it is imperative for my staff outside of the wine cellar, especially in sales and wine making, to taste and understand exactly what I like in wines. This education is vital to our wines and our business. I want everyone at the winery to become learned true believers, imbued with the same passion and commitment I feel.

No matter how serious our tastings were in the early years of the Robert Mondavi Winery, sometimes we succeeded with a given wine and sometimes we did not. But each year we were drawn deeper and deeper into the complexities of making fine wines. And this was always true: Nothing ever turned out to be as simple as it first appeared. For instance, when I visited the great châteaux in France in 1962, I noticed that the top-quality wineries, those producing Premier Cru, or what we call First Growth wines, were using brand-new barrels almost exclusively. And I detected no off-character flavors in their wines. In the wineries producing Second, Third, Fourth, or Fifth Growth wines, though, they were using older barrels, with

many years of use behind them, and in most cases I could detect off characters and other signs that the oak was spent. So I became convinced that using new barrels would produce better wines. In fact, I decided we should use only brand-new oak barrels. A good operating principle, seemingly. When we began working with French oak back home, however, I found the advantages of using new oak varied according to the length of time you aged in the barrel. If you have a good year, with good fruit and low yields, you can use 100 percent new barrels and be fine. But if you have a lesser year, then the oak taste becomes too predominant in the wine. So you always need to find the right balance. Sometimes older barrels that have been properly cleaned can be used to advantage. I did not learn this in one year, or two years, or even several years; I've spent most of my life trying to master the variables and subtleties of tasting and making fine wine. And I'm still learning!

One of a wine maker's most valued companions is patience. It took the Europeans many generations to develop great wines; I knew we weren't going to do it overnight. The beauty of it, though, was that we usually learned more from our gaffes and off years than we did from our successes. Take 1967, for example. This was our second year in operation and it was a killer. It rained constantly. Right through harvest. We were picking grapes in the worst mud you ever saw; it was so bad we had to get big boards, two-by-twelves, for our tractors to roll on so they wouldn't sink. Then, in some of our vineyards, we found a strange sight. Many of the grape bunches had skins that were

141

withered and discolored. The culprit: mold. *Botrytis cinerea.*

To an uneducated eye, botrytis looks like a rot, which would have meant that our entire crop was ruined. Botrytis, though, is what we call noble mold. Instead of ruining the flavor of the grape, it draws off a portion of the water inside, leaving behind high concentrations of sugar and other elements that give the grape its flavor. If you taste a grape affected by botrytis, it doesn't taste bad; it tastes wonderfully sweet. In fact, this is the mold that gives Sauternes its fabled velvety texture and nectarlike sweetness. Still, botrytis can be difficult to manage in wine making. And its appearance can be disconcerting. In fact, we were afraid the inspectors from the federal Bureau of Alcohol, Tobacco, and Firearms, who regularly came by to check our operations, might raise questions about that ugly-looking mold. So we harvested and transported the grapes in the evening to escape inspection. Then we took those grapes, botrytis and all, and made wine from them. No one, though, was very confident about the outcome, especially me!

How did we come out? With the rain and the mold, the harvest of 1967 had all the makings of a disaster. Indeed, the quantity of wine we produced that year was very disappointing. Along the way, though, we were able to learn firsthand about noble mold and we learned how to exploit its natural virtues. As a result, while our overall quantity was poor, the quality of some of our wines turned out to be absolutely outstanding. God bless that rotten botrytis; it brought forth one of the best chenin blancs we had ever tasted or produced, an irony almost as sweet as the wine itself.

A SENSE OF HERITAGE

Francis Ford Coppola

My adventure with the Napa Valley began in the early '70s. We were coming back from making *The Rain People*, and my young assistant George Lucas, who was from Modesto, suggested we drive back through northern California, through the Napa Valley. I had always heard of the area, because my grandfather made wine from Napa Valley grapes, and I pictured this as a little Italian community in the middle of the fields of grapes.

A few years later, after our family had moved to San Francisco, my wife and I thought it might be nice to have a little house and maybe an acre or two of grapes so that we could make wine in the Italian-American tradition. We came and looked for cottages and the realtor told us they were going to auction off the Niebaum estate, part of the great Inglenook. He said, "It isn't for you, but it would be fun to see it." At the end of the road was this stunning Victorian mansion on this enormous wine estate. It was like that George Stevens film, *A Place in the Sun*, with rich people sitting around a pool and a Mercedes out front. To anyone not raised with these things it was unbelievable. This was what everyone considered the queen of the Napa Valley, perhaps *the* great American château. We ended up being able to buy it, but it was a far cry from that little cottage we thought we wanted.

I have had the pleasure of meeting Francis Ford Coppola on many occasions, from his hot tub in Napa to his charity wine dinners in New York City. Like many of you, some of the most important movies of my lifetime have been produced and directed by him, such as Apocalypse Now *and* The Godfather. *But his other passion is wine. One of the dozen or so wineries I first visited in the early seventies was Inglenook, which Francis purchased in 1975. He turned it back into its once magnificent self, and is now called Niebaum-Coppola Estate.*

As I began to learn about the heritage of the estate, I realized that we had—by accident—come into possession of something extraordinary. It was like a family who inherits a racehorse and realizes it would be absurd not to race such a thoroughbred. We quickly realized that it was crazy not to make wine from this legendary property.

We had the privilege of tasting some very old Inglenook wines and could taste the greatness of the estate. Buying the rest of the property in 1995 and restoring the estate to its historic dimension is truly a dream come true. I didn't care that the Inglenook name didn't come with the purchase. It had been irreparably damaged anyway. What I wanted most was the heritage that makes the property unique— Gustave Niebaum's legacy, which was the creation of a world-class wine estate—the vineyards, of course, that grand château, the collection of old Inglenook wines, and all the other medals, awards, and memorabilia that are now in our museum. Heritage is everything. If you have the heritage and

respect it, it is an endless source of inspiration.

In America, very few things that are split apart are ever put together again. There seems to be no incentive to respect heritage and tradition. My family and I have vowed that this place will never be split up or sold again. In *A Sense of Place: An Intimate Portrait of the Niebaum-Coppola Winery and the Napa Valley*, Steven Kolpan tells the stories behind this estate's founding, ascent to greatness, eventual dissolution, and final reunification with great care, insight, and passion for this irreplaceable heritage.

When you have the land, you have the grapes, and when you have the grapes, you have the wine. This land has produced world-class wines for over 100 years, so if we can continue to do that under our stewardship, it would be a tremendous achievement. I've lived here for 25 years, surrounded by my family and beautiful nature. There are mushrooms on the mountains, vegetables in the garden, and fruit on the trees within arm's reach. This place is truly heaven on earth.

EXCERPT FROM *A SENSE OF PLACE*

Steven Kolpan

"I would question if money alone could buy this place. I came into possession of this place by accident. A place like this is not about having money. You have to be lucky, and you have to have a bit of vision. Traditionally, people who owned a place like this wouldn't want to sell it at any price.

"But in 1975, when we bought the original property and house, it loomed as a bit of a white elephant. Everyone in those days were afraid of maintenance and upkeep, and today, of course, this property has become extremely valuable. Always the phrase back then was 'white elephant,' but I don't think it was a daring financial transaction even in those days.

"The reason we got both properties was not our money, but our passion. We've been approached several times, especially recently, with the idea of selling a piece of the estate or all of it. And it would be a lot of money, but what would we do with it? If we had a lot of money I don't know what we would do with it, beyond wanting to live here. I mean, you could be Bill Gates and you couldn't buy this place. I have no motivation to sell it."

But how is it that the Coppola family was able to buy the most historically significant vineyards in the Napa Valley, not once, but twice? Why, in 1995, twenty years after the Coppolas bought the original piece, and the California wine industry was beginning to shine, why were they able to buy the front property and the Inglenook château? Surely the family and corporate vignerons of the Napa Valley wanted to own a piece of valley history. This is a question that engages Francis Ford Coppola's personal world view.

"I am a very big believer that there are things in the makeup of the universe that we don't understand, and so it builds a lot of room for such phenomena as fate and

Of all of the authors in this collection, I have known Steven Kolpan the longest. We both started our wine careers at the Depuy Canal House in High Falls, New York (a four-star New York Times–*rated restaurant). He also lives the closest to me in Woodstock, New York. He has been a good friend and advisor, and we have shared many great wines and meals together. Steven is professor and chair of wine studies at the Culinary Institute of America (CIA) in Hyde Park, New York, and the coauthor of* Exploring Wine *and* WineWise, *which won the 2009 James Beard Foundation award for best book.*

intuition and things that are hard to explain. But beyond that, a property like this would only become available to so-called 'rich people,' and I've noticed that rich people have a very ironic habit of trying to figure out how to prevent their last dollar from getting away, rather than focusing on the hundreds of millions of dollars that they make. By nature, they're cautious, stingy people, and I think that's why rich people lost the opportunity to buy and own this property.

"There were a number of wealthy people, some of them very well known, who considered buying this property, but they lowballed it. They just couldn't stand the idea of just coming out and buying it no matter what the price was.

"So, all the wealthy and wine-interest people made lowball offers. We made a bid and lost it, and were able to buy it on the rebound. So, when we bought it, it wasn't a matter of price; we just wanted to buy it. It wasn't in my mind to negotiate; it was just to get it."

If this sounds like the voice of someone who is not a good businessperson, someone who believes that with enough money you can buy anything, even if it doesn't make sense on the balance sheet, you may not be really listening. Coppola is passionate about this land, and as far as the bottom line, he is far smarter than someone who is just throwing movie money around because he wants what he wants.

Confirmation of Francis Coppola's view comes from Dennis Fife, owner of Fife Vineyards in Napa and Konrad Winery in Mendocino. He had worked in Heublein's fine wine division starting in 1974, and was the president of Inglenook from 1984 to 1989. Heublein owned the 100 acres of Inglenook vineyard fronting Highway 29 and the Niebaum-built château, as well as the Inglenook brand name. They also owned (and still own) the Napa Valley's other historic jewel, Beaulieu Vineyards.

According to Fife, "Coppola got the first piece, the Niebaum/Daniel estate, in 1975, because Heublein thought they were going to get a good deal, and we offered a ridiculously low bid. It was particularly stupid because that piece of property was very important to them; they could own all of Inglenook. *And it was a matter of somewhere between ten and fifty thousand dollars on a multimillion dollar piece of land that made them lose it.* Really stupid."

Francis and Eleanor Coppola bought that property, about 1,500 acres, including 110 acres of Inglenook vineyards, for approximately $2.2 million. In 1995, they bought the rest of Inglenook—including 110 acres of vineyards and the stone château—from Heublein for about $11 million. Although the Coppolas knew that they were destined to buy the property from Heublein, negotiations were rocky,

"The sellers knew we were willing to pay their price, so they tried to take advantage of us. They kept coming back to the deal, trying to build in things, like 'We won't sell you the vineyards, just the château'! It was outrageous.

"This is still an issue in my mind, because I feel they were unfair with me as owners, and now I'm the owner, but part of the deal is I have to sell grapes to them until the year 2000, which I'm not happy about.

"The reaction by some people in the Valley when we started making wine seriously was that we were crazy, and when we began to restore the château, some people used to call this 'Francis' Folly.' Can you believe it?"

When things were tough at Niebaum-Coppola, after Francis took on more than $16 million in debt to Chase Manhattan Bank in 1980 to bail out *Apocalypse Now*, many of the cognoscenti of the Napa wine industry believed Francis might fail, and ironically he was allowed to pursue his dream of a Grand American Wine without interference and without community support.

"I think among some of the people who live in the Napa Valley, I'm still considered a Hollywood filmmaker and a celebrity, even though this has been our home since 1975, and our kids went to school with their kids. And because I paid a lot to reunite Inglenook, I'm considered a patsy by some people.

"I am startled to feel that our family would be treated with anything other than the same goodwill we were years ago. I think there were rumors that this place would become available, because I zigged when I should have zagged financially. But lately, we're getting a little more power with the media, who know that we have *the* place, and our reputation may be coming into conflict with their expectations.

"Now that we've emerged from a boutique winery to a real château estate in America, and these same people see that we have the most historically significant wine estate in America, and they see that we have this beautiful and popular public place, and we're a real company, I feel there's a bit of dirty pool with me by the regulators, the people in power. They're tougher on us than they are on themselves. It's like, 'Hey, he gets all the publicity.' And although some people, like Robert Mondavi, are as helpful and gracious and supportive as they ever were, right from the beginning, I guess other people are worried that the boob has become formidable."

Coppola's complaints seem to have some merit. He must go through a tremendous amount of permit-seeking and board approvals to restore the estate to what it was in the era of John Daniel. Napa County seems intent on protecting the alterations of the Heublein era, which include the hideous storage building that blocks the view of the majestic Inglenook château from Highway 29. Perhaps even more important, Coppola will have to jump through many hoops to bring the winemaking back to the château, because Heublein stopped producing wine altogether at Inglenook in the mid-1970s.

"The winemaking team is so passionate, and I want them to have a beautiful facility. I want drawings, and I want to know how much, and then we'll have to pay for it as a capital outlay. That will be the last frontier of the winery. It's good that we built the visitor's center first, because it shows a strong interest and demand, and so will benefit the winemaking team to get what they way."

Clearly, Francis has decided that he will have his winery, and he knows where that winery must be located, because the history and heritage of Inglenook dictate that the winery be sited in a specific place.

"We are building a winery, and it will be built at the Inglenook château. Rubicon is our wine that is all about this property, this

147

place. I insist that we make Rubicon in the historic Inglenook winemaking facilities, in the château, and I'm told that we don't have the right permits, and again I say, 'Guys, don't hold me by what Heublein did here. They didn't care about making wine here.'

"How can the county not let us make wine in the Inglenook winery? It feels like they have their hands around my throat, holding us to the state of affairs that existed when Heublein shut down the winery. Legally, we're helpless if they tell us that we can't make wine in that building.

"They're saying we're a new winery because we bought this from Heublein in 1995, and as far as the county is concerned there was nothing here before. They're even telling us that Heublein was doing certain things without the right permits, and now that becomes my problem.

"It's all politics in a way. The people have been discouraging us from restoring and improving the property since day one, and I still don't know why. They just say, 'Oh, it's the rules.' And we have to be cautious because we don't want to make application for something and be turned down."

Getting a permit to build a new winery in Napa County is a bureaucratic nightmare. Building a new winery that conducts public tours and tastings, sells wine-related merchandise, and serves food is a virtual legal impossibility. Francis Coppola argues that what he proposes is not a new winery at all, but a return to winemaking at Inglenook in the original building to fulfill the original promise of Captain Niebaum and John Daniel—to produce American's finest wines.

"Gustave Niebaum and John Daniel made wine here for almost one hundred years. Let's face it, the county stood by and watched as this place, Inglenook, was destroyed. Now they want to treat us as though we're nothing more than Heublein's replacement, and I'm saying, 'Hey, we're not Heublein, we're the original Inglenook.' I would hope that we'd be treated like Inglenook, not a post-'90s Heublein.

"We're good for the valley, we're good for heritage, we're good for conservation. Yet, I'm beginning to feel there's a sentiment that I'm not a celebrity boob after all, and that we are serious about the wine, and that we might disturb someone else's financial situation.

"I'm all for no-growth policy, but I think there should be more policy concerning heritage. Right now, there's a lot of financial incentive for breaking things up, selling off pieces, taking companies public. There's no incentive for people who want to keep the original heritage, preserve a family-owned business. Why isn't the county's position to encourage preservation? I would never ask for liberal growth laws, but I would like to see intelligent heritage laws. There should be incentives not to sell to investment bankers.

"What I would like the county to say is 'OK, Francis, you can be as Inglenook would have been had it not been divided.' Then we have to look at what Inglenook would have become. That division impacted it greatly. It's like a kid has a terrible auto accident when he's nine; for years he can't walk or talk. Then, a miracle operation comes along and he's thriving. So, I would like the opportunity to see this place blossom consistent with its heritage. I don't want to mall-ize it.

"There are far more wealthy people than me in the Valley. The fact is we're a 100 percent family-owned wine estate with very little debt, and for that to work, I've got to focus my attention here. A lot of other people have portfolios, investments, etc., but I'm just willing to risk it all here. And now that the château is finished, people really like it, and all of a sudden they realize here was a vision, and here is a vision for the future. So now, we have public support.

"I have to be patient. I have to be optimistic. I think that policy will become more enlightened over the next several years, and I think, I hope, that lawmakers will see that with the act of preservation of vineyards, our uniting of the Inglenook Estate, we should be allowed to have traditional rights of usage. I think our view will prevail."

Jumping back from the future to the present and the not-so-distant past, Francis Coppola is not quite so sanguine, and his tone is not so optimistic or hopeful. He wants answers to some important questions.

"Isn't this county, by doing things like protecting that storage building out front, trying to assure that we don't leave the Heublein era? Why? Heublein had carte blanche. Where was the county then?"

The creator of the three *Godfather* films paises, then delivers a piercing blow to those who do not appreciate his dreams, labors, goals, historical perspective, and overall vision for Niebaum-Coppola.

"It's like a little Mafia here, and that's annoying."

DOODAH! DOODAH!

Baron Philippe de Rothschild

I come down dah wid my hat caved in,
Doodah! doodah!
I go back home wid a pocket full of tin,
Oh! doodah day!
STEPHEN COLLINS FOSTER

I arrived on October 22, 1922, the first Rothschild to move into the Médoc, the new manager, the boss. It was the fair weather that always follows the harvest. There was a dying fire in the courtyard. One or two of the men were standing looking at it. The boy Roger was with them. "What's this?"

They stared at me, one of them raked over the ashes. I looked. Someone had been burning the books. I could see the remains of bills and accounts on blackened scraps of paper blowing all over the place.

"Who did this?"

The men said nothing for a long while.

One of the greatest wine personalities ever, Baron Philippe de Rothschild was able to resurrect Château Mouton Rothschild beginning at the age of twenty. His winemaking philosophy was to make only the highest quality wine, and created many innovations that are still followed by the other great châteaux in Bordeaux. Besides buying other Bordeaux châteaux such as Clerc Milon, he formed a partnership with another wine icon, Robert Mondavi, to create the Opus One Winery in Napa Valley. His Mouton Rothschild wine labels have been designed since 1946 by famous artists such as Salvador Dalí, Henry Moore, Marc Chagall, Pablo Picasso, and Andy Warhol. He also created one of the first and greatest wine museums in the world.

Finally Émile Gerbaud shook his head and looked toward the village.

"No names, no pack drill. Your man has gone anyway, vamoosed, vanished."

"It wasn't only the house he built for himself," said the boy Roger. "He bought land for a vineyard with your money, and used all your materials to work it, all your machines and tools, even the vines he planted were pinched."

The local police came. I said I wanted no prosecution. Let him go, forget it. We had been absentee landlords, no one had cared a damn about the place. He knew it and took advantage of our lack of interest. Well, from now on things would be different.

But first I had to win the confidence of the men who were left, they still looked at me suspiciously. At least he can't uproot the vines, I heard one of them say.

They knew I knew nothing. I'd have to watch my step. All the same, some decisions had to be made, without delay. The work team badly needed a boost; morale was very low. At some point I would have to be ruthless, and I've never been a ruthless person. All the same, the wastrels and idlers would have to go, but how was I to separate the wheat from the chaff? Over the years this small society had become a closed shop, and on top of that everybody seemed to be related to everyone else. I took the plunge, sacked people from every rank, and at once earned the respect of the rest. There was no resentment; a firm hand was welcome. I had not realized the importance of direction till then. These tough *vignerons* of Mouton had been making wine all their lives, and their fathers before them; they knew nothing beyond the little

world of Pauillac; even their work isolated them. Tending the vines, lost in that lonely landscape, they hardly seemed to speak, even to each other, but among them there was enough skill and know-how to raise the whole standard of wine growing—if I could get it out of them. I invited a representative from each section of the work to my office, or what passed for my office. They sat uneasily on the edge of their chairs, caps on knees. I told them that we should share our problems and find solutions together. Nobody said a word. Of course I didn't realize that they'd never spoken to a boss in their whole lives. I tried a few jokes. There was a long silence, then somebody gave a grunt of approval.

I called them together every week and, slowly but surely, the ice was cracked. Someone would make a tentative suggestion, and they'd be surprised when I tried it out. Soon I found a title for them: my Commission Technique. They approved of that and the name stuck. That original band stayed with me all their lives, and it would be impossible to estimate how much Mouton owes to them. The commission still functions and, wherever I am, I receive their weekly report.

My father's new manager never did materialize. In fact I may have told him not to bother, I can't remember, probably I did. The doddery old gentleman at Bordeaux, the Baron de Miollis, who had been looking after the business since Moses was in the fire brigade, was on his way out anyway. He should have been retired years before. That side of things didn't bother me. I would sell the wine myself; two or three days in Bordeaux would fix that. I let it be known that I wouldn't be introducing any newcomers. There were some cagey looks—all the same I felt I was making some progress with the Moutonards. I wanted to win them over, I needed their devotion, but sometimes when I came out with a bright idea, they would listen, gazing over my shoulder into the distance, and say nothing. Then as I wandered off I'd hear them exchanging dry comments in that private language of theirs. I was still a foreigner, but they sensed that we had something in common. You see, I'm a peasant myself, a peasant in a silk nightshirt if you like, but I don't puke at the smell of steaming dung, or blench at the sight of a newborn calf; I can live without perfumed baths, pocket handkerchiefs, and Bach on a harpsichord before breakfast. I like the smell of fresh woman, horseflesh, and garlic, and my dogs sleep on my bed. So now you know why I liked Mouton.

Merilda spoiled me, preparing my favorite dishes, heaped with truffles and frogs' legs, and petite Odette put the hot brick wrapped in flannel in my bed on cold nights. All the same it was lonely. I read Ovid by the light of a spirit lamp, awakened at four in the morning by the schemozzle in the yard, oxen being yoked, horses harnessed. I began to savor the wine, to distinguish between the ordinary and the good; the exquisite was yet to come. I brooded over the state of the place. A lot of changes would have to be made, but it would take time and good planning: anything drastic would be disastrous in that eighteenth-century world where people went to bed with candles at nine o'clock, and deep silence descended on us all. If anyone owned a clock, it was a family heirloom, and I doubt whether they had ever seen a calendar. As for me I had only just learned that it takes five

years for a vine root to blossom and give fruit. I decided to invest in a new racing car.

I stayed at Mouton long enough to be sure my team was pulling together. If I knew nothing about wine making, I'd had enough sense to winkle out the men who did and give them my confidence. At the same time I made it my business to study the methods of work, in field and shed, surveying the working areas, taking note of stumbling blocks, snags, time-wasting routines. I also bought myself a micro-scope and took a long look at the vine bugs.

Sometimes I'd listen to the old vign-erons, who knew that land like the backs of their hands—a job getting them to talk but once started there was no stopping them. It was generally the taciturn old blokes who had pearls to scatter, if you caught them in the right mood at the right time, walking home at the end of the morning's work, or sheltering from a heavy rainstorm. . . .

Quand les hirondelles volent très bas,
C'est signe qu'il va pleuvoir.

Ah! And he'd give a great spit.

Or, looking over at the horizon, squinting at the sky before making his pronouncement, so often wrong, but still repeated like an old refrain. . . .

Quand le ciel est rouge
Vent ou plouge.

He speaks with a twang no one has ever tried to set down on paper. Imagine it round and rolling like broad Devonshire in England, or a midwest burr if you know that one better. Occasionally he'll bend to pick up a handful of small pink and gray pebbles rounded by water, over a million years.

"You're standing on a great limb of land thrown up once, some while ago mind, by the fierce Atlantic Ocean. It's all stones, stones that give the soil its nature and hold the sun's warmth. Good for the grape, especially in this climate.

"You can't get good wine if the soil isn't right. The nature of the soil is the most important part of your wine growing, then comes good husbandry naturally, and the rest is heaven's work.

Il n'y a pas un samedi en France
Sans que le soleil fosse sa révérence.

"You want to know the seasons? Then start with St. Vincent in September.

Quand St. Vincent est beau,
Il y a plus de vin que d'eau.

"Then comes Toussaint, when the sun is almost gone. Toussaint, All Saints' or All-Hallows', call it what you will, it's known all over the world. We go to mass that day to pray for a good year and we're no sooner by our own fireside than winter is down on us. You reckon there's nothing to do in winter, the earth asleep, the vineyard all bare and empty? You're wrong. You're pruning for a start, forever pruning. And I'll tell you why—if you like old stories. For it was once upon a time, as the saying goes, that a certain donkey, a very intelligent beast, content with his lot grazing away up on a mountainside, strayed one day down to the lower slopes quite by chance. And there his blue eyes lighted on

the vines and the tender shoots which sprout from the branches. He tasted one and he liked it and he went on to the next and the next, munching away till the owner of the vineyard happened to see him, ran out and beat him and chased him away. But, when the harvest came round, the owner found that the vines the donkey had pruned for him yielded grapes much richer and juicier than the rest. From that time on, we pruned, and that's how the main secret of fine wine was discovered, by a donkey. Donkeys wouldn't do that nowadays, mind you. Pruning has become an art. You have to know which shoot to cut and which to leave and you have to be right every time.

"Look at the vine in winter, all you see is two withered branches, two stretched-out arms. You can't believe that come July you'll be waist high in green leaves.

"Summer's a fine bustling time, but it's ordinary when you contrast it with the vine in winter, bare and elegant as she is.

Noël au balcon
Pâques aux Tisons.

"December's for muck spreading and in January the women are out gathering the bits fallen from the pruning, brown twigs now, fit for nothing but burning, though they make a sweet-scented fire. You never tasted anything so good as meat grilled on vine wood.

"February is men's work again and it's heavy. You don't need all your wrappings against the cold. The work will warm you. All those rows of stakes you see have to be repaired or renewed. They're there to support the lengths of wire, where the vines trail.

"March? Wrenching up the dead leaves. Vines last many a year, if they get the attention they should, up to a hundred sometimes, but like us they don't give much fruit in their old age. When they do, it's good still. They're at their prime when they're about twenty-five or thirty. And April?

Quand il tonne en avril
Foncez cuves et barils.

"Those vines beyond the Carruades have only just been planted, it'll be five or even seven years before they give us wine. You'll have to learn patience now you've come to Mouton.

"In April or thereabouts the vines begin to bud. It's a pretty sight, reminds you of nothing so much as a small bird alighted on a bough. That's when we have to watch out and do our best to protect them from the pests the Lord sends to try us. Oh yes, we've got a few treatments, but against naughty worms we can't do much.

"May's the time for following the plow, turning over the soil between the vine rows. Five or six plowings in the year there are. Used to be at the pace of oxen or sturdy horses, but in the last twenty years, tractors—faster and far more efficient, they say.

"June, and the women are back, tying up. July we're looking for grapes among green foliage, and August sees us cleaning the paths and ditches preparing for a good harvest. The grapes are turning red and we're weeding. Now come the critical days. Frost may kill everything. Sun and rain won't harm us, but with frost the grape can die on the branch.

"Autumn is here. It's October and every owner is wary, watching his neighbors. 'Well, she's just about ready. When do we start?'

"Decision time and everything depends on that decision. A day late and rain and frost may spoil the grapes, a day too soon and the fruit may not be ripe.

"They start calling round to see each other. 'Lafite has already started, when is Mouton going to begin?' 'Pedesclaux starts tomorrow.' 'Pantet Canet hasn't made up its mind.' And all the while the boss goes round sampling the grapes.

"It's a great time and a lively time, when you've been working on your own all year. The people come from far and near to gather grapes. The girls wear their kiss-me-nots, sun bonnets they wore when the British soldiers were here so their young faces wouldn't be seen."

I asked him which war that was in.

"Oh, the Hundred Years' War," he told me.

"When the harvest is done," he went on, "we go to the Big House with a handsome bouquet of flowers for the owner's wife. The Gerbaude of the harvest we call it. Mind you there's been no owner at Mouton for many a long year, let alone a wife."

Well, I knew a little more about the seasons after all that, but the ways he had learned were not eternal. The oxen with which he plowed, the beautiful shire horses you saw everywhere and the kiss-me-nots have disappeared long since. Now tractors plow and helicopters spray and soon the harvest will be brought in by machine. Nevertheless, Mouton will always be Mouton.

HARVEST AND WINEMAKING

Joy Sterling

According to ancient lore, grapes ripen with the waxing of the moon, which would put harvest at mid-month. The weather is cooperating. It seems as if we are going to luck out, and the dire predictions were unwarranted. This close to maturity, the Pinot Noir clusters, usually the first to be harvested, have turned completely, from green to purple. The Sauvignon Blanc is softening and becoming translucent. Cabernet and Chardonnay are still a ways off, but the flavors of all the varieties are developing day by day.

September 14. First day of harvest. It is a winemaking decision where and when to pick. This is the time that, when you taste the juice from a berry, you can in fact taste the wine. You can taste the intensity and the length. You taste the grapes, not only for sweetness, but for their balance and the lingering flavor. If you can actually taste the flavor of the grape for four, five, ten seconds after you put it into your mouth, the wine made from those grapes is going to have the same degree of intensity. The essence of harvest is to pick the grapes when they have reached the optimum of flavor maturity, not necessarily chemical maturity as it would be defined by Brix, acid, or pH measurements. You have to understand what the flavor character is for each section of the vineyard that you farm. You actually develop a track record and a palate memory, so that when you wander through a vineyard and taste the

berries, you compare them much as you do individual vintages of wine. What to pick and where is up to Forrest, and he tells Manuel. Manuel's talent is how to coordinate crews so they cover the whole vineyard without overlapping or neglecting any rows; and, also because of the terrain, you want to deploy the crews so they have lighter loads on the way up the hills.

"The idea," says Forrest, "is to achieve a wine that tastes like what I taste in the vineyard when the grapes are at their height of maturity. Once we get the fruit into the winery the idea is to just not screw it up."

At 6:30 a.m., Forrest went up to the equipment yard where the pickers had congregated. Manuel was taking the roll, writing down Social Security numbers, and assigning picking crews. There were some new faces, but most of the guys come back year after year.

156

We pick up between twelve and sixteen additional workers for harvest. Migrant workers start coming up to the winery looking for work in late August, just as the local apple harvest is waning. Having our harvest so late this year has kept many of them out of work for almost a month. Fortunately, it looks like they will be rewarded with a good crop in '91—easy to pick and bountiful. Pickers are paid by the bin. They were very badly hurt in short years like '88 and '90, but this harvest a fast worker could easily make $14 an hour.

Once the full crew is assembled, Forrest speaks to the men in Spanish. He explains the work rules, safety rules, and our bonus system for quality. He holds up two bunches of grapes. "This is mature fruit," he says, "and this is not. This is bonus fruit and this is not." Each picker comes equipped with his own knife. If he doesn't, we'll supply him one at cost. A picking knife is about six inches long and it has a curved, serrated, stainless-steel blade. Each picker has a particular way he likes his knife—either with a string attached to the handle so it dangles on his wrist between cuts, or tape around the handle to make it more comfortable. It needs to be very sharp to cut through the stems. The best picker will harvest fifty lugs a day. Each lug holds thirty-five pounds. About 7,000 clusters.

It is exciting when the first grapes are brought to the winery. Everybody wants to have a look and taste. It takes about two hours for a full press load to be assembled. We all just stand around—not quite sure whether we should go back to our offices or wait for the next ceremony.

Every winery has some sort of ceremony commemorating the beginning of harvest. Robert Mondavi invites the bishop to come and bless the grapes. We usually toast with sparkling wine, but this year we brought in Sauvignon Blanc before Pinot Noir for sparkling, so we had to quickly change our toasting wine and glassware. Obviously, you can't fall into any routines with farming. We sort of muddled through a modified version of pouring our 1990 Fumé Blanc over the first press load with our nondenominational blessing: "Here's to a great harvest, cheers!"

From here on out, the winery crew really shines. There's so much to do and the pace is fast. There's a certain misconception among city dwellers that country living is nice and easy. That's actually rather true during much of the year, but not during harvest. We don't walk about our business, we run. The men picking in the field get paid by the box. They get into a rhythm that sends them flying down the rows. You can see the tops of the vines shaking while the men are hacking off the clusters. Then they run to load the bins onto the back of the tractor. The bins get tied down with bicycle straps. It's not easy getting up and down our hills, and the bins tip over easily. The first day we brought in twenty tons.

Once harvest is in full swing, we fall into a routine of waking up early, checking the sky, checking the barometer, and checking the weather channel. Forrest goes up to the winery for a quick look at 7:00 a.m. It is just beginning to have that wonderful smell of fermenting wine—sweet fruit with a tinge of carbon dioxide that pricks your nose. Because it is cool and the doors have been shut, the smells accumulate in the winery overnight. The floors are damp from being hosed down. And it is quiet. The men are in the fields. Forrest ducks into the lab, where two interns, usually U.C. Davis students, are measuring the temperature, sugar, pH, and acidity of the juice in all of the tanks. Then they rack the juice that was pressed just the day before and allowed to settle overnight in a chilled tank. The clear juice gets pulled off and is pumped to a clean tank. The lees or solids—the pips and the dirt that sifted to the bottom of the tank—are filtered and recombined with the juice. The leftover cake of heavy sediment is composted and put back into the vineyard. We add yeast to the tank to induce fermentation.

Each wine requires a specialized strain of yeast. For sparkling wine, we use a bayanus strain, which we get from Champagne. The selection of yeast is purely subjective. There is a perpetual debate about the ideal yeast for each wine. The result is that, with modern freeze-dry technology, we are able to experiment with specialized yeast strains isolated from all the great wine-producing regions of the world. For sparkling wine, you want the first fermentation to be very clean, not overly agitated, and to start up within two days. It should take off slowly at about 20 degrees Brix sugar, and accelerate as the yeast cells multiply. It should then slow down again as the sugar decreases and the alcohol increases—a bell-shaped curve that lasts about ten days to two weeks. For our Cabernets, we want a very vigorous fermentation that can keep going at a higher alcohol level and that tends to extract more color and flavor from the skins. By about 8:00 a.m., Forrest heads out into the vineyards with Manuel to check how harvest is going, if everyone in the crew has shown up, and to say good morning to the harvesters and tractor drivers. He walks down the rows, tasting the grapes, mentally comparing this harvest to years past for flavor and yield. If he feels too much mature fruit is being left on the vine, or fruit is being dropped on the ground, or if the workers are gathering too many leaves, Forrest will advise the tractor drivers and reinforce their responsibility to oversee the picking crews. The drivers get paid by the hour, plus a bonus according to the picking quality of their respective crews.

157

September 25. The first grapes of the day come into the winery between 8:00 and 9:00 a.m. The harvest boxes are stacked on a pallet in the field and brought in by tractor no more than an hour after the grapes have been picked. The pallets get weighed on a portable electronic scale. Shirley is in charge. She sets up a card table, a chair with a cushion on it, her record books, and a calculator. Forrest, Raphael, John, and my father look over her shoulder throughout the day, trying to calculate a load for the press, figuring the yield per acre, and how much wine we will make. The press holds 4.5 metric tons of grapes and we want to keep each block of the vineyard separate. Coordinating the harvesting with the maturity of the fruit, running the presses at capacity, having the tanks available to keep the juice separate, and setting a pace so the picked grapes do not sit out in the sun, is like playing with a Rubik's Cube.

The yields per acre vary from vintage to vintage. Every day as the grapes come in we rewrite our sale projections. We have to keep an open mind. How the harvest goes in terms of quality and quantity determines how much Chardonnay and Pinot Noir we will make versus sparkling. Most of the vineyard is fairly clearly delineated as to which grapes are best for still or sparkling wine. As the new vineyards come into production, the balance is changing in favor of sparkling wine. But Forrest might still look at a particular block—say in a dry year, if the vines are stressed or stalled at 20 degree Brix sugar, which would be perfect for sparkling, but nowhere near maturity for Chardonnay. Conversely, there may be a block traditionally picked for sparkling which by some quirk begs to be left on the vine for a few more weeks for still wine.

Forrest makes a gut decision on what will make the best wine. Business considerations also come into play. We have invested in barrels and equipment and a staff for a projected amount of wine. And we like to keep a certain market position by maintaining a degree of continuity—as much as we can, since we are an estate-bottled winery. From the very beginning, Forrest and my parents decided we would not buy grapes and even the painfully lean vintages have not changed our minds.

The grapes for sparkling are stacked in boxes on pallets in front of the winery, attracting thousands of bees. Everyone on the winemaking staff gets stung at least once a year. We all pick at the grapes as we walk back and forth. The concentration of flavors and the texture of the skins give us an inkling of what the wine will taste like.

The pallets are forklifted through the front doors of the winery and down the main aisle that is lined with steel tanks on either side to a conveyor belt. A bucket brigade of all the winery personnel loads the grapes onto the conveyor as gently as possible so they do not bruise or rupture. The first boxes are put on the concrete pad alongside the conveyor to catch any grapes that fall off the sides. And two people—Raphael and either Forrest or my father—sort through the grapes as they go into the press, discarding leaves and underripe fruit or any clusters with rot. This is where they can check each picker's work to determine who will receive bonuses for quality at the end of the day. After the first press load, Forrest can usually tell who is doing a good job and who is not and soon he will go back out into the vineyard to rein-spire the men.

It takes about thirty minutes to load the press—ten tons of whole grape clusters falling loosely into a stainless steel cylinder that is highly polished and designed by a French firm in Champagne to give the most delicate juice possible. Inside the press is a white, Teflon-coated membrane that looks like a boat canvas and is about an eighth of an inch thick. When it is inflated slightly, it gently pushes the grapes together and juice flows through slotted screens out of the bottom of the press.

The press cycle lasts from one and a half to two hours and yields 140 gallons per ton, which is then separated into two parts: free-run juice and press lots. The first ten gallons go into the press tank because the first gush of juice out of the press is murky. The last twenty-five gallons are the most extracted. The free run in between is the cleanest, most delicate, and most flavorful. It is the best grape juice you will ever taste, though you should not drink too much of it. One glass is like two bunches of grapes.

The Chardonnay for sparkling is almost green, not quite clear and slightly frothy as it gushes out of the press. It smells like green apples and spice and it tastes something like apples with citrus, both sweet and tart. The Pinot Noir comes out a pale salmon color. It smells like berries and cherries with a wonderful tang in the finish. It is difficult to taste many nuances at this point. You are looking for balance and a long finish. The intensity of the fruit you taste now should always be there throughout the whole wine-making process unless bad wine making strips it of flavor.

The juice is pumped into a refrigerated tank and left to settle. The pomace—spent skins and seeds—is dumped into the back of a flatbed truck. It is astonishing how much juice flows down the sides of the truck onto the gravel—probably thirty gallons a ton. This is useless to us, because if we pressed any harder we would extract too much harshness and bitterness from the skins. For sparkling wine, you are trying to get the juice from the heart of the grape between the skin and the seeds, and if you walk over to the truck and pick up a fistful of pomace, you will see that the action of the press is so gentle that the skins of any slightly hard, immature grapes are not even broken. Now the press is cleaned out and ready for another load. If the weather is cool and the picking is going well, we can do four press loads a day.

Raphael is at the press watching the juice flow out. "Are you happy?" "Yes," he says. "The juice looks good and smells good." Forrest is also pleased by how smoothly harvest is running. No glitches. I mention this to John and he crosses his fingers. "Let's just hope it stays this way." Shirley is ecstatic about the size of the crop. So far, we're up 20 percent. Laurence figures we should make about 7,000 cases of Chardonnay. That

159

would mean 22,000 cases of sparkling. Forrest and I agree that this ratio fits the image of the winery. Besides, the 1990 Chardonnay is going to be so successful. It will set up the 1991 nicely. Forrest takes me out in the vineyard. He wants the crews to stop for today. Block L is next, but he'd rather hold off until tomorrow morning so the grapes will be "right there." It takes two to two-and-a-half weeks to harvest all of the grapes for sparkling. It depends on how the individual blocks ripen. Some days you have to stop to wait for the fruit to mature. It is hard to say "We are not picking today." The crew is so wound up they do not want to quit.

During our years of wine making, just about every conceivable disaster has occurred including a tractor blowing up and power failures in the winery, which become critical if they last for more than a day because we lose all our refrigeration. We even survived having our state-of-the-art, very sensitive German wine press die on us with a full load of grapes one Sunday afternoon. We had to Rube Goldberg it back together ourselves.

September 30. The Sauvignon Blanc from Forrest's property [T-T] usually overlaps with the sparkling. We have a second press and sufficient tanks and barrels to handle it. We pull two tractors and two crews from Iron Horse and send them to T-T. The grapes get trucked back to the winery. Sauvignon Blanc is easy to harvest because of the way it hangs on the vine. It is very exposed. The pickers love it. They can fly right through it, but because it gets very warm at T-T, we only

want to pick from 7 to 10 in the morning, which limits the crews to only ten to twelve tons a day.

The first load usually arrives at the winery around lunchtime. Forrest is always especially proud to see the fruit arrive from his vineyard, and Victor, his foreman, knows exactly how Forrest wants it presented—perfectly mature fruit and no leaves, prompting *oohs* and *ahs* as we all look over the bins. The grapes are fat and round and usually a honeydew-melon green. Forrest hedges the vines to let more sunlight through to the grapes, which turns the skins a honey color when they are ripe. The natural grassy tendency of Sauvignon Blanc seems to be concentrated in the skins. The heart of the grape tastes like melons, figs, pineapple, papaya, and peach—very exotic, and if you suck on the skins of the grapes, it is like chewing on a blade of grass. The more golden-colored grapes tend to have less of that grassiness and a much more floral, perfumelike quality.

Forrest also keeps the crop small. Sauvignon Blanc is a very heavy producing variety. It can comfortably produce, on good soils, up to eight tons to the acre. The average yield throughout the North Coast is five to six tons to the acre, Forrest's vineyard averages about four. His theory is that if the vines are not working all that hard, they will set more flavor in the berries. Also, growing a smaller crop means there is little need for supplemental irrigation, even on the marginal soils at T-T. The added water would merely plump up the berries and take away from the intensity of flavor.

The crews load the Sauvignon Blanc in 1,000-pound gondolas, steel bins that stack easily on the back of a flatbed truck for the thirty-mile drive over country roads to Iron Horse. The most critical factor in hauling the grapes is not to macerate the fruit before it gets to the winery. If the fruit gets mashed, the juice will oxidize in the gondola and could set off a spontaneous fermentation. As soon as the grapes arrive at the winery, the bins are unloaded by forklift, weighed, and taken over to the stemmer-crusher—an ingenious machine that pulls the grapes off the stems. The forklift raises the bin twelve feet off the ground, empties it into a stainless-steel hopper with a six-inch auger at the bottom that moves the grapes into a cylinder with a slow-turning, slotted screen on the outside and paddles on the inside, which turn at very high revolutions. The paddles knock the grapes off the stems and push them through the slotted screen and into another hopper. The stems are about four to five inches long, too long to get through the slots. The centrifugal force of the paddles drives them out the end of the machine, where they pile up in a heap.

The crushed grapes are pumped through a rather clumsy-looking piston pump that chunks away as the juice is pumped into stainless-steel pipes that wrap around the upper inside wall of the winery and then out the back to the presses. Half go directly into the press and the other into overhead holding tanks positioned high above the presses, in contact with the skins and the seeds so that they pick up more flavor for six to eight hours. We come back to the winery at midnight. By then, the seeds and skins have settled to the bottom of the holding tank, and the juice has risen to the top, so we first can draw off the free-run juice relatively cleanly and then open a big valve gate at the bottom of the tank to let the pomace fall into the press.

When Forrest is playing ringmaster for all the action during harvest, he often does not get to stand at the press and be a wine maker. It is a special occasion when he and I go up to the winery together. We bring a thermos of coffee, a bottle of brandy, turn on the radio and with an intern and one of our permanent employees, Pony, press fifteen to sixteen tons of Sauvignon Blanc by the light of the moon. Pony usually gets night duty because he has a car that is reliable and he does not seem to mind getting up in the middle of the night.

Forrest hooks up a hose to a valve on the outside of the holding tanks, opens the valve, and the juice flows down into a stainless steel cart. I hold the hose. The juice that comes out is this fabulous green-gold color and it smells like freshly mown hay. It is wonderful to taste a glassful taken straight from the hose. It flows at a good rate for nearly half an hour, then it starts to peter out. When it stops, Forrest shuts off the valve and lowers the snout of the holding tanks directly into the press to release the remaining pomace. Despite the high-tech design, we end up wrapping plastic bags around it so the must—the lees—does not go flying. The bottom of the holding tanks have 18-inch gate valves that are pneumatically driven. If you open the valve too fast, it will flood the whole area. When Forrest opens the valves, there is this *whoosh!* and you can see the pomace start to flow out of the tank. These tanks are about thirty feet high. There is a

161

very strong force of gravity, and you can fill the press with fifteen tons of crushed grapes in twenty seconds. The guys kneeling on top of the press, holding down the snout and the garbage bags around it, have to judge when the press is full and tell Forrest when to shut the valve. If it sticks or you do not close it fast enough, you could flood the whole platform with a sticky mess of grapes.

Losing five gallons of juice is not the end of the world, but hundreds of gallons could get wasted if you are not careful. Is the compressor running properly? Is air getting to the cylinders? Are all the valves hooked up properly? Is the pump hooked up correctly? Is the press locked into position? Is the top of the draining tank open? If it is not, the opened 18-inch valve at the bottom of the tank would suck in the sides of the stainless steel tank, and could end up looking like a crumpled beer can.

Once the press is loaded, Forrest sets the controls. Even though it is an automatic, he prefers to run it manually so he can constantly check the quality of the juice. Forrest presses his Sauvignon Blanc to 130 gallons of free-run juice and twenty-five gallons of press juice.

The pressing cycle takes from one to two hours, depending on how slowly he wants to go, how many times he opens the press to look inside to see how dry the fruit is. You have to look at it. You cannot just push a button. You have to stop, climb up there, feel it, smell it, taste the juice as you press harder, then make a subjective decision as to when it is ready. Meanwhile, we chat, drink coffee and brandy, and dance to some bluesy, sexy love songs on the radio.

Those numbers—130 gallons of free run and twenty-five gallons of pressed juice—are very conservative. Traditionally, Sauvignon Blanc is pressed to 170–180 gallons per ton. We throw away 25–30 gallons of juice, but we know from experience the extra 25–30 gallons of juice of Sauvignon Blanc detract from the overall quality of our wine. Technology is at the point where now you can get every last little drop out of the grape. In the old days, when the ancient little guy was stomping it with his feet, he was getting 130 gallons a ton at most, maybe 125, and he was beating his brains out; we jumped from that to the technology of having a press that could extract over 200 gallons a ton. By the end of the press cycle the grapes were ground down as dry as sawdust. Just as you can use technology to improve quantity, what is exciting about winemaking today is using it to get the most delicate juice possible.

When Forrest decides that the grapes have been properly pressed, we pull up the truck alongside the press and dump the pomace—the spent grapes—into the truck to be composted the next morning. We clean out the press, make a few small checks, the sulfur dioxide (SO_2), the acidity, and the pH, leave some notes for the morning crew, and go home.

Thank goodness, Iron Horse doesn't depend on making Pinot Noir. Forrest didn't make any in 1981 or 1984. He bottled the 1989 as a Tin Pony wine and in 1990 he made so little—only 100 gallons, about forty cases worth—that it was not enough to fill the press. We crushed the grapes by hand.

There is one shy bearing knoll—the top

of block G—behind the winery that Forrest used for a great string of Pinot Noirs in 1985, 1986, 1987, and 1988. He got about two and one half tons an acre off that knoll, which translate into 800 or so cases a year. He liked the knoll for still wine as opposed to sparkling because the grapes are smaller, more concentrated, and the skins are thicker, more tannic. The knoll is composed of very rocky shale and is relatively steep, so that drainage is good. It has easterly exposure—little afternoon sun—so a longer growing season. And the nights are cool. In warm climates, Pinot Noir results in thin-skinned grapes and bland-tasting wines.

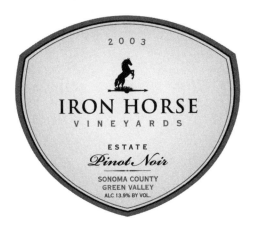

Pinot Noir is the most difficult grape to grow. It is the most site-specific of all the grape varieties. Whether the grapes are from the top of the knoll or the bottom makes a big difference, and you never know what you are going to get. One year it will produce a very good crop and the next year nothing.

Now Forrest has transferred all his affection to a new knoll— two acres on the next hill over, which Forrest planted in 1986 as one big Pinot Noir experiment with two different clones—a Pommard clone from David Adelsheim's vineyard in Oregon and a Giesenheim clone that we call clone N from the research center in Germany. The knoll is called Laurence's knoll because, some years back, Laurence and I were standing behind the winery looking across the property when Laurence mused, "You know, I can see my house on top of that knoll." He didn't move fast enough and now it's covered in vines. Forrest hopes to get his first commercial-size crop off Laurence's knoll in 1992. Mother has warned him that if he doesn't make any in '92 she'll make it herself. "And don't think I don't know how," she said, shaking her finger. Pinot Noir is her baby.

163

PART V

OLD WORLD

FRANCE

The Major Wine Regions of France

Alsace	Burgundy	Languedoc-Roussillon	Provence
Bordeaux	Champagne	Loire	Rhône

My first French wine was an easy-to-drink 1969 Louis Jadot Beaujolais-Villages. I enjoyed it. But the experience that turned me on to wine was being the bartender and "wine guy" at the Depuy Canal House Tavern in High Falls, New York. Peter Bienstock, a regular customer there, was kind enough to share with me his wine cellar. He was a lawyer and a wine lover. Peter had a tremendous collection of Burgundy and Bordeaux wines. I was lucky that, over the years, he brought bottle after bottle of his wines to try. These were eye-openers. He shared with me bottles of wines from the early 1900s to the 1950s. That's when I made the jump from Budweiser to Burgundy and Bordeaux, and decided that I wanted a life in wine. Peter was very influential in my life, and I am very grateful for his introducing me to the great world of French wine.

The French make anywhere from 7 to 8 billion bottles of wine each year. It is the second largest producer of wine in the world. Because most French wines are named not for their varietal but for the region from which they come, it is most important to remember geography when discussing French wines. Here are the major wine-producing regions in France and what grape or grapes they specialize in.

Let's start in the north. The Champagne region makes the world's best sparkling wines, primarily from Pinot Noir and Chardonnay grapes. The Loire Valley is known for its brilliant white wines that are made from Sauvignon Blanc and Chenin Blanc, and their reds from Cabernet Franc. Alsace is mostly known for citrusy, fragrant whites like Riesling and Gewürztraminer. The Burgundy region is known for whites made from Chardonnay and reds made from Pinot Noir and Gamay (Gamay Beaujolais).

Going south we find Bordeaux, which produces some of the most coveted red and white wines in the world. Their white wines, made from Sauvignon Blanc and Sémillon, can be dry, austere, and flinty; or deep, thick, and sweet. Their reds, made from Merlot, Cabernet Sauvignon, and Cabernet Franc, are some of the best in the world. Wines from the Côtes du Rhône are known for intense character from Syrah and Grenache grapes. And the reds and whites of Languedoc-Roussillon and Provence are beginning to make high-quality wines.

French wines are regulated by the strict laws of the Apellation d'Origine Controlé. (Of course, many people simply prefer to say "AOC.") The AOC regulates wine production in the winery and in the vineyard to maintain authenticity within the region, governing which grapes can be grown, quantity per hectare, and alcohol content.

—KZ

167

BORDEAUX

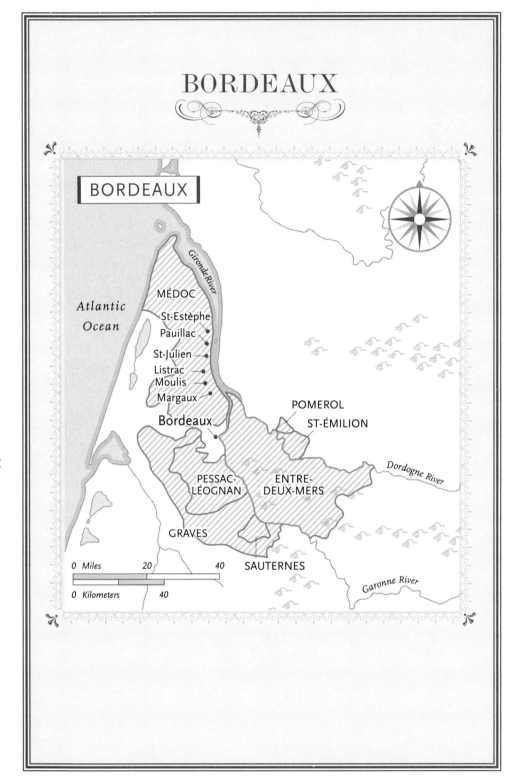

I HAVE PROBABLY SPENT MORE time in Bordeaux than in any other wine region. Maybe that is why Bordeaux is one of my favorite wines. With all of its history, culture, magnificent châteaux, and spectacular wines, for me Bordeaux has it all. Every year in June, one château hosts what is called the Fête de la Fleur (Feast of the Flower). The first one I ever attended was at Château Beychevelle, a second growth St. Julien and one of the most spectacular châteaux in the region. It was held in the "backyard" of Beychevelle, an intimate dinner for 1,000 wine lovers. The final of the 10 wines of the evening was Château Beychevelle 1961!

Bordeaux is a city located in the Aquitaine, one of the twenty-six regions of France, in the southwestern part of France. It is bounded on one side by the Atlantic Ocean and on the other by the Pyrenees mountain range on the Spanish border. Bordeaux is a city of more than one million people, and its outlying area is one of the most celebrated wine regions in the world. The region has about 287,000 acres of vineyards, 57 appellations, 10,000 wine-producing châteaux, and 13,000 grape growers, with an annual production of approximately 850 million bottles.

Bordeaux wine is all about history. The Romans first began making wine sometime after 48 CE, during their occupation of Saint-Émilion. The Romans established vineyards to cultivate wine for the occupying soldiers. The popularity of Bordeaux wines soared after the marriage in 1152 of Henry Plantagenet and Eleanor of Aquitaine. Once the English king had married the landed French noblewoman, copious amounts of Bordeaux claret (as the English called it) became all the rage on that isle. Through the next 900 years Bordeaux's vintages became some of the most sought-after wines in the world.

Many of Bordeaux's best vineyards are located near the Gironde River, where well-drained rock soil is most prevalent. The old saying in Bordeaux is that the best estates in the region can all see the river from their lands.

The three main grapes for red wine are Merlot, Cabernet Sauvignon, and Cabernet Franc. White wines from Bordeaux include Sauvignon Blanc and Sémillon. The latter two are used in dry wines, and are also notable for their use in the great sweet wines of the Sauternes region.

—KZ

BORDEAUX

Michael Broadbent

If the essence of this piece is "who makes what and where," my purpose is to explain why, and for how long, the fine wines of Bordeaux have dominated the market.

For me, Bordeaux is the "Mecca of wine." The world is now awash with wine, much produced in countries and regions where, hitherto, vineyards did not exist. Moreover much is of increasingly high quality, as my ever expanding tasting books attest: a gamut of surprises, delights—and abject awfulness. But however good and interesting, I always come back home to Bordeaux, not just because it dominated my early days in the wine trade but for over forty years as a wine auctioneer, red Bordeaux, "claret" to the English, still dominates the international fine wine market.

First of all, the basics. Where is Bordeaux? In the southwest of France, a vast acreage of vineyards owned by well over 10,000 winegrowers in surprisingly varied and contrasting districts within the Gironde *Département*. Bordeaux itself has long been one of the biggest cities in France and, despite it being 60 miles from the sea, one of its most important ports.

By a convenient quirk of history, Bordeaux and the entire west coast of France were, from the mid-14th century and for almost exactly 300 years, ruled by the English kings. Not surprisingly the wine, both red and white, was exported to England in vast quantities, enriching the merchants in London, Bristol, and many other British ports.

It was, however, Dutch engineers who, in the 17th century, drained the low-lying area along the banks of the Gironde estuary, enabling wealthy, mainly aristocratic landowners to plant vineyards in what is known as the Médoc; and by the middle of the 18th century, high-quality red wines were being produced under châteaux names. It was at that time that James Christie's first-ever auction, in December 1766, for a "nobleman deceas'd," included substantial quantities of "fine Claret" and "Fine old Madiera" (sic). Just three years later, on February 8, 1769, specific vineyards first appeared in a Christie's catalogue, at initially just two, "Lafete" (sic) and "Chateau Margeaux" (sic).

But it was Thomas Jefferson, soon after his appointment as American envoy in Paris in 1784, who set himself up in appropriate ambassadorial style. Jefferson, an American icon, was a gentleman of high intellect, refinement—and profligacy. He also harbored a passionate love of wine. Among nearly 20,000 letters received and copies retained are invaluable records of his wide-ranging interests and specific wine purchases. In 1787 he embarked on a lengthy journey, visiting all the major wine regions of France. One of his most important stops was Bordeaux, where, in just four days in May, he meticulously made notes of the châteaux he visited, their owners, climate and soil, vinicultural methods, even the laborers' wages. Most important of all, he recorded that "Of Red Wines there are 4 vineyards of first quality, viz. 1. Chateau Margau, 2. La Tour de Segur (Latour), 3. Hout Brion, 4. Chateau de La Fite (Lafite)" and, of sweet white wines that "the best crop belongs to M. Diquem (Château d'Yquem)." His initial order request via his agent in Bordeaux was for 250 bottles of the renowned 1784 vintage.

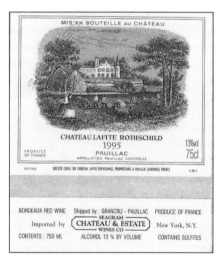

171

But Lafite, above all, was the first choice of the English aristocracy, rich merchants, bankers, and the like. Until Pétrus hit the headlines, Lafite consistently fetched the highest prices in the international market. It is worth stating that throughout the 1920s and 1930s, because the vineyards of Pomerol were so small, their production did not warrant the attention of the princely merchants of Bordeaux, their British importers, and wealthy customers. Despite the high reputation of Pétrus (a "*1er grand cru*") it was consumed almost exclusively by "citizens of the low countries," mainly the

Belgians. It was not until the great postwar vintages, 1945, 1947, and 1949, and the enterprise of the Mouïex family, that the vineyards of Pomerol and their resuscitated star, Pétrus, began to be appreciated by importers and connoisseurs. The rest, as they say, is history.

Space does not allow me to detail the elaborate network of middlemen, the *courtiers* (brokers) between the producers and négociants, the wine merchants of Bordeaux; the "shippers" and wine merchants of the importing countries. Thanks to Prohibition, the once rich American market received a setback. The renewal of serious interest began in the 1970s, at which period the British middle classes, who had long enjoyed even the first growths at drinkable prices, were priced out. Now it is the turn of the global market.

But what is the secret of Bordeaux's success? A combination of climate, soil, grape varieties, and centuries of experience and expertise. Perhaps not fully appreciated is the beneficial and moderating influence of a maritime climate, and the unpredictable weather throughout each growing season. For, importantly, these variations are entirely responsible for the quality of the vintage— assuming that viticulture, the care of the vineyard, selection of grapes and, of course, competent wine making, apply.

The inimitable style of Bordeaux results from a unique combination of several grape varieties (unlike red Burgundy, where only the Pinot Noir is used). First and foremost the now universally cultivated Cabernet Sauvignon; next Merlot (in volume the highest producer); finally Cabernet Franc and Petit Verdot. All four varieties are grown

on the "west bank," the Médoc, while on the "east bank," Pomerol and Saint Émilion, mainly Merlot and Cabernet Franc are used, though some châteaux also include Cabernet Sauvignon. Pétrus is virtually 100% Merlot.

The superb and ubiquitous Cabernet Sauvignon is the king of red wine grapes, giving the wine depth, complexity, and a dominant character. Merlot, an early ripening variety, despite its depth of color, on the whole, has a softer, fleshier, influence. In the Médoc, Cabernet Franc, late ripening and at best fully ripe, plays a supporting role, as does a small percentage of Petit Verdot, said to add a soupçon of "pepper and salt."

No matter the number of vines planted, the proportion of grapes used will vary from year to year. The percentage of each depends on the quality and ripeness of the crop, which, as few realize, can vary enormously. For example, at a recent extensive tasting of vintages from a classed growth Margaux, Cabernet Sauvignon was sometimes as high as 80% though, rarely, as low as the mid-twenties; a Merlot can also vary to a similar degree. However it is generally accepted that the average *cépage* mix in the Médoc is around 70% Cabernet Sauvignon, 20% Merlot, 8% Cabernet Franc, and 2% Petit Verdot.

As important as the vineyard site itself, soil and subsoil—happily not directly affected by the vicissitudes of weather—is also crucial to the quality of grapes, and wine. Drainage too, which is why many, if not most, prime vineyards are on a slope. Much has been said about *terroir* and much of it nonsense, at least ill-informed. It is not a fanciful French term but does, subtly and by implication, embrace the sum total of climate, weather, soil, and grape—all the components a vineyard manager and winemaker have to cope with. As a demonstration, take Lafite. With the wine-making skills and Rothschild wealth, Château Lafite, the *Grand Vin*, cannot be replicated if the same grapes are grown on lower ground, the *palus*, nearer the Gironde or on a site in the Landes to the west.

Quality and the market: I have already mentioned that the growing conditions, the weather, have a direct effect on quality, but what my historical researches reveal are distinct correlations between weather and market, demand and prices. Briefly, the following have in common a period of good weather, and increasing demand leading to over high, prohibitive prices, followed by unsuitable weather and a slump. For example the renowned pre-phylloxera period in Bordeaux, 1844–1878, with prices escalating in 1870, was immediately followed by bad weather, phylloxera, mildew, and a severe recession which lasted from 1879 to 1899 (1893 was a freak hot year like 1921 and 2003). The burgeoning affluence of the decade of the 1920s was followed by three execrable vintages in the early 1930s and a world slump. Variable vintages and dramatic inflation led to high priced 1970 and 1971 followed by an equally dramatic collapse of the market with the poor and unwanted 1972, 1973, and 1974. It is dangerous to interpolate, but one should be aware of an overprice stampede. It usually ends in tears.

1945, 1947, and 1949, the miraculously great postwar trio following the wartime years, with widespread shortages, of vines tended by old women and young boys, new casks unheard of, was due to traditional wine making—and no consultant enologists (the renowned Professor Peynaud was not yet on the scene). This period, and the next decade, produced wines of character and elegance. Name dropping, I once suggested to Baron Philippe de Rothschild that surely his favorite wine must be that which I had described as a "Churchill" of a wine, namely the 1945 Mouton. Yes, he said, but he preferred to drink his 1949, a wine of delicacy and finesse. Its alcoholic content 10.5%!

The remorseless elevation of alcoholic content is the bane of my life. Prewar vintages of claret were not uncommonly 11 to 11.5%; in the 1950s and 1960s the alcohol content ranged from 12 to 12.5% (the latter being ideal). Now, thanks to riper grapes and "superior" wine making, 13 to 13.5% is the norm. But 14.5 and over? Global warming cannot be denied but the "global" taste for deeply colored reds, fruit-laden, sweet, and unsubtle, is becoming the norm. Richness and sweetness tend to mask both the high alcoholic content and the life-preserving tannin. The plain fact is that the higher the alcohol, the lower the recognition of origin;

PRODUCE OF FRANCE
MIS EN BOUTEILLE AU CHATEAU
GRAND VIN DE CHATEAU LATOUR
PREMIER GRAND CRU CLASSÉ
PAUILLAC
12.5 % Vol.   750 ml
DEPOSE   APPELLATION PAUILLAC CONTROLÉE
STE CIVILE DU VIGNOBLE DE CHATEAU LATOUR, PROPRIÉTAIRE A PAUILLAC (GIRONDE) · LG 93

modern blockbusters, if not all identical, have the similar deadening character and headache-making effect.

Which is why I always come back to red Bordeaux. Claret is a civilized wine, perfect, as intended, to accompany food; and in the higher range, youthful claret initially laden with mouth-drying tannins—a healthy oxidant—has an unequaled ability to achieve harmony and extra dimensions with bottle age. What could be better?

WHITE BORDEAUX

Although red Bordeaux, claret, has always dominated the market, the production and sales of white Bordeaux have always been significant, the dry whites for more or less immediate drinking—as are virtually all of the world's dry wines; the sweet wines, in particular Sauternes, at best are in a category of their own.

The principal dry whites are produced in the extensive Graves district to the south of Bordeaux with a separate *appellation*. Pessac-Léognon is at its northern end, Léognon being a modest village with the larger number of leading producers such as Domaine de Chevalier, Carbonnieux, the Château de Fieuzal, Malartic-la-Gravière, and Bouscant—all of which, like most of the châteaux in the Graves area, produce red as well as white wines (a notable exception is the excellent Haut-Bailly, which is red only). The other portion of this *appellation* is Pessac, now virtually a suburb of Bordeaux but home to what is arguably the oldest château in Bordeaux, Pape-Clément, and the stars of the dry white wine firmament: Haut-Brion and Laville-Haut-Brion.

Both dry and sweet Bordeaux have the same two grape varieties in common, Sémillon and Sauvignon Blanc, the first providing what I think of as a firm foundation, the second a floral zestful character.

In my early days in the wine trade, back to the mid-1950s, and doubtless before that, "Graves" covered a multitude of sins. To be frank, most commercial Graves was of inferior quality, drab yellow, too long in old casks—or concrete vats—and flabby, lacking zest. The past thirty years have witnessed a renaissance thanks to better viticultural practice and superior wine making: paler in color, starbright, fragrant, vibrantly dry and refreshing; moreover, with the exception of the deservedly fashionable and top growths, reasonably priced. The advantage of these châteaux making both red and dry wines is that the latter, bottled and sold sooner, provides the proprietors with useful cash flow while the reds are *éléve*, time and finance required, not to mention the expense of new oak *barriques*.

GRAND CRU CLASSÉ

CHÂTEAU CARBONNIEUX
PESSAC-LÉOGNAN
APPELLATION PESSAC-LÉOGNAN CONTROLÉE
GRAND VIN DE GRAVES
PRODUCE OF FRANCE
MIS EN BOUTEILLES AU CHATEAU

Though dry white Bordeaux is made and marketed on an ongoing annual basis, some vintages, thanks to Bordeaux's fairly unpredictable climate, stand out as being superior, the best such as the highly successful 2005 which will benefit from further maturation in bottle.

SAUTERNES

By definition "Sauternes" is always sweet. And although the same grape varieties, Sémillon and Sauvignon Blanc, there is no such thing as a "dry Sauternes," though some châteaux in this relatively rustic, unsophisticated, southerly region produce a dry wine, in the case of Château d'Yquem, "Y" Ygrec.

Château Yquem warrants a chapter of its own. It was renowned as the finest of all Bordeaux sweet whites as long ago as the mid-18th century. The aristocratic Lur-Saluces family acquired it by marriage in 1785, and descendents owned and managed the estate until only recently. It was one of Thomas Jefferson's favorite wines, which he first purchased when he was the American envoy in Paris, writing to "M. Diquem" via John Bondfield, the U.S. Consul in Bordeaux, for a modest (!) 250 bottles of the vintage 1784. (Jefferson's letters

are well documented and are also confirmed by the original sale ledgers in Yquem's archives.)

In 1855, Yquem was the only white wine to be included in the classification of the wines of the Médoc, its status being recognized as *1er grand cru classé* whereas the four Médoc first growths were merely *1er cru classé*.

Unlike dry white Bordeaux, Sauternes not only keeps well but develops extra nuances with maturation in bottle. Yquem has a unique track record of particularly good vintages (and from well-kept cellars) and has been superbly drinkable for over a century.

But what is it that makes Sauternes special? It starts in September or October with the confluence of two rivers, the stately Garonne and the almost insignificant Ciron. This creates morning mists which, when burned off by the mellow autumn sunshine, produces a mold, *Botrytis cinera, pourriture noble*, noble rot, which settles on the skins of the ripening grapes, and when unpeeling the shriveled grapes, it reveals intensely rich and concentrated juice. Unhappily for the grower, not every autumn will produce botrytis; the wines will be sweet but lacking the extra depth and nuance. Fermentation is slow, the wine developing in cask for two—or in the case of Yquem—to over three years.

Other leading châteaux include de Rayne-Vigneau, Rieussec, Lafaurie-Peyraguey, and Suduirant, equaling Yquem in the excellent 1967 vintage and producing outstanding 1975s and 1976s; also two from the commune of Barsac, Châteaux Coutet and, above all, Climens, which I now rate the most highly after the inimitable Yquem. Château d'Yquem 1921 is one of the great

wines of all time; 1928 and 1929 both excellent but of different styles; 1937, 1959, and 1962 outstanding, and all scarce but superb to drink now; then come the outstanding 1971, 1975, 1983, and 1989, all at their peak, and the universally successful vintage 2001, still developing.

The most frequently asked question is, When does one drink Sauternes?

The French drink it as an aperitif, or, ideally with foie gras—and cheese. However, it is most customarily considered a dessert wine. But matching a superb vintage of Sauternes with a talented pastry chef's confection can be disastrous: it has the effect of emasculating the sweetness and richness of a superb—risky and expensive to make— wine.

My first taste of Yquem was in my student days with a cultured friend of the family: it was on a warm summer evening and accompanied by ripe nectarines. Memorable. Was it this that induced me to abandon architecture for a noble trade? Possibly.

SHALL THE OLD ORDER CHANGE?
The Case for Reclassification

Alexis Lichine

The 1855 Classement des Grands Crus de la Gironde, as it was called, was an ambitious work from the outset. Napoleon III was adamant in his desire for a classification of the wines of Bordeaux, the greatest of French wines, for the Exposition Universelle de Paris—the world's fair of the day—where the best France had to offer would be on display. Charged with the task of drawing up the rankings, the Bordeaux Chamber of Commerce delegated the work to the Bordeaux Brokers' Association, an official body attached to the Bordeaux Stock Exchange. What was required in effect was a listing of the wines of the Bordeaux region in order of excellence as demonstrated by the prices they had fetched over the years.

This type of list according to price existed long before 1855. From the time that wines began to emerge under their own names in the eighteenth century, price hierarchies had been established, based on the demand for the wine in the market. By the end of the eighteenth century, the four wines that were later designated First Growths in 1855 were already recognized as the very best that Bordeaux had to offer, and the prices paid for them were correspondingly high. Brokers often made informal classifications of their own to serve as buyer's guides of a sort. In 1824 and 1827 individual brokers drew up classifications with four major categories of growths (the 1855 list has five). The lists differed in significant ways from each other and from the 1855 Classification—each reflecting the limitations of its compiler.

Still, no group was better qualified to rank the wines of the region than the brokers. Since their job was (and is) to act as

Alexis Lichine has had the most influence on my wine-writing career. When I first went to visit the wineries of Europe I took his 700-page Encyclopedia of Wines and Spirits, *which I stuck in my backpack. And today it still sits on my desk as a reminder of my early years as a student of wine. He was truly a Renaissance man, carrying three passports: Russian, French, and American. He also served in the United States military intelligence in Europe during World War II. Besides his many books, he was also an importer and owned his own château in Bordeaux, Château Prieure-Lichine. I spent many a late evening at the château by his fireplace in the kitchen where we would cook our dinner over vine cuttings. And when he came to New York I did the same for him.*

the intermediary between the *propriété* and the shipper, they were familiar with all the wines of any commercial importance on the Bordeaux exchange. But this familiarity led to one inevitable and distorting limitation— wine which had little or no exposure in the Bordeaux marketplace received no attention, no matter what their quality. Therefore the great districts of today—Graves (except for Haut-Brion, which was classed along with the First Growths of the Médoc), Saint-Émilion, and Pomerol—were out of the running, because in 1855 they had no commercial or public recognition. The fact is that they were minor wines at the time. The brokers had no way of knowing that a century later Pétrus, Cheval-Blanc, and Ausone would all command prices equal to and often surpassing those of the First Growth Médocs. Whether these wines were in fact so little worthy of attention remains debatable, however—after all, the world of the Bordeaux wine trade was closed and snobbish and Saint-Émilion and Pomerol were on the wrong side of the river, so to speak. Between Bordeaux and Libourne (the wine center for Saint-Émilion and Pomerol) there are the Dordogne and Garonne rivers to cross, and until the early nineteenth century there was no bridge across the Dordogne. More than one château owner in Saint-Émilion and Pomerol has insisted to me that the only reason his region and wine were excluded in 1855 was that the Bordeaux trade in those days considered Libourne a social backwater. But that is another story.

The fact remains that there were only two notable wine regions at the time: the

Médoc for the red wines and the Sauternes-Barsac for the sweet whites. Château Haut-Brion in Graves was an exception to the all-Médoc lineup because it was too well known and too well sold to be ignored by brokers.

In establishing the criteria for the new classification, although price was the most important factor, the prestige of both the wine and the owner was taken into account. The quality of the soil and the exposure of the vineyard were also considered, because they remain more or less constant from generation to generation regardless of who the owner is. In 1867, only twelve years after the official classification, Charles Cocks, author of his own respected rating of the wines of Bordeaux, underscored the need for ongoing reassessment:

> Like all human institutions, this one is subject to the laws of the time and must, at certain times, be rejuvenated and kept abreast of progress. The vineyards themselves, in changing ownership, may often be modified. A certain vine-site, neglected by a careless owner, or by one who has run into debt, may fall into the hands of a rich, active, and intelligent man, and because of this, give a better product. The opposite can also happen. . . .

It is apparent that Cocks was and is right, and the time for a new classification is very much at hand.

Although the quality of the vineyard soil will remain the same, the owner may be forced to sell it or rent it out, or he may trade it for better vineyard parcels elsewhere. For these two reasons alone—the changes in ownership and the changes in vineyard holdings—updating is constantly necessary. The vineyard area of Médoc château is not fixed in the same way as the boundaries of a Great Growth (*Grand Cru*) vineyard of Burgundy, such as Latricières-Chambertin. Any of the First Growths of Pauillac, for instance, could buy hectares of the poor land within the Appellation Pauillac Contrôlée (all communes have select as well as less desirable areas of soil) and include the wine made from that land in the château-bottling. Given the character of the owners, this is not likely to happen, but the point is that no plot of vines within Pauillac (or Saint-Estèphe or Saint-Julien or Margaux, for that matter) is reserved for or classified under a specific château name. Instead, each vineyard parcel takes on the prestige of the château that owns it. Hence it is not uncommon for a given vineyard parcel to change classification from a First to a Fourth to a Second to a Fifth Growth as it is bought and sold by different châteaux. The character and quality of the château's wine are directly affected as a result.

The greatest variable in the greatness of wine, however, is ultimately the owner himself and the effectiveness of his management as reflected in the know-how and dedication of his workers in the vineyards and the cellars. Hundreds of small but crucial steps have a bearing on the quality of the wine. Does the owner see to it that the vines are properly pruned to limit the harvest, and properly safeguarded against disease? Is his vinification equipment clean and in good repair? Is he willing (and able) to buy new vats and barrels as they are needed? Is he prepared, in his search for the best quality, to sacrifice the lesser vats of his wine and reserve only the best to go out under the château label? Will he take the trouble to make soil analyses in order to ascertain the right types of fertilizers and vine clones to use? Will he buy only the best parcels of land within the *appellation* to plant with vines? The answers to all of these questions and more will indicate the depth of the grower's dedication, and determine the excellence of his product. Although the most conscientious grower in the world cannot overcome poor soils and unfavorable climate, he can have an influence—for the better—on all other aspects of the wine-making process.

With the changeability of these two factors—geography and management—in mind, it is especially remarkable that the form of the 1855 Classification was in strict order of merit, even within the five categories of growths. Within the Second Growths, for instance, the châteaux Ducru-Beaucaillou, Cos d'Estournel, and Montrose were listed in that order of excellence. But the owners themselves—even, probably, in 1855—would have hesitated to maintain that this order was the correct one year in and year out.

In recent years, after much agitation on all sides, the Syndicat des Crus Classes petitioned the INAO for an update of the 1855 classification. There were two choices: either the 1855 classification should be amended to reflect changes in production and market value, or else it should be left untouched and a completely new classification drawn up. In 1960 the INAO declared that the rankings in the 1855 classification had been prizes for quality at a given time and that they had no authority to, in effect, take the prizes back. So the INAO established guidelines for a new ranking; but even these were hotly disputed, and the Institut lost heart in the project.

In the meantime, four prominent and extremely able wine brokers were delegated the task of a new classification. The result was three categories of excellence, instead of the five used in 1855. Eighteen of the châteaux classified in 1855 were omitted and thirteen new ones were added. The judges concluded that it would be necessary to update the classification every five years.

The reaction was explosive outrage. Château owners demoted or entirely deleted gave vent to their intense distress and condemned the ranking as malicious, incompetent, and unjust. The fact is that at present Bordeaux simply lacks the courage and the leadership required to push through the necessary modifications. Moreover, the economic wine crisis of 1973–74 left Bordeaux badly shaken and—ironically— more apprehensive than ever of change, however urgently needed.

I was a member of the original committee on amending the rating, and when I saw that progress was not being made I decided to move ahead on my own. My classification, in its first version, was completed in 1959. In the course of preparing it, I interviewed more than seventy experts privately and off the record. We found that there were no real differences on the key issues. Investigations of the land records in the various communes

revealed that some of the châteaux no longer occupy the same terrain as they held in 1855, and in some cases no longer made any wine. Some classified as Fourth or Fifth Growths deserved to be sold as Seconds or Thirds, while certain Bourgeois Growths (the general group of vineyards which were not included in the 1855 classification) had earned elevation to Fourth or Fifth Growth status. Here the grower and consumer (who is misled by the wine's rating) lack a realistic basis for evaluation. It should be emphasized that even in 1855 a wine ranked as a Second, Third, Fourth, or Fifth Growth was *not a second, third, fourth, or fifth-rate wine*. This terminology has always been confusing. Actually, since 161 among approximately three thousand vineyards were considered worthy of being named Great Growths—whether First or Fifth— as a group they comprise a majority of the world's finest red wines. To be second only after Lafite, Latour, Margaux, and Haut-Brion is vastly different from being second-rate. Moreover, it is only on average that the First are the best; in certain years others equal or even surpass them.

I thus found general agreement on avoiding the invidiousness of a ranking by number—First, Second, Third, and so on. It goes without saying that in today's age of publicity and competitive salesmanship a Second, Third, Fourth, or Fifth Growth would be unfairly handicapped. When the vineyards of Saint-Émilion were classified in the fifties, the officials at that time used the simpler categories of "First Great Growths," "Great Growths," and "Other Principal Growths." I adapted this format to my needs. It was also decided that within each category the listing should be alphabetical rather than strictly hierarchical. This, too, is patterned on the new classification of Saint-Émilion.

To measure the effect of changes in ownership of vineyard châteaux demanded great delicacy, to say the least. It often happens that vineyards are passed on to less energetic sons or to inexperienced owners, and the change is reflected in the wine, as Cocks correctly foresaw. If there is no reassessment, the wine will coast along on its former reputation and ranking. For some châteaux, the problem remains chronic; in others the difficulty passes quickly, in the time it takes to find a new *maître de chai* or to employ an oenologist. Happily, vineyards that have fallen on hard times will frequently pull themselves together and surpass the wines of their rank. It was to encourage and reward those who work hard for the best quality that I undertook the new classification.

My ranking was published for the first time in 1962, and has been brought up to date many times since then—most recently in March 1981—and always in collaboration with the local experts of each region.

We should note, of course, the official reclassification of 1973 that gave Mouton-Rothschild the long-deserved accolade of First Growth status. Unfortunately, the Ministry of Agriculture stopped there. Others who deserve upgrading or even initial ranking will have to wait.

The following is the only classification that dares to combine the best red wines of all four important Bordeaux regions. In assimilating wines with varying characteristics it becomes increasingly difficult to identify peers as one moves toward the lesser growths. It is easy, for example, to compare the very best wines of Saint-Émilion and those of the Médoc, as one might contrast the masters of different schools of painting; but the more common and undifferentiated the wine, the narrower the base for comparison.

Because wine is a product of nature and of man's skill, any such classification is bound to be ephemeral and somewhat arbitrary, and several wines in the following list could be raised or lowered for any particular vintage.

With the exception of the Outstanding Growths, the wines in each category have been listed in alphabetical order.

181

Outstanding Growths
(Crus Hors Classe)

HAUT-MÉDOC
Château Lafite-Rothschild *(Pauillac)*
Château Latour *(Pauillac)*
Château Margaux *(Margaux)*
Château Mouton-Rothschild *(Pauillac)*

GRAVES
Château Haut-Brion *(Pessac, Graves)*

SAINT-ÉMILION
Château Ausone
Château Cheval-Blanc

POMEROL
Château Pétrus

Exceptional Growths
(Crus Exceptionnels)

182

HAUT-MÉDOC
Château Beychevelle *(Saint-Julien)*
Château Brane-Cantenac *(Cantenac-Margaux)*
Château Calon-Ségur *(Saint-Estèphe)*
Château Cos d'Estournel *(Saint-Estèphe)*
*Château Ducru-Beaucaillou *(Saint-Julien)*
Château Gruaud-Larose *(Saint-Julien)*
Château Lascombes *(Margaux)*
Château Léoville-Barton *(Saint-Julien)*

Château Léoville-Las-Cases *(Saint-Julien)*
Château Léoville-Poyferré *(Saint-Julien)*
Château Montrose *(Saint-Estèphe)*
Château Palmer *(Cantenac-Margaux)*
*Château Pichon-Lalande *(Pauillac)*
Château Pichon-Longueville (Baron) *(Pauillac)*

GRAVES
*Domaine de Chevalier *(Léognan)*
*Château La Mission-Haut-Brion *(Pessac)*
Château Pape-Clément *(Pessac)*

SAINT-ÉMILION
*Château Figeac
Château Magdelaine

POMEROL
Château La Conseillante
Château l'Évangile
Château Lafleur
Château La Fleur-Pétrus
Château Trotanoy

Great Growths
(Grands Crus)

HAUT-MÉDOC
Château Branaire *(Saint-Julien)*
Château Cantemerle *(Haut-Médoc)*

Château Cantenac-Brown *(Cantenac-Margaux)*
Château Duhart-Milon-Rothschild *(Pauillac)*
Château Durfort-Vivens *(Cantenac-Margaux)*

These wines are considered better than their peers in this classification.

*Château Giscours *(Labarde-Margaux)*
Château d'Issan *(Cantenac-Margaux)*
Château La Lagune *(Haut-Médoc)*

*Château Lynch-Bages *(Pauillac)*
Château Malescot-Saint-Exupéry *(Margaux)*
Château Mouton-Baronne-Philippe *(Pauillac)*
Château Pontet-Canet *(Pauillac)*
*Château Prieuré-Lichine *(Cantenac-Margaux)*
Château Rausan-Ségla *(Margaux)*
Château Rauzan-Gassies *(Margaux)*
Château Talbot *(Saint-Julien)*

GRAVES

*Château Haut-Bailly *(Léognan)*

SAINT-ÉMILION

Château Beauséjour-Bécot
*Château Belair
*Château Canon
Clos Fourtet
Château la Gaffelière

Château Pavie
Château Trottevieille

POMEROL

Château Gazin
Château Latour-Pomerol
Château Petit-Village
Vieux Château Certan

Superior Growths
(Crus Supérieurs)

HAUT-MÉDOC

Château Batailley *(Pauillac)*
Château Boyd-Cantenac *(Cantenac-Margaux)*
Château Chasse-Spleen *(Moulis)*

Château Clerc-Milon-Rothschild *(Pauillac)*
Château Gloria *(Saint-Julien)*
*Château Grand-Puy-Lacoste *(Pauillac)*
Château Haut-Batailley *(Pauillac)*
Château Kirwan *(Cantenac-Margaux)*
Château Lagrange *(Saint-Julien)*
Château Langoa *(Saint-Julien)*
Château Marquis d'Alesme-Becker *(Margaux)*
Château La Tour-Carnet *(Haut-Médoc)*

GRAVES

*Château Carbonnieux *(Léognan)*
Château de Fieuzal *(Léognan)*
Château La Louvière *(Léognan)*
*Château Malartic-Lagravière *(Léognan)*
Château Smith-Haut-Lafitte *(Martillac)*

SAINT-ÉMILION

Château l'Angélus
*Château Balestard-la-Tonnelle
Château Beauséjour-Duffau-Lagarrousse
Château Cadet-Piola
Château Canon-la-Gaffelière
Château La Clotte
Château Croque-Michotte
Château Curé-Bon-la-Madeleine
*Château La Dominique
Château Larcis-Ducasse
Château Larmande
Château Soutard
Château Troplong-Mondot
Château Villemaurine

POMEROL

Château Beauregard
*Château Certan-Giraud
Château Certan-de-May
Clos l'Église
Château l'Église-Clinet
Château Le Gay
Château Lagrange

Château La Grace
Château Nénin
Château La Pointe

Good Growths
(Bons Crus)

HAUT-MÉDOC

Château Angludet (*Cantenac-Margaux*)
Château Beau-Site (*Saint-Estèphe*)
Château Beau-Site Haut-Vignoble (*Saint-Estèphe*)
*Château Bel-Air-Marquis d'Aligre (*Soussans-Margaux*)
Château Bel-Orme (*Haut-Médoc*)
Château Belgrave (*Saint-Laurent*)
*Château de Camensac (*Haut-Médoc*)
Château Citran (*Haut-Médoc*)
Château Cos Labory (*Saint-Estèphe*)
Château Croizet-Bages (*Pauillac*)
Château Dauzac (*Labarde*)
Château Ferrière (*Margaux*)
Château Fourcas-Dupré (*Listrac*)
Château Fourcas-Hosten (*Listrac*)
Château Grand-Puy-Ducasse (*Pauillac*)
Château Gressier-Grand-Poujeaux (*Moulis*)
Château Hanteillan (*Haut-Médoc*)
Château Haut-Bages-Libéral (*Pauillac*)
Château Haut-Marbuzet (*Saint-Estèphe*)
Château Labégorce (*Margaux*)
Château Labégorce-Zedé (*Margaux*)
Château Lafon-Rochet (*Saint-Estèphe*)
Château Lamarque (*Haut-Médoc*)
Château Lanessan(*Haut-Médoc*)
Château Lynch-Moussas (*Pauillac*)
*Château Marbuzet (*Saint-Estèphe*)
Château Marquis-de-Terme (*Margaux*)
*Château Maucaillou (*Moulis*)
Château Les-Ormes-de-Pez (*Saint-Estèphe*)
Château Pédesclaux (*Pauillac*)
Château de Pez (*Saint-Estèphe*)
*Château Phélan-Ségur (*Saint-Estèphe*)
Château Pouget (*Cantenac-Margaux*)
Château Poujeaux (*Moulis*)
Château Saint-Pierre (*Saint-Julien*)
Château Siran (*Labarde-Margaux*)
Château du Terre (*Arsac-Margaux*)
Château La Tour-de-Mons (*Soussans-Margaux*)

GRAVES

Château Bouscat (*Cadaujac*)

Château Larrivet-Haut-Brion (*Léognan*)

Château La Tour-Haut-Brion (*Talence*)

Château La Tour-Martillac (*Martillac*)

SAINT-ÉMILION

Château l'Arrosée

Château Bellevue

Château Cap-de-Mourlin

Château de Châtelet

Clos des Jacobins

Château Corbin (*Giraud*)

Château Corbin (*Manuel*)

Château Corbin-Michotte

Château Coutet

Château Dassault

Couvent-des-Jacobins

Château La Fleur-Pourret

Château Franc-Mayne

Château Grâce-Dieux

Château Grand-Barrail-Lamarzelle-Figeac

Château Grand-Corbin

Château Grand-Corbin-Despagne

Château Grand-Mayne

Château Grand Pontet

Château Guadet-Saint-Julien

Château Laroque

Château Moulin-du-Cadet

Château Pavie-Décesse

Château Pavie-Macquin

Château Saint-Georges-Côte-Pavie

Château Tertre-Daugay

Château La Tour-Figeac

Château La Tour-du-Pin-Figeac

Château Trimoulet

Château Yon-Figeac

POMEROL

*Château Bourgneuf-Vayron

Château La Cabanne

Château le Caillou

Château Clinet

Clos du Clocher

Château La Croix

Château La Croix-de-Gay

Domaine de l'Église

Château l'Enclos

Château Gombaude-Guillot

Château La Grave Trignant de Boisset

*Château Guillot

Château Moulinet

Château Rouget

Clos René

Château de Sales

Château Tailhas

Château Taillefer

Château Vraye-Croix-de-Gay

185

BURGUNDY

BURGUNDY, OUTSIDE OF THE CITY OF DIJON, is real farm country. The Côte d'Or is only thirty miles long and every bit is covered vines. It was in Burgundy that I learned the importance of soil. During one of my trips to Burgundy, it rained for five straight days. On the sixth day, I saw workers at the bottom of the slopes collecting, with pails and shovels, the soil that had run down the hillside, and returning it to the vineyard. I have never forgotten. Every time I have a bottle of Burgundy, I always remember the importance of the soil to the Burgundian wine producers.

Of all French wine, the most complicated for me to understand is Burgundy. Many people, intimidated or confused by the many wine names in Burgundy, say, "There's so much to know with the many villages and vineyards." However, while this is true, there are other ways to understand Burgundy. If you were to memorize only fifteen to twenty-five names, you be able to speak intelligently about the region.

The major wine-producing areas of Burgundy are the Côte D'Or (which consists of the Côte de Nuits and the Côte de Beaune), Chablis, Maconnais, Chalonnais, and, of course, Beaujolais. Burgundy is noted for both red and white wines. Close to 80 percent of Burgundy wine is red. Under the rules and regulations of the AOC, Pinot Noir is the only red grape of the Côte d'Or, Gamay is the only red grape allowed in Beaujolais, and Chardonnay is the only white grape of the Côte d'Or, Chablis, and Maconnais.

—KZ

THE WINES OF BURGUNDY

Clive Coates

Today's Côte d'Or is the most exciting wine region in the world. There has been an explosion in quality over the last 25 years. The villages are vibrant with a new generation of qualified, talented, committed men and women, infinitely curious about all the wines of the world, willing and able to share their experience and expertise with their neighbors and to taste their wines one with another, and continually seeking to fine-tune their techniques of viticulture, vinification, and *élevage* in order to further increase the quality of the bottles they are producing. There is one goal: perfection.

Moreover, while no one would call Burgundy cheap—the wine cannot be inexpensive for all sorts of reasons, not least of which are the price of land, the pitifully small scale of the operations, and the impossibility of making top quality wine without reducing yields to a minimum—prices have remained remarkably stable, despite increasing demand for the starry wines. [. . .]

And there has been a further cause for celebration. Since 1985 Burgundy has enjoyed a 21-year (as I write this [. . .]), and perhaps continuing, run of good to very fine vintages. Though one could argue that the average vintage standard for white wines has been not as high as that for the reds, the reds have not produced a less than "good" vintage year since 1984—and the best 1984s, though aging now, are by no means to be decried. God seems to be smiling on the resurgence of modern Burgundy. In 1985, again in 1988 and 1989, triumphantly so in 1990, again in 1991, 1993, 1995, 1996, 1998, brilliantly in 1999, partially in 2001, in 2002, 2004, and spectacularly in 2005, we have seen red wine vintages which are very good if not very fine. Even in the softer and less consistent vintages, such as 1997 and 2000, and in the

I have been lucky enough to know Clive Coates for over twenty-five years. He is a Master of Wine and one of the most prolific wine writers, especially on the subjects of Burgundy and Bordeaux. He is a true expert of both regions. In 2008, he released Wines of Burgundy, *the sequel to the book* Côte d'Or: A Celebration of the Great Wines of Burgundy. *He also has a great sense of humor, and is one of the best lecturers on the subject of wine. Prior to his wine writing career he spent twenty years as a professional wine merchant, and also helped create wine programs for many hotels.*

vintages of the heat-wave conditions of 2003, there is much to enjoy, and these wines can be enjoyed soon, thus preventing the infanticide that occurs in the greater years.

Burgundy has evolved considerably since the early 1980s. Growers now act like négociants, bottling and commercializing their wares, as well as tending the vines and making the wine. Increasingly, perhaps to make up for land they have lost as estates are split up in the natural process of being passed down from one generation to another or as leases and sharecropping arrangements come to an end, some growers have set up in a small way as merchants who buy others' fruit, must, or finished wine.

Merchants, for their part, are increasingly acting as growers. Most now prefer not to buy finished wine but to contract for the fruit and vinify it themselves, alongside the produce of their own estates, these estates having themselves been enlarged by acquisition over the years. In their dealings with their suppliers, négociants are more and more frequently taking an active role in the vineyards, a partnership which hitherto did not exist.

Unlike their fathers and grandfathers—and unlike today, in previous generations, it would have been unheard of for women to take an active role in winemaking—today's Burgundian winemaker has been to wine school. While not all one is taught at the Viti in Beaune or at the University of Dijon is entirely compatible with the demands associated with the role of a producer of serious premier or grand cru, growers today do have the technical background to help them comprehend why it is that they do what they do and what the result would be if they modified their approach. Today they have the knowledge and the confidence to help them experiment in their search for improvement, and what could be a greater impetus toward higher standards than the fact that one's name is eventually going to be on the bottle?

A generation or more ago, Burgundy was on its knees. Overfertilization in the 1960s and 1970s, the introduction of high-yield, low-quality clones, and the clampdown on bolster wines from the south of France and Algeria all led to wine which was thin, pallid, fruitless, and short-lived. The vineyard is still weak in this respect, for it takes time and money to replant, and Burgundy's reputation has taken a long time to recover. But at least the problems are being faced. Good husbandry, *biologique* if not *biodynamique*, is the order of the day. Growers understand the crucial importance of low yields. Today's clones are judged by quality rather than quantity. Action can be taken to reduce erosion, sterilize the vineyard against viral diseases, improve drainage, counteract the effects of past fertilization mistakes, space out the fruit to reduce depredation, protect it against rot, increase the efficiency of the ripening process, mitigate against the effects of last-minute rain, eliminate all but the very best fruit before vinification begins, concentrate the must by equalizing the solid-liquid ratio, control the fermentations, improve the wine's ability to settle out its impurities naturally, and prevent it from contamination and deterioration during the process of *élevage*: in short, to translate as purely as possible the very best fruit into the very best wine.

Combined with a new understanding, a new mind-set, and new techniques is new

188

equipment. Cellars are temperature-controlled where necessary, and so are the fermentation vats. There are all sorts of new machines to help the winemaker in his task, to reduce his physical labor in the vineyard and in the cellar and to enable him to control the winemaking process in exactly the way he wishes. Moreover, today's winery is increasingly spotlessly clean. The old, bug-infested barrels have been taken out and burnt, and if there is sometimes a little too much new oak, this problem is not as bad as it was a few years ago.

Winemaking, at least for great Burgundy, does not, however, involve as much creativity of approach as most outsiders think. Winemakers can destroy, you will be told, through incompetence or ignorance, but they cannot make any better wine than the potential quality of the fruit, the *matière première*, will allow in the first place. The winemaker's role is one of preventive medicator. And increasingly, the move is toward a hands-off approach. The more you manipulate the wine, the more you risk reducing what is good and individual about it. The greater the quality of the fruit at the time of the harvest, the better the possibility of the wine. The last 30 years have seen a revolution in the cellar and in the understanding of winemaking. We are now in the middle of just as important a revolution out there in the vineyard.

A MARKED INCREASE IN QUALITY

Ten years ago, in Côte d'Or, I awarded stars (one, two, or three: in the Michelin Red Guide style) to the top domaines. In the Côte d'Or, 17 domaines earned three stars, 29 two stars, and 97 one star. I have repeated this exercise in *The Wines of Burgundy*. Within the Côte d'Or again, we now have 11 three-star estates, 29 two-stars, and 99 one-stars. Overall, there are now more than 50 percent more domaines worthy of a star rating than there were 10 years ago. This is good for Burgundy and good for the customer, and it shows the progress that has been made in the last decade.

BURGUNDY: THE ARCANE AND THE FRAGMENTED

Burgundy is considered complicated, difficult, and confusing. It is certainly complex, with an extraordinary variety of individual vineyards, estates, and winemaking styles and techniques crammed into a very small region.

In the Côte d'Or there are some 5,550 hectares producing some 250,000 hectoliters (2.75 million cases) of wine a year (all figures exclude generics), of which 75 percent is red wine from the Pinot Noir grape and 25 percent is white wine from the Chardonnay grape. There are two village-overlapping appellations (Côte-de-Beaune-Villages and Côte-de-Nuits-Villages), and twenty-five village appellations, most of which can produce both red and white wine (plus Côte-de-Beaune, not to be confused with the above). Within the villages there are a total of 539 premiers crus, probably an equal number of *lieux-dits* which are not premiers crus and thirty-two grands crus. Moreover, there are quite a number of special wine place-names

189

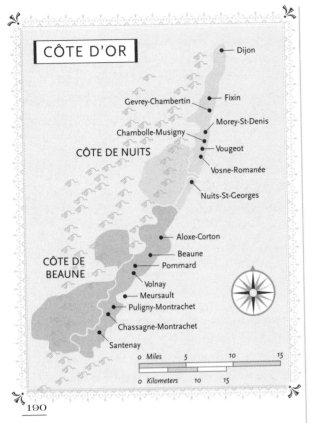

spread over a number of different *climats*, producing everything from various generics to, if they are lucky, grands crus. And of course the quantities of each wine produced will be miniscule, in Bordeaux terms. Château Lafite produces 21,000 cases a year of *grand vin* and 15,000 cases of Carruades. Romanée-Conti the vineyard yields 540 cases and Romanée-Conti the domaine 8,310. A typical top Burgundian domaine, today marketing most of its produce in bottle—although a little may be sold off in bulk at the outset to help with the cash flow—would probably be one like that of Michel Lafarge in Volnay, which comprises only 11.5 hectares, but commercializes fifteen different wines.

individual to particular growers—such as Bouchard Père et Fils' Vigne de l'Enfant Jesus, from Beaune's premier cru Les Grèves, or Louis Latour's Château Corton-Grancey.

While there are a couple of dozen important monopolies—whole appellations or vineyards within the fief of a single owner—most vineyards (or *climats*, to use the Burgundian expression) are divided up among a number of individual owners. The most commonly cited example of this is the 50-hectare Clos-de-Vougeot, which has 100 plots and eighty owners, with an average of 62 acres each.

It is this fragmentation which causes the confusion. Unlike Bordeaux, an area of large estates producing (usually) a single *grand vin*, Burgundy is a region of small domaines

Burgundy seems perplexing because of its nomenclature. During the 80 or so years after 1848—Gevrey was the first, Morey the last—the Côte d'Or villages complicated matters by tagging the name of their best vineyard onto that of the village, in order to raise the prestige of these lesser wines. Thus Gevrey became Gevrey-Chambertin, and Aloxe, Aloxe-Corton, while both Puligny and Chassagne chose Montrachet, whose *climat* straddles their borders, as a suffix. Meanwhile in Gevrey, but thankfully only in that commune, certain *climats*, later to be confirmed as grands crus, claimed Chambertin, to which they were contiguous, also as a suffix. Thus Gevrey-Chambertin is a village, Charmes-Chambertin a grand cru. The only solution to these complications is knowledge.

There is another tradition, now a legal rule, which needs appreciation. The thirty-two grands crus exist in their own right. No further geographical clarification is necessary. A name such as Le Musigny says it all. The premier cru and *lieu-dit* designations, on the other hand, need to be preceded and qualified by the name of the village. Thus, a wine from Les Amoureuses is described as Chambolle-Musigny, Les Amoureuses, with or without (this is optional) the mention that the *climat* is a premier cru. Each premier and grand cru is an appellation in its own right.

So if Burgundy seems difficult to comprehend at first, a little perseverance will soon clarify matters. And the solution to the fact that, on the face of it, a number of people seem to be offering the same wine is to understand that, even more than the geographical origin, it is the name of the domaine which made the wine that is important. Bordeaux châteaux names are brand names, and the top ones have a classification, which is a help to the consumer, even if that of 1855 is somewhat out of date. It is the land in Burgundy, not the winemaker or his estate, which is classified. The classification is based on geographical possibility, not on the quality in the bottle. And there are good winemakers and bad. One grower's Chambertin can be sublime, another's beneath contempt.

191

CÔTES DU RHÔNE

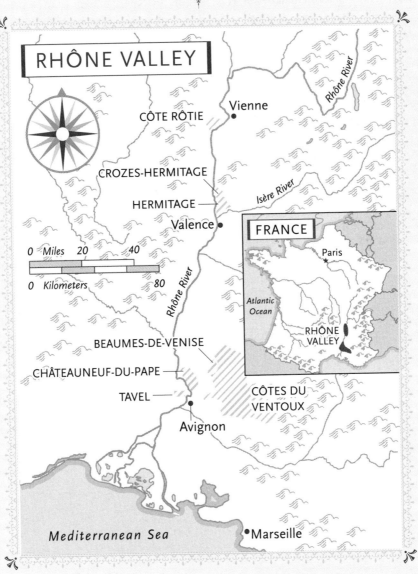

RHÔNE VALLEY

CÔTE RÔTIE

Vienne

CROZES-HERMITAGE

HERMITAGE

Valence

Rhône River

Isère River

Rhône River

FRANCE

Paris

Atlantic
Ocean

RHÔNE
VALLEY

BEAUMES-DE-VENISE

CHÂTEAUNEUF-DU-PAPE

TAVEL

Avignon

CÔTES DU
VENTOUX

0   Miles   20   40

0   Kilometers   80

Mediterranean Sea

Marseille

ONE OF MY GREAT EXPERIENCES OF VISITING the Rhône Valley in France was seeing the village of Châteauneuf-du-Pape, which means "new house of the Pope." The major period in history that the Vatican was not located in Rome began in 1309 when Pope Clement V, who was the archbishop of Bordeaux, moved the papal court to the Rhône Valley city of Avignon. For the next seventy years, seven popes ruled the Catholic Church from France. This period is sometimes referred to as the Avignon Schism, and at one point in time there were actually two popes (one French and one Italian). This was a very difficult time for the Catholic Church, with much dissension and controversy over legitimate popes and "antipopes."

The Rhône is separated geographically into two regions, southern and northern. Northern Rhône's most famous regions are Hermitage, Crozes-Hermitage, and Côte Rôtie. The south's most famous appellations are Châteauneuf-du-Pape and Gigondas. Some of the oldest vineyards in all of France are located in the Rhône Valley. One, Hermitage, has been in existence for almost two thousand years!

The AOC requires that all Côtes du Rhône wines have at least 10.5 percent alcohol, while specific appellations such as Châteauneuf-du-Pape require at least 12.5 percent. Ninety-one percent of all wines made in the Côtes du Rhône are red. Grenache and Syrah are the two dominant grapes of the region, but Cinsault and Mourvedre also play significant roles.

Rhône wines are usually bigger, deeper, and more robust than the Burgundian reds of the north. The Côtes du Rhône is located just north of the city of Avignon. Because of its southerly location, the region gets warmer breezes (known as the Mistral) near the Mediterranean Sea. The Côtes du Rhône gets more days of sun than northern regions. The vineyards here are covered in stones, which help retain heat after the sun goes down, resulting in higher alcohol levels and stronger flavors.

—KZ

SOUTHERN RHÔNE VALLEY

Kermit Lynch

Rhône wine, we say, but it is badly said because a Rhône wine can be red, white, or pink, sweet or dry, still or sparkling. It can be from one grape variety or a blend of several. It can be among the handful of France's noblest wines, or it can be a simple wine whose proper place would be in a carafe alongside a quick steak and french fries.

Rhône tastings are conducted in which such diverse wines as Gigondas, Saint-Joseph, Hermitage, Châteauneuf-du-Pape, and Côtes du Rhône are tasted blind, as they say, then judged and ranked. Such a grouping has a single characteristic in common: the grapes that produced them are grown near or somewhat near the Rhône River. There is as much difference between a Gigondas and a Saint-Joseph as there is between a Saint-Joseph and a Beaujolais, yet blind tasters would never square off a Saint-Joseph against a Beaujolais. The fact that Gigondas and Saint-Joseph are lumped together in Rhône tastings is a symptom of confusion,

an unfortunate confusion, because each wine expresses itself in its own language, and in the Babel-like jumble of such a blind tasting one misses what each has to say. The

winner is usually the most powerful wine, the one that speaks in the loudest voice, so one leaves having learned nothing.

Sorting out the Rhône is not difficult, and several wine books explain the different *appellations*. Dividing the Rhône into north and south is the first step. Such a division is altogether practical and natural. The two regions,

---

I have always had a tremendous admiration for the wine selections and writing style of Kermit Lynch. He began his wine career as a retailer in California and then began importing small artisanal-style wines from known and unknown wine regions of France. He is now a part owner of Domaine les Pallières in Gigondas. A true lover of all wines, he spends half of his time in Berkeley and the other half in Provence.

north and south, are about an hour's drive apart. There are profound differences between the two in terms of landscape, soil, climate, and grape varieties employed (although they overlap a bit as we shall see), and finally in the taste of the wines themselves.

South of Lyons (the French spell it Lyon), a few hundred yards past the limits of the old Roman city of Vienne, the vineyards of the northern Rhône commence in grand fashion with the Côte Rôtie, or "roasted hill." For the great *appellations* of the north, it is best to keep in mind two dominating factors: *Syrah*, which is the only red grape permitted, and *steep*, because the vines are planted on dramatic terraced hillsides that rise from the narrow valley floor. One does not see these dazzling carved mountainsides in the southern Rhône. The dominant grape variety in the southern reds is the *Grenache*, which is usually blended with other varieties, and the terrain is comparatively *flat*.

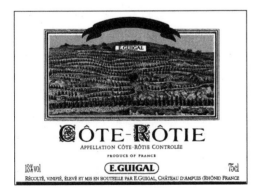

The northern Rhône consists of a long, narrow, stingy stretch of vineyards along the river between Vienne and Valence, the source of such exalted growths as Côte Rôtie, Hermitage, Saint-Joseph, and Cornas. I hesitate to include Crozes-Hermitage because the committee that defines the limits of the controlled *appellations* has allowed commerce to be its guide, and most Crozes today comes from flat, sandy soil. An extraordinary Crozes is hard to find, and it is objectionable that the growers have the right to tack Hermitage onto their name.

By contrast, the southern Rhône is a vast, productive, almost circle-shaped area, and here one finds the vineyards of Châteauneuf-du-Pape, Gigondas, Tavel, Cairanne, Rasteau, and countless others. The most important city of the southern Rhône is Avignon, but the most important for the wine lover is Châteauneuf-du-Pape.

In terms of worldwide renown and prestige, Châteauneuf-du-Pape is the greatest *appellation* in southern France, which is not to say that it is always the source of the finest wine. A perfect Côtes du Rhône will inspire more pleasure than a badly made Châteauneuf-du-Pape. It is well to remember that the system of Appellation d'Origine Contrôlée (AOC) is not a rating, not a judgment of the wine in bottle, but a definition of the terrain, the soil, the grape varieties . . . the raw materials!

Over the years, wine writers have yielded to the temptation to classify the top domaines of Châteauneuf-du-Pape much as the Bordeaux châteaux were classified in 1855. However easier such a ranking might appear to make the life of the wine consumer by helping him decide what to buy, such a classification is dangerous work. In 1832 a French writer, A. Jullien, placed La Nerthe at the top of the Châteauneuf-du-Papes. More recently an American author, Robert Parker Jr., left La Nerthe out of the top category

195

and rated Vieux Télégraphe, Beaucastel, and Fortia grand cru classé. Vieux Télégraphe's vines are planted on a very privileged site. Thanks to this site, their vinification, and their consistency, it is one of the two or three finest domaines producing Châteauneuf-du-Pape today. But what is to prevent Vieux Télégraphe from buying another block of vines in a less privileged part of the *appellation* in order to pump out more wine and take advantage of the commercial possibilities created by their new grand cru status?

Classifying a domaine or a château rather than the soil or terrain misses the point. Rating the specific vineyards of Châteauneuf-du-Pape is a good idea, overdue, in fact, because the area of the *appellation* is so enormous (over seven thousand acres) and includes nobler and less noble sites. If domaines had plots of vines in several parts of the *appellation*, which is often the case, they would have to vinify their grand cru separately if they wanted to name it on their label. A perfect example of such a system can be found in Burgundy. La Romanée-Conti (the vineyard) is a grand cru, but the Domaine de la Romanée-Conti (the winery) is not. If it were, the proprietors could bottle a simple Bourgogne *rouge* and call it grand cru.

Henri Brunier of Vieux Télégraphe agrees that the vineyard site is of supreme importance. The source of his wine's quality, he says, is his stony terrain, situated upon the slope of the highest ridge in the Châteauneuf-du-Pape *appellation*. Because of the superior elevation, it was on this ridge that a telegraph tower was constructed in the eighteenth century, one of the relay points for communications between Paris and Marseilles. The crumbling stone ruin of this tower gave Vieux Télégraphe its name, and there is a rendering of it on the domaine's label. To the eye there is no soil here and one would think it is barren, but living vines poke out from the thick layer of smooth, oval stones. Walking the Côte Rôtie vineyards, one is impressed by the difficulty of climbing such steep hills. In Brunier's vineyard it is hard to walk because the stones slip and slide underfoot. An unreal landscape, it sticks in the mind like the volcanic Kona coast of Hawaii or the surface of the moon. It is totally unprotected from the elements. I have been there in the summer when the stones are too hot to touch. I have heard the sound of vine branches cracking in a fierce mistral. Nowhere does the mistral blow with such force. It can knock you over, and when it turns cold, the mistral cuts right through you. You cannot move your fingers, your teeth chatter, your nose and ears turn red. You are glad you are an importer who can head for the fireplace and a glass of Vieux Télégraphe and not the poor fellow out there pruning the vines.

One visitor from California revealed perhaps the difference between the American and French mentality when he asked, "Why did they move all those stones into the vineyard?" The French cultivated this ridiculously stony site, this nearly impossible surface, because it gives a special character to the wine. Typically American would be to plant on the valley floor and use land-moving equipment to move in a layer of stones.

They look like Sierra riverbed stones and were formed by the same geological process. They are glacial deposits, shattered and shaped by the weight and crunch of the glacier's movement, then rounded and polished by the flow of water as the ice melted.

One tastes the influence of the stones in the wine. Experienced tasters in the area recognize a Vieux Télégraphe by its expression of *pierre à feu*, or gunflint. A great Châteauneuf-du-Pape tastes almost as if it had been filtered through the stones, and indeed rainwater is filtered by this thick stone layer before it reaches the underlying soil which nourishes the plants. In addition, the stones account for Vieux Télégraphe's characteristic power and generosity

because they reflect and collect heat, and it is believed that during the ripening season this store of warmth works throughout the night contributing to the grapes' maturity. Brunier considers adding some sandier parcels to his holding because in hot years he wonders if his wine is not too alcoholic, lacking perhaps a certain finesse, which a proportion of less-ripe grapes would palliate. Americans who buy Vieux Télégraphe are not at all of this opinion. The hottest years producing the strongest wines, such as 1983, are the object of a real buyers' scramble. A more elegant vintage like 1984, by no means a light wine and which Brunier prefers to his massive 1983, is slower to disappear from the shelves.

One is immediately at ease with Henri Brunier. He typifies the Provençal qualities of warmth, friendliness, and candor. The rugged cut to his features and his ruddy, sunbaked cheeks attest to the years he has spent outdoors with his vines. He looks the way the winemaker of a robust wine like Vieux Télégraphe should look.

When he shows off his new vinification cellar, completed in 1979, he stands back with his hands on his hips gazing up at the towering stainless-steel *cuves* like a sculptor regarding a grand new work. "*Eh, voilà*," he says, as if letting the installation speak for itself. He is still awed by his creation. The envy of many of his neighbors because it is so rational and functional, Brunier's new winery permits him unusual control over the elaboration of his wine no matter what the vagary of the vintage. Each harvest means different problems, yet most winemakers are predestined to a certain vinification by

197

virtue of the equipment at hand. Their vinification will be essentially the same whether the grapes are shriveled, thick-skinned, and sugary, or plump with water from unseasonal showers. Brunier's cellar is built up against the hillside next to his house. The grapes arrive at the rear and enter on conveyer belts, a rather gentle reception. They can be partially or totally destemmed, or not at all. They can be partially or totally crushed, or left intact. Henri is free to decide according to the constitution of each variety as it arrives. By an ingenious system of movable bins, the grapes then fall directly into whichever vat he chooses, without having suffered the stress of mechanical pumping. Once the must is in the fermentation tank, Henri can control its temperature, which is of exceeding importance in the south of France, where it is often brutally hot during the harvest. In 1985, for example, many growers saw their wines cooked right from the start because temperatures soared in the vats during an unusually ebullient fermentation. The result is a wine lacking freshness and fruit and marred by excessive volatile acidity. At Vieux Télégraphe, Brunier kept the fermenting mash down around 30 degrees centigrade, and his wine shows splendidly ripe fruit without a trace of volatility.

Dwarfed by this costly, gleaming, high-tech facility, one might imagine that Brunier had forsaken the chewy, old-style wine that made his reputation . . . until he explains that here the wine spends only the first twelve to fifteen days, the most tumultuous days, of its life. It could be compared to an obstetrics ward, because during this initial fermentation a wine is born and it can develop certain faults or virtues that will remain with it and mark its personality.

The second fermentation, the malolactic fermentation, takes place in glass-lined tanks under the most sanitary conditions possible. Brunier then has a clean, healthy wine which is racked into his huge oak casks, or *foudres*— the traditional aging vessel of the Rhône—to develop slowly for six to eighteen months.

When I arrive in the fall after the new vintage has finished the initial fermentation, we begin our business by tasting the new wine drawn directly from the glass-lined tanks. There are several cuvées to taste. The final assemblage will occur when the wine is racked into the oak foudres.

We usually begin with a cuvée of 100 percent Grenache. The aroma is reminiscent of pit fruits, like cherry, plum, and apricot. Certain years produce a sumptuousness that is blackberry-like. Typically, there is an extravagance of alcohol (sometimes between 15 and 16 degrees) and a lack of acidity. The wine fills the mouth, but there is no center.

The next sample is from a cuvée with a high proportion of Syrah. Disputes occur because I often arrive with the aftertaste still lingering from tastings of the noble Syrahs of the northern Rhône. The Syrah expresses itself in more vulgar terms in the southern soil and climate, where it seems more peppery and earthy, often leaden with rude tannins. The Bruniers see the violets and raspberry, the stuffing and length of it.

Mourvèdre dominates the next cuvée with its wilder (the French say *sauvage*), more vegetal aromas of *garrigue* and herb. The Bruniers value the Mourvèdre for its structure, nervosity, and, in contrast to the Grenache, its resistance to oxidation. However, there is also a sapid, delicious fruitiness recalling black cherries picked ripe off the tree, and an intriguing soulfulness, a darker, more mysterious nature than expressed by the pure Grenache. Mourvèdre has a leaner, intense feel to it, and in fact it normally ripens to only 12.5 degrees to 13 degrees alcohol.

Brunier still has some Cinsault in his vineyard, but little of it is destined for the final *assemblage* of what will be sold as Vieux Télégraphe. For the most part, it is blended with Syrah to make the Bruniers' everyday house wine. A pure Cinsault passes over the taste buds without sticking, almost like water.

In a normal year Vieux Télégraphe is 75 percent Grenache, 15 percent Syrah, and 10 percent Mourvèdre. Recently, they planted five more acres of Mourvèdre, which, when the vines are old enough, will significantly alter the proportion of Mourvèdre in the final assemblage.

Then we move into the old cellars to taste the previous vintage. The walls are humid and moldy, lined with *foudres*. From twelve to twenty *foudres* contain wine, depending on the size of the year's crop. Each *foudre* differs in size, but the average in Brunier's cellar holds about seven thousand bottles of wine.

Henri's son Daniel does the work of drawing the samples from the *foudres*. He has a robust, self-assured presence like his father. In his mid-twenties, he is curly-haired and well built, with a firm cut to his jaw. He has an irrepressible mischievous streak that grows more and more effective as he learns how to disguise it behind a serious expression. "Which one do you want to taste?" he asks, tossing a glance at the row of casks.

"Well, all of them," I reply.

He grimaces. "They're all the same."

"Let's taste them and see."

Theoretically, each *foudre* contains the same wine because the final blend was made when the *foudres* were filled. However, the *foudre* itself has an influence, subtle or profound, on the wine as it ages. Therefore, I like to taste each and select the ones to be bottled and shipped to me.

Daniel grabs the wooden ladder and slams it up against a *foudre*. He pounds down on it once or twice to make sure it is secure, and climbs up on top, crawling between the cask and the roof.

All of us taste, Henri, Daniel, his brother Frédéric, and I, but they don't contribute much in the way of opinion. I wish they would because they certainly know their wine better than I do. On the other hand, they appreciate *all* their offspring. How often do you hear a father say, "This child I don't like"? And perhaps they like to stand back and judge my judgments.

Each sample means Daniel must scramble up and down the ladder one-handed because he has to carry the glass "thief" with which he draws the wine from the top of the cask. After the fifth or sixth cuvée he starts acting like it is a real pain in the ass, but over the years it is always the same routine; it is a playful pose for the sake of his father and brother.

Henri says, "*C'est bon, ça,*" about one cuvée, "This has the aroma," about another. If I comment that one *foudre* seems to me the

199

most complete, he says, "That cask always makes a good wine, but it really is strange because they were all exactly the same to begin with." Each year he seems to learn anew that the evolution within each *foudre* is different.

As usual, when we went through the 1984s I jotted down a quick note on each *foudre* to remind me later on of the differences among the twelve to twenty tasted:

1. Spicy, a bit hard.
2. Lacks nerve.
3. Closed. Excellent palate. Finishes dry.
4. Nose lacks charm.
5. Spice and black pepper. Ripe, stony, long.
6. Most complete so far. Spicy, vibrant, deep, long.
7. Closed. Quite round but finishes abruptly.
8. Still full of CO_2. Difficult to judge today.
9. Deep purple. Classic V.T. nose. Powerful, tannic, long.
10. Short.
11. Well balanced, a bit dumb.
12. A bit tarry; lacks finesse.
13. Lovely robe. Finesse. Typical flavors. Finishes a bit short.

And so it continues. Finally Daniel marks *foudres* 5, 6, and 9 with a KL in chalk. One cannot say that I necessarily receive the best. For one thing, returning three months later, I might replace one of my selections with #8, which was that day so difficult to judge. Or another might develop unexpected qualities, which often happens. Finally, it would be surprising to find two tasters who could agree on a ranking of so many similar wines.

However, I do get my preference, which adds a certain personal involvement to my work.

When I reminded them to bottle my *foudres* without filtering, our annual to-filter-or-not-to-filter discussion begins. With the 1982 vintage they began bottling my selections unfiltered, but the rest of their production was filtered. We have been arguing filtration a long time. Daniel sums up their position when he says, "There are filtrations and then there are filtrations. And then there is the system we use. It doesn't change the wine at all,"

"If it doesn't change the wine, why do it?" I ask.

"Just to take out the heaviest sediment."

"Oh, you have a filter that thinks, that looks through the constituents of your wine and decides what needs removing? That is quite an advanced system."

Then they surprise me by pulling out two bottles of 1983. "One is filtered, one unfiltered," says Frédéric, the quiet Brunier whose expression tells you more than his utterances.

For years I have been waiting for just such a face-to-face comparison. Bizarre as it seems, it is the first time I have been provided with two glasses of the same wine, one filtered, the other unfiltered. Up to this moment, my lecturing winemakers all over France has been theoretical. One would think all winemakers would bottle such samples as a matter of course in order to experience with their eyes, noses, and palates the results of their manipulations.

The entire family is assembled for our blind comparison. Maggie Brunier leaves her *pot-au-feu* on the stove to join us. There is silence as we taste, then a secret ballot.

"It is unanimous," Daniel announces, and pauses dramatically. "The unfiltered wins."

What a victory! It is not astonishing, after all, because the difference between the two bottles was striking. The filtered was a limpid, one-dimensional ruby color, boring to the eye. The unfiltered was deeper-colored, shimmering with glints of purple and black.

The filtered smelled as clean as it looked, but what little nose it had seemed superficial compared to the unfiltered, and it gave an impression of fatigue, which is not illogical because filtration involves pumping, or pushing, the wine through a long series of cardboardlike plaques. The less you work a wine, the more vitality it retains. The unfiltered had a deep, healthy aroma. One might say that its aroma had *texture*; it seemed dense and full of nuances of spice and fruit. It smelled as good as the wine fresh out of the *foudre*.

On the palate, too, the filtered bottle lacked texture. It had body, but it didn't coat the taste buds with flavor like the unfiltered, which was chewy and substantial.

The difference in the aftertaste was dramatic. The filtered wine clunked dryly to a halt. In the unfiltered, the typical Vieux Télégraphe perfumes kept returning.

The Bruniers are keeping a stock of each bottling in order to compare the evolution over the years.

The difference between the two was dramatized by the face-to-face comparison. The filtered is not a bad wine. The Bruniers are conscientious and skilled; they do not practice severe or sterile filtrations.

However, side by side, the filtered seemed merely decent, the unfiltered grand. There was more wine in the wine!

"But look at this," Henri says, and he holds up to the light an unopened bottle of the unfiltered. "That's what I don't like, that *petite tache*."

There was a *petite tache*, or smudge of deposit, that had settled on the underside of the bottle. Already. Even though the wine had very recently been bottled.

"What's wrong with that, Henri?"

"It's worrisome."

"It's nothing. I like it. it shows that you respect your wine too much to subject it to filtration."

"The clients don't like it."

"Wait, I'm a client and I like it. For someone who doesn't understand fine wine you are going to trade the color, the aroma, texture, and flavor for a spotless appearance?"

"What can one do? They return bottles like this. They think the wine is not clean." He shrugs helplessly.

"Don't sell to clients like that," I insist. I could see that even after my secret-ballot victory the battle was not yet won. "Almost all my reds arrive now with this *petite tache*. People who love wine prefer to have it intact, even if it means there is a little sediment, which falls harmlessly to the bottom anyway. You watch, Henri. Soon it will be fashionable, the sign of a serious winemaker, to bottle without filtering. Your customers will be demanding an unfiltered wine."

Daniel speaks up. "We'll have to uncork our bottles and add a little deposit to make them happy!"

It is a relief to terminate with laughter what is actually a dispute of passionate importance to both of us.

One must not have the impression that the problem of filtration is easy to resolve. It is not as simple as saying, "I shall, or shall not, filter." Foremost is the problem in the marketplace. If a vintner chooses not to filter, he limits himself to the minority of wine buyers, the true connoisseurs who care about quality and will accept some gunk at the bottom of the bottle. For superstar producers like Brunier, the problem is not as big as he makes it out to be, because there is never enough Vieux Télégraphe to supply the demand. He has certainly reached the point at which he can choose his clientele and bottle the finest, most natural wine possible.

But there is also the question of how to bottle a wine without filtering. One cannot proceed just like that, leaving out the filter. Above all, it is a matter of clarification by natural methods: fining, racking, and time, allowing the unwanted material to fall to the bottom of the cask and drawing off the clear wine. The ancients understood how to do it; they had to because they had no filters. However, today's is a hurry-up world, time is money, and fining and racking require more patience, care, and attention than mashing one's wine through a filter pad.

Also, winemakers in France pay a tax on their stock. Thus, today's scarcity of old bottles and the rush to bottle and sell as quickly as possible. Châteauneuf-du-Pape used to spend three to four years in *foudre*. Some growers today bottle before a year has passed. No one likes taxes, especially a Frenchman.

Vieux Télégraphe was not filtered until the 1979 vintage. One might claim that they earned their reputation with unfiltered wine, but in fact very little Vieux Télégraphe was bottled at the domaine until the 1978 vintage. For the most part, it had been sold in bulk to négociants.

The domaine's origins go back to the turn of the century, according to Henri. "My grandfather, Hippolyte Brunier, was a peasant, meaning he lived off the land. He grew melons, lettuce, almonds, apricots, wheat, and he had two acres of vines in the heart of this plateau, which was known as the Royaume des Craux." (Royaume means realm or kingdom. Crau is an arid plateau dressed in stones which supports little in the way of vegetation.)

"My grandfather put a little of his wine in bottle. He saw that it pleased the clients, so he and my uncle purchased another forty acres. Forty acres of *garrigue*, scrubland, woods. After the first war, they began to transform it to vines. My grandfather worked the land, my uncle handled the business side of it, and my father built the original *chais* with his own hands."

Henri began working with them in 1940 at age seventeen. During World War II, they acquired additional acreage. "It was cheap. No one wanted it. There was no market for wine then. Some simply gave us their land. It was believed worthless because it was covered with scrub. To clear it by hand . . . Then you Americans arrived and introduced us to the bulldozer." He lets out a deep chuckle. "And then, after the war, people began to ask for the wine again.

"When I sold my wine to the négoci-ants, I always received the highest price," he says proudly. "Our wine was called a *vin de médecin* because the négociants used it to remedy the ills of their less successful cuvées."

Henri Brunier is a proud man without a trace of haughtiness or self-importance. Such a man, who rightfully takes pleasure in his achievements, is rare and a joy to behold. With so many people who have attained success, one has the impression that their thirst for it will never be quenched because they never take the time to celebrate their

blessings. Above all, the source of Henri's pride is his family; they are close yet notably individualistic and independent, and they love him. As he surveys the great plateau, the Royaume des Craux, one sees his pride now that it is planted and productive. He succeeded in introducing modern tech-nology into his cellar without compromising the robust, old-fashioned character of his wine. He guided the commercialization away from bulk sales toward domaine bottling with his name on the label. And you see his pride when he says, "It is a wine that pleases."

CHAMPAGNE

CHAMPAGNE

ENGLAND

BELGIUM

LUX. GERMANY

Seine River

Paris ★

CHAMPAGNE

Atlantic
Ocean

FRANCE

SWITZERLAND

ITALY

0 Miles   300

0 Kilometers   300

SPAIN

Mediterranean Sea

~ WHEN TO DRINK ~ CHAMPAGNE

Champagne is ready to drink as soon as you buy it. Nonvintage Champagnes are meant to be drunk within two to three years, and vintage and prestige cuvée Champagnes can be kept longer, about ten to fifteen years. So if you're still saving that Dom Pérignon that you received for your tenth wedding anniversary fifteen years ago, don't wait any longer. Open it!

I SPEND A LOT OF TIME IN CHAMPAGNE because of its proximity to Paris. It is a must visit every time I'm there even if it is just a day trip, which can easily be done by train to Epernay. Champagne has the most fascinating and natural cellars in the world with miles upon miles of underground cellars going down hundreds of feet below the surface of the white chalk soil. On one of my visits I heard what I thought were gunshots and our guide quickly led us into an inner tunnel. The "shooting" lasted for about five minutes. Fortunately, no one "died" since it was the Champagne bottles themselves that were exploding. With 90 pounds per square inch of pressure, Champagne producers lose over a million bottles a year due to breakage. So if you are going to visit the cellars of Champagne, the first thing you must do is look for a place to hide!

Champagne, first and foremost, is a region in France. The country's northernmost winemaking region, to be exact—and it's an hour and a half northeast of Paris. Why do I stress its northern location? Because this affects the taste of the wines. In the Champagne region, the grapes are picked with higher acidity than in most other regions, which is one of the reasons for Champagne's distinct taste.

In my opinion, the Champagne region of France makes the best sparkling wine in the world. The region has the ideal combination of elements conducive to excellent sparkling winemaking. The soil is chalk, and the grapes (Pinot Noir, Chardonnay, and Pinot Meunier) are the best grown anywhere in the world for sparkling wine. The houses of Champagne have worked tirelessly for centuries honing an image for their region and their wine. Several of the great houses, for example Veuve Clicquot, started shipping their wines thousands of miles around the world, creating markets and inspiring enthusiastic loyalists as far back as the late 1700s.

> ⁓ **OPENING** ⁓
> **CHAMPAGNE CORRECTLY**
>
> 1. Chill the bottle well before opening it.
> 2. Cut the foil around the top of the bottle.
> 3. Place your hand on top of the cork, never removing your hand until the cork is pulled out completely.
> 4. Undo the wire. Either leave it on the cork or take it off carefully.
> 5. Carefully put a cloth napkin over the top of the cork. If the cork pops, it will go safely into the napkin.
> 6. Remove the cork gently, slowly turning the bottle in one direction and the cork in another. Cracking open the bottle with a loud pop and letting it foam, rather than easing out the cork gently, allows the escape of the carbon dioxide that gives Champagne its sparkle. A bottle opened gently can be opened hours before your guests arrive with no loss of carbon dioxide.

Today, *Champagne* is a brand name that can be applied only to wines made within that region. Some American producers have borrowed the name *Champagne* to put on the label of their sparkling wines. These cannot and should not be compared with Champagne from France.

The Champagne region is divided into four main areas: the Valley of the Marne, Côte des Blancs, the Mountain of Reims, and Côte des Bar. Three grapes can be used to produce Champagne: Pinot Noir (red) accounts for 38 percent of all grapes planted; Pinot Meunier (red) accounts for 35 percent of all grapes planted; Chardonnay (white) accounts for 27 percent of all grapes planted.

There are three major types of Champagne. *Nonvintage/multiple vintage* is a blend of two or more harvests: 60 to 80 percent of the base wine comes from the current harvest and 20 to 40 percent of the wine comes from previous vintages. *Vintage Champagne* is a bottling of a single vintage. The most expensive champagne is called *prestige cuvée*. This designation assures a higher quality of grape and requires longer aging.

There are five main differences between nonvintage and prestige cuvée Champagnes. Prestige Champagnes are usually made from the best grapes of the highest-rated villages; made from the first pressing of the grapes; aged longer in the bottle than nonvintage Champagnes; made only in vintage years; and made in small quantity. Price is dictated largely by supply and demand.

I am often asked, "How do I buy

~ WHICH GLASSES ~ SHOULD CHAMPAGNE BE SERVED IN?

There are three classic shapes: the coupe, the flute, and the tulip. For centuries, the glass of choice was the coup, said first to be molded in the shape of the breasts of Helen of Troy, and later molded to fit the more buxom Marie Antoinette, Queen of France.

Despite the rich heritage of the coupe, today's more favored glass is the flute. The coup's wide brim dispels quickly the effervescence of the wine. The flute and the tulip-shaped glasses form the wine into more of a column, with less wine-to-air ratio, slowing down the escape of the bubbles inside and ensuring longer sparkling. It also focuses more of the aroma of the wine to the nose.

or find a good Champagne?" First determine which style you prefer most. Do you like sparkling wine to be full-bodied or light-bodied? Then buy your Champagne from a reliable shipper/producer. Each producer takes pride in its distinctive house style, and strives for a consistent blend, year after year.

Sparkling wine is produced in many areas of the world outside Champagne, and the quality varies from country to country. The Spanish produce sparkling wines, known as *cavas*: the popular Codorniu and Freixenet are both excellent values and of good quality. The German version is called *Sekt*. Italy has *spumante*, which means "sparkling," and also Prosecco, which is the name of a sparkling-wine grape grown primarily in the Veneto region. New York State and California are the two main producers of sparkling wine in the United States.

—KZ

PUTTING ON THE STYLE

Tom Stevenson

Contrary to belief in some parts of the world, Champagne is not a generic term for any sparkling wine; it is the protected name of a sparkling wine produced from certain grape varieties grown within a specific, demarcated area of northern France. If not all sparkling wines are Champagne, then it is equally true that Champagne is not just one style of wine. There are many different styles, from the most basic division between vintage and non-vintage, to *blanc de blancs, blanc de noirs, rosé, crémant,* non-dosage (extra brut), prestige *cuvées,* red, sweeter styles, and aromatic styles. This applies to sparkling wines wherever they are produced.

NON-VINTAGE

In theory this is a blend of wines from two or more years, although many Champagne growers also sell a wine from a single year as non-vintage, which is perfectly legal because they are not actually claiming it comes from any particular year. Non-vintage sparkling wines are common in Europe, especially Champagne, but they are almost non-existent in parts of the New World where the connotation of a vintage is such that a product not bearing one is automatically deemed inferior.

In Champagne a non-vintage blend is always based on wines made from the current harvest, to which the reserve wines are added, so providing the second most fundamental level of potential complexity to a sparkling wine (the first level being achieved by blending different grapes and areas), and a certain instant maturity. The amount and age of the reserve wines can vary from just 5 or 10 percent of wine from the previous year, to 40 or 50 percent from six or seven vintages going back 15 years or more.

The term "non-vintage" sounds derogatory to many people, yet a blend of different

When it comes to Champagne, Tom Stevenson is your go-to guy. His credentials are outstanding—author of twenty-three books, he also created and was the editor for the annual Wine Report. He has received some of the top awards given to wine writers, including the Wine Literary Award, America's only lifetime achievement award for wine writing. This piece gives some insight about the style of Champagne.

years is the most classic of Champagnes, and the equivalent French term of *sans année* or "without year" provides a subtle but important difference in emphasis. All good non-vintage Champagnes benefit from an extra year or two cellarage and the very greatest (often prestige *cuvées* that are referred to as a multi-vintage or a blend of vintage years) can improve for as long as a great vintage Champagne.

VINTAGE

Vintage Champagne must by law be 100 percent from the year indicated, but other sparkling wines in the EU need only be 85 percent (which, ironically, is more of a blend than some non-vintage Champagne *cuvées*!). Elsewhere it varies; 95 percent in California, 85 percent in Australia, 75 percent in South Africa, and so on. The vintage of any wines produced in a country with regulations that are not as strict as those in the EU must, however, be at least 85 percent if they are imported into any EU member state. The opposite applies in the USA where any imported wine merely has to conform to the standards set in the country of origin, even if they are inferior to domestic American regulations.

The implication of a vintage in Champagne is that the harvest in question was especially good and the wine produced does not require blending with other years. Some Champagne houses stick rigidly to declaring a vintage in only the greatest years, but many, sadly, do not, which is why we have seen vintage Champagnes from less than ideal years like 1978, 1980, and even 1984. There are certain cooperatives and growers who produce vintage Champagne virtually every year and in such circumstances the year merely becomes an indication of age, not quality. However, even in an authentic vintage, vintage Champagne is the result of selection and is thus a deliberate exaggeration, rather than a reflection, of the year in question. If vintage Champagne is superior to non-vintage, logic dictates that it is only because superior wines have been selected for its production; volume-selling non-vintage Champagnes are still produced in even the greatest vintages. Any reserve wines added in the blending of non-vintage Champagnes are supposed to improve the product, thus the only difference between vintage and non-vintage Champagnes produced from the same year can only be the selection process of the base wine.

The character of a vintage Champagne is more autolytic than a non-vintage of the same age because it has no reserve wine mellowness. If you like those biscuity or toasty bottle aromas then you must store the vintage until it is eight to ten years from the date of harvest and has had at least three years aging after it was purchased.

All the following styles of wine can also be either vintage or non-vintage.

Blanc de Blancs

Literally, "white of whites," a *blanc de blancs* simply means a white wine produced from white grapes, and it does not have to be sparkling. In Champagne this wine is produced entirely from Chardonnay, but for sparkling wines produced elsewhere it may be made from any white grape, either as a pure varietal or a blend.

A *blanc de blancs* Champagne possesses the greatest aging potential of all sparkling wines, and although it may be made from grapes grown in any district of the region, the best examples are made with grapes from a small part of the Côte des Blancs between Cramant and Les Mesnil-sur-Oger. Like the Côte des Blancs, the Côte de Sézanne also specializes in grapes for *blanc de blancs* Champagne, but the wines from these grapes are much more precocious, with attractive, tropical fruit flavors.

A classic *blanc de blancs* from the Côte des Blancs is a much tighter, more reserved style of wine that can appear to be austere and lacking in fruit in its youth. However, with sufficient age it develops a toasty richness that fills the mouth with a singular intensity of its fruit. Some of the classiest *blanc de blancs* from the best area of the Côte des Blancs develop a biscuity creaminess with complex aromas of hazelnuts, walnuts, or brazil nuts.

Outside Champagne, pure Chardonnay *blanc de blancs* are generally the most successful classic brut style sparkling wines.

Blanc de Noirs

Literally "white of blacks," a *blanc de noirs* simply means a white wine produced from black grapes, and it does not have to be sparkling. In Champagne this wine is produced from either Pinot Noir or Meunier, or a blend of the two, but for sparkling wines produced elsewhere it may be made from any black grape, either as a pure varietal or a blend.

Throughout the New World, and in California in particular, *blanc de noirs* is used to describe slightly colored wines that range from a sunset gold through various shades of rosé. But in France, where the term originated, the skill has always been to produce as light and as white a wine as possible by natural means.

In Champagne, a golden hue is acceptable, but any hint of pink would be regarded as clumsy by professional winemakers. The yardstick *blanc de noirs* Champagne is Bollinger's incredibly expensive Vieilles Vignes Françaises, a unique example of super-ripe grapes from ungrafted Pinot Noir vines. This famous wine has given people the notion that all *blanc de noirs* are big, burly wines, but nothing can compare with it, and most other *blanc de noirs* Champagnes are unremarkable.

Rosé

Champagne rosé is an anomaly in the EU wine law, as it is the only pink wine that may be made by blending white wine with a little red. All other rosés, whether still or sparkling, must be produced by macerating the juice and skins to extract pigments just as red wine itself is produced, but for a much shorter period. Some rosé Champagnes are, in fact, produced by maceration of the skins, but most are produced by adding a little red wine. Some critics believe that maceration is superior to blending white with red, but this is simply not true. It is possible to find good and poor quality examples produced by both methods, just as one can find rosé Champagnes that are light or dark in color, and rich or delicate in flavor. Whenever I hear someone claim that maceration is intrinsically superior, I always issue a challenge: I'll set up a blind tasting of 20 rosé Champagnes and you tell me which ones have been made by maceration—no one has ever taken me up on it!

If there are fairly common traits to pink Champagnes, whatever their method of production, it is that they have slightly less acidity than white Champagnes and are best drunk as young as possible. There are exceptions, of course, but the lower acidity is due to the higher Pinot content and/or the addition of red wine. The reason why most rosé Champagnes should be drunk young is not because they won't last, but because they generally have a delicate, floral, perfumed style that has nothing to gain from laying down other than turning orange.

Many houses simply add a little red wine to their basic non-vintage or vintage Champagne *cuvées,* which is a cop-out and generally tends to produce the least inspiring wines of this category. Pink Champagne is a style, albeit a most varied one, and every winemaker has a duty to make something specific. Furthermore, if the non-vintage or vintage *cuvée* is a balanced product, it cannot be properly balanced again after red wine has been added.

The trouble is that most Champenois do not take pink Champagne seriously—not even those who make the greatest pink Champagnes. In other sparkling wine areas the quality of this style is second only to that of *blanc de blancs*, but generally there is an inverted snobbery about rosé wines, whether they are still or sparkling.

Crémant

Although a traditional Champenois term, *crémant* disappeared from Champagne labels in the early 1990s by voluntary agreement. This occurred after the term was adopted for various French sparkling wines appellations, such as Crémant d'Alsace and Crémant de Bourgogne, following the EU ban on the use of the term *méthode champenoise*. Since only a small number of Champagne producers were actually using the term *crémant* at the time (just Besserat de Bellefon, Alfred Gratien, Abel Lepitre, Mumm de Cramant, and De Venoge spring to mind), having to drop it was of little commercial consequence, although historically it is a pity that it is no longer used in its appellation of origin. The few Champagne *crémants* that did exist are still made in the same style, and have merely been renamed. The most famous, Mumm's Crémant de Cramant, for example, is now sold as Mumm de Cramant.

A *crémant* should have a softer mousse; most Champagnes are fully sparkling or *grand mousseux*, with an internal pressure of between five and six atmospheres, but the old regulations determined that a Champagne *crémant* should have a pressure of just 3.6 atmospheres. To be a true *crémant,* however, it was not sufficient to have just a lower pressure; the word itself literally means "creaming" and the mousse should unfold slowly, leaving a creamy *cordon* at the top of the wine around the inside of the glass, something that is very difficult to achieve. Beyond the various French sparkling wine appellations, the term is occasionally seen elsewhere, but few producers have a reputation for the style.

Non-Dosage (Extra Brut)

This was a fad in the early 1980s, but not an entirely new one, as Laurent Perrier sold *"Grand Vin Sans Sucre"* over a century ago. Officially designated throughout the EU as Brut Extra or Extra Brut, this style has been commercially labeled variously as *Brut Zéro, Brut Savage, Ultra Brut,* and *Sans Sucre.* The late 20th century fashion for these wines emerged when consumers began seeking lighter, drier wines and were influenced by wine snobs who despised *Demi-Sec* and thought that Champagnes without any *dosage* must somehow be superior. Although such Champagnes still exist (most notably Laurent-Perrier Ultra-Brut and Piper-Heidsieck Brut Savage), most *cuvées* were austere, and lacked generosity, being tarts and unpleasant to drink. Furthermore, without a *dosage* a Brut Extra *cuvée* does not develop the mellow, complex bottle-aromas that devotees of mature Champagnes adore. Not surprisingly, the trend of these wines died a quick death, and the style has not taken off anywhere else.

Prestige Cuvées

These are the most expensive *cuvées* sold by sparkling wine producers. In Champagne, prestige *cuvées* are epitomized by the likes of Dom Pérignon, Roederer Cristal, and Belle Epoque, but are they the greatest sparkling wines you can buy or just a marketing opportunity to increase profit margins?

The most important common factor that defines a prestige *cuvée* is selection. It is, or should be, the ultimate expression of the strictest selection that a particular producer can undertake. If vintage Champagne is superior to non-vintage only because higher quality wines have been selected for its production, then selection must be even more important for a prestige *cuvée*. And whereas the wines selected for a vintage Champagne logically result in a deliberate exaggeration of the year in question, then it is rational to assume that the wines chosen for a prestige *cuvée* are selected to exaggerate the house style or winemaker's philosophy. This is why prestige *cuvées* are produced in tiny quantities which inevitably determines their high price.

The expensive price is not, therefore, a ploy to increase profit margins, although whether the wine is worth the money is another matter entirely. The best most certainly are, but intensive selection alone cannot produce a great sparkling wine. Selection for selection's sake easily leads to *cuvées* that are over-refined and lack the vibrant balance that makes great sparkling wine so exciting. Perversely, there comes a point when the greater the selection, the more difficult it is to blend a sparkling wine of any finesse. The key to any prestige *cuvée* is selection, selection, selection, but a great prestige *cuvée* still requires a great winemaker.

Red

This style is illegal in Champagne, where only rosé or white wines are permitted. However, there are no color intensity parameters written into the regulations, thus the dividing line between a dark rosé

211

and a light red wine is a matter of opinion. Veuve Cliquot's 1976 Rosé was the deepest colored Champagne I had come across until I discovered Leclerc-Briant's huge, crimson 1989 Rosé Rubis.

The earliest sparkling red wines were probably made in Burgundy in the 1820s, and the style has always been light and soft. Henry Vizetelly, who tasted a number of such wines as a juror at the Paris Exposition in 1878, stated that, "Although red wines, they had the merit of being deficient in that body which forms an objectionable feature in sparkling wines of a deep shade of color."

There are today many sparkling red wines produced in France and beyond, but the most famous and probably the most serious is Australia's sparkling Shiraz. This style started off as so-called Sparkling Burgundy, which a company called Auldana first produced in 1881. It was much lighter in both body and color than today's sparkling Shiraz which, as a generic style, can loosely be taken to include sparkling red wines made from Cabernet Sauvignon, Merlot, and other grape varieties, both pure and blended. They are deep purple-red colored, pungently-flavored, full-throttle wines that invariably have a somewhat sweet finish and come in two distinct styles: oaky/fruity or fruity/fruity, with all the tannin and body that Vizetelly found so objectionable.

Sweeter Styles

As Brut sparkling wines should have a balanced *dosage*, they rarely taste as austere as the term suggests, and the next level up—extra-sec or extra dry—is obviously sweeter. Some retailers have cottoned on to this and, knowing how many people "Talk dry, drink sweet," they have deliberately imported Champagnes and sparkling wines at this level of sweetness instead of brut. When the *dosage* is properly balanced, extra-sec *cuvées* can be excellent, and the word "*sec*" or "dry" helps psychologically for people who want to be seen drinking a dry wine.

The same could be said for sparkling wines sold as *sec* or dry, which are sweeter still. But on its own, the word *sec* hints at Sekt, with all its bad connotations. The additional word "extra" does allude to something extra, better, improved, thus *sec* is not used as heavily as *extra-sec*.

In theory the sweetest Champagne style is *doux* or sweet, which must contain at least 50 grams of residual sugar, but this style has not been widely available since the turn of the century, and the very last commercial production was made by Roederer in 1983 under its famous Carte Blanche label. That wine had 60 grams of residual sugar, which is not really sweet by *doux* standards, although ten years earlier Roederer's Carte Blanche was an 80 gram wine, while 100 years ago it was 180 grams.

Roederer's Carte Blanche today is just 45 grams, which puts it at the high end of the *demi-sec* range. A *demi-sec* Champagne may contain between 33 and 50 grams of residual sugar, but most average just 35 grams, although a few are as high as Roederer's Carte Blanche. Although a *demi-sec* is indeed sweet, it is not as intensely sweet as, say, a top Sauternes, which in great years will average 90 to 108 grams of residual sugar. It is thus neither one thing nor the other and because most who buy it are more concerned with experiencing a certain sweetness rather than a definite quality, the Champenois have gradually been able to get away with using more and more inferior base wines.[. . .]

Aromatic Styles

The use of aromatic grapes for dry sparkling wine will always be difficult for regular Champagne drinkers to come to terms with, but once the style is accepted for what it is, the best examples shine out.

The most important dry sparkling wine made from an aromatic grape is of course Riesling Sekt, but until very recently the number of these wines showing any quality at all was very small indeed. There has, however, been a surge in the quality of some of these wines recently, although they still represent a tiny minority of the Sekt industry as a whole. Most of them are produced by small, go-ahead wine estates rather than the old-established Sekt factories and they are invariably bottle-fermented.

Keeping wines made from aromatic grape varieties on their yeast does nothing to help or increase the quality. In fact it detracts. Yeast-contact merely obscures the varietal purity of aromatic grapes, thus such wines should be disgorged as soon as possible after the second fermentation. Even the best of the new breed of Sekt could be made just as well by *cuve close*, but Sekt is so cheap that it is not considered a serious wine, even by those who drink it, thus the producers of the best Riesling Sekt have to use bottle-fermentation in order to persuade customers that the wines are worthy of far higher price than their competitors.

The easiest way for a Champagne drinker to enjoy the best quality Riesling Sekt is to forget Champagne and think of a fine Riesling because in the Sekt format the classic petrolly and honeyed character of a mature Riesling comes through.

The greatest sweet sparkling wine in the world is, without a doubt, Asti. Although it is a fraction of the price of a *demi-sec* Champagne, the best Asti is ten times the quality, making it one of the great fine-wine bargains in the world. Virtually every bottle of Asti is made by *cuve close*, which is far superior to *méthode champenoise* for an aromatic, as mentioned above. This is particularly so for a sweet sparkling wine because, in all but a few exceptions, freshness of fruit is the key to a great sweet sparkling wine. No extra quality is gained from extended yeast contact.

The best Asti wines have a fine mousse of tiny bubbles, a fresh, grapey aroma, a luscious sweetness, and a light yet rich, flowery fruitiness that should be vivacious and mouth-watering. The greatest examples will be reminiscent of peaches, and may even have a hint of orange, but Asti is not a wine that should be kept. One of the most important compounds in the Moscato aroma is geraniol, which is wonderful when fresh but which, with bottle-age, assumes an unpleasantly pungent geranium odor.

ITALY

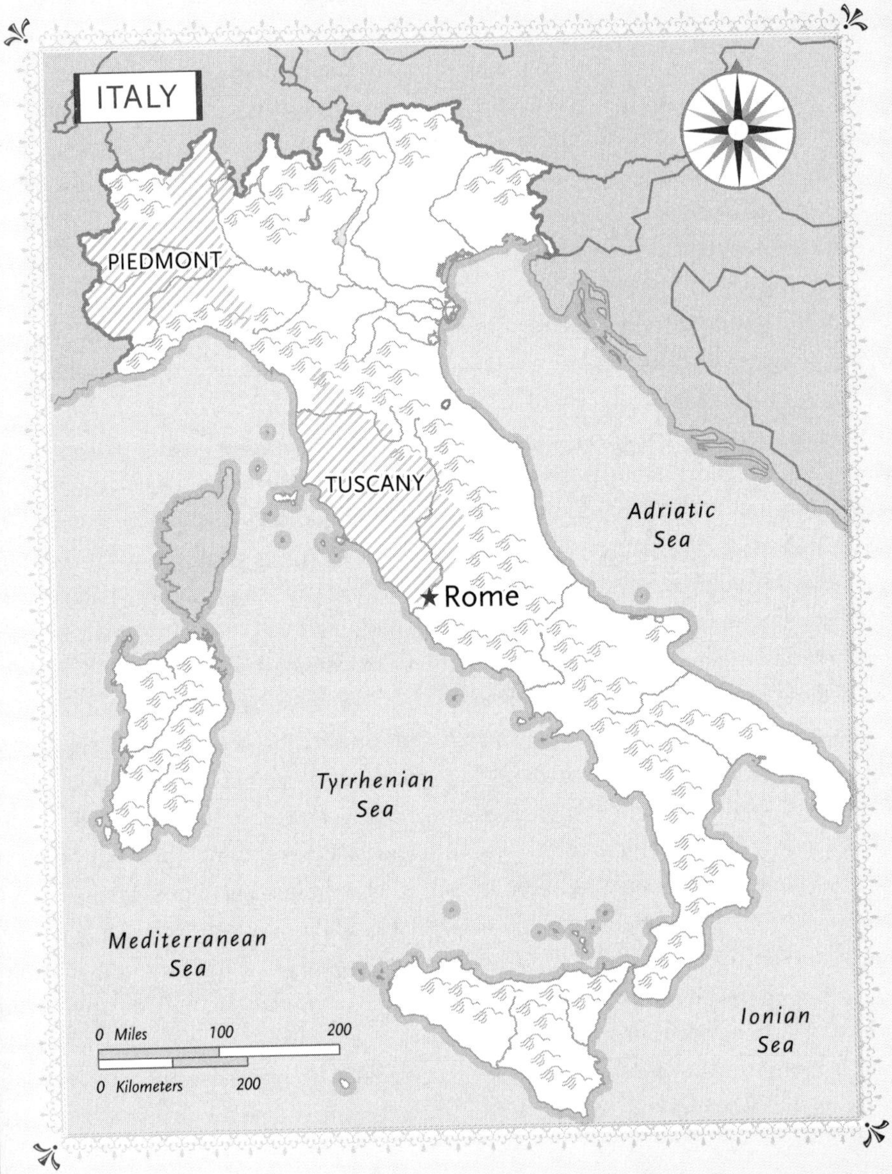

ITALY

PIEDMONT

TUSCANY

★ Rome

Adriatic
Sea

Tyrrhenian
Sea

Mediterranean
Sea

Ionian
Sea

0 Miles   100   200

0 Kilometers   200

214

EVEN UP TO THE EARLY 1980S, most Italian wines were made to be consumed in Italy, by Italians, with no thoughts of the export market. Italians love their wine, which are a part of the afternoon and evening meals. They've been making wine on the Italian peninsula for thousands of years, since the Etruscans and the Greeks dominated the landscape, long before the Romans. By 2008, Italy was the foremost producer of wine, eclipsing longtime rival France. It made nearly six billion liters of wine that year. There are nearly 1 million vineyards under cultivation, in almost every region.

For many years, Italian winemakers had focused on making medium-bodied, casual, food-friendly wines aimed at their home market. Today they are making much better, more complex wines, and they are very fashionable around the world. They have created these new wines by using modern technology, including modern vinification procedures, and updated vineyard management as a basis for experimentation.

Throughout this book I have shared my own personal experiences of the many wine regions that I have visited. There are more than 100 different Italian stories that I could talk about but the most important was the influence Italians had on me in my early days. The most asked question I get is, "How did you get involved with wine?" Many people think that I am joking with my answer . . . but as a twelve-year-old altar boy, my first taste was a sacramental wine! My parish priest was Italian, Father Salvatore Matarazzo. He was not only my spiritual advisor but guided me to think "out of the box" in life and in business. We are still friends today. At nineteen, as a freshman in college, I got a job as a waiter in a restaurant which received a four star rating from the New York Times. The Italian owner and the chef, John Novi helped me understand the restaurant world and the relation-ship between wine and food. His love and passion for food was infectious. Finally I married an Italian and have three bambinos and one bambina!!

As one retailer of fine Italian wine once told me, "There is no country. Italy is one vast vineyard from north to south." For simplicity's sake, I have chosen to concentrate on two of my favorite wine regions—Tuscany and Piedmont.

—KZ

TUSCANY

TUSCANY

EMILIA-ROMAGNA

LIGURIA

SAN MARINO

MARCHE

Rufina

Carmignano

Pisa   Arno River   Florence

Livorno   CHIANTI

San Gimignano

Siena

Bolgheri   TUSCANY

Tyrrhenian
Gulf   Montepulciano

Montalcino

ITALY

UMBRIA

Miles   50

Kilometers   100

Maremma   LAZIO

AFTER GRADUATING COLLEGE, I left for a year's study in Europe with a Eurail pass and a directory of youth hostels. When I got to Tuscany I found my way to the Ruffino winery in Greve to set up an appointment for the following week. I was very well received by the receptionist, who asked me to wait as she called the export manager. Ten minutes later he appeared and asked me if I was interested in lunch. In Tuscany, lunch is something you never refuse. Little did I know that he was inviting me to lunch with five hundred of Rome's top restaurateurs. He stopped the lunch, which was already in progress, to introduce me. I have no idea what he said since I didn't speak Italian, but the next thing I knew I received a standing ovation—for reasons still unknown. That lunch was one of the highlights of my first European wine trip.

Tuscany, with its rolling hills, gorgeous Italian villas, and ubiquitous undulating vineyards, is one of the most beautiful wine regions in the world. Tuscan wines are delicious. Tuscany is in central Italy, along the coast of the Tyrrhenian Sea. Some of the world's most famous wines and wine regions are located there. Some notable wines include Chianti, Brunello di Montalcino, and Vino Nobile di Montepulciano. These are primarily made from the Sangiovese grape.

The 1980s and 1990s saw the ascendance of new wines called Super Tuscans: grape varieties and blends beyond the traditional limits of Italian wine-labeling codes. This was a peak period for the Tuscan wine region, and gave rise to an international taste that elevated the name and reputation not only of Tuscany, but Italian wines in general.

—KZ

TOSCANA:
The Center of the Italian Wine Universe

Joseph Bastianich and David Lynch

BUSHWHACKING IN BOLGHERI

Daniele is chewing on the remains of a cigar as he tramps through the Bolgheri woods, a battalion of hunters in fatigues trailing behind him. He is a gamekeeper at the Tenuta San Guide, and every Sunday from November through January he runs the *caccia al cinghiale*, or wild-boar hunt, at the estate. Tenuta San Guido is known to wine lovers as the home of Italy's first Super-Tuscan wine, "Sassicaia." But only 150 of its 6,200 acres of land are vineyards; the rest is a vast nature preserve around Bolgheri, which Daniele and two partners are charged with maintaining.

Joseph Bastianich is a true family restaurateur, working together with his mother, Lidia Bastianich, one of the great U.S. chefs and food personalities. His innovative and creative restaurants have been extremely successful. With renowned chef Mario Batali, Joe has integrated all the great aspects of food, design, service, and wine lists. He is now an owner of vineyards in Italy and Argentina and an importer of their wines to the United States.

After graduating from Boston College, David Lynch worked as a senior editor for Wine & Spirits *magazine. He received a James Beard journalism award in 2001 for his writing. David has a knack of combining a sense of place in his writing, which besides wine includes food, culture, and traditions. He combines all of these in his book* Vino Italiano: The Regional Wines of Italy.

Bolgheri is about a half-hour south of Livorno on Tuscany's Mediterranean coast, part of a band of maritime hills that stretches down past Grosseto. This area, known as the Maremma, may be Italy's most densely populated with *cinghiale*. They take refuge in the thick Mediterranean scrub, called *maicchia*, or in the woods farther inland in Chianti and Montalcino, usually coming out only at night. Omnivorous and stealthy, they are known to like ripe wine grapes—in fact, vintners often lament that boars are true grape connoisseurs, choosing only the best-quality fruit when they raid a vineyard. And of course their looks don't win them any sympathy: With those prehistoric faces, they're like mythic beasts come to destroy the village, even though all they really want is to be left alone.

Still, boar are mean when provoked and armed with those fearsome tusks, which can slice a dog from stem to stern. The *caccia al cinghiale* is often described as a war, and Daniele, with his three-day beard and Clint Eastwood stogie, fits his role perfectly: Like a grizzled sergeant heading into a firefight, he positions his hunters about twenty yards apart along a hillside trail. There are nearly thirty riflemen (*fucilieri*) in all—most of them older men, huffing and puffing as they try to keep up—lining up across the ridge like a firing squad. With his hawk's eyes Daniele glares at the new guys, explaining in no uncertain terms where they can and cannot shoot (should someone track a boar too far to his right or left, he could shoot the neighboring rifleman—not uncommon in the loosely regulated world of Italian boar-hunting).

On the other side of the crest. Daniele's friend Loris struggles through the thicket with six dogs, all of them howling and straining at their leashes. Loris is the head of the *bracchieri*, a group of about ten dog handlers whose job it is to flush the *cinghiale* in the direction of the firing squad. Stumbling along with a rifle on his back, walkie-talkie in one hand and dogs in the other, Loris curses and yanks hard on the leashes as he and his crew get into position.

When he's finally ready, Loris barks to Daniele over the speaker. At the sound of Daniele's horn from the other side, the *bracchieri* begin unchaining the dogs one by one. Loris exhorts each mutt like a boxing trainer, shouting "*Avanti!*" and "*Vai!*" and "*Attenti alla strada!*" and shooting birdshot into the air. The crazed dogs fan out in search of *cinghiali*, and for a moment the ridge becomes strangely calm.

Meanwhile, Marcello, the white-haired manager of the Sassicaia estate and one of the *fucilieri*, sits on a camp stool, his rifle in his lap. Surrounded by the fragrant *macchia*— a mix of holm and cork oaks, evergreens, juniper bushes, wild herbs—he listens to the commotion of the dogs off in the distance. At first the howls are diffuse, disorganized, but soon they concentrate, and then the roar is on the move and getting closer. Marcello hops up, aiming his rifle at a tiny clearing a few yards away, the racket of the dogs now right in front of him. He readies his gun, lowers it, then readies and lowers it again, in concert with the crescendos.

Twenty yards up the ridge, there's a rifle blast. Then another one. The barking subsides and the panting dogs squirt out of the brush, one of them bloodied from a tusk to the chest. After only about fifteen minutes

219

of action, it's all over—and this is the last of three passes before lunch—so Marcello packs up and trudges up the path. Everyone assembles in a small clearing where the two dead *cinghiali* have been dragged, and it's at this point that the one-sidedness of the battle becomes clear: There are more than forty men and as many dogs, all for two boar of about 120 pounds each. The only one who still looks like much of a warrior is Danielle, who hoists the bloodied boar into a small pickup truck.

At lunch, the hunters settle into a happy Tuscan domesticity, breaking out their packed pasta lunches and bottles of homemade wine. There are steaks on the grill, and hunks of pecorino sliced with big hunting knives. One of the *fusilieri*, a chain-smoker named Bacci, pulls back the tinfoil on his wife's "famous" chestnut torte, making his way around the tables like Martha Stewart. Of all the hunters' picnics in all the world, only an Italian one includes a five-minute debate on the type of flour used in a *castagnaccio*.

A hired hand begins to field-dress the two boar, both of which are males. He starts by disemboweling them, rather casually tossing their testicles into the bushes. "Aw, they shouldn't throw those away," remarks Alfio, one of the older men in the group— and also the most dapper in his corduroy car coat, green wool pants, and matching fedora. Only a few nod in agreement when Alfio refers to the testicles as "*molto delicati*."

The head, heart, and liver of a *cinghiale*, all of which are considered delicacies, are given to the hunter who shoots it. Alfio hooks the arm of one of the successful shooters— a tall, younger guy dressed head to toe in

camouflage—and begins to explain the finer points of boar-head cookery: "It's not very big, so use a little more oil. Wash it good, and on the last wash use some red wine vinegar." The young guy seems only mildly interested.

"Bring it to my house and my wife'll do it," Alfio blurts. The camouflaged one laughs at this left-handed invitation. "You know what? Bring the liver, too."

Most people are content to have some spicy *cinghiale* salami or a *ragù di cinghiale* over polenta and forget about those grizzled snouts staring at them from the butcher-shop walls. But they certainly lend atmosphere to a region that has become the tourism capital of Italy. People these days would rather shop for porcini mushrooms in the hills of Chianti than walk through a *duomo*, or so it seems by the sounds of all those English and German voices in the wine-country restaurants.

No doubt part of the appeal is Tuscany's importance as a wine region. Some people rank the wines of Piedmont higher, but from a commercial standpoint, there's no comparison—Tuscany's brand recognition is far greater. Tuscany is Italy's Bordeaux, Piedmont its Burgundy: One is worldly and market-minded, the other more insular and scholarly. And both seem to like it that way.

Only Piedmont, in fact, outdoes Tuscany in enological complexity, with a whopping fifty-two DOC(G) zones to Tuscany's forty. Yet when you factor in the vast array of Super Tuscan wines with only a *nome di fantasia* (fantasy name) to identify them, Tuscany may ultimately take the prize as Most Confusing Region. In both cases, though, appearances can be deceiving.

As freighted as Tuscany is with history,

geographic diversity, and an encyclopedic array of great wines, the region is nevertheless dominated by two grapes: the white Trebbiano and the red Sangiovese. They are the two most-planted varieties not just in Tuscany but in Italy as a whole, and they share a number of similarities: Both are believed to have been native wild vines that were domesticated by the Etruscans; both are large families of varieties and clones that cover a broad area (Trebbiano is also diffuse in France, where it is known as ugni blanc); and both can be used, in varying percentages, in thirty-one of Tuscany's forty DOC(G)-classified wines.

Vini Bianchi

Of course, Tuscan whites don't begin and end with Trebbiano. The Vernaccia of San Gimignano is another native grape with more star power, although that may have more to do with San Gimignano itself, a medieval village whose hilltop locale and lofty towers are a big tourist draw—there's also a museum devoted to medieval instruments of torture. The Vernaccia grape (the name comes from the Latin word for "indigenous," which is why it is attached to unrelated grapes elsewhere in Italy) is more aromatic and structured than Trebbiano, but it too falls on the lighter side of the white wine spectrum.

Vernaccia is one of Tuscany's most historic wines, first cited in San Gimignano town records in the thirteenth century. It was also celebrated in literature, including poems by Dante and Francesco Redi, whose *Bacco in Tescana* (1685) lavished particular praise on it. The weight of all this history may have

factored into Vernaccia di San Gimignano becoming Italy's first DOC in 1966, and to its subsequent elevation to DOCG in 1993—the latter despite the wine having become a fairly insipid, mass-produced product by the 1980s. At its best, Vernaccia can be a floral, crisp white with a note of bitter almond on the finish. But for American drinkers it's hardly the big mouthful of fruit that a California Chardonnay is. Most producers these days, including local giant Teruzzi & Puthod, add body and complexity by including Chardonnay and Vermentino in the mix; both play a big role in Teruzzi & Puthod's well-known "Terre di Tufi," although that wine is labeled as an IGT, not DOCG (the DOCG regulations permit only 10 percent of grapes other than Vernaccia).

Vini Rossi

Even now, coastal Tuscany is a frontier, both for winemakers and tourists; much of the southern Maremma, in fact, was malarial marshland until Mussolini drained it in the 1930s. While the islands of Giglio and Elba and a handful of towns along the southern coast have their share of visitors, most of the action (and this goes for wine, too) is centered in the thickly forested hills around Florence and Siena.

Wines notwithstanding, it's hard to compete with some of the images: like winding along the Strada del Chianti (SS 222) in Chianti Classico, cresting the hill at Panzano and descending through the Conca d'Oro (golden bowl), a sun-splashed arc of vineyards that seems to open onto the entire south of Italy; or approaching the bulky mass of Montalcino, which sits like an island in an undulating sea of wheat fields and pasture; or peering over the east wall of Montepulciano and taking in nearly all of the Vino Nobile DOCG zone in one shot. These three areas are the "big three" of Tuscan red wine, showcasing the many faces of the Sangiovese grape—the most diffuse, most intensely studied, and along with the Nebbiolo of Piedmont, most important native red of Italy.

The origins of the Sangiovese name are widely debated. One theory is that Sangiovese derives from *sangue di Giove* ("blood of Jove") or *di Giovanni* (Saint John), while another suggests *sangue da giogo/gioghetti* ("blood of a crest, or ridge"); the latter ostensibly refers to the Apennines between Tuscany and Emilia-Romagna, where the variety is thought to have originated. In any case, an author named Soderini, in a 1590 book on viticulture, describes a "Sangiogheto," the first known written reference to the grape.

The origins of Sangiovese have long been unclear. Most experts traditionally concluded that it was a native wild vine of the Italian peninsula. But in 2004, a researcher from the prestigious winemaking institute at San Michele all'Adige, in the Alto Adige, determined through DNA testing that Sangiovese is descended from another Tuscan grape, Ciliegiolo, a bright, fruity variety found mostly in coastal areas. Sangiovese's other parent was an obscure variety identified as Calabrese Montenuovo, of which very little is known.

In spreading throughout Tuscany and elsewhere, Sangiovese has picked up different names in different places—Prugnolo Gentile in Montepulciano, Brunello in Montalcino, and Morellino near Grosseto, all of which are said to be individual strains of Sangiovese. Generally speaking, though, these subvarieties fall within two basic categories of Sangiovese: one with large berries (Sangiovese *Grosso*, which includes Prugnolo and Brunello) and another with small ones, Sangioveto, Chianti's version.

Is this really important? Well, some say that Sangiovese *Grosso's* thicker skins are what give Brunello a more tannic bite and thus a greater capacity to age. Others say that the idea of a distinct, widely propagated clone such as Brunello or Prugnolo is nonsense—that the varying personalities of the wines come from planting the same grape in different places. What everyone can agree on is the unique character of the variety: In Sangiovese you get not only a telltale aroma and flavor of black cherry but a distinctive savor that roots the wine in Tuscany. A good Chianti, or Brunello di Montalcino, or Vino Nobile di Montepulciano, has a foresty, smoky quality; drinking it is like eating berries in the woods, the spicy scents of the underbrush mingling with the sweetness of the fruit.

Sangiovese is very vigorous (meaning that it has to be closely pruned to produce concentrated fruit), sensitive to its environment, and difficult to get fully ripe, which is one of the reasons old-style Chiantis had such an acidic kick. The variety also tends to be low in anthocyanins, the natural phenolics in the skins that give a wine color (Brunello seems to be an exception). This is why lesser-known grapes, such as Canaiolo and Colorino, found their way into Chianti blends in the past—and it's why Cabernet Sauvignon and Merlot have become nearly as important as Sangiovese in Tuscany over the last thirty years. In looking at the current red-wine scene in Tuscany, it's these last three—perfumed Sangiovese, powerful Cabernet, and plump Merlot, either alone or in combination—that have come to define the region.

Chianti and Chianti Classico

Since the Middle Ages, when Florence was probably the most powerful of the city-states, the hills south of the city have been the epicenter of commercial winemaking in Italy. Although there are other wine zones that are equally if not more historic (including San Gimignano and Montepulciano), Chianti was the first real "delimited" wine zone as we know it today.

The Florentine Republic identified the hills between Florence and Siena as "Chianti" in the fourteenth century. Years later, in 1716, the Grand Duke Cosimo III de' Medici created what is considered the first "legislation" governing wine production. He identified the communes of Greve, Radda, Gaiole, and Castellina as a discrete production zone. Later still, in the 1870s, Gaiole nobleman Bettino Ricasoli (the second president of unified Italy and an ancestor of present-day Castello di Brolio scion Francesco Ricasoli) devised what became a "formula" for Chianti-area reds: a base of Sangiovese, with a touch of the softening Canaiolo and a significant dose of white grapes for those who wanted fresher wines (or, later, for those who wanted to stretch their production).

In the twentieth century, three bad things happened to Chianti. First, the original zone, now referred to as the Classico, was expanded to include a huge swath of central Tuscany, as the government envisioned Chianti as a "brand" more than as a site-specific wine. Second, the Ricasoli recipe became doctrine in Chianti, and when the DOC production formula was created in 1967 it allowed for up to 30 percent white grapes in the blend. And third, as elsewhere in Italy, there was a mass exodus from the Tuscan countryside in the fifties, which in turn prompted the Italian government and the European Community to finance large-scale replantings of Tuscany's vineyards in the sixties—all geared toward mass production.

At present, the Chianti DOCG zone takes in more than forty-two thousand acres, of which seventeen thousand are the

223

original Classico. There are now seven Chianti subzones: Colli Aretini, near Arezzo; Colli Fiorentini, south of Florence, north of the Classico; Colli Senesi, all around Siena to the north and south; Colline Pisane, south of Pisa; Montalbano, west of Florence; Rùfina, east of Florence; and Montispertoli, also west of Florence.

So then, what were you drinking if you drank Chianti in the seventies and eighties? Probably a mouth-puckering, browning-at-the-edges red in a straw-covered *fiasco*—the cheap pizza-parlor wine that became world-famous, enticing producers to crank out even more. There's still a good amount of it around today, and the down-market image of the *fiasco* with a candle melting over its edges still haunts the industry.

"For so long, our wine culture was based on quantity, not quality," says Marchese Piero Antinori, head of one of the many noble families that have anchored the Tuscan wine scene. Antinori was one who bucked the trends in the seventies, chafing at what he and others saw as shortsighted Chianti DOC regulations. He followed the lead of his uncle, Marchese Mario Incisa della Rocchetta of Sassicaia, and in 1971 introduced "Tignanello," a blend of 80 percent Sangiovese and 20 percent Cabernet Sauvignon aged in French oak barriques. Because Cabernet Sauvignon and barrique aging were not allowed in the DOC regulations of the day, he labeled Tignanello as a *vino da tavola*. Along with "Sassicaia" and a raft of other nontraditional reds, it came to be known as one of the Super Tuscans—most of which were either 100 percent Sangiovese (which also wasn't allowed in the Chianti disci-

pline), or a mix of Sangiovese with international varieties like Cabernet or Merlot.

"In the past, Italy produced mass quantities of wine because we were an agricultural economy and people used wine to quench thirst," says Antinori. "After the Second World War, consumption went way down as we became more industrialized. But our mentality toward winemaking did not change: Even now I'd say a high percentage of the vineyards in Chianti Classico are the old-style, high-production vineyards of the sixties."

That may well be true, but Chianti—and Chianti Classico especially—is not the wine it once was. In fact, it has undergone a more profound change in the last twenty years than practically any other wine in Italy. The Chianti Classico zone is now a source of world-class reds, bottles you should stick in your cellar for a few years, not stick candles into.

It started in 1984, when Chianti and Chianti Classico were upgraded to DOCG, which adjusted the blending formula to include a minimum of only 2 percent white grapes and allowed "foreign" varieties such as Cabernet and Merlot to be included in percentages up to 10 percent (in 1996 it changed again, eliminating the minimum for white grapes and upping the amount of "foreign" grapes to 15 percent). Further, the DOCG placed tighter restrictions on yields in the vineyards, essentially forcing people to cut excess fruit in the summer to produce more concentrated grapes.

In the cellars, winemakers not only benefited from the enriching effects of Merlot and Cabernet, but more and more of them adopted controlled-temperature fermentation in stainless steel (to preserve aromas) and aging in smaller, newer oak barrels instead of big, musty *botti* made of chestnut (stabilizing the wine's color and adding richness and tannin). People began striving for more power in their wines, employing longer contact with the skins of the grapes during fermentation to extract more color and tannin.

But the biggest change has come in the vineyards. Since 1989, the Chianti Classico *consorzio*—a producers association whose symbol is the *gallo nero,* or black rooster— has overseen a viticultural research project known as "Chianti Classico 2000." Originally headed by Carlo Ferrini, now the most famous winemaking consultant in Tuscany, the project centered on a series of experimental vineyards planted at the estates of *consorzio* member-producers. The principal aim was to identify new clones of Sangiovese that had thicker skins, higher anthocyanins, and sparser grape bunches (Sangiovese grows in a notoriously tight bunch, which prevents light from entering and ripening all the grapes evenly).

Parallel to the Chianti Classico 2000 project, any number of producers were making their own clonal selections and also replanting their vineyards more densely so that each vine could be more closely cropped to produce less. The basic idea behind planting vines more densely is that the vines are not only producing a smaller quantity of fruit per vine, but that they are competing with one another for nutrients in the soil. In theory, these struggling vines will produce fruit that is more deeply flavorful, since all of the plant's energy is being directed toward a carefully controlled number of grape bunches.

So, concurrent with the Chianti Classico 2000 research, noble estates such as Antinori, Badia a Coltibuono, Fonterutoli, and Castello di Brolio, along with smaller producers such as Fontodi and Isole e Olena, ignited a minirevolution in the Chianti Classico vineyards, aggressively replanting their

properties with the intent of transforming Sangiovese. Rather than have a vineyard with about two thousand vines per hectare, producing four or five kilos (or more) of grapes per plant, they were upping the number to five thousand vines or more, but with only one to two kilos per plant as an ideal. And with new clones at that. The quality implications are pretty obvious.

As some Italian-wine fans are aware, the vintages 1997 through 2000 were great years in Chianti Classico—especially '97, which was hailed as the vintage of the decade. Many producers say that this was not just the luck of weather, but a refinement of the raw ingredients. "One reason '97 was great was because it was a point of convergence— of good weather and years of improvements in the vineyards," says Roberto Stucchi, winemaker-proprietor of Badia a Coltibuono in Gaiole. "That was probably the first year when a good number of the vineyards replanted in the late-eighties and early nineties were coming into production."

Stefano Porcinai, the current in-house enologist at the Chianti Classico *consorzio*, is a little more conservative in his estimates of the effects of replanting in the nineties. The results of the Chianti Classico 2000 project, for one, have only recently had an impact: Actual seedlings of the four new clones the *consorzio* isolated were only put on the market in 2001. As for the replantings carried out privately, Porcinai says that maybe 20 percent of the Classico's seventeen thousand acres have been replaced in the last decade. The best is yet to come.

"Super Tuscans were very important for gaining world recognition of Italian wines,

but they also created some anarchy in the marketplace," Porcinai explains. "With the changes in the laws, Chianti is technically a Super Tuscan. But if the progress with Sangiovese continues, you'll probably see more Chianti wines that are 100 percent Sangiovese instead of being blended with other grapes."

So then, what are you drinking if you drink Chianti Classico in the twenty-first century? From the heights of Gaiole, Greve, Castellina, Radda, and Panzano, where the crumbly, schist-like soil called *galestro* dominates, you get a wine that captures not only the perfume of Sangiovese but also its power. Often the wines have a sheen of new oak, and are sweetened with Merlot and Cabernet. They're denser, darker, more ageworthy reds, but in comparison to other wines of the world they're still angular and firm rather than fat or musclebound. The best Chianti Classicos are about grace, which doesn't fade with age.

Brunello di Montalcino

Not far from the southern reaches of Chianti Classico, the commune of Montalcino towers over the surrounding area, one of those trademark Tuscan towns that seems to perch on a ledge. Its only about twenty-five miles south of Siena, but in that short span the climate shifts from the damper, cooler continental climate of the Chianti Classico to a dryer, hotter, more Mediterranean environment. While Montalcino's altitudes are similar to those in Chianti (vineyards are usually found from three hundred to five hundred meters), the soils are different, generally containing more limestone and sand than the soils farther north.

It's these differences, along with the purported superiority of the Brunello clone, that make Brunello di Montalcino the most powerful Sangiovese around. Not only is the climate hotter—Montalcino is always the first of the "big three" to start the harvest in the fall—but the soils are, too: Where cooler clays and marls tend to slow down ripening, sandier soils speed it up. Potentially disastrous October rains, always a concern in Chianti Classico, aren't much of problem in Montalcino, since the harvest typically finishes in mid- to late September. Along with Barolo and Barbaresco from Piedmont, Brunello di Montalcino has become one of the handful of DOC wines hunted by wine collectors, because its depth of flavor and tongue-curling tannins give it the potential to age for decades. The lighter-styled Rosso di Montalcino, sort of a younger, "declassified" Brunello (and usually a great value), was created so people could drink a more immediately accessible Montalcino wine while they waited for their Brunellos to age; DOCG law requires a minimum of four years before Brunello can go on the market.

Most experts credit the discovery of Brunello to Clemente Santi, who is said to have isolated the clone in the 1840s. When his grandson Ferruccio Biondi returned to the family farm in Montalcino after fighting in the Risorgimento (the movement for Italian unification), he planted the vineyards with Brunello and created the Biondi-Santi brand in 1888. It wasn't until the 1950s that Fattoria dei Barbi, Costanti, and a handful of other estates joined Biondi-Santi on the scene, and in general Montalcino was relatively unknown well into the seventies. According to the Brunello di Montalcino *consorzio*, there were some 800,000 bottles of wine made in the zone in 1975, from about 25 producers; in 1995, that number had ballooned to 3.5 million bottles, from more than 120 estates.

In fact, where Chianti Classico was already well-developed in the 1970s, Montalcino was still the boondocks—sort of like the way Grosseto is today. The exodus of the area's farmers in the fifties and sixties left Montalcino landowners holding the bag, and many were content to unload property inexpensively. Among the early investors in the zone were the vermouth-making Cinzanos of Piedmont, who bought the Col d'Orcia estate in 1973, and the American wine importers John and Harry Mariani, who started acquiring property for their Banfi estate in 1978.

Although they're regarded by some as interlopers, there's no measuring the impact the Marianis had on Montalcino. Having

ROSSO DI MONTALCINO

Denominazione di Origine Controllata

2006

COL D'ORCIA

made their fortune importing Riunite Lambrusco, they did things in Montalcino on a big, international scale—building one of the most high-tech wineries in Italy, planting a California-sized tract of vineyards, and making the whole place tourist-friendly. Banfi's compound may be an example of American excess, but the buzz it created spurred new investments in the area. The Frescobaldi clan of Chianti Rùfina fame bought the Castel Giocondo estate in 1989, and both Piero Antinori (Pian delle Vigne) and Barbaresco legend Angelo Gaja (Pieve di Santa Restituta) arrived in the nineties. Along with these bigger players came a raft of newer, more boutique estates, including Siro Pacenti, Uccelliera, Le Machioche, and Salvioni, and once-quiet Montalcino grew thick with high-end wineries.

Generally speaking, Brunellos are described as bigger, "blacker" wines than Chiantis or Vino Nobiles. But Giacomo Neri, winemaker-proprietor at the well-regarded Casanova di Neri estate, puts a finer point on Brunello style. He, like many

of his peers, believes there are differences between the wines grown in vineyards north of Montalcino and those from vineyards to the south. The Montalcino commune, which takes in smaller villages such as Torrenieri (northeast of Montalcino) and Castelnuovo dell'Abate (southeast) is like a big circle, with Montalcino in the center. The vineyards that fan out to the north, characterized by cooler calcareous clays and a slightly cooler microclimate, produce, in Neri's view, more perfumed, elegant wines. In vineyards facing south, such as in Castelnuovo dell'Abate and Sant'Angelo in Colle, the soils are significantly sandier and the climate more full-on Mediterranean. This, says Neri, creates denser, fuller-bodied wines with less acidity.

"When you cross over Montalcino and start heading south toward Castelnuovo, it's like going into a different world," says Neri. "The vegetation actually changes. On the north side, it's more like the Chianti forests, with lots of oaks and pines. On the south side it turns into the *màcchia*, more scrub brush. Go in October—on the south side of Montalcino the olives are turning black; on the north side they're still green."

To put Neri's hypothesis to the test, you might try a side-by-side comparison of a Brunello from the northern part of the zone (like Tenuta Caparzo, Biondi-Santi, Silvio Nardi, or Altesino) with one from the south (maybe Mastrojanni, Banfi, Col d'Orcia, or Casanova di Neri). Given the wide array of techniques being applied these days (types of wood aging, lengths of macerations) it may be difficult to sort out the intricacies of *terroir*, but it sure would be fun trying. Most important of all is this: While the Chianti,

Vino Nobile, and Carmignano DOCGs all allow for other grapes to be blended in with Sangiovese, Brunello is the grape unadorned. For a thick *cinghiale* or rabbit *ragù*, a classic pasta topping of the Tuscan hills, there may be nothing better.

Vino Nobile di Montepulciano

Somewhere in the middle of Chianti Classico and Brunello di Montalcino, literally and figuratively, lies Vino Nobile di Montepulciano. It is the smallest of the "big three" DOCGs, with about twenty-five hundred acres under vine. And despite having a history at least as illustrious as Chianti's, it tends to be the forgotten middle child in the group.

Montepulciano itself is like a mini-Florence, and for that reason alone it's worth a visit. But some would argue that this is the only reason. Like Chianti and Brunello, the modern Vino Nobile industry developed in the 1920s and '30s (Fanetti and Contucci are two estates from that era still making wines). And, like Chianti, the establishment of the Vino Nobile DOC in the sixties led to a dramatic surge in vineyard plantings and wine production. The main difference is that in the seventies the largely mediocre Vino Nobile wines didn't become famous in spite of themselves, as Chianti wines did. As Burton Anderson writes in the *Wine Atlas of Italy*: "Even when enjoyable, [Vino Nobile] tended to vary so radically from one vintage—or even one bottle—to the next that it was hard to determine a Vino Nobile personality or define any one house's style."

It wasn't until the beginning of the eighties that Montepulciano began to gain momentum, thanks in large measure to the Avignonesi and Poliziano estates, both dynamic marketers as well as forward-looking producers. Avignonesi, run by brothers Ettore and Alberto Falvo (the name and the original property in Montepulciano comes from Ettore's ex-wife, Adriana Avignonesi), began as a small-scale producer of Vin Santo but eventually grew into a force. The Falvos, whose family was in the hotel business, not only invested heavily in the area—their properties in Montepulciano and neighboring Cortona now include 375 acres of vineyards—but created a more international array of wines. Ettore Falvo, a passionate viticulturist, focused on getting the most out of his Sangiovese (Prugnolo), introducing his first Vino Nobile in 1978. But he wasn't shy about planting Cabernet, Merlot, and other "international" varieties, particularly in Cortona. His Cabernet-Prugnolo blend "Grifi" (discontinued after the '96 vintage) and the Merlot-Cabernet "Toro Desiderio" weren't Vino Nobile wines, but they did what Tignanello did for Chianti a decade earlier: show what the zone was capable of.

In the case of Poliziano, which was founded in 1960, it was a question of shifting focus. Poliziano was a big producer of fairly mundane Chianti Colli Senesi until Federico Carletti, son of the founder, got a degree in agronomy and began directing the estate in 1980. His vineyard holdings have ballooned to about 300 acres in Montepulciano and Torrita di Siena (for Chianti, which he still makes). And with the help of consultant Carlo Ferrini, he has created probably the slickest Vino Nobiles on the market. He uses traditional varieties but adds a substantial amount of new barrique for aging. He also

229

RISERVA GRANDI ANNATE

1999

MONTEPULCIANO · CORTONA

AVIGNONESI

VINO NOBILE DI MONTEPULCIANO

DENOMINAZIONE DI ORIGINE CONTROLLATA E GARANTITA
IMBOTTIGLIATO DA **AVIGNONESI** SPA, MONTEPULCIANO, ITALIA

750 ML ℮ ITALIA · NON DISPERDERE IL VETRO NELL'AMBIENTE ALC. 13,5% BY VOL.

makes a Super Tuscan, "Le Stanze," a super-charged Cabernet-Merlot blend.

Since the early eighties, Montepulciano's development has been similar to Montal-cino's, albeit on a smaller scale. Big-name investors came in, including the Marche's Fazi-Battaglia winery (their estate in Montepul-ciano is called Fassati); the SAI insurance company (Fattoria del Cerro); the Ruffino wine house (Lodola Nuova); and Antinori (La Braccesca). There's also a new genera-tion of smaller producers, many of them as yet undiscovered: Valdipiatta, La Ciarliana, Salcheto, and Il Macchione, to name a few. Relatively speaking, there are some great values to be found among this group.

Still, the style of Vino Nobile remains stubbornly difficult to pinpoint. One reason for this may be the DOCG discipline for Vino Nobile, which even now isn't as closely prescribed as Brunello's or Chianti Classico's

when it comes to the grape mix. Although a Vino Nobile di Montepulciano can now be 100 percent Sangiovese (thanks to changes in the law in 1999), the official formula still allows for up to 20 percent Canaiolo and/ or up to 20 percent other grapes, including a maximum of 10 percent white varieties. Another development has been a liberalizing of the aging requirements for Vino Nobile, in that producers are no longer required to age their wines a minimum of two years in wood. Depending on the producers' choices, you'll find some Vino Nobiles that are more resiny, spicy, and herbal, and some that are more forwardly fruity and rich—although that could be said about Chianti Classico, too.

If there's any broad, sweeping generaliza-tion to be made, it's that Vino Nobiles have softer tannins than Brunellos and broader, less acidic profiles than Chianti Classicos— while maintaining the appealing aromas of Sangiovese. The slopes of Montepulciano are more open and gently rolling than the tight, steep pitches of Chianti Classico or Montalcino (allowing in more sunlight), and the soils are generally sandier and more alluvial than either of the others (advancing ripening), yet the elevations are the same. Like most middle children, Vino Nobile strikes a balance between its more extreme siblings, and is often the more interesting because of it.

PIEDMONT

OF COURSE ALL ITALIAN WINES ARE MEANT TO be had with a great meal. I will never forget visiting two of the top producers, one in the morning and one later in the day. After the first visit we were invited to lunch at one of the most spectacular restaurants in Piedmont. The lunch began at twelve noon and continued until 4 p.m. It wasn't just the length of the lunch, which is fairly normal; it was the amount of food that was placed on the table. After that lunch I didn't think I would ever eat again, at least for another week, and really needed a siesta—but I had to go to my second appointment. After visiting our second winery, the owner asked us to join him for dinner, and as fate would have it, he chose the same restaurant we had had lunch at: another four-hour meal equaling eight hours of eating and drinking. Some say my job is difficult, and sometimes it really is!

Piedmont, which the ancient Greeks called *Oenotrua* (meaning "land of vines"), was eventually cultivated by the Romans. In the foothills of the Alps, it is in the northwest corner of Italy that shares a border with France, with Turin as its capital. The most widely planted varietal in the region is Barbera. Nebbiolo and Dolcetto also are popular, and are used in a sizable portion of the red wines produced in the region. France, particularly the region of Burgundy, has had significant viticultural influence on the region, which can been seen in the styles of many Piedmontese wines.

BAROLO VS. BARBARESCO

Barolo	Barbaresco
Nebbiolo grape	Nebbiolo grape
Minimum 12.5% alcohol	Minimum 12.5% alcohol
More complex flavor, more body	Lighter; sometimes less body than Barolo, but fine and elegant
Must be aged at least three years (one in wood)	Requires two years of aging (one in wood)
"Riserva" = five years of aging	"Riserva" = four years of aging

—KZ

PIEDMONT:
A Land, a Grape, a People

Mary Ewing-Mulligan and Ed McCarthy

If you want to know something about our taste in wine, here's a hint: we honeymooned in the Langhe hills of Piedmont. We didn't know the area as "Langhe" at the time. It wasn't until sometime in the 1990s that wine lovers began using that local name to refer to the territory that encompasses the Barolo and Barbaresco wine zones, around the town of Alba, in the southeastern part of the Piedmont region. In 2001, the Langhe name became codified into Italy's wine lexicon as a DOC territory—the "fallback" DOC name for wines that do not, or cannot, carry the name of the older, more traditional DOC/G zones in that area. At the time of our honeymoon, we just called it the Barolo-Barbaresco area.

Although we each had been to that part of Piedmont before, separately, we essentially discovered it together, and over the years have formed deeper and deeper bonds with that land, its wines, and the people who live there. We are convinced that Langhe is one of the most precious wine regions on earth. It is beautiful beyond description. (On a clear day, depending on where you stand, your vista could stretch seven ridges of hills deep, all the way to the Alps that divide Italy from France.) The Piedmontese people are hardworking, principled, humble, and, once you get to know them, welcoming. The wines are glorious.

The Langhe hills produce wines from several different grape varieties, overwhelmingly

I first met Mary Ewing-Mulligan when she worked for the Italian Trade Commission, which was located in One World Trade Center, the same tower as Windows on the World. We were both at the beginning of our careers. She was one of the first outside lecturers for the Windows on the World Wine School. Mary went on to become the first female Master of Wine (MW) in the United States and also became the U.S. director of the Wine & Spirits Educational Trust (WSET) which she runs out of the International Wine Center in New York City where she is the president.

Ed McCarthy and I have been tasting wines together at various wine and food events for more than twenty-five years. He is one of the best wine tasters I know and coincidentally met Mary at an Italian wine tasting in, of all places, New York City's Chinatown! Not only did they get married but they went on to co-author six wine books in the Wine for Dummies series. One of their great loves is the wines of Piedmont and they have actually named one of their cats Dolcetto, one of the grapes of Piedmont.

red. Barbera and Dolcetto are noteworthy varietal wines, the cornerstones of the regional table. But the Nebbiolo grape is the glory. It is a variety that excels only there, along with very limited areas in northern Piedmont and neighboring northern Lombardy. In the hills of the Barolo and Barbaresco wine zones, it makes wines that are not only world class in quality and longevity, but also unique in style among the world's great red wines.

The Nebbiolo grape, the only grape permitted for both Barolo and Barbaresco wines, requires a long growing season. It buds earlier than Dolcetto and Barbera, but it is always the last grape to ripen. Harvest can occur as late as November, when thick fog often envelops the hills at night and farmers hunt down the world-famous Alba white truffles.

Nebbiolo's demanding ways continue after the harvest. The grape is high in both acid and tannin, but unstable in coloring matter. Traditional winemaking techniques to soften the tannin—such as extended maceration times—can diminish the color of the wine. Modern winemaking techniques to stabilize the color of the wine—such as aging the wine in small barrels—can compound the grape's own tannin with oak tannins. Either way, the acidity remains a force to reckon with. By regulation, the wines must age before release: two years for wines from the Barbaresco zone (with a minimum nine months in wood) and three years for wines from the Barolo zone. Wines designated as *riserva* age an additional year.

But the structural characteristics that the Nebbiolo grape brings to its wines tell only half the story. Nebbiolo's aromatics are truly magnificent. A Barolo from a good vintage can have aromas and flavors of fruit, especially strawberry; herbs, especially mint, camphor, and anise; earthiness, exhibited as mushroom, white truffles, or tar; and floral elements, especially roses. With age, the wines can develop notes of tobacco, coffee, and leather.

Barolo and Barbaresco are sometimes compared to Burgundy, and in many ways the comparison is apt: both are hilly areas with small individual landholdings, where the red wine is made from a single grape variety, and the wines' aromas and flavors are complex, specific to the grape and terroir, and critical to the quality of the wine. But Nebbiolo-based wines have a Piedmontese soul. They can be a bit austere at first, opening up to you only with time. They are sturdy. They have character, guts, and perseverance—and yet are refined and stylish.

Just as a great Burgundy wine speaks of the particular plot of land where its grapes are grown, so too are the wines of Barolo and Barbaresco expressions of specific terroirs, and often of individual crus. (Italian wine regulations call an individual vineyard a *vigna*, not a *cru*—but the Piedmontese, being so close to France geographically and historically, when their Kingdom of Savoy encompassed western France, usually refer to their single vineyards as *crus*.) Barbaresco and Barolo are distinct areas, the former north of Alba and the latter south. Barbaresco is considerably smaller than the Barolo territory, with only about 35 percent as many producers as Barolo. In general, its wines are more elegant than Barolo and approachable at a younger age, although wines from certain vineyards made by certain producers in great vintages can age for decades. Barolo, being a larger territory (but still small, with annual production of about half a million cases), can make wines that are less consistent in quality from producer to producer, but in general Barolo wines are a bit bigger than Barbarescos, more powerful, longer-aging, and slower to develop.

Terroir differences exist not just from Barolo to Barbaresco, but also within each zone. The Barbaresco zone encompasses vineyards around just three villages: Barbaresco, Neive, and Treiso. The vineyards of Neive tend to make the most full-bodied and tannic Barbarescos; those of Barbaresco itself make wines that are known for their perfume and their structure, even if they are often a bit lighter than those of Neive; wines from vineyards around Treiso are a bit lighter yet, and very finessed. (Three Barbaresco producers who stand out, in our experience, are the very traditional Bruno Giacosa and Marchesi di Gresy and the renowned modernist, Angelo Gaja.)

Within the Barolo zone, the main territorial categorization that exists is that of the

western villages and the eastern villages, based on differing soil types in each of the two sections. Altogether the zone encompasses vineyards in eleven villages, but five communities account for 87 percent of Barolo production. The eastern vineyards include the hilltop villages of Serralunga d'Alba, Castiglione Falletto, and Monforte d'Alba; here the Barolos are the most powerful, fullest-bodied, most austere, and most ageworthy. The western vineyards of La Morra make Barolos that are usually more perfumed, more elegant, less tannic, and more precocious. The vineyards of Barolo itself extend across both soil types and can vary in style according to the location of the specific vineyard. (Favorite producers of ours from the eastern vineyards include Giacomo Conterno, Giuseppe Mascarello, Vietti, Aldo Conterno, and Cavallotto; from the western vineyards and/or from Barolo itself: Giuseppe Rinaldi, Bartolo Mascarello, and Renato Ratti.)

Throughout the Barolo zone, but especially within the territory of these five villages, are dozens of cru vineyard sites. In the early 1990s, when a change in Italy's national wine regulations opened the door for official recognition of individual vineyard sites, the Piedmontese were well ahead of other regions, having thoroughly documented and registered nearly all their vineyards. The vineyard names that appear on Barolo wines are too numerous to describe individually. Through years of research, however, we have satisfied ourselves that most of the cru Barolos do have specific, recognizable traits, whether that be the power and minerality of the Rocche di Castiglione cru, for example,

235

GAJA ®

BARBARESCO
DENOMINAZIONE DI ORIGINE CONTROLLATA E GARANTITA

IMBOTTIGLIATO DA · BOTTLED BY GAJA, BARBARESCO, ITALIA
RED WINE, PRODUCT OF ITALY
e 750 ML 14% VOL.   ALC. 14% BY VOL.

or the supreme elegance and balance of the famed Cannubi cru in the village of Barolo.

Weather creates yet another layer of complexity in the picture of Barolo and Barbaresco. Although the quality of a vintage can vary from one area to another, certain vintages stand out for their general excellence and longevity. In the 1980s, the years 1982, 1985, 1988, and 1989 were outstanding. The wines of '88 and '89 are still not at their peak in 2010.

The 1990s ushered in a wave of very fine vintages, especially in the latter half of the decade. The 1990 wines are very good and ready to drink. The 1995s, from a powerful year, need more time. Likewise the wines from 1996 need another decade to reach

their best drinking; it was a classic year, one of the greatest vintages, with austere and tannic wines. Both 1997 and 2000 were precocious and many wines are past their best moment. The 1998 vintage was very good, and 1999 even better, almost on a par with 1996. More recently, 2001, 2004, and 2006 stand out as excellent—but 2006, like 1996, will need decades to reach its zenith.

And this finally is our fascination with Piedmont's Langhe hills: It is a breathtakingly beautiful area, where a challenging but truly noble grape variety meets its match in determined, dedicated growers and winemakers who respect the potential of individual vineyard sites and produce wines of majesty, longevity, and mystery.

GERMANY

GERMANY

North Sea

DENMARK

• Hamburg

Berlin ★

POLAND

NETHERLANDS

BELGIUM

Rhein River

MOSEL-SAAR-RUWER

• Bonn

RHEINGAU

• Frankfurt

LUX.

RHEINHESSEN

FRANCE

Mosel River

PFALZ

Rhein River

CZECH REPUBLIC

Munich •

0 Miles 100 200

0 Kilometers 200

SWITZERLAND

AUSTRIA

MY FIRST TRIP TO GERMANY COINCIDED with one of their big national holidays, May Day. The export manager for a major German wine producer said we would be unable to visit the wineries since they were all closed, but suggested that a cruise up the Mosel to Koblenz would be a great way to spend the day. It was like one of those party cruises that you go on when you are vacationing in the Caribbean, except that the beauty of the vines along the steep hills of the Mosel are still vivid in my memory. On this all-day cruise I learned that one of the German traditions is to clear your palate with a beer before every glass of wine. Needless to say there was much consumption by all including the export manager, who after getting off the boat had no idea where he had left his car. We missed the ferry home, and I am not sure what happened after that!

Beer, not wine, is the national beverage in Germany. However, Germany does produce 2 or 3 percent of the world's wines. Germany is the northernmost country in which vines grow with any success in Europe. And 80 percent of the quality vineyards are located on hilly slopes. Germans can forget about mechanical harvesting.

Two to three percent is a lot when you consider that the volume depends largely on the weather. Why is this? German vintners must contend not only with the hilly conditions, but also inclement and uncooperative weather in order to grow grapes that produce the highest-quality wines in Germany.

If memorizing the Grand Crus of France, the more than 2,000 wineries

～ THE THIRTEEN ～ WINEMAKING REGIONS OF GERMANY:

1. Ahr
2. Baden
3. Franconia or Franken
4. Hessische Bergstraße
5. Mittelrhein
6. Mosel (previously known as Mosel-Saar-Ruwer)
7. Nahe
8. Palatinate or Pfalz (until 1992 known as Rheinpfalz)
9. Rheingau
10. Rheinhessen or Rhenish Hesse (largest)
11. Saale-Unstrut
12. Saxony or Sachsen
13. Württemberg

of California, and the multitude of Italian DOCs isn't enough of a challenge for you, then Germany presents the ultimate memory challenge. There are more than more than 1,400 wine villages and 2,600-plus vineyards in Germany. That's approximately 4,000 names to have to memorize. Believe it or not, there were almost 30,000 names you would have had to remember before 1971. Before that, Germany's wine industry was split up into very small parcels of land owned by an assortment of different people. And the names used to be very involved. In 1971, the German government passed a law in an effort to make German wine less confusing (even to German consumers). The new ruling stated that a vineyard must encompass at least twelve and a half acres of land. This law cut the list of vineyard names considerably, but it increased the number of owners.

In Germany today there are thirteen winemaking regions. Riesling is the most widely planted grape in Germany. It is easily their most popular and recognized grape. Müller-Thurgau, also widely found, and is a cross between two grapes (Riesling and Chasselas) and accounts for 13.5 percent of Germany's overall wine output. And the third most popular variety is Silvaner, which accounts for another 5 percent of all German wines.

—KZ

THE RIPENESS LEVELS OF GERMAN WINE

As a result of the German law of 1971, there are two main categories, Tafelwein and Qualitätswein.

Tafelwein: Literally, "table wine." The lowest designation given to a wine grown in Germany, it never carries the vineyard name. It is rarely seen in the United States.

Qualitätswein: Literally, "quality wine," of which there are two types.

1. *Qualitätswein bestimmter Anbaugebiete:* QbA indicates a quality wine that comes from one of the thirteen specified regions.

2. *Prädikatswein:* This is quality wine with distinction—the good stuff. These wines may not be chaptalized. In ascending order of quality, price, and ripeness at harvest, here are the Prädikatswein levels:

KABINETT: Light, semidry wines made from normally ripened grapes. Cost: $15–$25.

SPÄTLESE: Breaking up the word, *spät* means "late" and *lese* means "picking." Put them together and you have "late picking." That's exactly what this medium-style wine is made of: grapes that were picked after the normal harvest. The extra days of sun give the wine more body and a more intense flavor. Cost: $20–$35.

AUSLESE: Translated as "out picked," this means that the grapes are selectively picked out from particularly ripe bunches, which yields a medium-to-fuller-style wine. You probably do the same thing in your own garden if you grow tomatoes: You pick out the especially ripe ones, leaving the others on the vine. Cost: $25–$50.

BEERENAUSLESE: Breaking the word down, you get *beeren*, or "berries"; *aus*, or "out"; and *lese*, or "picking." Quite simply (and don't let the bigger names fool you), these are berries (grapes) that are picked out individually. These luscious grapes are used to create the rich dessert wines for which Germany is known. Beerenauslese is usually made only two or three times every ten years. It's not unheard of for a good Beerenauslese to cost up to $250.

TROCKENBEERENAUSLESE: A step above the Beerenauslese, but these grapes are dried (*trocken*), so they're more like raisins. These "raisinated" grapes produce the richest, sweetest, honeylike wine—and the most expensive.

EISWEIN: A very rare, sweet, concentrated wine made from frozen grapes left on the vine. They're pressed while still frozen. According to Germany's 1971 rules for winemaking, this wine must now be made from grapes that are at least ripe enough to make a Beerenauslese.

GERMAN WINES

Frank Schoonmaker, with Peter Sichel

An invisible line, a frontier much more enduring than any national boundary or iron curtain, runs across Western Europe, traced by the sun. It starts north of Nantes on the Atlantic coast of France, parallels the Loire as far as Orléans, and continues east to Auxerre, cuts abruptly north to Château-Thierry and the Marne hillsides, runs on east to Luxembourg and thence northeast to the Rhine; beyond the Rhine it turns sharply south to Würzburg, Stuttgart, and the Black Forest. This line is not, although it sounds like it, a tourist's itinerary—it is the northern limit of the vine.

Beyond this line grapes will not ripen in an average year; along this line, close to it but south of it, are produced the lightest, the most delicate, the most fragrant, the loveliest white wines of the world.

The Mosel and Rhine wines are the undisputed queens among these "border vintages"—fine, pale, cold-country wines, so light in alcohol that many of them could not legally be classified as wine if they were produced in California. The vineyards from which they come are on the same latitude as Land's End and the Isle of Wight. There is already snow in the Hunsrück and the Eifel and the Black Forest by the time the grapes are ripe on the lower hillsides in late October; and there is still a danger of frost when the first timid leaves appear and the days of the "Ice Saints" come round in mid-May.

When my first book, Windows on the World Complete Wine Course, *came out in 1985, I asked Peter Sichel to write the foreword. As anyone in the wine business will tell you, Peter is always there to help, especially for new wine lovers. I remember, as a student of wine in my twenties, going to a lecture on German wines that Peter conducted at the Culinary Institute of America, and from that moment on I wanted to learn everything that he could teach me not just on the wines of Germany but on the wines around the world. He has authored many books and countless articles on wine, and though now in his mid-eighties continues to speak on wine. Many of you would know his famous wine Blue Nun, which he helped establish as a top-selling wine in the American market, but beyond that he was one of the great experts on Bordeaux and until recently owned Château Fourcas Hosten. One of my fondest memories of Peter was his surprise sixtieth birthday party organized by his wife, Stella, and his daughters, which was held at Windows on the World.*

There are four of these *Eis-Heiligen,* or Ice Saints, in the German calendar; May 12, St. Pancratius; May 13, St. Servatius; May 14, St. Bonifacius; and May 14, *die kalte Sophie,* or cold St. Sophia. According to tradition, the vines are safe from freezing once these days are past, but a sudden cold snap during the Ice Saints' days has ruined any number of otherwise excellent vintage years. You will see smudge pots out in many German vineyards by May 10, ready to be lit at short notice if the Ice Saints live up to their reputation; although they are listed as saints in the calendar, cold St. Sophia and her friends are regarded as hardly fit subjects for canonization by the average wine grower.

A hundred days of full sunshine are needed between May and October, the Germans say, to produce good wine, and a hundred and twenty to produce great wine. They get their hundred about every other year, and their hundred and twenty perhaps twice in a decade.

Germany is not, therefore, a wine-producing country in the same sense as Italy, France, and Spain. Grapes are grown and wines are made commercially on only a few southern slopes in certain favored valleys. Actually the Bordeaux district of France, with its Graces, Sauternes, and clarets, produces a greater variety of wines than all the vineyards in Germany put together, and the annual production of a single French department, the Hérault, is three times that of all Germany. Yet Germany, despite the fact that her wines are limited, in quantity and also in range, ranks, in the special field of fine wines, almost on par with France.

Leaving out of consideration the German red wines (few of which could be described as fine by even the most charitable of judges, with one or two notable exceptions), it can be said that *all* German wines, from the most inconsequential Gutedels and Kleinbergers of Southern Baden and the Neckar Valley to the noblest and most aristocratic Rieslings of the Rhine, have a decided and unmistakable family resemblance. German vintners, in other words, do only one thing—but they do that one thing supremely well. German wines have, beyond any questions, a higher average level of excellence than the wines of any country in the world.

THE LAND

"Rhineland," says an old German proverb, is "wine-land," and certainly, as far as Germany is concerned, this is gospel. Every German wine of the slightest consequence, from the Drachenblut, that rather anemic "Dragon's Blood" which the slopes of Drachenfels, near Bonn, yield in the north, to the pleasant little Seeweine produced on the shores of Lake Constance in the south, is, in the last analysis, a Rhine wine, or at least a wine produced in the Rhine basin. Not only the Rhine Valley itself, but the valleys of almost all its tributaries, have their wines. Thus the picturesque and charming little valley of Ahr, which joins the Rhine some 20 miles south of Bonn, has acquired a special and largely local fame for its red wines, which can be most agreeable on a restaurant terrace in summer. The Mosel of course needs no

241

introduction; its waters meet those of the Rhine at Koblenz—the name Koblenz, incidentally, comes directly from the Latin and means confluence. A little farther south, there is the Nahe: along its precipitous and rocky banks is produced a whole collection of wines which are little known outside Germany but which are often admirable. The Main, which gives its name to Mainz (or Mayence) winds down out of the Franconian highlands, but way of Würzburg and Frankfurt; the vineyards of Hochheim, although classified as belonging to Rheingau, actually overlook the Main, not far from its junction with the Rhine; and along the upper Main are the hills which produce the Frankenweine which comes to us in the characteristic *Bocksbeutel*. Lastly there is the Neckar, Heidelberg's river, which between Heilbronn and Stuttgart is flanked with vines.

And, in addition, of course, in all their unending numbers, there are the wines of the Rhine Valley itself.

Most of this vineyard country, oddly enough, has a trace or a whiff or a what-you-will of Southern Europe in its makeup. The villages are typically and charmingly German, with half-timber houses and high gables, old, painted wrought-iron signs over the tavern doors, ruined castles on a good many of the hills, and window-boxes full of flowers along every main street of every important town. And yet this feeling of the South persists—you will see fig trees and almond trees and apricot trees in the sheltered gardens, and life seems a good deal less rigid and less stern than it is in Prussia. Constantly, and almost everywhere, you will find something reminiscent of Northern

Italy or Southern France or Spain, and even now, after 1,800 years, something that will make you remember that most of this Rhine country, this vineyard country, was once part of the Roman Empire, influenced by Latin customs and subject to Roman law.

There are the remains of Roman buildings or the relics of Roman life almost everywhere: bronze pruning knives, eighteen centuries old but very like those used today, in a museum; the great dark indestructible mass of the Porta Nigra in Trier; a carved stone signpost across the river from Piesport; a ruined amphitheatre, a wine amphora in a private collection; even the Latin names of towns—Cologne, from *Colonia Agrippina*, Mainz, from *Moguntiacum*, Trier, or Trèves, from *Augusta Trevirorum*.

But even more than all these, there is, in the life of this wine country, something ancient and good, a feeling of an old civilization, of well-tilled and well-loved soil.

THE VINE

The Rhine Valley is one of the rare districts in Europe where the vine grows wild—as if Nature had set out to prove that the Rhineland had been destined from the beginning to be a "wine-land." This wild vine, however, is not of course the conventional *Vitis vinifera*, the "wine-bearer" of almost all European vineyards—it is *Vitis silvestris*, very similar to the familiar *Vitis labrusca*, the wild grape of the New England woods. German geologists have even found the clear print of grape leaves in fossils of the Tertiary period; these seem to belong to an unknown species which has been christened *Vitis teutonica*, and is presumably the earliest German vine. We can safely assume that it was a less good wine grape than the Riesling.

For the Riesling, in Germany, is king. To it, and to it alone, the wines of the Mosel and Saar and Ruwer owe the floweriness of their bouquet and their extraordinary delicacy of flavor. Its tight little bunches of yellow-green grapes, which become deep golden as they ripen, are responsible for practically all the great wines of the Rheingau and the Nahe, and for all the best of those of Rheinhessen and the Pfalz. This may, incidentally, be as good a time as any to point out [. . .] that the name is pronounced "reece-ling," not "rye-sling."

it yields wines not unworthy of their great name. It is grown to a certain extent in the vineyards of Soave, which is perhaps the best of Italian white wines, and in Alsace, of course, overlooking its native Rhine, it is completely at home. There are even unlikely stories to the effect that one or two of the better Graves, in the Bordeaux country, owe their finesse to a proportion of Rieslings planted among the Sémillons and Sauvignons which predominate in their vineyards.

Despite this ability to survive and prosper in other countries, the Riesling is at its best in Germany, as no one who has ever tasted a great Scharzhofberger, or a great Marcobrunner, or a Forster Kirchenstück, can for a moment doubt.

243

Even transplanted to other countries, the Riesling preserves a good deal of astonishing quality and breed. In California it is known as the white Riesling, or Johannisberg Riesling, and from it come some of the best wines produced in the country around San Francisco Bay. It is called the Johannisberg (presumably after Schloss Johannisberg) in Switzerland, and along the upper reaches of the Rhône Valley, east of Lake Geneva,

This, of course, is partly a matter of climate (the Riesling needs warm weather and can subsist with a minimum of moisture), partly a matter of soil (the Riesling is not fussy about the soil and does well in infertile and stony ground), and partly a matter of the loving care with which the vine is cultivated and the grapes picked, sorted, and pressed. Such loving care the Germans give the Riesling, full measure and running over. And what the Riesling gives in return is beyond praise.

The Riesling accounts for slightly more than 23 percent of the white grape varieties grown in Germany. Vastly more German wine is made from other, more productive, less distinguished grapes than from the Riesling itself. Most of these have the virtue of a high yield per hectare, plus an ability to ripen more quickly, a necessity in a northern vineyard area. The two other main grape varieties are Müller-Thurgau, today the most prevalent white variety grown in Germany and accounting for fully 31 percent of total white grape planting, and the Silvaner, which accounts for 17 percent. The Müller-Thurgau carries the name of the scientist who created it in 1882 from crossing two clones of Riesling, and it was first planted commercially in 1913. It produces on average at least one-third more per hectare than the Riesling and ripens early. Its wines are light and fruity with a slight Muscat taste and with less acidity than the Riesling. It requires better soil and more rain than Riesling, but it is less fussy about sun and heat. When limited in its production it can produce wines of elegance and charm, reminiscent of the Riesling. The Grüner (Green) Silvaner was the dominant grape variety only ten years ago, and is still the second variety after Müller-Thurgau in the Nahe, Rheinhessen, the Rheinpfalz, and Franconia. It ripens some fifteen days before the Riesling and produces full, though somewhat neutral, wine. It is the most copious producer after the Müller-Thurgau. Ideal as a blending wine, it also makes an admirable everyday wine, quite drinkable when only a few months old. Like the Riesling, which it in no way resembles, the Silvaner has a confusing multiplicity of names. In the Rheingau, where

it is little grown, it is called the Österreicher, which would seem to indicate that it originated in Austria. In the Pfalz it goes by the name of Franken, or "Franconian." Around Würzburg, in Franconia, the Steinwein country, it is sometimes even called the Franken Riesling—but this name is almost in the nature of a joke, like Welsh rabbit or Scotch woodcock. However, in the United States, the Silvaner has had the effrontery to call itself simply "Riesling," instead of Franken Riesling, and this absurd misnomer has received, alas, official sanction, so that in order to get a true Riesling wine from California, the consumer now has to ask for Johannisberg Riesling. It would be hard to find a more illegitimate appropriation of a great name. It is also rather amusing to note that Swiss usage is the exact opposite of American in this connection: a Swiss wine labeled "Johannisberg" may be made from either Silvaner or Riesling; one labeled "Riesling" may be made only from the true Riesling grape.

Germany would not produce the quality or quantity of wine it does if it did not benefit from the most advanced scientific research. It is the only country where clonal selection is used both for the rootstock and the grafted scion. This has resulted in greater vine productivity, disease resistance, and development of new crossings.

There is a permanent scientific effort to develop grape varieties that combine the elegance and taste of the Riesling without its long maturing period. Other varieties are developed for blending wines in order to enable an unripe Riesling grape still to produce an elegant and fine wine when nature has not permitted it to mature fully.

Some of these varieties may indeed become prevalent thirty or forty years from now, just as the Müller-Thurgau achieved this distinction only recently. It is a fascinating game of man against nature, requiring patience and ingenuity. [...]

THE VINEYARDS

The vineyards of Germany are very ancient. Many of them, certainly those of the Mosel, Hessia, and the Pflaz, date back to the dawn of the Christian era, a century or so after Caesar's conquest of Gaul. At the beginning, their expansion was limited by very severe laws forbidding the planting of the vine in Roman colonies—perhaps the first but certainly far from the last protectionist legislation in the field of wine. These laws were finally abrogated in the third century AD by the Emperor Probus, who is today regarded as the father of German viticulture, although whether he ever tasted a glass of German wine is at least doubtful.

In any case, a hundred years later, the Latin writer Ausonius, who gave his name to Château Ausone, in France, published a famous descriptive poem about the *Mosella* and its wines, and many of the Roman relics that have been unearthed date from approximately the same period.

There exist dozens of stories and legends about these historic vineyards, but it is a little difficult to say how many of them are worthy of credence. Thus it is told that Charlemagne, from the great palace he built at Ingelheim on the Rhine near Mainz, perceived that there was one slope across the river, in what is now called Rheingau, on which the snow melted earlier than elsewhere; he ordered that it be planted with vines, and this is now the steep vineyard of Schloss Johannisberg.

As everywhere in Europe, the early history of the vineyards is closely bound up with the history of the Church and of the monastic orders, particularly the Cistercians and the Benedictines. A surprisingly high proportion of the great German vineyards was created by monks and was at one time ecclesiastical property despite the fact that most of these holdings have long been secularized; it is still possible to buy a wine (and a very good wine, too) produced and bottled by the Cathedral of Trier.

Through the ages more than 20,000 individual vineyard names were registered in their communities, and at least a quarter of them became famous among the wine-drinking public in Germany. The new German wine law of 1971 decreed that no single vineyard should be less than 5 hectares in size and that its soil and climate should be homogenous enough so that wines grown in any part of the vineyard would be similar in quality and taste. [...]

An outline map of Western Germany, showing only the rivers, is surprisingly like a wine map of the country. There are differences, of course. The Rhine north of Bonn runs through flat land unsuited to vines. But German vineyards, as a whole, are river vineyards and hillside vineyards; in the northern latitude the grape requires a maximum of sun, which only a hillside vineyard, facing south, can provide, and most such slopes are along river valleys. The majority of German vineyards, for the same reason, are steep, and have to be created, cultivated, and maintained by hand labor. Each individual vine, on the Mosel, has its stake, taller than a man; along the Rheingau and in Rheinhessen and the Pflaz, the vines are strung on wires and tailored until they look like hedges in a formal garden.

An enormous amount of care goes into the selection of the vines themselves. Along the Mosel you will quite often see colored rings painted on the vine stakes; these, like ribbons at a dog show, are the marks of a champion, a particularly sturdy or particularly productive vine, and it is from these that cuttings are taken for propagation.

Like practically all the wine-producing vines of France, those in Germany are for the most part grafted, and on American roots. In the latter half of the last century, an insect pest invaded Europe from the United States, probably carried on some native American grape cuttings brought over for experimental purposes. The name of the pest is *Phylloxera vastatrix*; it is a tiny louse which lives on the roots of vines. In the eastern United States, the roots of the hardy native vine are rough enough to survive. In Europe (as in California, where the vineyards are planted with

European varieties) its arrival was a major catastrophe. It devastated and destroyed three-quarters of the famous vineyards of the world in less than fifty years. The remedy was found at last—to bring over to Europe, and from the eastern States into California, the wild, native American vine, or a hybrid descended from it, and to graft on this resistant stock the Rieslings, the Silvaners, etc., which unlike the wild American vine, produce grapes for fine wine. [...]

THE VINTAGE

The vintage, or harvest, in Germany rarely begins before mid-October, and in certain extraordinary years it continues through November, long after the wine has been pressed out and fermented and safely stored away in its cellar in other countries. The truth is, of course, that most grapes would simply not ripen at all in the pale, cool autumn sunshine of the Mosel and Rhine. Yet it is this same process of long maturation under a sun that never bakes the grapes which gives German wines their incredible elegance and flavor. A whole family of new grape varieties that mature early has been developed by German scientists, the Müller-Thurgau being the most famous and most successful. Unfortunately the Riesling takes a long time to mature, yet its hardiness and superb, fragrant fruit make it the best of the fine grape varieties the Germans grow. The Silvaner matures earlier than the Riesling, but later than the Müller-Thurgau, which is why it has been supplanted by the latter.

This question of ripeness is an exceedingly important one: in the field of German wine, it is the key to everything—to vintage charts and vineyard ratings, to nomenclature, and even price. The most expensive wines are those made from grapes that are not only ripe, but overripe; the cheapest from grapes so green and sour that sugar has to be added to their juice in order to produce something that can pass for wine. The great vintage years are those in which a high proportion of grapes achieve full maturity, just as the great vineyards are those favored slopes on which grapes ripen more often and more completely than on neighboring hillsides.

German wines are the only wines in the world which are classified not only by geographic origin and by vineyard, but also by degree of ripeness at the time of picking. Prior to the new German wine law the vintners, and particularly the estates, had many gradations describing ripeness, based not as much on the existing regulations as on the growers' dedication to diversity. All that has been done away with, and today there are strict regulations as to the degree of grape sugar a wine must have at time of picking to be allowed to be sold as wine at all, or to be entitled to one of the other designations identifying quality and type. In addition there are strict regulations forcing the grower not only to report each lot as it is picked, but also to submit the wine to an official panel for approval before releasing it for sale. Before 1791 the wine law was so complex and diverse that it was almost impossible to set a guideline as to the different designations. Now it is so specific that the consumer can have no doubt that the wine he buys is legally entitled to its name of origin and designation of quality.

There are set minimum sugar requirements for every region, grape variety, and quality designation. The Riesling has the lowest requirements since it is the last to ripen and is the most ambrosial of all grape varieties. It is what the Germans call *extraktreich* (full of essence).

SPAIN

SPAIN

FRANCE

RÍAS BAIXAS

RIBERA DEL DUERO

RIOJA

PENEDÈS

RUEDA

PRIORAT

Barcelona

PORTUGAL

★ Madrid

Mediterranean Sea

Sevilla

SHERRY

Atlantic Ocean

0 Miles 100 200

0 Kilometers 200

I THINK I MIGHT HAVE BEEN ONE OF THE FIRST young Americans ever to go to Rioja. My hair was much longer than it is today and I was twenty-four years old, fresh out of college. Rioja back in those days was very rural, and Francisco Franco was still running the country. I am sure many locals were wondering what I was doing in their region. In one of my visits to a bodega, no one spoke English and my Spanish was very poor. Finally the winemaker decided he would give me a tasting. He started with wines from the 1960s, the 1950s, and then back to the 1940s. When I finally asked him why he was being so generous with such older vintages, he surprised me by stating that the wines really weren't that old. He had just labeled them with the birth years of his children! Anyhow, I was happy to be in Rioja and it was still a great tasting.

There are 2.7 million acres of land planted to grapevines in Spain, the most acreage dedicated to grapevines than any other country in the world. Spain is the world's third largest producer of wine (behind Italy and France).

Tempranillo and Garnacha are the two main red grapes of Spain, and there are three main quality levels of Spanish red wine: Crianza (released after two years of aging, with a minimum of one year in oak barrels); Reserva (released after three years of aging, with at least one in oak); and Gran Reserva (released after five to seven years of aging, with a minimum of two years in oak). The most popular white grapes are Viura and Albarino.

The main wine-growing regions of Spain are La Rioja, Cataluna (Penedes and Priorato), and Ribera del Duero, all of which are north of Madrid and west of Barcelona; and also the Sherry district south of Sevilla and east of the Strait of Gibraltar. Other wine-growing regions are Rias Baixas, Toro, and Jumilla. A real treat is to try the great rosés of the Navarra region. In Penedes and Priorat, the main grape is Garnacha, while in Rioja, Tempranillo is king.

The renaissance of Spanish wine has been nowhere more prevalent than in Rioja! Since the 1800s, Rioja had always been influenced by its French neighbor, Bordeaux, in techniques and traditions. Rioja is less than 250 miles from Bordeaux. I often think there's more to that than people realize. During the 1870s phylloxera caused many of Bordeaux's winemakers and owners to relocate to Rioja, where the blight had yet to appear and whose climate and growing conditions were similar to that of Bordeaux. As they established their own wineries and vineyards, they influenced how Rioja wine was made. This influence is still apparent in Rioja wines today.

Rioja benefits geographically from its northern mountain ranges, whose protective ring shields it from cold, northern sea winds; and the southern end of the region, which is open to the warm air currents from the Mediterranean Sea. Its microclimate is unique.

—KZ

SPANISH WINE: A Brief History

John Radford

If Noah really planted the first vineyard around 5000 BC on Mount Ararat, then Spain was a relative latecomer to the practice. Despite the fact that an ancient people known as the Phoenicians dominated trade around the Mediterranean for centuries, they did not establish the city of Gadir (modern Cádiz) until around 1100 BC. Even then, wine was a commodity, traded along with olives and wheat.

In those days, wine was transported in clay containers called amphorae, which were heavy, leaky, and fragile (fragments are still being fished out of the estuary at Sanlúcar de Barrameda). Sooner or later, it must have seemed more sensible to the Phoenicians to make wine themselves and ship it out of Gadir, rather than to lug it all the way into the city from what is now called the Middle East.

Farther inland from Gadir and away from the fierce, westerly coastal winds, the land was low and fertile and the climate hot—an environment that must have seemed similar to the Phoenician traders' own homeland. Such conditions were ideally suited to growing the tough-skinned, sweet grape varieties that were the stock-in-trade of the traveling vintner 3,000 years ago, and this is probably the origin of the "golden triangle" we now know as Sherry Country.

The next major shift in winemaking style and skills came with the Romans, who ruled Spain (or most of it) from about 100 BC until the collapse of the Roman Empire in the fifth century. As was their usual practice in conquered lands, the invading legions planted vines; more important, they brought new viticultural methods with them. As a result, the local tribes—mostly Celts in the west and Iberians in the center and east—quickly adopted the Roman practices of fermentation in stone troughs and storage in smaller, more manageable amphorae made of finer (and therefore tougher and less porous)

John Radford is another great British wine and food writer with special emphasis on the wines and food of Spain. Since 2004 he has been the Spanish editor for the annual Wine Report, which has been an invaluable, up-to-date guide to understanding what's happening in Spain. His books have won international prizes including Best Wine Book in the World in 2008 by the Gourmand World Cookbook Awards, and his articles appear in many publications including Decanter magazine.

clay. This style of winemaking is still in use in the Spanish countryside, where it is known as the *método rural*, or rural method.

The Moorish Invasion

After the fall of the Roman Empire, Spain came under the domination of the Moors of northern Africa, whose occupation lasted from the eighth century until their defeat in 1492. Although the Moors perfected the art of distillation, as a Muslim people they used it mainly in the manufacture of perfumes and cosmetics from plant materials—though undoubtedly stumbling upon various alcoholic distillations in their medicinal research. Wine, meanwhile,

was probably made by individual farmers, who may even have traded it with parts of Christian Europe. In terms of advancement, however, Spanish wines remained in a period of stasis until the country was reunified and wine became an export commodity in huge demand in the developing Americas.

Spain's first wines were heavy and heady—a reflection of their eastern Mediterranean heritage—and they were made in either a sweet or *rancio* style (literally "rancid," that is, fully oxidized and heavily reduced): the sort of thing that could survive intact if its container were neither airtight nor spotlessly clean. By the sixteenth and

seventeenth centuries, however, wine was being made all over northern and central parts of the country, and the styles of both red and white wines were much more similar to the wine styles of today.

As always, oxidation posed the main problem for all wines, and a number of methods were devised to prevent it. The first (and most obvious) solution was to develop a taste for *rancio* wines. Although it admittedly takes some getting used to, this style is still made and enjoyed by a small but enthusiastic market in northern Spain.

Prevention and Cure

As to ways of keeping air out: the Greeks had already set a precedent by sealing their amphorae with pine resin, a practice that gave birth to retsina. Similarly, Spanish *viñeros*, or winemakers, developed large clay vats known as *tinajas*, with narrow openings at the top. These they filled to the brim and sealed with a heavy lid to exclude as much air as possible. Even if oxidation did take place, the small surface area meant that its effects were minimal. Old earthenware *tinajas* are still found in parts of southern Spain.

Useful as they were, such vessels were simply too large and cumbersome to move about; they were especially unsuitable as cargo for ships bound for the expanding colonial markets. For this reason, wine was transported in dried animal skins which could be filled and tightly sewn together to prevent oxidation. Given that the curing and cleansing process was a little on the primitive side, however, the wine inside such skins would hardly have remained unaffected, and the several weeks it took to sail from Cádiz

to the new colonies inevitably took their toll on the contents.

The late fifteenth century brought some progress in the form of the butt or cask. Round wooden containers had been used to transport foodstuffs for years; once winemakers began to employ them, laws were passed around the year 1500 which stipulated that barrels made for wine must be of the highest quality, untainted by any other product.

Initially, butts were used for fermentation and storage because the wood swelled when wet, keeping the wine secure. They were little better than skins at keeping air from wine during long sea voyages, but they were hardy enough to keep the strong, fortified wines of Jerez in check—as Sir Francis Drake discovered when he "singed the king of Spain's beard" in 1587 (by attacking Philip II's armada in Cádiz) and made off with 2,900 of them. This incident coincided with a big demand for what had become known as "sheris sack" in Shakespearian England, as evidenced by the antics of such fictional characters as Sir John Falstaff. The real breakthrough in Spanish winemaking took place toward the end of the eighteenth century. In Bordeaux, cooperage had become much more of a fine art, with the great châteaux demanding (and being able to afford) the best workmanship. A *viñero* from Rioja by the name of Manuel Quintano was so impressed with the quality of Bordeaux casks that he purchased some and brought them back to his native vineyards. The French coopers had discovered the art of keeping barrels airtight by means of using a bung on the "belly" of the cask as well as one in the end. This prevented air from coming in and made it easier for wine to be withdrawn and racked; it also made the casks easier to clean and refill.

Quintano filled the barrels with Rioja wine and sent them to America. Not only had the wine arrived in excellent condition, but the time spent in cask rolling around on the deck of the ship had added a pleasantly "oaky" flavor to it—something modern Rioja-lovers would immediately recognize. His neighbors, however, were less impressed, refusing to have anything to do with him until he stopped using Bordeaux casks. Eventually, Quintano went back to using leaky buckets, but not before the seeds of progress had been sown.

The Rioja Transformation

Fifty years later, the foundations of modern Spanish wine were laid by two men who quite separately brought "Bordeaux technology" to Rioja. The first was the Peruvian-born Luciano de Murrieta García-Lemone (later the Marqués de Murrieta), who had fled Spain after fighting on the "wrong" side in the first Carlist war and spent time in Bordeaux, studying winemaking methods

there. He returned to Rioja in 1850 and made his first vintage in a borrowed bodega in 1852. Meanwhile another Spanish exile (because of his liberal political writings), Don Camilo Hurtado de Améxaga, the Marqués de Riscal, had been learning the Bordeaux trade at Château Lanessan in the Haut-Médoc. Both men had had the same idea: that the wines of Rioja could compete with Bordeaux in quality terms, given the right treatment. Riscal planted a vineyard in Elciego and created the first purpose-built bodega there in 1860. Murrieta went on to found his own bodega—the magnificent Ygay estate outside Logroño—in 1872.

253

These early experiments were ridiculed as being too expensive by some of the existing wine producers, but the local government office in the province of Álava saw the results and realized the potential. They hired the services of a French winemaker by the name of Jean Pineau to show this same Bordeaux technology to winemakers in the area in the hope of improving their wines, getting a better price for them, and developing an export market. However, the locals (with the odd honorable exception) would have none of this foreigner coming around telling them how to make wine, and gave him the cold shoulder. It's important to remember that they were still making wine by the stone-trough method, which had remained virtually unchanged since the Romans, 1,300 years before. That gives us some idea of how radical these proposed changes must have seemed.

Don Camilo's neighbors watched in amusement as he invested massive amounts of money in his new winery, but the smiles froze on their faces as they saw his wines fetch prices of which they had never dreamed. Jean Pineau's contract expired in 1868, and Riscal stepped in and hired him to supervise the winemaking at his bodega. The new technology had proved its worth, and most of the rest of Rioja's winemakers followed suit, sooner or later—although you can still buy *cosechero* Rioja made in the old style, even today.

A hundred years passed before the next great innovation, and the prime mover behind this was the late Miguel Torres, who had seen stainless-steel winemaking kits in France and Australia in the 1950s which gave winemakers pin-sharp accuracy in controlling fermentation temperatures. He installed the first tanks at his winery in Catalonia in the 1960s and such was their success that most of the rest of Spain followed suit. Indeed, Barcelona has become a world center for the manufacture of stainless-steel winemaking gear, and it's now cheaper to install water-jacketed tanks than to rebuild or even repair the old epoxy-lined concrete tanks which had been the nineteenth-century update of the Romans' stone troughs.

Spanish Wine in the Modern Age

At this point, Spanish winemaking history might well have ended. New-style winemaking existed alongside traditional methods: native and international grape varieties flourished in adjacent vineyards. From the customer's point of view, there was something for everyone. But Spain is not a country to stand still once it finally gains momentum. After centuries of stasis, the *viñeros* have the scent of innovation in their nostrils and they like the aroma. Even in the most obscure regions, at least one maverick is trying out a different type of fermentation, a new yeast strain or a forgotten grape variety. Sometimes their efforts come to nothing; sometimes they yield pure gold. The best news by far is that the *consejos reguladores* (regulating councils) are much more prepared to look at new ideas and innovation. Just twenty years ago, they might have thrown up their corporate hands in despair.

This forward-looking attitude has given rise to a new approach to Spanish wines, which could be dubbed "postmodern" wines, since they usually involve reinventing some ancient practice. Barrel fermentation is a good example. In the past, it was only in rare autumns, when the temperature fell sharply immediately after picking, that it produced great wines. With today's air-conditioned underground cellars, the coolness of those autumns can be reproduced artificially, with a resulting improvement inside the cask. Similarly, grapes such as the Verdejo, which traditionally oxidized so fast that it was normally used to make *rancio*-type wines, have proved to make outstandingly fresh wines when vinified under a blanket of inert gas. That is the range and panoply of contemporary Spanish wine.

THE NEW SPAIN

To understand any country's wine, it is first necessary to have a basic knowledge of its structure and geography. In 1978, Spain adopted a new constitution which restored the identity of the ancient kingdoms and regions which originally made up the nation in 1492. The result was a kind of "United States of Spain," consisting of seventeen *autonomías*, or autonomous regions, each with its own parliament and a number with their own languages. To complicate matters, the country is further subdivided into fifty *provincias*, or provinces, and Spain also controls two offshore outposts on the Moroccan coast. Some *autonomías* consist of several provinces; others, such as La Rioja and Navarra, consist of only one. Although man-made divisions go some way toward explaining how and why wines develop as they do, other, uncontrollable, influences (for instance nature and the human condition) play even more vital roles.

Regions and Wines

Three main factors influence the way wines develop. First, there is the climate: cool, wet

areas foster white-grape vines; warm, dry ones favor reds. A second factor is the food that was most freely available in the days before refrigeration: coastal areas and riverlands yield fish and seafood, while inland and mountainous regions offer game, cattle, sheep, and pigs. Finally, there are the cultures and origins of the inhabitants themselves. Celtic seafarers, for example, have very different eating habits to those of the isolated, land-locked shepherds of the Meseta. This evolution of climate, gastronomy, and culture has divided Spain into seven major regions.

GREEN SPAIN "Green" Spain stretches from Galicia in the lush, cool, rainy northwest through the *Costa Verde*, or Green Coast, of Asturias and Cantabria in the north, and finally into the Basque Country. These areas share weather influences from the Atlantic and the Bay of Biscay, a tradition of seafood, and a strongly non-Castilian culture—Celtic in the west, Basque in the foothills of the Pyrenees. In Galicia, they speak Gallego, a close relative of Portuguese. In the Basque Country, they speak Euskara, related to no other language in the world.

OLD CASTILE, or Castilla y León, is the historic heartland of Castilian Spain, where kings and bishops, princes and academics have disported themselves since the Middle Ages. Food comes on the hoof or on the wing, the climate is hot and continental, and the wine style is very "mainstream"—Spanish wines the way Spaniards drink them. This is traditionally where the best Castilian Spanish is spoken.

NORTH-CENTRAL SPAIN This part of the country lies in the shelter of the Cordillera Cantábrica mountains, which protect it from the excesses of Green Spain's maritime climate. Two provinces of the Basque Country are situated north of the mountain range; one—Álava or Araba—is located south of the mountains and produces Rioja wines.

La Rioja, Navarra, and, to a lesser extent, Aragón have been at the forefront of Spanish winemaking for a thousand years. After the phylloxera, or vine-louse, epidemic that devastated Frech vineyards between 1860 and 1890, these were also the nearest regions from which the French could buy wine. Then, as now, the Spanish *viñeros* worked hard to keep their customers happy. If these Spanish wines have been designed to please export markets, it must just be a coincidence that this region reflects a strong Castilian heritage, a dry, continental climate, and a history of prosperity.

CATALONIA AND THE BALEARICS There is a strongly independent outlook here, the legacy of the medieval Catalan empire (that included the Balearic Islands). The climate is Mediterranean maritime, the cuisine is based mainly on the sea, and the Catalan people are quick to point out that Spain is not all Castile. This inventive culture has produced some of the country's most exciting and innovative wines. The people of Catalonia speak Catalan, while those of the Balearic Islands use a Catalan dialect called Mallorquín.

THE LEVANT In terms of climate, the Levant (literally "the getting-up"—where the sun rises) is a hotter version of Catalonia, with similar weather and gastronomy, and an ancient tradition of seafaring and trade. It is divided between Valencia, where the locals speak a Catalan dialect called Valenciano, and Murcia, where Castilian is spoken.

THE MESETA, according to a Castilian proverb, suffers from "five months of winter and seven months of hell." This flat, semi-arid plain is hot and high (2,297 to 3,281 feet/ 700 to 1,000 meters), and only sheep and the toughest grapes survive here. Thus, local cuisine consists basically of sheep, sheep's-milk cheese, and sheep, and until the foundation of Madrid in the sixteenth century, the local culture was one of isolation. This section covers the wines of Madrid province, Castilla-La Mancha (post-*Reconquista*, or reconquest, Castile), and Extremadura, on the Portuguese border. Castilian is the main language, with regional dialects.

ANDALUSIA Andalusia is Spain's oldest wine-producing area, dominated by sherry. Its climate is fully Mediterranean, but the style of wine has been determined more by several centuries of export markets than by the local gastronomy. Andalusia is highly traditional, and Castilian is its main language, though seasoned with the usual regional dialects.

THE CANARY ISLANDS have a subtropical climate, a seafood-eating history, and an interesting cultural mix of islanders that is skewed annually by a massive tourist industry. Its wines, however, are astonishing in many ways, ranging from the most modern, cool-fermented styles to those derived from ancient vines that have been cultivated since the Romans left. Here, they speak a soft, gentle dialect of Castilian, and refer to mainland Spaniards as *peninsulares*.

This is how Spain's wine-country breaks down culturally, gastronomically, and climatically—but real life is never as well-organized as we might prefer. If ever there were a country in which every rule proves to be an exception and every exception proves to be a rule, then this is it.

PORT

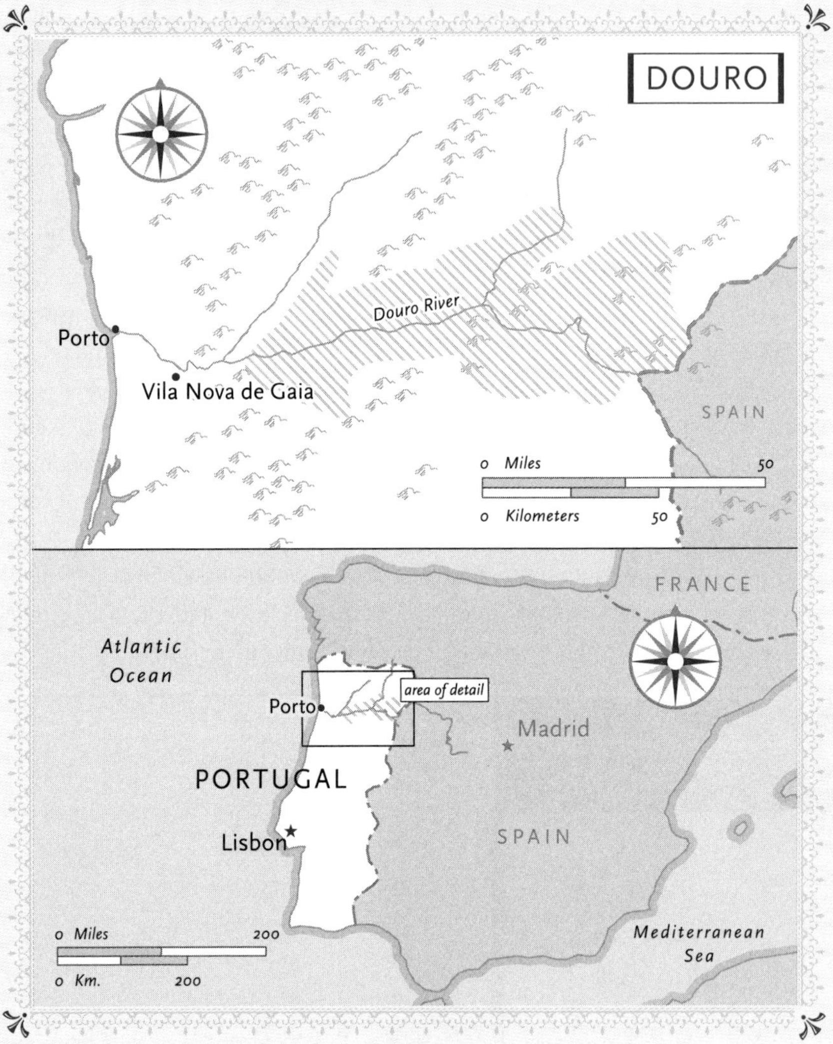

DOURO

Porto

Vila Nova de Gaia

Douro River

SPAIN

o Miles 50

o Kilometers 50

FRANCE

Atlantic
Ocean

Porto

area of detail

Madrid

PORTUGAL

SPAIN

Lisbon

Mediterranean
Sea

o Miles 200

o Km. 200

ON MY VERY FIRST TRIP TO OPORTO, I was lucky enough to visit many of the great port producers, and one of them was Niepoort. One of the reasons I was drawn to study wine and have continued it for the last forty years is because of the hospitality and generosity of wine families. The Niepoort family insisted that I stay with them in their home instead of a hotel. They also went through a tasting with the vintages going back to the early 1900s. One of them was from the 1927 vintage which I had explained to them was the birth year of my father. At the end of my stay they gave me a bottle of the 1927 to give to my father for his next birthday. I can assure you my father and I bonded with the taste of that vintage.

Port is one of the great wines of the world. It has a rich tradition and history that begins in the Douro, a region in northern Portugal. The names *Port*, *Vinho do Porto*, and most recently *Porto* (named for the main city in the Douro from which the wines are traditionally shipped), have been trademarked within Portugal. No new wines made outside of the Douro in the Port style may use these names.

The producers of Port that are renowned in Oporto are labeled by their firm's name, such as Niepoort or Fonseca. Early in the history of the Douro region, many of the most powerful shipping families were British. Over the years Dutch, German, and Scottish as well as Portuguese-owned shippers have also become prominent in the Port industry. For hundreds of years the houses have shipped wine around the world. Once, the *barcos rabelos*, a type of old wooden sailboat used for shipping, were used to transport barrels of Port wine down the Douro River for storage and aging in caves. Today, the *barcos* are used more for promotion, and the Douro region celebrates that tradition with races and festivals celebrating their heritage every mid-summer.

Port may vary from a sweet, rich, deep ruby to a light, rusty, dry tawny. But one thing remains consistent between them: the process by which they are made. Neutral grape brandy is added to Port during fermentation, which stops the fermentation and leaves behind a high percentage of residual sugar. This is why Port is on the sweet side. When making drier ports, the neutral spirits are added after the wine ferments, leaving behind less sugar. Also, when making tawny ports, the wines are aged in oak for a longer period—some for ten, twenty, or thirty years—letting the wine oxidize more.

—*KZ*

POSTCARD FROM PORTO

Mike DeSimone and Jeff Jenssen

In all history, there is no instance of a country having benefited from prolonged warfare.

So stated Sun Tzu, the ancient Chinese general, military strategist, and author of *The Art of War*. There is no argument among intelligent people as to the absolute horror of any war; yet many would agree that without the War of Spanish Succession, the world may never have benefited from the seemingly accidental creation of Port Wine. One of the results of this war, fought among the major European powers from 1701 through 1714, was the signing of the Treaty of Methuen between England and Portugal in 1703.

The primary alliance between England and Portugal was no doubt the 1662 marriage of Charles II, King of England, Scotland, and Ireland, to Catherine of Braganza, the Portuguese Infanta and sister of Peter II, King of Portugal. Catherine is historically noted as being a strong supporter of the formal agreement solidifying military and trade alliances between the two countries. The Treaty of Methuen—also known as the "Port Wine Treaty"—allowed woolen cloth from England to be transported to Portugal duty-free, and it lowered the duty on Portuguese wines brought into England. Several years prior, Charles II had prohibited the importation of all French goods, including wine, into England. In late seventeenth century England, it was impossible to purchase wine from France! Thus wine from Portugal became an available replacement for French wine. A well-known ditty by Jonathan Swift probably best sums up the British sentiment at the time:

Be sometimes to your country true,
Have once the public good in view;
Bravely despise Champagne at court,
And choose to dine at home with Port.

Mike DeSimone and Jeff Jenssen write about travel, food, wine trends, and culture. I've know Mike and Jeff since they took my course, and I have had them back to speak to my students. I see Mike and Jeff all around New York City, where we often run into each other at tastings and other events. But these are two well-traveled gentlemen, who've visited almost as many wine producing countries and regions as I have. They are fun, insightful, and a wonderful team. Their writing is not only informative, but filled with entertaining stories as well.

As English traders in Porto searched for Portuguese wines suitable for shipment to England, the logical source was just upriver, in the Douro Valley. Douro translates as "River of Gold," and it seems to be exactly that to those whose families have made their fortunes on it in the intervening years. One of the first successful merchants to source from this area was Job Beardsley, whose firm formed the basis for Taylor Fladgate and Yeatman. Among the other English Port Shippers listed in early trading documents are Warre's, Phayre and Bradley (later known as Croft), and Kopke. The first Port wines were dark, dry reds, and merchants got into the habit of adding a small amount of brandy to their barrels prior to shipping, in order to preserve them for the overseas voyage. This "small amount" gradually increased, and is today part of the wine-making rather than shipping process. It is in fact one of the very things which makes port wine into Port Wine.

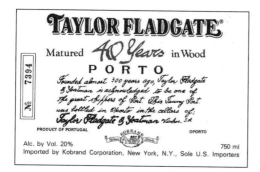

THE FACTORY HOUSE

Short of taking a long boat ride with many stops up the twisting Douro or visiting every Port Lodge in Vila Nova de Gaia, the history of Port is best appreciated through a visit to the Factory House, a grand four-story Georgian

structure on the Rua do Infante Henrique, just near the bridge connecting Porto to its neighbor across the river. In fact, even the street name itself bears testament to the seat of British trade in Portugal: It was formerly named Rua Nova dos Inglezes, which translates as "New Street of the English." It was originally built by the British Association, a merchant's group of English and Scottish traders based in Porto, who dealt not only in Port but other types of goods, such as wool and textiles. The merchants were also known as factors, leading to the origin of the name. (Each merchant's group had its own Factory House, although this is the only one remaining in the world.) The first mention of the British Factory is from the year 1666. After relocating from its original site, built in 1727, it was used by its members from 1790 to 1807, with an interruption from 1807 through 1809, due to the invasion of Portugal by France's Napoleonic armies. Although the British recaptured Porto in 1809, it took until 1811 for the Factory House to reclaim its position as the center of the British Port Trade. On November 11, 1811, a dinner was held celebrating the reopening of the Factory House, and a 100-year anniversary dinner was held on the same day in 1911. Plans are already underway for the 200th anniversary dinner in 2011.

We had the privilege of dining there late last summer, with Adrian Bridge, CEO of the Fladgate Partnership, and his wife, Natasha Robertson Bridge, a seventh generation descendant of the Yeatman family, who is the Chief Port Blender for the group, which includes Taylor Fladgate, Fonseca, Croft, and Delaforce. After passing through

261

the grand pillared entrance, we began with a tour of the cellar, which contains bottles from every major Port Shipper, and reads like a *Who's Who* in the history of Port. Fonseca, Croft, Symington, Graham's, Warre's, Taylor, Cockburn's, Sandeman—bottles of all these and more are arranged in neat little dust-covered stacks, in stark contrast to the young, vibrant, and very attractive First Couple of Port who steered us through low-ceilinged stone alcoves in which rest probably the finest collection of rare vintage ports known to man. Upon joining the Factory House, each new member gives twenty-four cases in order to stock the cellar. In addition to Tawny and Vintage Port, members also pull from their personal selections of Bordeaux and dry Portuguese wines so that there is always a broad choice of wines to serve with Wednesday lunch.

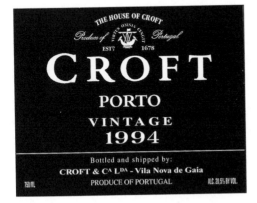

After our cellar tour, we visited the library and kitchen; the Factory House serves for its members as a University Club might in other cities; gentlemen can often be found reading newspapers or books, or engaging in polite discourse. Although this is, strictly speaking, the headquarters of the British Port world, discussing business over meals is frowned upon. White Port cocktails were served in the large yellow antechamber, and we were then summoned to the richly paneled dining room, where we started with avocado and prawn salad, paired with 2007 Quinta de Carmo, a dry red blend from southern Portugal, whose plummy attack was balanced nicely by a chocolate finish, before moving on to duck confit with mushroom risotto, served with Quinta de Roriz Reserva 2002, a delicious dry red blend, which contains two of the main grapes used in Port, Touriga National and Touriga Francesa.

After dessert of crème brûlée with raspberries, on its own, we each carried our napkin, as is the custom, into the twin dining room opposite the first, and took our same position at the table for the main event of the evening—drinking Port. We first passed a bottle of velvety Fonseca 20 Year Old Tawny. While we are on the subject of passing the Port, if you ever find yourself in the company of members of British Port families, you will do well to remember that a bottle or decanter of Port is always passed to the left, and as you receive the bottle, you pour a glass for the person on the right. It is said that the leftward passing is a means of always keeping the right hand free to grab one's sword. Another Port tradition states that at the end of a meal, fine Tawny is served before Vintage Port, in order to "rinse" the mouth of the tastes of food and wine. Vintage is then served blind, in a handsome cut crystal decanter around whose neck hangs an oval silver tag emblazoned with grape bunches and engraved with the words "Port 1." (In a multiple blind tasting, ascending versions of the same tag are placed on a series of decanters.) On this occasion, we were treated to a Fonseca 1970 Vintage, whose almost 40 years in bottle were obviously well-spent, as its luscious toasted red and black fruits were perfectly rounded out with notes of mint and licorice. The last wine came with a bit of work—we had to play "Guess the Vintage." Fortunately, we didn't have to play too long as we guessed the correct vintage in under two minutes. If we remember correctly—albeit through a haze—we were offered jobs in the Port trade that evening.

"Guess the Vintage" is a game played after every Wednesday lunch, a tradition as old as the house itself. Members from Port Shipping families meet weekly, for both social and business purposes. Through the years, many families have inter- and cross-married, and it is hard to find someone among the members of the Factory House who is not somehow or however distantly related to at least one other person in the room. Past treasurers, or directors, include Bill Yeatman, William Warre, and John Delaforce. Our good friend Robert Bower is another seventh-generation Yeatman descendant. Robert, a dashing young man with piercing blue eyes and a posh British accent, is a cousin of Natasha; his paternal grandmother was a Yeatman. Although the company is now known officially as the Fladgate Partnership, it is also known as Taylor Fladgate Yeatman. Robert was born and raised early on in Porto, went off to boarding school in England at age eight, and now lives in New York, managing the family's portfolio for their American importer, Kobrand.

Natasha's husband, Adrian, has been responsible for the development of the family's new luxury hotel, The Yeatman, in Vila Nova de Gaia, which offers stunning views of Porto, including the upper levels of this historic meeting place. Robert recently described Wednesday lunch to us, which may include those he counts among his closest friends, including Paul Symington, Johnny Graham, and George Sandeman.

"Lunch at the Factory House, we always come over with some friends or some colleagues from work. We're all great friends with many of our competitors, and we get to see them and get to find out how their families are doing. We're all often traveling at the same time, and the Factory House is a good way to connect while in between all of our travels. You come into the Factory House, and we normally have all of the newspapers there, and we'll always have a newspaper from one hundred years past, so we'll have today's papers and one from one hundred years ago, and it's always quite interesting to read the news and then compare.

"And then we'll go upstairs to the anteroom, and we'll have a glass of Sherry or white Port. We'll have a drink and some roasted almonds, and then when everyone is ready, Olga, who runs the Factory House, will give the treasurer a tap on the shoulder, and then he will shout out to us, sort of tell us, 'Come on, bad boys, get into lunch.' And actually, a little trivia, Olga is Robin Reid's daughter—Robin Reid was the Managing Director for Croft in the eighties and seventies.

"So you and your guests will be together, but that's the only seating plan. We kind of

263

mix it up, but generally you stay with your guests, and although there is a wine list, we will already have ordered the wines in advance, and quite often Paul Symington will have his wines, I'll have mine, and we'll switch around and compare, so it's a good excuse for a wine tasting as well. Then, after the meal is done, you will have your Port Wine and cheese. It's always Tawny Port, followed by your Vintage Port, and that's where I was taught by Michael Symington. I was sitting next to him at my first Wednesday lunch—I was eighteen—and he was the one who said, 'Okay, now you've got to guess the Port.' I went in, I was a kid, and this was my first introduction to this, and I sort of stuck my nose into it, and I was asked to guess what the wine is. You've got all these wonderful wine experts all around you, and there I am, eighteen, praying, *Please don't ask me, please don't ask me.* Michael Symington was very helpful: He leaned over and said to me, 'Don't worry about it. I'll teach you a trick. You just keep *umming* and *arrghing* until they get so bored they move on to the next person. And if you have to say something, always say something good about the wine, because you never know, it might be yours.'

"I find those Wednesday lunches amazing because you get to try somebody else's wine that you're not normally used to, and all of these wines will have come up from the cellar at the Factory House. All of those wines are given when you join. They are given over to the Cellar Master, and you give some of your own best vintages, plus some Bordeaux or Sauternes. Once they are down in that cellar, you know they are going to age amazingly well."

Robert's maternal grandfather and a great-uncle were directors of Cockburn's, which is no longer a family-owned company. Founded by Samuel Cockburn, a Scotsman, in 1815, the house is now part of Fortune Brands' portfolio, after previously having belonged to Allied Domecq and then Pernod Ricard. As the twentieth century notion of marriage for love rather than political alliance or consolidation of family wealth has proliferated, corporate mergers and acquisitions have altered the face of this once wholly family-dominated industry. Quinta de Noval, which sits at the heart of the Douro Valley, has been making world-class Port since 1715, and continues to do so even under the umbrella of the French insurance giant AXA. This is not surprising, considering the fact that AXA's assets also include Château Pichon-Longueville in Bordeaux and Disznoko in Hungary's Tokaj region.

The Symingtons, also major players in the sphere of Port, are able to trace their Port ancestry back thirteen generations, through their great-grandmother Beatrice Atkinson, who married Andrew James Symington in 1891, but was also directly descended from the merchant Walter Maynard, who is recorded as having shipped 39 Pipes of Port from Porto in 1652. (Although they may vary in size, a standard pipe is equal to 550 liters, or 733 bottles of 750 ml each.) Through a series of alliances and mergers begun in 1905, Symington now owns Warre's (established in 1670, and among the oldest British Port firms), Dow's, W & J Graham, and Smith Woodhouse. There are currently seven Symingtons in the family business, which enables them to have a family member

264

actively working in every aspect of production, all the way from the vineyards through blending and bottling. Certainly the jewel in their crown is the one-thousand-plus acre Quinta de Vesuvio, at which they make the eponymous Symington's Quinta de Vesuvio Vintage Port.

THE QUINTA

Quinta de Vesuvio is inarguably among the very best of the *quintas,* or estates, in the Douro, known for producing the very highest quality Ports in both widely declared vintages, or, in undeclared years, Single Quinta Vintage Ports. It is often compared side by side with Taylor Fladgate's Quinta de Vargellas. At the 2007 Vintage Declaration at the Four Seasons Restaurant in New York, the good-natured rivalry among the Port families was evident to us as each presented their finest wines from that year to a select group of guests; taking the microphone to present his wine, he made sure to mention its superiority to that of his competitors. If a bottle from either of the above (or Quinta de Noval, for that matter), from a vintage year, either widely declared or single *quinta*, should pass into your left hand, quickly pour a glass to the person on your right, and hand the bottle of rarified nectar on to the person on your left, so that your glass may be filled as well. And if the bottle stalls before it makes its way to you, remember to ask the person in front of whom the bottle sits, "Do you know the Bishop of Norwich?" If, like yourself, the bottle-staller is well versed in Port etiquette, he will be immediately prompted to hoist

the bottle and resume its passage around the table. If he responds in the negative, you may then inform him, "He's an awfully nice fellow, but he never passes the Port."

THE DOURO

It was hard to appreciate the breathtaking beauty of the Douro Valley on our recent visit to this venerable region with our speedboat captain careening down the Douro River at 40 knots per hour. It was all we could do to hold on to the gunwale with both hands, clinging for dear life itself. The captain refused to comprehend the idea that we wanted a leisurely cruise to take photographs of the steep verdant terraces. Only when the boat came to a halting stop mere meters away from the dam and ensuing waterfall did we loosen our grip long enough to grasp a Chip Dry White Port and tonic to toast our arrival. We raised our glasses to Baron Joseph James Forrester, who died on May 12, 1861, while traveling down the Douro by boat. Locals claim he drowned because the money belt he was wearing, filled with gold coins, pulled him to his death. The bronze plaque near the dam stands as a memorial. His companion, Dona Antonia Ferreira, the largest landowner in the region, was saved by the buoyancy of her fashionable hoop skirt. Looking back over our shoulders for the first time, our brains were etched evermore with the unforgettable panorama of one of the world's most beautiful wine regions.

Located approximately 50 miles upriver from the cities of Porto and Vila Nova de Gaia, both of which are just inland from the

265

Atlantic Ocean, Port wines are produced in the north of Portugal in an area known as the Demarcated Region of the Douro. The region is comprised of three separate areas, the Baixo Corgo (Lower Corgo,) Cima Corgo (Upper Corgo), and the Douro Superior (Upper Douro). The area known as the Lower Corgo is bordered by the towns of Barqueiros, Barro, and Requa. It has a total area of about 45,000 hectares with 14,500 hectares under vines. There are approximately 15,000 farmers in this region. The Upper Corgo continues upstream from Regua to Cachao de Valeira and consists of a total area of just about 95,000 hectares. Approximately 20,000 hectares of vines are tended by 16,000 farmers. The Upper Douro begins above Cachao de Valeira and extends eastward to the Spanish border. Only 10,000 of the total 110,000 hectares are planted with vines. More than 7,000 farmers call this region home.

Of the total land planted with vines, only 26,000 hectares have been authorized for the production of Port Wine. The vines must be at least five years old and are selected according to a strict set of criteria. Vineyard classification is based on a standardized scoring method that rates them from A to F. Grape variety, vine training, productivity, soil type, amount of stones, altitude, geographic location, slope angle, exposure to sun, age of the vines, and vine density are all taken into consideration. Vines are trained close to the ground using the single Guyot, double Guyot, unilateral cordon, or bilateral cordon system. Trellises, while popular in many wine growing regions, are not permitted for Port.

THE VINEYARDS

The vineyards of the Douro are terraced due to the steep incline of the river valley. Initially, vineyards were planted on very narrow terraces which resembled stairs. This terracing, combined with the Douro's many hairpin turns, only adds to the unique beauty of the region. After phylloxera decimated the area in the 1870s, it was customary to build broader, angled terraces. The 1960s brought bulldozers to the region to carve even wider and steeper terraces, or *patamares,* into the valley. Ramos Pinto's Quinta do Bom Retiro is credited as being the first house to use *patamares.* The planting technique was improved again in the late 1970s when the *vinha ao alto* system changed the planting orientation to perpendicular and was widely adopted.

The soil in this region is primarily schistose in nature. Much of it has been created by breaking the upper layers of sedimentary rock with dynamite. The soil type has been officially identified as aric anthrosoil. Areas that have had less aggressive intervention have Precambrian, Leptosoil, and Riverine soils. Particles of broken schistose rock and clay comprise the majority of the topsoil. The Douro is protected from the Atlantic winds by the Montemuro and Marao Mountains, leading to hot, dry summers; conversely, winters are cold and wet. Rainfall is heaviest in the winter months of December and January and is lightest in the summer. Vines in this region are known to extend their roots downward more than twenty-five feet in search of water.

PORT WINES

Port Wine is also known as Porto, Vinho do Porto, or simply Port. Although many winemakers in other countries (including Australia, India, South Africa, and the USA) bottle wine which is labeled "port," European Union guidelines protect the Designation of Origin of Port and Porto Wines from Portugal. Port Wine is a fortified wine that is produced by adding distilled brandy, or *aguardente*, to fermenting wine. The introduction of alcohol kills the yeast, effectively stopping the fermentation process, resulting in a wine with higher levels of residual sugar and alcohol. The fermentation process can last as little as forty-eight hours, as opposed to about one week to ten days for dry wines. A high level of maceration is important to extract the flavors, color, and tannins from the grape skins in this short period of time. For this reason, grapes have been trodden by foot for centuries, and only recently has mechanization taken over to simulate this effect.

The styles of Port include: Ruby Style, Tawny Style, White Port and Rosé Port. Ruby style Ports include Ruby, Reserve, Late Bottled Vintage, and Vintage. Ruby is the youngest and most fruit forward of the Ports. They are usually blends of a few years and are aged two or three years before bottling. Reserve Rubies are made from premium grapes and are generally aged for three to five years. Late Bottled Vintage (LBV) Ports are from a single harvest year and are aged four to six years before bottling. Vintage Ports are made from the best wines from a single exceptional harvest. They are aged in wood for approximately two years prior to bottling,

and will continue to age in the bottle for many more years. Vintage Ports come only from "declared" years. Both Late Bottled Vintage and Vintage Ports are capable of being stored and aged while Ruby and Reserve should be enjoyed earlier. All of these ruby-colored Ports make excellent dessert wines and can accompany a variety of cuisines.

White Ports are made from the free run juice of white grapes and are usually more off-dry rather than sweet. There are an increased number of Light Dry White Ports on the market that have lower (16.5%) alcohol levels. White Ports are excellent as an aperitif or mixed in a pre-dinner cocktail.

The newer style of Rosé Port is obtained by gentle maceration of red grapes. These pink-colored Ports are delicious served chilled, on the rocks, or in a cocktail.

Tawny Ports are wines that have been aged in either vats or barrels. They pick up their tawny color and oxidative character both from time and wood. The four types of Tawny Port are Tawny, Tawny Reserve, Tawny with an Indication of Age (10, 20, 30 and 40 years old), and Colheita. Only Colheita is from a single harvest year and must be aged in wood for at least seven years. The other three types may be a blend of different harvest years.

Aged Tawnies have remarkable complexity due to the long barrel aging.

There are thirty varietals of grapes that are commonly used. The most common red grape varietals that are planted in the region are Tinta Amarela, Tinta Barroca, Tinta Roriz, Touriga Francesa, Touriga Nacional, and Tinto Cao. The popular white varietals are Malvasia Fina, Viosinho, Donzelinho, and Gouveio. By law, the maximum yield per hectare is 7,500 kilograms of grapes, but most producers striving for quality limit their yields. The average yield of 4,100 kilograms per hectare is more common.

The change of the seasons and agricultural calendar are very much a part of life in the Douro. The entire year is filled with many chores and responsibilities, each contributing to the production of a fine Port Wine. In the cold winter months you can find workers pruning the vines by hand. Each vine is treated as an individual, and is pruned according to its needs in an attempt to coax the correct number of grape bunches the following summer. Farmers who do not use herbicides can be found digging up weeds at this time. February is time for fertilization and replanting. In March, vineyard workers can be seen laying out the training wires and posts as well as grafting new vines onto rootstock. April is a time of growth for both the vines and the surrounding grass. The latter must be kept short so that it does not compete with the vines, while still preventing erosion. May is when the flowering begins and the new growth must continuously be tied to the wires by hand. By June, you can find clusters of hard, green berries hiding under the thick, lush leaves. In July, the excess shoots must

be removed, and by now the grapes are the size of black-eyed peas. Their color begins to change in a process known as *veraison,* which marks the beginning of ripening. By the time August arrives, the grapes have stopped growing in size, but they continue to ripen, increasing their sugars, tannins, acids, and pigments which are necessary components for the wine yet to come.

THE HARVEST

Mid-to-late–September brings the harvest that we've waited so patiently for. Workers descend upon the vines to pick the grapes and place them into flat, shallow containers, so as not to crush the skins before their time. The grapes are then transported to the winery and gently crushed before being tipped into shallow granite tanks, or *lagares.* Villagers, migrant workers, winemakers, college students, and field hands alike roll up their pants, wash their feet and jump into the *lagares* to crush grapes to the sounds of accordion and drums. The smell of yeast and sweet grapes fills your nostrils as the crushed grapes begin to warm under your feet, signifying the start of the fermentation process. At the precise moment when half of the grape's sugars have been converted into alcohol, neutral brandy is added to stop the fermentation, thus giving Port its characteristic voluptuous sweetness.

As children, most of what we learned about making wine came from watching re-runs of the grape-stomping episode of *I Love Lucy.* Think about it: In your mind's eye—can't you see the Queen of Comedy in the oversized wooden vat with the other peasant women, her hair in a kerchief, and skirt hiked up? Come on, you remember this episode when Ricky and Lucy traveled to Italy and Lucy wanted to audition for the great Italian movie director, Vittorio Felipe. Isn't it every child's dream to crush grapes with their bare feet? The only problem with this romantic idea is that so few wine makers in the world still tread grapes by foot—we might not have been able to see it—until we were invited by Alistair and Gilly Robertson to join them at Quinta de Vargellas for their harvest. We could only hope, in our childish minds, that we would be invited into the *lagares* for some *I Love Lucy* grape stomping of our own.

Young men and women from all around Portugal earn seasonal money by stomping grapes, but what we didn't realize was that this is a time honored mating ritual with complex rules and mores. Once the province of migrant workers, young people are finding it fashionable to connect to their country's winemaking roots. They are also finding it a great way to meet a new boyfriend, girlfriend, husband, or wife.

We were seated high above the banks of the Douro while enjoying dinner on the Robertson's terrace. The sounds of music and laughter from the winery below taunted us like the Sirens' call. We kept asking our hosts if it was time to go down to the *lagares*—much like small children asking their parents, "Are we there yet?" It was evident there would be no grape stomping until we ate a proper— very British—meal.

Dinner at Alistair and Gilly's was a formal, multi-course affair. A chilled aperitif of crisp and refreshing Taylor Fladgate Fine

White Port started the evening off right. A first course of smoky *chourico*, peppers and onions, served with a delicious Croft Pink whetted our appetites for the meal yet to come. A main course of spiced roast pork and oven roasted potatoes, paired with a perfectly balanced and elegant 2000 Chryseia Douro dry red, gave us the sustenance we would need to carry out the duties of the night. Only after a delicious dessert of Portuguese style crème caramel and a nutty, silky smooth Fonseca 20 Year Old Tawny Port were we invited into the main parlor at midnight, to receive our "treading outfit." Each of us was handed a clean white T-shirt and a pair of navy blue running shorts. We were instructed to quickly change into these clothes and scrub our feet and legs with lots of soap and water. The final antibacterial rinse would occur right before we stepped into the *lagares*. When we emerged from the dressing room, we were happy to see that our hosts were wearing the uniform as well— they were going to join us in the tanks. We wouldn't stand out as strangers—or so we hoped—stomping grapes while they politely stood by and watched.

The walk from the porch down to the winery was treacherous due to the steepness of the hill, borrowed flip-flops, and the high level of Port in our bloodstreams. Nonetheless, the music, laughter, and bright lights continued to coax us downward. Stepping through the winery door was a moment that we will never forget. We entered an enormous stone room with four swimming-pool-sized *lagares*, all containing grapes. Three of them were filled with people dancing, singing, and stomping, while one of them lay waiting for

269

our arrival. Alistair and Gilly, and we, their childlike American guests, were greeted with cheers, laughter, and applause. It means a lot to the workers when the owners get into the tanks to do some of the dirty work. The band immediately perked up and started to play music that can only be described as traditional Portuguese meets disco.

The four of us stepped into tubs of disinfectant, and then climbed the ladder up and over the *lagare* wall. The initial squish of grapes through our toes was exhilarating. Soon we found ourselves standing thigh-high in crushed grapes. Rhythmically, one by one, we started to march in place to the beat of the drums and eventually started dancing to songs such as the Chicken Dance and Portuguese Hustle. Happily dancing, yet oblivious to all danger, the four of us were suddenly surrounded by our fellow grape stompers. Like Zombies in *Night of the Living Dead*, they were poised to pounce upon us at any moment. Outstretched grape-stained hands began aiming for our clean white T-shirts. Only when we discovered that "hand-printing" was the local custom to welcome newcomers did we realize that this would not turn into a grape tossing smack-down of *Italian Peasant Woman versus Lucy McGillicuddy Ricardo* proportions.

Three hours of dancing and stomping (and too many songs to count) passed before we dragged our tired legs out of the heavy must. We hosed down our purple legs, walked back up the steep hill to the English-style manor house, and chatted and laughed for another hour as we soaked our legs in the Quinta's pool before tottering off to bed, glass of Port in hand. Our only regret is that harvest comes but once a year. It is customary for guests at Quinta de Vargellas to write a poem in the guest book prior to leaving, and ours elicited a few good-natured chuckles when read aloud over breakfast:

> *While visiting Alistair and Gilly*
> *Drinking gallons of Port, don't act silly.*
> *Please no breaking of glass*
> *Or behaving low class,*
> *And don't stumble, no matter how hilly.*

BARCOS RABELO

After the fermentation is stopped by the addition of neutral spirits, the wine is stored in great oak casks at the wineries where it was made, and rests over the winter months. The wines are tasted in the following spring. They are then transported to Vila Nova de Gaia, opposite Porto. At one time, wine was brought down river by sailing vessels called *Barcos Rabelo*; however, the last commercial voyage to Vila Nova de Gaia was in 1964. Sadly, times have changed and many wines are now carried via refrigerated trucks, but the *Barco* races on the Douro River still stand as a reminder of those earlier days. The races occur on the day of Saint John, Patron Saint of Porto, which is the 24th of June, and are a sight to see. They are organized by the *Confraria Do Vinho Do Porto*, or Port Wine Brotherhood. There are about fifteen *Barcos*, one from each Port house, entered in the race. The square-rigged sails sport the famous logos such as Warre, Dow, Taylor, Croft, and Sandeman. The *Barcos Rabelo* are fashioned to resemble the ancient Roman flat-bodied boats that plied the Douro during the days of pre-Christian Iberia and are still built according to traditional measurements. The race is not meant to be a serious regatta—much Port wine is consumed—but the competitive spirit among the Port houses makes for an exciting day. If you're lucky enough to be standing next to members of the Port Wine Brotherhood, you may hear them loudly declare: "LONG LIVE PORT, LONG LIVE THE CONFRARIA, LONG LIVE THE BROTHERS!"

Upon arriving in Vila Nova de Gaia, those wines that are destined for Ruby, Late Bottled Vintage, or Vintage are transferred to 10,000- or 20,000-liter vats. Those that are destined as Aged Tawnies are stored in 550-liter barrels, or pipes, to mature. Wines that show they have Vintage Port potential are aged in oak vats for "two winters in the wood." After standing this test of time they are tasted again, blended, tasted, then re-tasted again and again. If all or most of the Port houses decide to declare a vintage, this is known as a "general declaration" of a vintage year. Bottling usually occurs in the early summer. The Vintage Port wines are shipped to wine merchants all around the world relatively soon after bottling. Most collectors eagerly await the arrival of Vintage Port shipments.

VINTAGE PORT

There is much confusion as to the difference between a generally declared vintage year, and single *quinta* vintages. In a declared vintage, a majority of producers, upon tasting their Port in the second spring after the harvest, determine that they are in the process of aging Port which will bottle-age exceptionally well on its own, rather than being further barrel-aged and blended into another type or style of Port. (For example, the 2007 Vintage Declaration was made in the spring of 2009.) Only the finest grapes are used in Vintage Port, from either the producer's own *quinta* or that of one of their most highly-valued suppliers. This decision may be made over a series of Wednesday lunches, but it is not always unanimous; there have been cases of "split vintages," wherein one group of producers declares a vintage in one year, and their neighbors declare in the next, as happened in 1991–1992. The most recent declared vintages are 1970, 1975, 1977, 1980, 1983, 1985, 1991, 1995, 1997, 2000, 2003, and 2007. Although there is no set rule, in general, a vintage is declared three times per decade. A formal declaration of a vintage year traditionally occurs on St. George's Day, April 23. Vintage Ports age for up to two years in oak barrels, and are then transferred to bottles, where they will age gracefully for ten, twenty, thirty or more years, to be opened and enjoyed at peak perfection.

In the event that there will not be a general declaration, some shippers choose to bottle Single Quinta Vintage Ports from their finest parcels. This makes sense, given that annual unanimous vintage declarations would dilute the very meaning of the declaration, rendering it next to useless both in real terms as a determination of quality, and in consumer marketing terms as well. A Single Quinta Vintage Port is the bottling of a very small amount of Port from a specific plot of land, because the end product from this parcel is just too precious to be blended into a non-vintage Port.

Although styles and taste vary widely, the following are considered by most (including ourselves) to be some of the world's best Ports: Burmester, A.A. Calem & Filho, Churchill's, Cockburn Smithes, Croft, Delaforce, Dow, A.A. Ferreira, Fonseca, Fonseca-Guimaraens, Gould Campbell, C.N. Kopke, Martinez Gassiot, Niepoort, Offley Forrester, Manoel D. Pocas, Quinta do Bomfim, Quinta

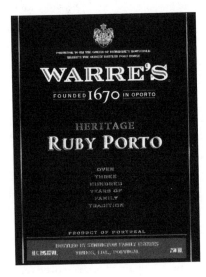

da Cavadinha, Quinta do Noval, Quinta do Noval Nacional, Quinta do Panascal, Quinta da Roeda, Quinta de Vargellas, Quinta de Vesuvio, A. Ramos-Pinto, Robertson's Rebello Valente, Sandeman, Taylor Fladgate, and Warre.

Not too long ago, we had the good fortune to taste barrel samples of three of the finest Single Quinta Vintage Ports from 2008: Croft Quinta da Roeda, Fonseca Quinta do Panascal, and Taylor Fladgate Quinta de Vargellas. As would be expected,

each had its own unique character and flavor, but there was no clear concensus among our group as to which was the best. We elicited comments from our friends; among us was Robin Kelley O'Connor, former ambassador of the Bordeaux Wine Bureau, current Director of Sales and Education at Sherry-Lehmann, and one of the most knowledgeable personages in the wine world as you are ever likely to meet. He called the Quinta da Roeda "jammy, with strong flavors of plum tart and just a hint of mint," and thought it would "start drinking really well in about twelve years." He found the Quinta do Panascal "superb, yet very compact, with strong characters of blueberry and blackberry, but showing its youth." He then elaborated that he would advise holding a bottle of this until at least 2023. O'Connor also had nothing but praise for the Quinta de Vargellas, which was deep violet with a garnet edge, and tasted of "roasted plums, walnut, licorice, and a hint of vanilla."

Fonseca Technical Director and Wine Maker David Guimaraens, who is himself a sixth-generation member of the Fonseca-Guimaraens family, had this to say, speaking about the Fonseca Quinta do Panascal Vintage Port: "There is great purity in the way in which it expresses the style of the estate. The 2008 was a harvest of relatively low yields and produced wines with a lot of depth and structure. Virtually perfect picking conditions meant that great wines were made right up to the end of the harvest."

Although the latest generation of Port Shippers has a strong respect for tradition and history, they are definitely keeping their eye on the future. While Alistair Robertson is widely credited for developing Late Bottled Vintage Port, it is his son-in-law, Adrian Bridge, who came up with the first Rosé Port, Croft Pink. In addition to their far-ranging Port holdings, the Symington family have branched out into dry red wines, the most noted of which is Chryseia, produced in partnership with Bruno Prats, the former owner of Cos d'Estournel in Bordeaux. After Johnny Graham's family sold their namesake Port company to the Symingtons in 1970, Johnny worked for several years at Cock-burn's, married Caroline Churchill, and started the first independently owned Port Shipper in many years. Churchill Graham Lda, which bottles under the Churchill's label, began experimenting with dry white wines in 2009. Widening the product base ensures that the grapes from the family's own vineyards and those of their suppliers have a market regardless of the popularity of Port in a given year. Family members and employees leave the Douro for schooling and training abroad, specializing in oenology, business, or marketing.

The history of Port is filled with innovation, from its accidental inception when brandy was added to shipping casks, to the Factory House, which features one of the first ballrooms in the world with a suspended dance floor, through the Taylor Fladgate Research and Development Program's creation of mechanized "port toes," which closely duplicate foot-treading. Quinta do Noval has just updated its staid image with Noval Black, which comes in a sleek black bottle and even has its own website. Far from its stuffy image as something to be drunk in front of a fireplace while wearing a tweed jacket with leather elbow patches and smoking cigars, the younger members of the Port world drink their family's heritage anywhere, anytime, mixed into cocktails and with a wide array of foods.

Attending cocktail conventions armed with bottles of their family's finest under their arms, they sponsor Port Cocktail contests which draw celebrity mixologists from around the globe. They maintain their families' websites, blogs, and Face-book pages, and Tweet the latest Vintage Declaration from their iPhones—held firmly in their right hand, so they may continue to pass the Tawny to their left, toast the Queen of England, the President of Portugal, and any prominent guests present, while preparing to play "Guess the Vintage."

PART VI

NEW WORLD

CALIFORNIA

CALIFORNIA

NORTH COAST

Napa

Sonoma

San Francisco

SAN JOAQUIN

Monterey

NORTH CENTRAL COAST

SOUTH CENTRAL COAST

Santa Barbara

Pacific Ocean

Los Angeles

0 Miles   100   200

0 Kilometers   200

I STARTED STUDYING WINES WHEN I WAS NINETEEN years old and taught my first wine class at twenty. Unfortunately, I could not go to California and taste their wines since the drinking age at that time was twenty-one (in New York it was eighteen). Finally, when I turned twenty-one, I took a semester off from college, wrote to the dozen or so quality wineries that existed, and, with very little money, hitchhiked to California. My first day of hitchhiking got me to State College, Pennsylvania, on Route 80—the direct route to the Pacific Ocean. As the sun was setting, a pickup truck driven by a young man in the military, who was in a hurry to get home to his girlfriend in California, picked me and my friend up and drove us straight to Santa Cruz, California! I feel lucky that I was able to get to the great wine regions of California earlier than planned. What a great experience it was to visit Napa, Sonoma, Mendocino, Livermore, etc., before the wine boom hit!

In the last fifty-odd years, California has gone from being an enological backwater to a world leader. Today California drives the marketplace. It is the hub of new agricultural theories, ideas, and practices. It sets the standards for winemaking innovation and experimentation. It has set the style for the last twenty years.

In the late 1960s and early 1970s, most California wine was bottled in and sold in jugs. Fine wine was an anomaly. The French drove the quality wine market. The Germans scooped up almost everyone else. But more than jug wine was fermenting in the Napa Valley. There was a movement that thought the region could produce fine wines. Frank Schoonmaker, an importer and writer and one of the first American wine experts, convinced some California winery owners to market their best wines using varietal labels. In Napa, there was a group of young, brash winemakers who thought they could make quality wine, including Warren Winiarski (Stag's Leap), Robert Mondavi, Mike Grgich, and others. Mondavi especially led the call for quality wine in the region, and became a lifelong ambassador for the wines from Napa and California. This small group helped turn Napa from a source for grapes into a mecca for great wine.

The biggest change in the 1970s was calling wines by their varietal names. It was no longer Chablis Blanc. It was now Chardonnay. It was no longer Claret, it was either Cabernet Sauvignon or Merlot. It was no longer a wine from Burgundy. It was now Pinot Noir. This was a seismic shift in the wine world at the time. Today, the rest of the world has adopted this labeling initiative as standard practice.

By the mid-1970s, the few quality wines made in California were almost solely the domain of serious wine collectors and local enthusiasts. Few were on the menu, at comparable prices, in well-known or well-respected restaurants— especially on the East Coast. Today, they stand toe-to-toe with their European counterparts all over the world. If California were a nation, it would be the third largest producer of wine in the world. No winegrowing area in the world has come so far so quickly as California.

The foremost reasons for California's winemaking success are location, weather, the University of California at Davis and Fresno State University, and finally money and marketing strategy.

The weather's warm sunny days; cool, dry nights; and long growing season delivered both tourists and working capital to San Francisco. Nearby, both the University of California at Davis and California State University, Fresno (Fresno State) have been great advocates for farmers and winemakers. Both schools' curricula emphasize the scientific study of wine, viticulture, and, most important, technology. Their research, focused on soil, different strains of yeast, hybridization temperature-controlled fermentation, and other viticultural techniques has revolutionized the wine industry worldwide.

Money and marketing cannot be overemphasized. Selling the wine was key. As the winemakers concentrated on producing the best wines they could, it was noted that wine consumers would respond. Several important leaps had to be made. One was changing the perception of being jug wine producers to that of quality wine producers. And the second was that big business discovered, in the late 1960s, that selling wine from California could be a good investment. When Almaden was bought by the now defunct National Distillers, many large corporations sought gold in the hills of Napa and Sonoma. Companies like Coca-Cola, Pillsbury, and PepsiCo started making huge investments, bringing yet more money and expertise to California. Soon, as sales rose, quality became more and more important.

The success in Napa and Sonoma was contagious, and now California is the winemaking capital of the United States, producing 90 percent of all the wine made in America. While Napa and Sonoma are the two most famous names in California wine, less than 12 percent of all wine from California originates from these two counties.

It's easier to understand the wines of California by dividing them into four major wine regions:

NORTH COAST Napa, Sonoma, Mendecino and Lake counties. This region is known for Cabernet Sauvignon, Sauvignon Blanc, Chardonnay, and Merlot.

NORTH CENTRAL COAST Monterey, Santa Clara, Stana Cruz, and Livermore counties. The best wines form this region include Syrah, Grenache, Viognier, Marsanne, and Rousssane.

SOUTH CENTRAL COAST San Luis Obispo and Santa Barbara counties. This region is known for Sauvignon Blanc, Chardonnay, and Pinot Noir.

SAN JOAQUIN VALLEY This region is historically known for the production of "jug" or "box" wines.

—KZ

THE DAY CALIFORNIA SHOOK THE WORLD

Frank Prial

On May 26, 1976, six weeks before America's bicentennial celebration, there occurred in Paris a tasting that American winemakers and cultural historians have come to characterize as a defining moment in the evolution of fine wine in this country.

The effects on the California wine industry, as well as on its distributors and their customers, were profound. The winemakers had known they could make great wine; wineries like Beaulieu and Inglenook had been doing it for many years. What the Paris tasting did was bolster American self-esteem. It encouraged many who had been content making mediocre wine to go for it, to make the very best. More important, it showed American consumers that they no longer had to look abroad for fine wine. Little more than a decade earlier, a general

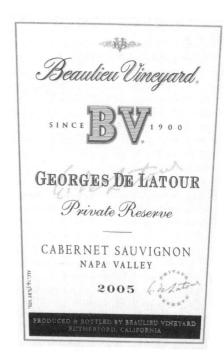

When I was an early student of wine, the highlight of my week was reading Frank Prial's "Wine Talk" column in the New York Times. *Shortly after I began working at Windows on the World in 1976 I got to meet him in person and the Windows wine program became a subject of many of his future articles. He was able to express wine in a simple, common language that all could understand, which was a major inspiration for my* Windows on the World Complete Wine Course *book. Frank and his family were also regular customers of Windows on the World and he was there in 1977 when New York City experienced a blackout. Since he worked for the New York Times, we were able to get updated information on the status of the blackout and how to evacuate our hundreds of customers.*

American embarrassment had greeted President Lyndon B. Johnson's decree that American embassies serve only American wines.

At that now-famous tasting twenty-five years ago, nine judges, all prominent French food and wine specialists, gathered in the enclosed courtyard of the Paris Intercontinental Hotel and tasted twenty wines, red and white, French and American. The tasting was blind; all the bottles were covered; no one was told which were French, which were American.

When the bottles were unwrapped, the tasters were astonished to discover that the highest scorers were American: a 1973 Cabernet Sauvignon from Stag's Leap Wine Cellars and a 1973 Chardonnay from Chateau Montelena, both from the Napa Valley. Under the headline "Judgment of Paris," *Time* magazine said the "unthinkable" had happened: "California defeated all Gaul."

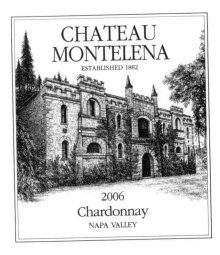

The tasting had been arranged by Steven Spurrier, a thirty-four-year-old Englishman who ran a wineshop and wine school just off the Place de la Madeleine. The idea sprang from his association with his young American customers, many of whom worked at I.B.M.'s French headquarters just across the street.

In 1975, intrigued by his clients' talk of American wines, Mr. Spurrier sent an assistant, Patricia Gallagher, to California to investigate. She was so impressed that Mr. Spurrier soon made his own pilgrimage westward. He returned to France excited by what he had found and determined to arrange a tasting event. He hoped to twit the xenophobic French, publicize the fine California wines he had discovered, and, understandably, win some publicity for himself.

He succeeded on all three counts. The French tasters, who included the owners of two famous Paris restaurants, the sommelier of a third, and the editor of France's best-known wine magazine, were true to form. They lavished praise on the wines they thought were French—and derided those they assumed to be American.

The California reds were all Cabernet Sauvignon; the French reds all Cabernet-based Bordeaux. The California whites were Chardonnay; the French whites all Burgundies, all Chardonnays as well. The reds, in order of finish, were: Stag's Leap Wine Cellars, 1973; Mouton-Rothschild, 1970; Haut-Brion, 1970; Montrose, 1970; Ridge Vineyards Monte Bello, 1971; Léoville–Las Cases, 1971; Mayacamas Vineyards, 1971; Clos du Val, 1972; Heitz Cellars Martha's Vineyard, 1970; Freemark Abbey, 1969. The whites, in order of finish, were: Chateau Montelena, 1973; Domaine Roulot, Meursault Charmes, 1973; Chalone Vineyard, 1974; Spring Mountain Vineyards, 1973; Joseph Drouhin, Beaune

Clos des Mouches, 1973; Freemark Abbey, 1972; Ramonet-Prudhon Bâtard-Montrachet, 1973; Domaine Leflaive, Puligny-Montrachet, Les Pucelles, 1972; Veedercrest Vineyards, 1972, and David Bruce, 1973.

"The egg on the judges' collective faces," wrote Paul Lukacs in *American Vintage*, "came from their inability to discern what until then everyone assumed was obvious—namely, that great French wines tasted better than other wines because they tasted, well, French."

Still, there is one notion that the tasting should have dispelled, but didn't: that California wines do not last. I don't know why the doubt persisted, but, perhaps because

it did, Mr. Spurrier decided to re-create the red-wine tasting in 1986. By then the wines were thirteen to sixteen years old. The French wines were in perfect condition, but so were the Americans. And again a California wine placed first—this time Clos du Val—and the Ridge Monte Bello was second. The Stag's Leap 1973 was sixth, after three French wines, but hardly because of age. Warren Winiarski, who owns Stag's Leap Wine Cellars, served it at a dinner I attended at Stag's Leap recently, and at twenty-eight years of age it was in beautiful condition.

For the French, the impact of the 1976 tasting and its 1986 re-creation has been subdued. One early result was that it became easier for French and American winemakers to overcome their mutual suspicion and begin to exchange visits and information. It's a rare California winery these days that doesn't employ a French apprentice or two, while young Americans can be found pulling hoses and scrubbing tanks in wineries all over France. One unexpected effect: American wines may still be rare in the French market, but the French wines that come here taste more and more like California wines. Once Bordeaux winemakers strived for restraint, elegance, and subtlety in their wines. They were proud to say their wines took thirty years to mature. Many still are, but many others in recent years have begun to make California-style full-bodied, high-alcohol, extra-ripe wines that they say are ready to drink in three or four years. Could it be a case of "if you can't beat 'em, join 'em"?

One thing that has changed for both countries over the last quarter-century is prices. In its June 7, 1976, article on the Paris tasting, *Time* magazine noted: "The U.S. winners are little known to wine lovers since they are in short supply even in California, and are rather expensive."

Time's definition of "rather expensive"? "$6 plus."

NAPA

ON MY FIRST VISIT TO NAPA VALLEY, I was twenty-one years old. I was staying in Santa Cruz and had hitchhiked my way to Napa for an appointment I had made with Inglenook Winery. My traveling friend and I were walking down the half-mile driveway to the Inglenook chateau when a pickup truck with a handlebar-mustached driver stopped. Without saying a word he motioned to us to jump in the back for the ride down. When we got to the entrance he asked us what we were doing and I told him that I was here to see the president of Inglenook Winery. He found this very funny because the president was an older, distinguished, well-dressed gentleman, and he wasn't expecting anyone with our casual appearance and longer hair. When the president arrived down the entryway he looked around, saw us, and kept looking for someone else. Our driver thought this was even more hysterical. Anyhow, I established my credibility with the president, we tasted the wines, he thanked us for coming, and the pickup driver was so enthralled with all of this "play" that he invited us to stay with him in the Mayacamas Mountains. This man's name was Don Surplus, and he ended up creating the first cooperage company in Napa Valley and later went on to own a hot-air balloon company. We have reconnected many times over the last forty years.

Napa is the most popular tourist destination in California, after Disneyland. It wasn't always that way. John Patchett established the valley's first commercial vineyard in 1858, and Charles Krug established its first commercial winery in St. Helena in 1861. However, the region suffered serious setbacks with a phylloxera epidemic that crippled the region, and then the emergence of Prohibition and the Great Depression in the 1930s, which brought down the quality of production.

For much of the forties, fifties, and sixties, Napa was a quiet, grape-growing valley. Outside of farm stands, tourism was scant. However, the rebirth of Californian quality wine in the midsixties saw a huge increase of oenophiles coming to visit to taste the many wines that were flourishing.

Today, Napa Valley is a hotbed of great wine and culinary delights. It has some large, high-quality producers but mostly small, artisanal wineries. The beauty of the valley remains breathtaking.

—KZ

NAPA VALLEY

Karen MacNeil

About 55 miles northeast of San Francisco, the Napa Valley is California's best-known and most renowned wine region, even though it is responsible for an astoundingly small amount of all the wine produced in the state—just 4 percent. Its fame (and infamy) is derived from an eventful commingling of history and humanity. For almost a century and a half, the valley has attracted a majority of the most ambitious, dashing, and outspoken vintners in the United States.

Where else but in the Napa Valley would a palatial wine estate (Inglenook) be built by an adventurous Finnish sea captain named Gustave Niebaum and sold more than a hundred years later to a superstar film director named Francis Ford Coppola? Where else but in the Napa Valley would an Olympian monolith called Opus One be built by two of the world's leading vintners, Robert Mondavi and Baron Philippe

de Rothschild? Where else but in the Napa Valley would the first California wine to cost $100 a bottle be made, not to mention the first to cost $200? (The wines are Diamond

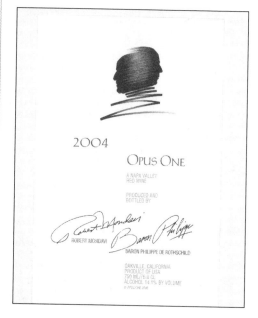

Karen MacNeil is one of the best American wine writers and the most articulate when it comes to her classroom style of teaching wine. I first met Karen when she was the wine and food editor of USA Today, *and since that time she has gone on to write one of the most successful wine books in the United States,* The Wine Bible. *Karen is the chair of the professional wine-studies program of the Culinary Institute of America in Napa Valley and has appeared on many television shows, including her own,* Wine, Food, & Friends; *as well as being featured in the* New York Times, *the* Los Angeles Times, Wine Spectator, *and many more.*

Creek Cabernet Sauvignon Lake Vineyard 1987 and 1992, respectively.) Where else but in the Napa Valley would the world's largest charity wine auction be held, raising millions of dollars [$4.3 million in 2010] each year?

Critics say Napa Valley has an ego. But what it really has is a gargantuan appetite for life and a palpable hunger for success. You can taste it in the wines. While the Napa Valley is not the only California region to make great wine, it consistently makes a good share of the most polished, classy, and complex wines in the state. The Napa Valley's reputation as the premier wine region in the United States is, however, not due solely to the quality of its wines and the hard-driving will of its vintners. Some of the credit must also be given to the relentless prophesying of a single man—Robert Mondavi, patriarch of the Robert Mondavi Winery and tireless crusader for California's place in the wine empyrean. Mondavi, whose father sold grapes to home winemakers during Prohibition, constantly rejected a second-place status for California behind the great wine regions of Europe. His credo that California wines belong in the company of the greatest wines of the world would eventually become—in the Napa Valley at least—not a goal, but a given.

The valley proper is small and neatly framed. Stretching 30 miles long and ranging between 1 and 5 miles wide, it begins at a bay, ends at a volcano (Mount St. Helena), and is flanked on each side by mountain ranges. The Napa Valley wine region, however, extends beyond these borders to incorporate parts of the mountains themselves and smaller valleys nestled high up in the mountains. Though the main valley looks geographically uniform, nothing could be further from the truth. The volcanic eruptions that occurred here two million years ago have left the valley with almost three dozen different soil types belonging to eight of the twelve major soil classifications found worldwide. The ground itself is also subtly irregular, with numerous benches, terraces, canyons, and fans that have been carved out or pushed up from the valley floor. This geologic potpourri coupled with highly independent winemaking styles means that wine estates next door to one another often make wines that taste totally different.

The valley's geologic diversity is underscored by its variable climate. A person standing at the southern end, which is open to the San Pablo Bay, might be pulling on a sweater at the very same minute someone in the north near Calistoga might be stripping down to a bathing suit. This said, much of the valley experiences the magical combination of days that are hot but not blistering and nights that are cool but not cold.

Napa Valley vineyard land is thought to be the most expensive agricultural land in the United States. As of 2000, a single acre of planted vineyards in a prime location might cost as much as $130,000 or more. Vineyards cover roughly 37,000 acres of the 485,000 acres that comprise the valley.

Though the Napa Valley is planted with numerous varieties, no grape captures the soul of the valley better than Cabernet Sauvignon. Chardonnay, Sauvignon Blanc, Merlot, and Zinfandel can all become very good and occasionally brilliant wines in the Napa Valley, but the top Cabernets are simply stellar. No other wine region in the country makes as many stunningly rich and complex Cabernets year after year.

Some of these top-notch Cabernet Sauvignons aren't made exclusively from Cabernet. Often small amounts of Merlot, Cabernet Franc, Petit Verdot, and/or Malbec—the so-called Bordeaux varieties— are blended in. (By law, the wine can still be called Cabernet Sauvignon as long as the other varieties make up less than 25 percent of the total wine.) These "not 100 percent" Cabernets are often the most complex Cabernet Sauvignons of all.

In 1974 this realization led Joseph Phelps Vineyards to take the concept of a blended Cabernet one step further. With the idea of making the very best wine they could—even if that sometimes meant using far less than 75 percent Cabernet—Phelps made the first Bordeaux blend. It was called Insignia. Several other top Napa Valley wineries followed suit, each giving their Bordeaux blend its own proprietary name. Today the Napa Valley is famous for such wines, collectively sometimes referred to as Meritage wines. Among the best are Opus One, Dominus, Rubicon, Trilogy, and, of course, Insignia.

NAPA VALLEY AVAs

In addition to the American Viticultural Area Napa Valley, there are thirteen smaller AVAs within the valley. The most important of these are Stags Leap District, Rutherford, Oakville, Spring Mountain District, Mount Veeder, Howell Mountain, and Atlas Peak. The AVA Carneros, at the southern tip of the valley, straddles both Napa and Sonoma counties.

Stags Leap District, a small pocket of land, is named for what looms above it—majestic, sun-dappled outcroppings of tortured rock over which, as fable has it, stags have leapt to escape hunters. The vineyards have a more auspicious existence, sprawled as they are on the rocky foothills below. The district lies in the southern part of the Napa valley along the eastern flank and is known mainly for Cabernet Sauvignons from such leading wineries as Shafer, Stag's Leap Wine Cellars, Stags' Leap Winery, Silverado Vineyards, Chimney Rock, and Clos du Val.

287

The two separate AVAs of Rutherford and Oakville are, geologically speaking, large alluvial fans sitting side by side and spreading out north and south from the towns of Rutherford and Oakville, smack in the heart of the valley. An alluvial fan is a sloping mass of sediments deposited by a river where it issues from its canyon onto the valley floor. The Rutherford and Oakville fans are composed of deep gravelly and sandy clay loam soil. Some of the most famous and historic of all Napa wineries are found here, including Beaulieu Vineyard, Niebaum-Coppola (the former Inglenook property), Robert Mondavi, Opus One, Caymus, Cakebread Cellars, and Grgich Hills.

Vines not only carpet the valley floor but are also sprinkled over both the Mayacamas mountain range on the west and the Vaca mountain range on the east. Some of the most famous, small viticultural areas within the Napa Valley are located on these mountains, including Mount Veeder and Spring Mountain on the Mayacamas range and Howell Mountain and Atlas Peak on the Vaca range. Napa's mountain vineyards are highly prized, for the wines that come from them can be superbly concentrated yet elegant at the same time. At up to 2,000 feet in elevation, the grapes in these vineyards ripen slowly, yet because they are above the fog line, the vineyards are also drenched in sun for long hours each day.

Examples of quality Napa mountain wines are numerous and include the Merlots from Beringer and the Cabernet Sauvignons from Dunn (both from Howell Mountain); the Cabernets from Mayacamas and Mount Veeder Winery (from Mount Veeder); the Cabernets from Diamond Creek (from Diamond Mountain, among the Napa Valley's most prestigious AVAs); plus Ridge's York Creek Zinfandels and one of the most legendary of all California Chardonnays, Stony Hill's (both from Spring Mountain).

⌐ THE THRILL OF THE GRILL ⌐

California may not have a full-fledged cuisine of its own, but as any Californian knows, there's a style and sensibility to the local cooking that's unmistakable. Grilled lamb with raspberry-mango relish doesn't exactly have Massachusetts written all over it, any more than grilled avocado salad with pesto is evocative of Arkansas. No, when it comes to culinary personalities, California's is clear. Take, for instance, California's unofficial religion: grilling. From peaches to porterhouses, no food is exempt from this beloved technique. Grilling is also one of the best things that can happen to wine, especially red wine. (Well, not to it exactly.) The sweet, charred flavor and slightly crusty texture grilling imparts make any food more red wine willing. Which is why—warm weather be damned—oceans of red wine are drunk all summer long in California. Three types of reds underscore the flavors of grilled foods best: Zinfandel, Syrah, and Petite Sirah. Zinfandel's simple jammy fruitiness is an easygoing match for grilled vegetables, grilled chicken, even grilled cheese sandwiches, which à la California, really are grilled. Then there's Syrah with its primal, peppery, earthy flavors just begging for grilled lamb or duck. As for Petite Sirah (don't be fooled by the name; there's nothing petite about it), the wine's massive structure and brooding, rustic, sensual flavors make it one of the best friends a grilled steak can have.

SONOMA

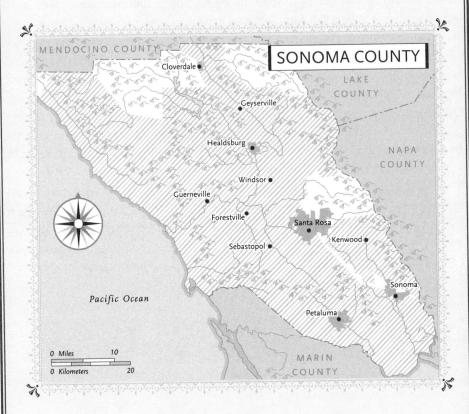

THERE REALLY WEREN'T MANY WINERIES in Sonoma when I first visited there. Most of the big names were in Napa Valley, but I ventured outside of Napa and into Sonoma to my first winery, Buena Vista. As a history major, going to the oldest active winery in California was a special treat. It was founded by a Hungarian nobleman, Count Agoston Haraszthy, who has been called "the father of California viticulture." In 1861 he was sent to Europe by the California government. When he returned, he brought back many thousands of vine cuttings that began the quality California wine industry.

The true birthplace of quality California winemaking is in the Sonoma Valley, which is located between the Mayacamas Mountains and the Sonoma Mountains. It is often called the "Valley of the Moon." Franciscan monks planted the valley's first vineyards in at Mission San Francisco Solano in 1823. In 1857, the Buena Vista winery was established by Haraszthy and became California's first successful commercial winery. Gundlach Bundschu was founded a year later in 1858.

The microclimates of the Sonoma Valley are unique, with the Sonoma Mountains buffering the valley from the wet and cool influence of the nearby Pacific Ocean. While the geography helps protect the valley from excessive weather and rainfall, the valley benefits from the winds that wind their way south from the Santa Rosa Plains, and from the cool air that reaches northward from San Pablo Bay through the Los Carneros region.

Like Napa Valley, Sonoma was crippled by the crushing effects of Prohibition, the Great Depression, and the spread of disease. However, they too rebounded by the 1980s. By 2010, there were 254 wineries, and over 65,000 acres under vine. Today, many wines in Sonoma are ranked among the world's best.

Sonoma's cool climate makes for excellent production, favoring varieties such as Sauvingon Blanc, Chardonnay, and Pinot Noir.

—KZ

SONOMA COUNTY

Matt Kramer

A mystery that magnifies the earth but does not lie. What is Pure Land to that?

—JACK GILBERT, *Monolithos, Poems 1962 and 1982*

Good poetry somehow answers unasked questions. As it happens, Jack Gilbert did not inquire, "What is fine wine?" Yet his is the most elegantly simple answer: *A mystery that magnifies the earth but does not lie.* The stature of such an accomplishment is revealed by what the poet asks instead: *What is Pure Land to that?*

Nowhere in California has there been more "pure land" for fine wine than in the sprawl of Sonoma County. Yet no wine area in California has waited longer to transform. Sonoma's longtime crops of melons and bulk wine grapes, among many others, offered little magnification of the earth, or much telling of its truth. That Sonoma lent itself

to winegrowing was apparent from the start: It was Sonoma County, not Napa Valley, that sparked some of the earliest wine interest in California settlers.

The nineteenth-century California humorist George Horatio Derby, writing under the pen name Squibob in what was once California's largest daily newspaper, *Alta California*, usually delighted in skewering what even then was California's pretension toward proclaiming itself heaven on earth. Yet even he felt compelled to acknowledge, in 1850, that "Sonoma *is* a nice place . . . enjoying an unvaryingly salubrious climate, neither too warm nor too cold. With little wind, few fleas, and a sky of that peculiarly blue description that Fremont terms *the Italian*, it may well be called . . . the Garden of California." He also noted that "The most luscious grapes [are] to be found there." (The fleas still are few.)

Just why Sonoma County took so long to transform from "pure land" to something

---

Maybe the best way to describe Matt Kramer's wine-writing style is that he "makes sense" of wine through all his books, Making Sense of Wine, Making Sense of Burgundy, Making Sense of California Wine, Making Sense of Italian Wine, *and, most recently,* Matt Kramer on Wine. *He has been a regular columnist for* Wine Spectator *for twenty-five years and his articles are many times entertaining; others educational; and many controversial, sometimes poking fun at all of us in the wine world.*

more articulate is puzzling. Some of the explanations are straightforward, such as its ability to support enormous grape yields thanks to easy irrigation and a high water table along the Russian River Valley. The restraint required for fine wine was no match against the ready market for high-yield bulk wines.

But part of Sonoma's slow crawl toward transformation is due to something less provable, but perhaps no less forceful. Why, for example, has neighboring Napa Valley, not Sonoma County, long been the place where wealthy newcomers to wine built their winemaking pleasure palaces?

After all, Sonoma County was where the northern California wine rush began. The town of Sonoma was the site of the last, and northernmost, Spanish Mission: the Mission San Francisco, founded in 1823. Only one year later, a vineyard of more than one thousand grapevines was successfully installed. It was this vineyard that supplied grapevines to George Yount in 1838 when he established Napa Valley's first vineyard in what is now Yountville.

By that time, what has since come to be called the Sonoma Mission was the private property of the army officer who originally secularized the Spanish-owned church holdings, then-lieutenant (later general) Mariano Guadalupe Vallejo. It was Vallejo who laid out the town of Sonoma. And it was Vallejo who established his own vineyard outside of Sonoma, which he named Lachryma Montis, or "Tears of the Mountain." The name referred to a mountain spring he used to irrigate his vineyard, making it one of California's earliest vineyard irrigation efforts.

After Vallejo came Agoston Haraszthy, who started the still-extant Buena Vista winery in 1856 with the purchase of 560 acres of land northeast of the town of Sonoma. Six years later, in 1862, Haraszthy had 300 acres of bearing vineyard. He also built himself a grand, Roman-style villa that no longer exists. Chinese laborers dug extensive tunnels, which do remain. (Making the picture neater yet, Haraszthy's son, Atilla, married Vallejo's daughter and started his own vineyard next to Vallejo's Lachryma Montis vineyard.)

Sonoma County was attracting attention, as well as investors of considerable worth. Jacob Gundlach started his Rhinefarm next to Buena Vista. Charles Kohler, who first brought California wine (grown in the then-larger Los Angeles vineyards) to a national market, created a grand winery and vineyard in the town of Glen Ellen. Grandest of all was Issac de Turk in Santa Rosa. By the 1880s, his was the largest business in Santa Rosa, as well as the largest winery in Sonoma County.

Yet despite this significant history, as well as no fewer than 118 wineries by 1891, Sonoma County never managed to rival Napa Valley in high-society esteem or architectural lavishness. It was to Napa Valley that wealthy San Franciscans came both to play and establish vineyards. More than Sonoma County,

Napa Valley was home to winegrowers of showy ambition, be they American-born or immigrant.

It was Napa Valley where Frederick Beringer built his imposing stone and timber mansion, where Gustave Niebaum erected his substantial brick winery for his Inglenook estate, and where San Francisco investor William Bourn built the enormous stone winery called Greystone. All three structures, among others, are still in use.

Then as now, Napa Valley was where wealthy owners built show-off wineries. Sonoma County, in contrast, was where people went to farm. Why was this so? And why did this pattern repeat itself in the 1970s, when winegrowing again became fashionable among wealthy Californians? Napa Valley boosters like to point to themselves as "keepers of the flame," noting such wineries as Beaulieu (founded in 1900) and Inglenook (founded in 1879), both of which managed to

get through the thirteen devastating years of Prohibition. Yet Sonoma County had its own survivors: Korbel (founded in 1862), Simi (founded in 1876), and Sebastiani (founded in 1904).

Nothing about the quality of the land distinguishes Napa Valley from Sonoma County. But something about the lay of the land does: The sheer sprawl of Sonoma County flavored its fate. No one has captured this better than the novelist Lawrence Durrell in his essay, "Landscape With Literary Figures":

> "You write," says a friendly critic in Ohio, "as if the landscape were more important than the character." If not exactly true, this is near enough the mark, for I have evolved a private notion about the importance of landscape, and I willingly admit to seeing characters almost as functions of a landscape. . . . You begin to realize that the important determinant of any culture is after all the spirit of place.

Perhaps more than any other element, it is Sonoma's "spirit of place" that best

explains why it evolved so very differently from Napa Valley. The most obvious feature is size. Sonoma County is more than twice as large as Napa County: 1,604 square miles compared to Napa's 744 square miles.

But size alone is not the cause of Sonoma's strikingly different spirit of place. Instead, it is the shape and feel of the landscape. In Napa Valley one has a feeling of being on display. Its narrow configuration is inherently public. Far from a detraction, it is this publicity that attracts—or at least lends itself to—a certain sort of ostentation. The configuration of Napa Valley allows one literally to be "in society." It is this delicious confinement of landscape that was then, and still is today, the appeal of Napa Valley for wealthy outsiders. After all, why build a show-off winery (or house), if no one can see it? And wealthy newcomers to Napa Valley in the 1880s, or in the 1980s, had no intention of going unnoticed.

In comparison, Sonoma County lends itself to an assured privacy—almost to fugitiveness. You can get lost in Sonoma County, in every sense. In the Russian River Valley, the river twists on the ground like a landed fish. Each bend of the river is its own world, isolated in sight and sound from the landfall of a neighboring bend. The result is a remove of the sort found in the mountain hamlets of Appalachia. (It should be noted that in the late 1800s some wealthy San Francisco families sought this privacy as well as the Russian River Valley's cool summer climate. But winegrowing was not their goal.)

The many landscape isolations of Sonoma County help explain why it—never Napa Valley—was the place of choice for winemaking communes. By their nature, they seek refuge from prying eyes. The most notorious was Fountain Grove, which was established outside of Santa Rosa in 1875. That year, Thomas Lake Harris, the English founder of a communal religious sect called the Brotherhood of the New Life, bought 400 acres of land north of Santa Rosa.

By 1883 the commune was devoted entirely to winegrowing; by 1888 the property expanded to 2,000 acres (400 of which were vineyard) and production reached 200,000 gallons of wine annually. It even published what was surely California's first winery newsletter, the *Fountain Grove WinePress*. (I am indebted to Thomas Pinney's *A History of Wine in America: From the Beginnings to Prohibition* for these and other details.)

Harris propounded some delightfully wacky religious ideas. According to Thomas Pinney, "Harris taught that God is bisexual, and that everyone, man and woman, has a celestial counterpart with whom to seek eternal marriage. Unluckily, the counterpart is elusive: it may move from one body to another, and in any case it is hard to know for sure where it dwells, and when." Perhaps the choicest bit was that Harris, according to Pinney, wrote about how "the world is filled with tiny fairies who live in the bosoms of women and sing heavenly harmonies inaudible to worldly ears." He was run out of town in 1892 and never returned.

Despite that, Fountain Grove remained and continued to produce wine under the guidance of a Japanese convert to the Brotherhood of the New Life, Kanaye Nagasawa. He owned the winery and vineyards until his death in 1934. Everything eventually died by

1951, although the Fountain Grove label still exists.

Farther north was another sect of sorts, the Icaria Speranza commune. Inspired by the Utopian communism of Frenchman Étienne Cabet's book *Voyage en Icarie*, the adherents eventually arrived in California, purchasing 885 acres along the Russian River near Cloverdale in 1881. The Icarians believed in what they called True Christianity, taught universal brotherhood, and—thanks to its original French members—required that all Icarians read and speak French as a prerequisite for membership. By 1887 the commune dissolved due to debt.

The most famous communal—really, cooperative—effort was the Italian Swiss Colony. Here the impulse was not religious, but idealistic social philanthropy. It was founded by a successful banker, Andrea Sbarboro, a native of Genoa. He figured that a way to help his fellow Italians was to create a grape-growing business modeled on the principles of the savings and loan societies where he made his fortune. Using payroll deductions, the workers could own shares in the company.

In 1881, Sbarboro bought 1,500 acres of land in Asti, a tiny town virtually within shouting distance of the Icarian commune in Cloverdale. Workers got $30 to $40 a month, plus room, board, and free wine. Despite the name, the community was virtually all Italians. However, they wanted no part of Sbarboro's scheme to deduct $5 a month from the wages to pay for shares in the company. They smelled a (nonexistent) rat. Not a single worker participated.

Eventually, the company became like any other, although still exceptionally paternalistic. It also went into winemaking, not Sbarboro's original intention, which was only to grow grapes. By 1900, it had become the largest single winery in California and by 1910 owned 5,000 acres of vineyard, much of it far afield from Sonoma County. Although a financial success, by 1913 it was absorbed into the California Wine Association cartel.

The fugitive, even furtive quality of the tucked-away terrain of Sonoma County is further demonstrated by its being the home of the Bohemian Grove. Located near Guerneville on the Russian River, the 2,700-acre Bohemian Grove is the site of a famously private retreat of San Francisco's Bohemian Club.

Every July approximately 1,500 men from around the country assemble at Bohemian Grove for two weeks (some stay only for one week or come only on the weekends) to enjoy each other's company, participate in elaborate theatrical productions, and listen to "lakeside talks" from distinguished speakers.

This is no ordinary club. And its speakers and entertainers are no ordinary performers. Bohemian Grove is perhaps the most exclusive assemblage of American corporate leaders, high-ranking political figures, top-level entertainers, and prestigious academics—at least those who are male, anyway. It also is famously secretive, indeed genuinely furtive. For example, when then President Richard Nixon was invited to give a strictly off-the-record "lakeside talk," the press was outraged and insisted on covering the event. The president was disinvited.

That Bohemian Grove was created in 1880, and that the chosen site was the dense, secretive redwoods of Sonoma's

Russian River Valley, speaks volumes. The publicness of Napa Valley was unthinkable. Even in 1880, when the Bohemian Grove was first established, Sonoma County felt right. Surely, Napa Valley was considered, as it was the playground of choice for rich and powerful San Franciscans. Yet even in those unpopulated times, Napa's publicity of place felt wrong. Sonoma's spirit of place is a sense of real or imagined isolation.

The force of the Sonoma landscape has also created a sense of place different from what is publicly perceived. In the public mind, there exists something called the Napa/Sonoma wine country, as if the two were one. Why is this so? Partly it's proximity. But mostly it's public relations, fueled by economics. It comes down to this: Sonoma County grapes fetch a price that can be as much as one-third less per ton, 17 percent less per ton than the same grape variety grown in Napa Valley. Such is the cash-on-the-barrel difference that a famous name can command for an otherwise anonymous bunch of grapes.

Like a local politician jostling for position next to a visiting national luminary at a public reception, Sonoma County finds it useful to be publicly associated with Napa Valley. Its growers want parity. And they are savvy enough to know Napa Valley grapes command a premium due to a perceived, rather than actual, difference in quality. If the public sees the two counties as equal, all the better for Sonoma County.

Yet Sonoma County really sees itself linked with Mendocino County. Witness the willingness of Sonoma wineries to use Mendocino County grapes. In comparison, Napa wineries do so infrequently. This is longstanding; it is a function of landscape.

It's landscape that makes Sonoma and Mendocino, if not blood relations, then kissing cousins. That both counties have always been largely rural environments devoted to farming adds to a sense of commonality. But landscape binds them. The Russian River runs south from Mendocino into Sonoma, where it eventually empties into the Pacific Ocean after meandering through the Alexander and Russian River Valleys.

Identical in effect, and in much of its path, is Highway 101. Along its Mendocino/Sonoma segment, Highway 101 is a fellow traveler with the Russian River for more than fifty miles from Ukiah to Healdsburg. Far from quarreling with the landscape, it falls in with it and in the process, becomes a natural feature.

In comparison, no ease of movement exists between Sonoma and Napa. The Mayacamas Mountains are a formidable wall. To this day, crossing the Mayacamas is not a carefree drive. The roads that span it are narrow, few, and twisting. Even with modern transportation and communications, a sense of identification and connection, real or imagined, between Sonoma and Napa still is effectively discouraged. Such is the persistence of place upon the spirit.

CANADA

CANADA

BRITISH COLUMBIA/
OKANAGAN VALLEY

QUEBEC

Ottawa ★

NOVA
SCOTIA

ONTARIO/
NIAGARA PENINSULA

ONTARIO

Toronto

Lake Ontario

BRITISH
COLUMBIA

NIAGARA
ESCARPMENT

NIAGARA
ON THE LAKE

Kelowna

St. Catharines

OKANAGAN
VALLEY

0 Miles   100

0 Miles   50

0 Kilometers 100

0 Kilometers 50

Lake Erie

I WROTE MY FIRST BOOK, the first edition of *Windows on the World Complete Wine Course,* in 1985. Most of the letters and e-mails I have received since then have come from Canadians who have been upset that I never included their great wines. The history of Canada's winemaking is very similar to that of the United States, starting on the east coast (Ontario) and eventually moving west (British Columbia). So I am happy to say that for the twenty-fifth-anniversary edition of my book, I finally got smart and added a chapter on the world-class ice wines of Ontario and the dry whites and reds of British Columbia.

Canada has been making wine for more than two hundred years. Its extreme winters originally made it hard to grow quality *vinifera* wines, putting Canadians at a disadvantage. Especially in the Niagara/Ontario region, they focused their efforts on making wines from winter-hardy *labrusca* grapes (Concord, Catawba, and Niagara). When using these grapes they concentrated on making fortified wines.

In the 1970s things began to change. Several small producers began to experiment with winter-hardy hybrids, producing better wines. Eventually they shifted, with the help of very careful farming techniques, to *vinifera* wines. And the regions that grew grapes and made wine also started to expand.

Today, there are many wines that originate mostly in southern Ontario on the Niagara Peninsula, and Okanagan Valley in British Columbia. The country has seen growth of small, quality producers in the Similkameen Valley, the southern Fraser River Valley, southern Vancouver Island, and the Gulf Islands, as well as the shores of Lake Erie and in Prince Edward County in Ontario.

Through hard work and perseverance, Canada produces much quality *vinifera* wine. In 2002, Canada produced 75.9 million liters of wine (0.3 percent of world production). However, the largest and most highly prized wine export from Canada is Ice Wine. Much of it is made in the Okanagan Valley and the Niagara Peninsula.

The first great Canadian wine I ever tasted was an Ice Wine—or *Eiswein*—made by the Inniskillin winery. Inniskillin, founded in 1975, was the first new winery founded in Ontario since 1927, and it produced its first Ice Wine in 1984 after a very cold winter. To make Ice Wine, grapes are allowed to freeze on the vine before being picked by hand. The grapes are then carefully pressed while still frozen, yielding a small amount of concentrated juice that is high in sugar and other components. Canadian law dictates that Ice Wine can be made using only *vinifera* grapes (usually Riesling and the French hybrid Vidal). It must also contain at least 125 grams of residual sugar per liter. Most Ice Wines are expensive and are sold in half bottles.

Ice Wine became so popular that many wineries followed their example, eventually finding shortcuts like placing grapes in large freezers before pressing instead of letting the fruit freeze on the vine. Many new laws then stopped imitators from mislabeling those wines as Ice Wine. Today, only wine made from naturally frozen grapes may bear that name.

—KZ

> ## ⟿ WHAT ARE THE ⟿ MAJOR WINE REGIONS OF CANADA?
>
> Canada has two major wine-producing regions: British Columbia on the Pacific Coast, and Ontario in the eastern Great Lakes region.
>
> ***Ontario/Niagara Peninsula:*** Chardonnay, Riesling, Pinot Noir, Vidal, Cabernet Franc
>
> ***British Columbia/Okanagan Valley:*** Chardonnay, Pinot Gris, Merlot, Cabernet Sauvignon, Syrah, Gewürztraminer, Pinot Noir

ICEWINE

~~~

Tony Aspler

Canada is becoming recognized as one of the world's best producers of Icewine. Ontario is the most prolific source of this gift of winter to the wine lover; virtually every winery in the province produces the honeyed nectar on an annual basis.

Inniskillin gave this fact global recognition at Vinexpo 1991 in Bordeaux when it won the Grand Prix d'Honneur for its Vidal Icewine 1989—one of only 19 such medals out of 4,100 entries. The message was further driven home when Stonechurch won a Grand Gold Award at Vinitaly, Verona, in 1994 for its 1991 Vidal Icewine, and Reif in 1995 for its Vidal Icewine 1993. Since then, Ontario Icewine has regularly won gold at international competitions.

Canada is, in fact, the world's largest producer of this vinous rarity. Ontario alone produces 15,000 to 20,000 cases. (Small amounts are made in British Columbia, Quebéc, and Nova Scotia.)

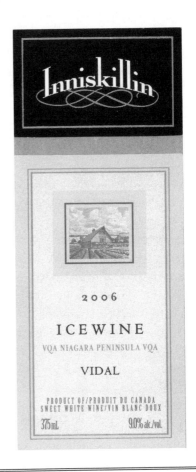

Tony Aspler is the Canadian wine expert and has also been the wine columnist for the Toronto Star *for twenty-five years. He has written fifteen books on the subject of wine and food, and nine novels with titles like* The Beast of Barbaresco, Death on the Douro, *and* Blood Is Thicker than Beaujolais. *Quite a collection of wine murder mysteries from a guy who really likes "Ice" wine!*

Icewine, or *Eiswein* as the Germans call it, is the product of frozen grapes. A small portion of the vineyard is left unpicked during the September-October harvest and the bunches are allowed to hang on the vine until the mercury drops to at least 19° Fahrenheit (-7° Celsius). At this frigid temperature the sugar-rich juice begins to freeze. If the grapes are picked in their frozen state and pressed while they are as hard as marbles, the small amount of juice recovered will be intensely sweet and high in acidity. The wine made from this juice will be an ambrosia fit for Dionysus himself.

Like most gastronomic breakthroughs, the discovery of Icewine was accidental. Producers in Franconia in 1794 made virtue of necessity by pressing juice from frozen grapes. They were amazed by the abnormally high concentration of sugars and acids which hitherto they had achieved only by allowing the grapes to desiccate on straw mats before pressing or by the effects of *Botrytis Cinerea*. (This disease is known as "noble rot"; it afflicts grapes in autumn usually in regions where there is early morning fog and humid, sunny afternoons. A mushroom-like fungus attaches itself to the berries, puncturing their skins and allowing the juice to evaporate. The world's great dessert wines such as Sauternes, Riesling Trockenbeerenauslese, and Tokay Aszu Essence are made from grapes afflicted by this benign disease.)

It was not until the middle of the last century in the Rheingau that German wine-growers made conscious efforts to produce Icewine on a consistent basis. However, they found they could not make it every year since the subzero cold spell has to last for several days to ensure that the grapes remain frozen solid during picking and the lengthy pressing process which can take up to three days or longer. Grapes are 80 percent water, and when this water is frozen and driven off under pressure as shards of ice, the resulting juice will be miraculously sweet. A sudden thaw causes the ice to melt, diluting the sugar in each grape.

This means that temperatures for Icewine are critical. In Germany, the pickers must be out well before dawn to harvest the grapes before the sun comes up. Some German producers even go so far as to rig an outdoor thermostat to their alarm clocks so as not to miss a really cold morning. But in Ontario there is no need for such dramatics. The winemakers can get a good night's sleep secure in the knowledge that some-time between November and February our climate will afford them a stretch of polar temperatures. As a result, Ontario Icewine is an annual event and as predictable as the turning maples. Sometimes the cold comes early, as it did in 1991. On October 29, in British Columbia, Hainle Vineyards, Cedar-Creek, and Gehringer Brothers were able to pick frozen grapes for Icewine when temper-atures plunged to 8° Fahrenhiet (-13° Celsius).

THE ROYAL TOKAJI WINE COMPANY

Royal Tokaji

ASZÚ ESSENCIA

Produced and Bottled by
The Royal Tokaji Wine Company
Mad, Tokaji Hegyalja

500 ml e 9 z

TOKAJI WHITE WINE PRODUCE OF HUNGARY   Alc. 8.5% by vol

Not all grapes can make Icewine. Only the thick-skinned, late-maturing varieties such as Riesling and Vidal can hang in there for the duration against such predators as gray rot, powdery mildew, unseasonal warmth, wind, rain, sugar-crazed starlings—and the occasional Ontario bureaucrat. The very first attempts at producing Icewine in Canada on a commercial basis were sabotaged by bird and man. In 1983, Inniskillin lost its entire crop to the birds the day before picking was scheduled. Walter Strehn at Pelee Island Vineyards had taken the precaution of netting his vines to protect them from the feathered frenzy. Some persistent blue jays, however, managed to break through his nets and were trapped in the mesh. A passing bird-fancier reported this to the Ministry of Natural Resources whose officials descended upon the vineyard and tore off the netting. Strehn not only lost $25,000 worth of Riesling grapes to the rapacious flock but, to add insult to injury, he was charged with trapping birds out of season—using dried grapes as bait! Happily, the case was dropped, and with the grapes that were left Strehn managed to make 50 cases of Riesling Icewine 1983.

Since those days, more and more Ontario wineries have jumped on the Icewine bandwagon. Their wines literally sell out the moment they reach the stores. To avoid disappointment, customers have been encouraged to reserve their bottles while the grapes are still hanging on the vine. In Japan, these wines sell for up to $200 the half bottle (the price in Canada ranges from $29.95 to $50). Note: Many Ontario wineries are making a second pressing of their Icewine

grapes to produce a more affordable and less concentrated dessert wine they call Select Late Harvest or Winter Wine.

But whenever you leave grapes on the vine once they have ripened, you are taking an enormous gamble. If birds and animals don't get them, mildew and rot or a sudden storm might. So growers reserve only a small portion of their Vidal or Riesling grapes for Icewine—a couple of acres at most.

A vineyard left for Icewine is really a very sorry sight. The mesh-covered vines are completely denuded of leaves and the grapes are brown and shriveled, hanging like so many bats from the frozen canes. The wrinkled grapes are ugly but taste wonderfully sweet—like frozen raisins.

The stems that attach the bunches to the vine are dried out and brittle, so a strong wind or an ice storm could easily knock them to the ground. A twist of the wrist is all that is needed to pick them.

Usually there is snow and a high wind which makes picking an experience similar to Scott's trek to Antarctica. When the wind howls through the vineyard, driving the snow before it, the wind-chill factor can make a temperature of 14° Fahrenheit (-10° Celsius) seem like -40° (-40° Celsius). Harvesting Icewine grapes is a torturous business. Pickers, fortified with tea and brandy, brave the elements for two hours at a time before rushing back to the winery to warm up.

And when the tractor delivers the precious boxes of grapes to the winery, the hard work begins. Since the grapes must remain frozen, the pressing is done *al fresco* or the winery doors are left open. The presses have to be worked slowly, otherwise the bunches will turn to a solid block of ice yielding nothing. Some producers throw rice husks into the press which pierce the skins of the grapes and create channels for the juice to flow through the mass of ice. Sometimes it takes two or three hours before the first drop of juice appears. These drops will be the sweetest since grape sugars have a lower freezing point than water.

Roughly speaking, one kilogram of grapes will produce sufficient juice to ferment into one bottle of wine. The juice from a kilogram of Icewine grapes will produce one-fifth of that amount and less, depending on the degree of dehydration caused by wind and winter sunshine. The longer the grapes hang on the vine, the less juice there will be. So a cold snap in December will yield more Icewine than having to wait for a harvest date in January when there will be a crop weight loss of 60 percent or more over normal harvest weights.

The oily juice, once extracted from the marble-hard grapes, is allowed to settle for three or four days and then it is clarified of dust and debris by racking from one tank to another. The colorless liquid is cold and will not permit fermenting to start, and a special yeast has to be added to activate that process in stainless steel tanks. Because of the very high sugars, the fermentation is very slow and can take months. But when the amber wine is finally in bottle, it has the capacity to age for a decade or more.

While Germany may be recognized by the world as the home of Icewine, ironically the Germans cannot make it every year. Canadian winemakers can. Klaus Reif, the winemaker at Reif Winery, has produced

Icewine in both countries. While studying oenology at the Geisenheim Institute in Germany, he worked at a government winery in Neustadt in the Pfalz. In 1983, he made his first Icewine there from Riesling grapes. Four years later he made Icewine from Vidal grapes grown in his uncle's vineyard at Niagara-on-the-Lake. "The juice comes out like honey here," says Klaus. "In Germany it drops like ordinary wine."

Robert Mielzynski, formerly of Hillebrand Estates, who had also studied winemaking in Germany, agrees: "A lot of the Icewines I tried in Germany were less viscous and more acidic that ours. We get higher sugar levels."

Neustadt is around the 50th latitude; Niagara near the 43rd. Although our winters are more formidable than those of Germany, we enjoy a growing season with more sunshine hours, resembling that of Burgundy. Our continental climate in southern Ontario gives us high peaking temperatures in July, the vine's most active growing month. This means that grapes planted in the Niagara Peninsula can attain higher sugar readings than in Germany, especially late-picked varieties because of dramatic fluctuations of temperature in the fall season. "From September on," says Karl Kaiser, winemaker and co-owner of Inniskillin, "the weather can turn cold and then suddenly warm up again. This warming-freezing effect makes the grapes dehydrate. Loss of water builds up the sugars. In January we have very windy weather that further desiccates the grapes so that when we harvest the Icewine we have very concentrated flavors."

So when the thermometer takes that first

303

plunge of winter, think of the grape pickers down on the Niagara Peninsula, bundling up to harvest the grapes of frost. Bat-brown and shriveled like the old men of the mountains, those bunches hanging precariously from the vine may look unappetizing but the lusciously sweet wine they produce is worth all the numb fingers and raw cheeks. At least the vintners have machines to press the juice from the frozen berries; they don't have go through the procedure in their bare feet!

The credit for the first Canadian Icewine must go to the late Walter Hainle in British Columbia who began making it from Okanagan Riesling in 1973 for family and friends. Tilman Hainle confesses that the family has one bottle of the 1974 vintage left ("in a glamorous Lowenbräu bottle with matching cap and homemade label"). "We have made Icewine every year since then, except in 1977. It is possible to make Icewine every year in British Columbia, although the picking dates and quantities vary widely. Usually, we have to wait until November or December for the appropriate temperatures."

Up until 1983, the Hainles used Okanagan Riesling to make their Icewine, but since then they have used a number of varieties including Traminer, Pinot Noir, and Riesling. "We felt that Riesling is the most successful variety for our Icewine," says Tilman. Over the years their sugar levels have varied from 33 Brix to 57.5 Brix. A range of 35 to 40 Brix is typical at a temperature of 15° Fahrenehit (-9° Celsius) to 10° (-12° Celsius).

The quantity of juice the Hainles got from their frozen grapes ranged from as little as 20 liters in 1990 to as much as 580 liters in 1987. "The maximum quantity for us is limited by our mechanical capability—one press will yield from 150 to 300 liters of juice, and we don't have the crop or the time to do more than one press." Tilman Hainle is also reluctant to produce large quantities of Icewine. The wine, he contends, is a curiosity which garners a lot of publicity, chiefly because of its rarity and because it is not sufficiently cost efficient to warrant making it a large part of their portfolio.

ARGENTINA

ARGENTINA

Pacific Ocean

BOLIVIA

PARAGUAY

CHILE

Cafayete

SALTA

ARGENTINA

BRAZIL

San Juan

MENDOZA

URUGUAY

★ Buenos Aires

UCO VALLEY

Neuquén

RIO NEGRO

Atlantic Ocean

0 Miles   400

0 Kilometers   800

> ## ～ WHAT ARE THE ～ MAIN GRAPE VARIETIES OF ARGENTINA?
>
> *The major white grapes are:*
>
> *Torrontés Riojano* (20,300 acres)
> *Chardonnay* (14,200 acres)
>
> *The major red grapes are:*
> *Malbec* (60,300 acres) *Merlot*
> (18,300 acres) *Cabernet Sauvignon*
> (43,700 acres) *Tempranillo* (15,775
> acres) *Syrah* (30,630 acres)

SOME WINE COUNTRIES ARE VERY protective and proud of their own wines, and don't usually talk about their neighboring countries'. I found this out the first time I went to Australia when the producers didn't like the idea of my next visit—New Zealand. I found this a little silly since the primary quality grape of New Zealand is Sauvignon Blanc and the primary quality grape of Australia is Shiraz. It's the same with Chile and Argentina since the major quality grape of Argentina is Malbec and the highest quality wine of Chile, in my opinion, is Cabernet Sauvignon.

Obviously I did not listen to my friends in Chile and decided to visit the wine region of Mendoza "just" on the other side of the Andes (the largest mountain range in the world). It was one of the greatest road trips I have ever taken, with picturesque views, snow-capped mountains, breathtaking waterfalls, and beautiful wooded areas. As in all my journeys around the world, it is not always about the wines.

Argentina is probably the one country I name most often when people ask me what is the newest and brightest-wine producing region. It's on the cusp of breaking out.

There are many reasons Argentina is primed for an incredible expansion. One is that Argentina has tremendous soil and incomparable weather. This is red wine country: arid climate, big soils, lots of sun. Also, Argentina is the second-largest country in South America. Since there are thousands more acres yet to be planted, its potential is enormous. But while land, soil, air, and sun are all important, all great wine countries need one thing to get to the next level: investment. And Argentina has it. Argentina's financial commitments come from countries all over the world, such as Spain, France, and Chile. And it also has people. Not just any people, but wine experts who are world-renowned, and have experience running their own vineyards and wineries.

Argentina's tradition of making wine goes all the way back to the 1500s, when the land was colonized by the Spanish. Jesuit missionaries planted and

～ WHAT ARE THE ～ MAIN WINE REGIONS OF ARGENTINA?

North

Salta: Torrontés Riojano, Cabernet Sauvignon
Cafayate

Cuyo

Mendoza: Malbec, Tempranillo, Cabernet Sauvignon
Uco Valley
San Juan: Bonarda, Syrah

Patagonia

Rio Negro: Pinot Noir, Torrontés Riojano
Neuquén

cultivated vines in Mendoza and also to the north in San Juan. For many years little Argentine wine, which was well made and inexpensive, left the country.

However, the last twenty years have seen massive changes in Argentine wine drinking. Average annual domestic consumption of wine dropped from twenty-four gallons to just eight. And the devaluation of the Argentine peso in 2001 made exporting profitable. These two factors caused many Argentine wineries to change their marketing. They also had the help of large investments of foreign capital and an influx of internationally renowned winemaking consultants, most notably Michel Rolland. Rolland, with his Clos de los Siete estate of five wineries, became a champion of Argentine wine. Other outside interest came from Bordeaux. For example, Château Léoville Poyferré invested in Cuvelier los Andes, as has Château Clarke in Flechas de los Andes. This helped prime Argentine wines for introduction to the international export market.

The introductory prices for Argentine wines were very low, and the wine world had tremendous fun discovering the main grape of Argentina, Malbec. Now Argentina had a place at the wine table with a signature grape that immediately captured the wine and food writers', not to mention the public's, attention.

The quality/price ratio continues to be among the best in the world! With the size of the country and the speed of its winemaking success, look for even more and better wines over the next twenty years.

—KZ

ARGENTINA

Christopher Fielden

Excellent secondary wines are made at Mendoza, at the base of the Andes, which form an article of considerable traffic with Buenos Ayres, a thousand miles distant across the Pampas. They are transported even during the summer heats, and so far from spoiling, they prove all the better from the journey. The wine is not carried in skins, which so taint and disqualify the produce of some districts in the mother-country, but is conveyed in small barrels slung on each side of a mule and the quantity thus sent is considerable.
—James L. Denman, *The Vine and Its Fruit,* 1875

Argentina is by far the most important wine country in Latin America, both in terms of the area that it has under vines: 209,000 hectares as opposed to the next largest, 132,000 hectares in Chile, and also in per capita consumption: 40.99 liters, as opposed to 31 liters in Uruguay. Despite all this it is difficult to comprehend that on all vinous sides, it is but a shadow of its former self. In 1973, the production of wine in Argentina was 27 million hectoliters; in 1997 it was exactly half this. In 1970 the annual consumption per capita of wine in Argentina reached 91.79 liters, now it is just 41. Like no other wine country in the world, the wine industry in Argentina has been through a torrid time and is only now just emerging from the ashes.

Geographically, there is no other country in the world that has a broader spread of vineyards than those of Argentina. They stretch in the lee of the Andes almost 1,600 km from Salta in the north to Neuquén in the south.

Christopher Fielden has been around wine all of his life from importing to education to writing. He was one of the first writers to cover the new and exciting world of Latin America, especially Chile and Argentina. I'm often asked by my students what will be the next wine region or country to emerge with quality wines. Argentina is my answer and I am not just talking about the Malbec grape. In 2010, Argentina is still only at a fraction of the eventual vineyard land that can be cultivated. Christopher writes about Argentina's past in relation to where the country's wine industry will be in the future.

In altitude, the vineyards range from 450 m above sea level in Río Negro to over 2,000 m in Salta Province. This means that there is a wide range of climatic conditions. As we shall also see the altitude of the vineyards plays perhaps a larger part than in any other wine country.

In many ways Argentina has much going for it as a wine-producing country. For a start, the family of the President, Dr. Saúl Menem, has a background in the wine trade in the province of La Rioja. It has a good climate and no shortage of water for irrigation. It has no shortage of land available for the expansion of vineyards. Indeed, as has just been mentioned, the area under vines could increase by almost 50%, just by replanting the area that has been grubbed up since 1972. Land is cheap. There is also a healthy domestic market of approximately 35 million consumers, most of them of Italian or Spanish origin, with a tradition of wine drinking. All this makes the country an attractive proposition and the wine industry has attracted inward investment more than any other country in Latin America.

Are there clouds on the horizon? The main one must be the question of economic stability. Since 1991, the Argentine peso has been pegged to the U.S. dollar in a bid to curb inflation and to give some solidity to the currency. While there is no doubt that in the short term this has achieved the desired effect, as I write this, questions are being asked as to whether the economy is about to implode with dangerous results. A further problem is that of the wine that Argentina exports, three-quarters is just ordinary "table wine." This is no more than a commodity and,

as a commodity, can easily be the victim of market circumstances beyond its control. For Argentina to be a truly major force in the world of wine, it must concentrate its efforts on the export of "fine" wine. Here it is having some success, with sales in Britain, for example, rising fast. It is in this field that the future of the Argentine wine industry must lie.

HISTORY

The colonization of Argentina took place in three different waves and from three different directions. The first colony in the country was established in 1536 at Buenos Aires, by the explorer Pedro de Mendoza, who arrived with a fleet of 16 ships and 1,600 men. However, largely due to the hostility of the local Querandí Indians, the settlement was abandoned and the Spaniards sailed up the Paraná River and built the city of Asunción, in what is now Paraguay. It was more than 40 years before the Spaniards established another bridgehead on the south bank of the River Plate.

The other two waves of exploration into what is now Argentina were financed by the wealth of the silver mines of Peru and Bolivia, and they came through the Andes. In 1553, Francisco de Aguirre, known as the "Mother of Cities" for his role as a colonizer (and who has given his name to a major Chilean winery) established the first Spanish city in the country, Santiago del Estero. This became an important stage on the route between the food-supplying region of the Pampas and the colonial cities in the Andes. The third "invasion" came from Chile through the Uspallata

Pass and led to the foundation of the city of Mendoza in 1561, by Pedro de Castilla, and of San Juan, by Juan Jufré, the following year. There is little doubt that all these expeditions will have included priests, who most probably brought vine-shoots with them.

It is Juan Cidrón (or Cedrón), however, who is credited with being the father of the Argentine wine industry. In 1553, the citizens of Santiago del Estero complained that there was no priest in their community and asked that one should be sent from Chile. This was the man who was sent and he is recorded as having arrived with a crucifix in one hand and a bundle of vine-shoots and cottonseed in the other.

Early winemaking was almost totally in the hands of the Jesuits, who primarily made wine for their own needs. However, trade developed, mainly across the Andes, and, to a lesser extent, to Buenos Aires. Notwithstanding the transport difficulties of the seventeenth century, Antonio Vasquez de Espinosa could report that in Mendoza, "there are very good vineyards from which they make quantities of wine which they export in carts via Córdoba to Buenos Aires." This business must have been very risky, for apart from the natural hazards of a month's journey by ox-cart, entry and exit duties had to be paid to each province through which the wine traveled. In addition, the prices in Buenos Aires were fixed by the City Council. For example, in 1620, the price per *arroba* was 14 pesos for wine from Castilla, 12 pesos for wine from Paraguay, and 10 pesos for wine from Chile (Mendoza and San Juan). In the same year the prices were reduced to 12, 10, and 6 pesos, respectively. By this time, there were officials deputed to check on the quality of any wine that was offered for sale in the city.

Morewood, writing in 1838, says, "The genial warmth of the climate and soil in the valleys and plains under the Andes, are particularly favorable to the growth of the vine. Some of the vineyards, especially those in the vicinity of Mendoza, are said to contain 60,000 plants. The grapes are large, black, and highly flavored, resembling the Hambro species more than any other. A duty of one dollar is imposed on every cask of brandy and four reals on every cask of wine. The wines and brandies of Mendoza, San Juan, and Rioja make their way to the Río de la Plata to the extent of 12,000 barrels annually, where they are bartered for English merchandise, besides which, large quantities are sent to Potosí, Santa Fé, and other places. In transporting these over the immense plains of the Pampas, oxen and mules are employed. The former to the number of six in a wagon, traveling about eight leagues in a day; and the latter laden with skins in pack-saddles, travel in troops together at the rate of ten or twelve leagues a day."

In 1776, the Spanish government created the Viceroyalty of the River Plate and, for the first time, the provinces of the Cuyo (Mendoza and San Juan) owed allegiance to Buenos Aires rather than to Chile. This situation was comparatively short-lived, for in May 1810 came the revolution, in which the country gained independence. This led to a bitter internal struggle between the Federalists, who believed that each province should have autonomous powers, and the Unitarists, who demanded a centralized government, with the power being firmly held by Buenos Aires. Overall, the Unitarists continued to dominate the political life of the country. Naturally, in such circumstances, things were not easy for a provincial, rural industry, such as wine.

There were three important factors in the creation of a truly national wine industry. The first was the power of an ever-growing immigrant community used to consuming and, often, making wine. The first of these had arrived in San Juan as early as 1777. They were Portuguese prisoners, as a result of the war between Spain and Portugal, and they included a number of agronomists and viticulturalists. The real immigrant movement did not get under way, however, for almost another century. As Dr. Emilio Maurín Navarro writes in his history of the Argentine wine trade, "In 1874, the last year of the Sarmiento presidency, there arrived in Mendoza fifty-eight immigrants, who were received with enthusiasm by the city which organized a great celebration in their honor." The following year there were 296 immigrants of whom 122 were Italian, 96 French, 30 Spanish, 18 German, and 11 Swiss. It must be assumed that many of these came from wine-growing regions. (There were also eight Englishmen and two Americans.)

One has only to look at the histories of the major wine companies still in existence, to see that this was the time when many of their founding families first arrived in Argentina. Taking a random selection of brochures, I see that Juan Carlos Graffigna began producing wine in San Juan in 1869, Pascual Toso in 1880, Luis Tirasso established Santa Ana in 1891, Rodolfo Suter arrived in Argentina in 1897, Enrique Tittarelli in 1898, and the Pulenta family, of Peñaflor, in 1902. For every potential producer who arrived in Argentina, it must be realized that a host of potential consumers also arrived. These lived mainly in the big cities, for wine was an urban drink; on the farms, spirits were much more popular.

The second major influence was Domingo Faustino Sarmiento, a native of San Juan, who became Argentina's first President from the provinces. During his presidency (1868–74), he established wine schools in San Juan and in Mendoza. He also brought to the country three foreign experts: a Frenchman, Aimé Pouget, who is credited with introducing many of the noble French varietals; an Italian, Schieroni, who established an experimental vine nursery with more than 200 varieties; and a German, Röveder, who ran one of the wine schools.

The final influence was the arrival of the Buenos Aires al Pacífico railway in Mendoza in 1885, with a line to San Juan established the following year. This meant that delivery times to the major market, Buenos Aires, were reduced from a month to two or three days. This naturally had a beneficial effect on the quality of the wine and also opened up the possibility of wines being shipped to European markets.

These factors all led to an increase in the quality of the wine and a move away from total reliance on the Criolla grape, which had been the backbone of the industry since its introduction by priests in the sixteenth century. The use of European varietals was particularly recommended by Tiburcio Benegas, who might be described as the creator of the modern wine

311

industry in Argentina. He recommended also that wines should be made in European styles and in one of his books that appeared in 1885, he gave recipes for producing "Burdeos" and "Borgoña." He was also the founder of the wine company Trapiche.

Tiburcio Benegas was also one of the driving forces behind the establishment of the Defensa Viti-Vinícola Nacional, which was created in 1904 as a vehicle to fight the sale of fraudulent or adulterated wines, on which taxes were rarely paid. This role is now the responsibility of the Instituto Nacional de Vitivinicultura.

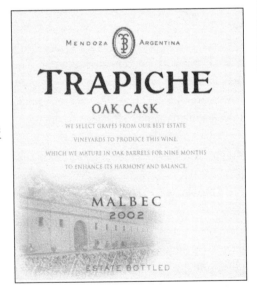

In the early years of the twentieth century, the Argentine upper-classes still insisted on drinking French wines; it was the new wave of immigrants who kept the local wine industry in business. The first Argentinean "Champagne," the brainchild of a German, Juan Von Toll, appeared on the market in 1905, and the writer Fernando Buzzi puts its instant success to the prolif-

eration of tango bars and brothels in Buenos Aires, providing solace to a predominantly male immigrant community.

During the middle of the twentieth century, there was a dramatic expansion in the vineyard area in Argentina. In 1936, there were 149,815 hectares of vines; in 1950 there were 175,013, but by 1977, at its peak, the figure had reached 350,680. Two other interesting peaks were that in per capita consumption (1970—91.79 liters) and in overall production (1976—27 million hectoliters). Interestingly, as a result of government policies, which resulted in the planting of low quality vineyards in Mendoza Province, a second peak in production was reached in 1987. Since then the decline has been rapid in all three fields. This has been brought about, as in many other traditional wine-producing countries, by a combination of factors. The first of these is the rapid rise in the consumption of beers, fruit juices, and soft drinks such as Coca-Cola. These are all very much brand dominated and have vast marketing budgets behind them. Also it might be said that, in hot climates, such as that of most of Argentina, they provide better "refreshment." Secondly, and this also comes with a growing market with higher aspirations, there is a move away from "table" wine to "fine" wine.

It is interesting that the first peak of production, in 1976, coincided with a dramatic leap in export sales which in that year shot up to 45 million liters from just 11 million liters the year before. However, this is accounted for very largely by sales in bulk to Chile, presumably because of a short harvest there. In the same year sales of "fine" wine increased from 2.05 million liters to 2.78 million liters; two-thirds of this was sold in just three markets in South America: Brazil, Venezuela, and Paraguay. The United States was the fourth biggest market.

Despite the fact that this increase was short-lived, it engendered certain optimism with regard to exporting. An article in the *Buenos Aires Herald* of October 12, 1977, was headed "Argentine Wines Among World's Best." Similarly, a month earlier a feature appeared in the *Financial Times* of London about Argentina and it included an article headed "Wine Begins to Travel." It finished up, "If the export trade in wines grows—as is likely as a result of Government efforts to increase the exports of all Argentine manufacturers—this should lead naturally to more discipline in the industry. The discipline will come all the more quickly if special efforts are made to export bottled rather than bulk wines and the Argentine producers see the necessity of establishing and safeguarding the names of the wines and their constant quality." Here two recurring problems in the Argentine wine trade were pointed out, the lack of constancy of quality and the pragmatism with which the wines were labeled. These are problems that are still present, though to a lesser degree than in the past.

For the first time eight of the largest producers jointly attacked the British market, until then just an importer of cheap wine, the equivalent of approximately 10,000 cases a year in bulk. These producers put on a tasting for the trade and the press at one of London's most exclusive clubs in October 1977. Overall the reactions were favorable

and for the first time the capacity of Argentina as a potential source for good wine came to be recognized. A period of expansion in sales began. This good work was totally destroyed on April 2, 1982, when the Falkland Islands were invaded. It was more than 10 years before the ground that was lost on that day was recovered.

The result of this gross over-production of "table" wine was a collapse in prices, which fell below 10c a liter. An interesting comparison can be made in looking at the figures for new vineyard planting; from 1985 to 1990 an average of 2,000 hectares of new vineyards were planted each year, in the following five years, this fell to less than 100 hectares. It is important to note also that Argentina has only had an open economy since 1990. The hard currencies were not available for the wineries to invest in modern plant. As it was put to me by a leading figure in the industry, "At the time, we did not have educated people who made wine for educated people."

During the past few years, many of the traditional companies, specializing in low-price wines, have gone to the wall. Those that have survived are those who have also produced quality wine, particularly if they have been able to develop export markets. In the Argentine world of wine, big is no longer necessarily beautiful.

Today, the wine industry of Argentina lies at a crossroads. It can no longer rely on the domestic market; it must invest in exporting. The multinational companies seem to have confidence in its future; let us hope they are right!

THE WINE REGIONS

While the vine is widely grown in Argentina, to all intents and purposes, wine is produced in the string of provinces that form the western border of the country, those that lie in the shadow of the Andes. As far as the Instituto Nacional de Vitivinicultura (I.N.V.) is concerned these are classified in four groups: the North-West; the Center-West; the South; and Others. Of these the Center-West, which comprises the Provinces of Mendoza and San Juan, accounts for more than 90% of production.

Argentina is the only country in South America to have a D.O.C. (Denominación de Origen Controlada) system. I would like to say that it has a well-developed D.O.C. system, but that is not the case. In fact the first wines to bear D.O.C. labels were Chardonnays from San Rafael in the 1992 vintage. At present there are just two D.O.C.s, both from the Province of Mendoza: San Rafael and Luján de Cuyo. Their relative unimportance in the Argentine wine scene suggests that their future is uncertain. Why should this be so? Perhaps most people think as did a spokesman for Bodegas Norton, when he said to me, "We don't trust any control; the cuisine is not as it was twenty years ago. Look at the French and the Spanish, they have handcuffed themselves."

While it does not imply any qualitative controls, the growers of the Province of Río Negro have adopted as a regional statement of the origin for their wines, "Los Vinos de la zona fría"—"Wines from the cold zone."

Generally speaking, the vineyard regions of Argentina have well-defined summers and winters. In summer the weather can be hot and there is little or no rainfall. The main climatic problem is hail, which can strike suddenly and devastatingly. While rockets are still occasionally used to break up potential hail-clouds, the main protection is netting. Winters can be cold, but frost in spring is rarely a danger. Annual rainfall varies between 150 and 400 mm, but this is supplemented by unlimited water for irrigation, either from the rivers flowing down from the Andes, or from artesian wells drawing on subterranean aquifers.

In Argentina, more than in any other wine-producing country in the world, altitude of the vineyards is a powerful factor. Indeed it has been the marketing point behind the launch of the Terrazas range of wines from Chandon. Each grape variety has its ideal altitude. The vineyards in Argentina range from about 450 m above sea-level in Río Negro, to just over 2,000 m in Salta. The advantages of higher altitudes include better exposure to ultraviolet rays and higher contrasts between day and night temperatures. Similar results can be obtained by planting in the valleys leading down from the Andes. Here currents of air also make for greater differentials between day and night temperatures.

There are three dominant winds in the vineyard regions. Of these two, the southerly Polar and the south-easterly Sudestada, are generally moderate and rain bearing. The Zonda, which comes off the mountains to the north, can blow from August to November, is very hot and enervating and causes a dramatic drop in humidity levels. It is a particular problem in San Juan Province.

Because of the dryness of the climate, except in Río Negro Province, fungal diseases, such as mildew, oidium, and botrytis are rare. Most vines are ungrafted, as *phylloxera* is not a common problem, though with the increase in drip irrigation, nematodes might become a bigger concern. Certain viruses, such as leaf-roll, are also present.

For the most part, the soils are sandy and drain well. As you get closer to the Andes, and particularly in historic riverbeds, stones play a more important role in the composition. The vineyards are planted overwhelmingly on the plains; very rarely on slopes that exceed 2%. There are very few of the hillside vineyards, that one might find, for example, in Chile.

A wine label might well bear the name of a province, a department, or a town—or any combination of the three. Alternatively, it might bear the name of a specific region. To give some examples of these:

Viña de Santa Isabel
Chardonnay
Mendoza
gives just the name of the province.

TRUMPETER
Merlot
Tupungato
gives just the name of a department, within the Uco Valley in the Province of Mendoza.

TERRAZAS
Cabernet Sauvignon
Perdriel, Mendoza
has the name of the town, Perdriel, and the name of the province, but no mention is made of the department, Luján de Cuyo.

THE WINES

The first thing that must be said about the wines of Argentina is that, while more white wine might be produced than red, the red wines tend to be more interesting than the whites. This may be because, with strict currency controls in the decade up to 1990, it was very difficult to buy modern winery equipment. In a hot country, such as Argentina, it is also much easier to make fine red wine than it is to make fine white wine. Similarly, the historical white grape varieties of the country, Pedro Gimenez and Ugni Blanc, produce very boring wines. Yes, there is plenty of Torrontés and Moscatel de Alejandría, but unblended they produce such powerfully flavored wines that it is difficult to drink any quantity of them.

We must also not forget that the history of the wine trade in Argentina for the past 30 years has been a roller-coaster ride. It was able to rely on a thriving domestic market, with one of the highest per capita consumption figures in the world. It could also rely on export markets, such as Eastern Europe, which would absorb vast quantities of basic bulk wine. Japan, too, needed such wines for stretching out its own domestic product. The area under vines grew to keep pace with demand from markets that were undemanding as far as quality was concerned. In 1976, for example, the country exported 42 million liters of table wine in bulk at an average price of 10.9c per liter; the previous year, the average price had been 16.2c. On the internal market, the wholesale price of a liter of wine in 1982 was, in real terms, a seventh of what it had been 10 years earlier.

315

The whole wine industry was in a catastrophic state.

Given these circumstances, it is not surprising that there was a dramatic decrease in the area under vines, from a peak of 350,680 hectares in 1977 to 209,102 hectares in 1989. Since then the figure has not changed much. The result is that a leaner wine trade is having to work harder to make a living. However, by arriving late as a "New-World" producer, Argentina has been able to learn from other people's mistakes. It has been able to move smoothly to the latest techniques. One example of this is the use of inner-stave treatment for the "oaking" of wines. This is widespread in Argentina, whereas the use of oak chips seems to be much less general than it is in Chile, for example.

Argentina suffers from one major problem that is current throughout South America. The wines that the locals drink are, for the most part, not acceptable in international markets. Both during my latest visit to Argentina and the subsequent Argentine generic tasting in London, I was offered wines that may have been highly regarded in Argentina, but were undrinkable in Europe. It does not need a great deal of research to find out what markets are looking for. As the Australian writer Alan Young says in his *Wine Routes of Argentina* (1998), "It has been heartening to observe this industry during this last decade when it moved from the darkest night to the dawning of a new tomorrow. Although a number of traditional bodegas produce a different style of wine, more than 95% of the 1,485 professional wineries registered with the National Institute of Vitiviniculture

(I.N.V.), still produce what could rightly be called old-fashioned style wines. Some could be classified as 18th century wines."

What role does the vintage play in the wines of Argentina? This is a subject that I have deliberately avoided [when writing . . .]. Some years ago, I was asked by a publisher to research a book on the question of vintages around the world. As a result, I wrote to a number of worldwide official bodies. By chance, I have just discovered the reply I received in September 1977 from Mario Rodriguez, then Director of the I.N.V. in Mendoza: "With regard to your question as to the variations in quality between the different vintages, I can tell you that given the climatic conditions we have in the wine regions of Argentina, the quality does not differ fundamentally from one crop to another as happens in some European countries. Because of this it is not usual to mention the vintage on the label."

Since then, international demand has meant that the vintage is generally mentioned on the labels of all wines for export. It is still probably true to say that, in most cases there is little difference between the vintages, either from year to year, or from region to region. There are, however, notable exceptions. Once of these was 1998, the year of El Niño. In Cafayate, in the north of Argentina, it was an outstanding year; in Mendoza, on the other hand, Las Terrazas were so disappointed with the quality that it sold no wine under its label bearing that vintage.

A number of forward-looking producers are now making one style for the domestic and South American markets, and a more appealing, international style, for the export markets of Asia, Europe, North America, and the Pacific countries. A smaller group has switched to only one style for all markets but these wines may come in different labels for different countries.

Where the country has been wise, or perhaps just lucky, is that it has been able to select two varieties, the Malbec and the Torrontés, with which it can attack the world markets and offer something distinctive. Furthermore, in such grapes as the Bonarda, the Sangiovese, the Tempranillo, and the Nebbiolo, it can draw on its European roots to offer a broad range of New-World wines that are distinctly different from the Big Four French varietals that everyone else seems to be offering.

Argentina has happily embraced the teachings of a succession of foreign experts, such as the Frenchman Michel Rolland in the field of winemaking and Richard Smart in vineyard techniques. They have been eager to learn. However, I foresee one potential problem. So many flying winemakers are now being sent out to Argentina that they may well make standard wines in which the Argentine character is subsumed. In the long run, this could do the country much harm, if a new source turns up which can provide such wines cheaper. Fortunately, though, there is little evidence that Argentine wineries are being forced to compete in price with the wines of Chile, for example.

What then is different about the wines of Argentina? As far as the red wines are concerned, many of the varieties could be described as being rustic. This means that they often have natural tannins which give them the ability to last. One gets the impression that all Chilean wines are made for immediate consumption as soon as they are released. On the other hand in Argentina, there are many Malbecs and Malbec blends that will benefit from further bottle aging.

I am the fortunate possessor of a quadruple magnum of Trapiche Milenium 1955, as far as I am aware, a one-off 70% Cabernet Sauvignon/30% Merlot blend, aged for 14 months in new French oak before bottling. If ever there was a wine destined for a long life, I imagined that it was this. However, when I visited the winery in August 2000, they expressed surprise when I said that I had not yet opened it. I hope that it is not over the top when I do finally take the expensive decision to draw the cork!

In Argentina, I do not think that I tasted any wines more than five years old, but traditional companies, such as Lopez and Weinert, still offer on their price lists older wines than that. The excellent Mendoza restaurant, 1884, still offers a Cabernet Sauvignon 1992 from Goyenechea at $16 a bottle and a 1991 from Cicchitti at $22. Malbecs of a similar age are also available at a similar price. This would suggest that older wines are appreciated and that a high price does not necessarily come with age.

Are there the same icon wines in Argentina that are receiving so much hype in Chile? The answer is that super-premium wines do exist and that newcomers, such as Salentein, are trying to raise the stakes with wines, such as Primus. Other wineries, which appear to have high-flying prices include Finca La Anita and Luigi Bosca with their Finca Los Nobles range. In the same restaurant the

317

SALENTEIN
RESERVE

MALBEC

Valle de Uco, Mendoza
ARGENTINA

ESTATE BOTTLED

most expensive wine is Catena Zapata 1990, a Cabernet/Malbec/Merlot blend. It may be that this is a wine released from personal reserves, as the restaurant is in cellars belonging to the Catena Group! (An interesting footnote at the beginning of 1884's wine list says, "Wines whose price is above $40 a bottle will be served from a Riedel decanter into Riedel glasses. Otherwise this will cost $3 per person.")

Perhaps as a generalization, it might be said that the best red wines of Chile are well-honed and smooth, while those of Argentina tend to have a more individual personality, but there is some truth in it. In the end, it depends what appeals to you!

I have already suggested that I have reservations about the Torrontés as much more than a novelty grape variety. While it has a fresh, fruity appeal to the novice wine drinker, it is difficult to take it too seriously. Can a Torrontés be a great wine? I doubt it.

As in Chile, even the best white wines do not seem to be as highly valued, or as highly priced as the reds. There are now some excellent Chardonnays coming out of cooler regions, such as Tupungato and Río Negro. There is no doubt that the availability of French barrels and grapes with sufficient acidity, is helping growers, such as Salentein to make great wines.

However, the white grape that appears to me to have the greatest potential is the Viognier. While plantings are at the moment limited, those wines that I have tasted have shown intense varietal characteristics. This may be a future winner for Argentine winemakers.

Like most New-World wines, those of Argentina can be relied on to be sound. They have the climate to see that the grapes are sufficiently ripe and enough new equipment has been bought in the past decade to ensure that the wines are well made. What is more, most of the wines are not in the common mold; they are different. Why select a Cabernet Sauvignon, when a Malbec has just as much character? In many ways, at the moment, Argentina is the most exciting wine country in Latin America.

CHILE

In 2009 I was honored to be invited by the government of Chile to be a judge at their annual wine award tasting. Chile, whose major grape is Cabernet Sauvignon, has come a long way since my first visit in 1997. Judging wines can be an arduous task, and in this case it involved over three days of tasting. On the final day, the top wine award came down to two red wines in one of the most heated discussions I have ever experienced at a wine judging. Since both wines were extremely high quality, the winning wine won by one vote. So everyone is very curious about both wines, but, as fate would have it, the winning wine for Chile 2009 was a Malbec (the major grape of Argentina). I don't think that any of the judges will be invited back to Chile anytime soon!

For years I referred to Chile's wine industry as a "work in progress." I say this with a smile because they have been making wine in Chile for centuries. But the industry has seen interruptions throughout its history. When I first visited Chile in 1997, I was impressed by some of wines I tasted. It was a country on the verge of producing world-class wine, primarily reds.

During my 2008–09 world wine tour I spent ten days in Chile. I judged more than 400 wines and then visited wineries throughout the country. What a difference twelve years had made. It wasn't just the wines! Chile's geography and landscapes illustrate the mixture of the old and new, such as in historic Santiago, Chile's capital, where over the past fifteen years the infrastructure has changed radically for the better. New hotel construction and highways have transformed this country into an exceptional tourist destination.

Chile is impressive. With over 2,500 miles of Pacific coastline and being, on average, only 109 miles wide, Chile has many different climates, from desertlike conditions in the north to glaciers in the south (in the southern hemisphere, the farther south you go, the colder it gets). In the middle of the country you will find the perfect Mediterranean climate for growing outstanding wine grapes: warm days, cool nights, and ocean winds. And one cannot write about Chile without mentioning the majestic snow-capped Andes, which supply all the necessary water through both flood and drip irrigation. The peaks average over 13,000 feet. It is the world's longest mountain range—over 4,000 miles extending into seven countries.

The vineyards and wineries of Chile blend the old with the new. Chile's first grapes were planted there in 1551. The first wine was produced in 1555, and the mid-1800s saw imports of French varietals such as Cabernet Sauvignon and Merlot. Some of the largest wine cellars in the country were built before the American Civil War.

But all these advances ground to a halt in 1938, when the government of Chile decreed that no new vineyards could be planted. Political instability in the twentieth century, coupled with bureaucratic regulations and high taxes, tempered the growth of the Chilean wine industry. Many of these laws were repealed or relaxed after 1974. The renaissance of the modern wine industry of Chile really began only in the early 1980s. The new technology of stainless-steel fermentors, the old technology of French oak barrels, better vineyard management, and drip irrigation were combined to produce higher-quality wines. Old vineyards were refitted, new vineyards were planted, and new regions were established.

Like its neighbor Argentina, Chile saw a huge influx of wealth and expertise flow into the country in the 1980s, with investments of prestigious houses from both the Old and New World, including Robert Mondavi, Miguel Torres, Kendall-Jackson, Château Lafite Rothschild, Bruno Prats, and Château Mouton Rothschild. The wineries' sizable investments of time, money, and expertise have helped to raise overall wine quality.

Chile is no longer "in progress": it is a wine nation that has arrived.

—KZ

INTRODUCTION TO
THE WINES OF CHILE

———⁓⁓⁓⁓———

Peter Richards

"Of bee, shadow, five, snow, silence, foam, of steel, line, pollen was built your tough, your slender structure."
PABLO NERUDA, TINA MODOTTI HA MUERTO, RESIDENCIA EN LA TIERRA

Chile is an extraordinary country. It is a thin strip of land, averaging less than 112 miles (180 kilometers) in width yet stretching over 2,600 miles (4,300 kilometers) along South America's southwest extremity. Its slender territory is hemmed in between the towering peaks of the Andes in the east and the vast Pacific Ocean to the west. The northern extremities are windswept, desiccated desert, but in the far south the air teems with rain and sea spray as the country fragments into bitter, iceberg-strewn Antarctic waters at the southernmost tip of the Americas. In between these extremes lies an intriguing, diverse, extraordinary world.

Such is the range of Chile's natural features that it almost seems too much for one nation to contain within its borders; it is certainly a challenge to try to put it into words. A Chilean friend once told me how his country's weird and wonderful nature was the result of divine thrift. It was, I was informed, all down to the fact that when God was nearly finished making the world, He had bits and bobs of everything left over— desert, mountain, ocean, lake, river, glacier, plain, island—and so He cobbled them all together and tacked them onto a part of the world where no one would notice. This was Chile.

I have always been fond of this story, not just because of its wonderful imagery but also because of the way in which it reveals a common feature of the Chilean character: self-effacing, imaginative, cheerfully fatalist. The Chilean novelist Isabel Allende put it in the following terms: "we're a people with poetic souls. It isn't our fault; that one we can blame on the landscape. No one who is

Peter Richards is one of the youngest writers included in this book, bringing a fresh approach to wine writing. He has written two books, Wineries with Style *and* The Wines of Chile. *He appears on many British television shows and BBC radio. He is also an international wine judge and chairman of the Decanter World Wine Awards.*

born and lives in a natural world like ours can resist writing poetry. In Chile, you lift up a rock, and instead of a lizard out crawls a poet or a balladeer." (*My Invented Country: A Memoir.*)

Having been lucky enough to live and work in Chile, to get to know its people as well as travel across its extensive territory, I can safely say two things. Firstly, I still have much more to learn and, secondly, it is hard to remain detached from Chile once you get to know the country and its people. It is at once a fascinating, frustrating, endearing, and contradictory country, where the memory of violence, both natural and human, is seldom far from a serene surface. It is a country that is worth getting to know.

One way that people have got to know Chile better in recent years has been through its wine. Although it is only ever a limited and vicarious introduction, it nevertheless affords some sort of an insight into the country, its climate and geography, soils and people. It is this vivid and varied picture that I hope to capture in the following pages and in doing so lend what momentum I can to the enjoyable task of creating an ever-greater understanding and appreciation of Chilean wine as well as the country and culture.

This introduction is not intended as a comprehensive picture of Chile. Rather, it is an attempt to situate Chilean wine in a brief and general context of nature, history, politics, geography, economics, society, and gastronomy. Wine is just one small part of Chile's big picture but it is nonetheless an element of increasing significance, renown, and interest both at home and abroad. This, then, is the beginning of the story.

A BRIEF HISTORY

Chile's earliest beginnings are thought to lie in the Palaeozoic era, around 300–400 million years ago, when tectonic activity caused by the collision of the Nazca and South American plates raised land from the ocean. Chile's oldest landscapes are to be found in the far north and on the summits of the coastal range of hills: this was the first land to rise from the waters. Some two to three hundred million years later, by which time dinosaurs were widespread, similar tectonic forces pushed up the Andes mountain range and Chile as we now know it slowly came into being.

Since then, the activity of volcanoes, earthquakes, and natural erosion has further molded Chile's form. Glaciers and rivers have scoured and deepened valleys; winds and rains have slowly worn away the rocky hillsides; volcanoes and magma vents have added their ash and lava to the changing landscape. The country is continually reminded of the underlying forces that have given rise to its lands: earthquakes are common, as are active volcanoes. Much of the country—around eighty percent—is mountainous.

Chile's climate is governed by two major factors: its mountains and ocean. Variations in altitude and exposure create differences in local climate (in the Andes, for example, higher means cooler and wetter). In central and northern parts, which are of most relevance to wine, the ocean plays a crucial role in determining the weather, primarily because of a cold Pacific water mass known as the Humboldt Current that runs northward along the coast from southern Chile. In

THE HUMBOLDT CURRENT

VENEZUELA

COLOMBIA

ECUADOR

PERU

BRAZIL

BOLIVIA

CHILE

PARAGUAY

Pacific Ocean

ARGENTINA

URUGUAY

0 Miles 500 1,000
0 Kilometers 1,000

Atlantic Ocean

sunny, dry conditions for much of the year followed by a short, rainy winter. (It is often referred to as a Mediterranean climate, though winemaker Ed Flaherty has suggested the term Eastern Pacific Cold Ocean climate as a more accurate alternative, noting the greater similarities between the Chilean and Californian climates.) During the grape-growing season, conditions during the daytime are usually warm and dry, turning cool at night.

Humans are believed to have started settling in the Americas from before the end of the last Ice Age. This may have been as early as 50,000–60,000 years ago, with people arriving either via the Bering land bridge from Asia or by sea from Polynesia. In any case, evidence exists to suggest that humans had reached the southern tip of South America by 12,000 BC. Indigenous cultures such as the Chinchorro, Molle, Ona, Diaguita, Aymara, and Mapuche subsequently developed within what are now Chile's borders. In the fifteenth century, the Inca invaded and assumed control over northern Chile, though they were not able to conquer the Mapuche in the south. It was a similar story when the Spanish arrived in the mid-sixteenth century.

The first conquistador to lead a foray into Chile was Diego de Almagro in 1535. This was a short-lived incursion, however, and in 1540 a new expedition under Pedro de Valdivia was launched. He founded Santiago in 1541. For the next three centuries, the settlers would be at violent loggerheads with

combination with the Pacific anticyclone (a stable high-pressure system that prevails in much of Chile's central and northern areas), this cooling influence in the ocean creates a temperature inversion, with cool air trapped beneath a layer of warm air, which prevents the formation of high rain-bearing clouds.

While this makes for clear, dry weather inland for much of the year, it also gives rise to morning fogs and low cloud cover as well as afternoon breezes, especially in areas on the westerly side of the coastal range or inland areas where these hills are less obstructive. These cooling afternoon winds are also a feature of the mountainous east, where cold air moves down the hillsides from altitude. The overall effect in much of central Chile is a temperate climate, with the Mapuche, the border between them for much of this time being formed by the river Bio Bio in the south. Nonetheless, the conquerors were determined to settle the land and did so by not only installing themselves but also encouraging émigrés from Spain to set up homes and establish managed estates. What was effectively slave labor was provided by the now disenfranchised indigenous underclass. The Mapuche were not officially defeated until 1881, though, when the overwhelming firepower of the Chilean army was finally brought to bear. The Mapuche had the majority of their land confiscated—estimated to be around five million hectares, or ninety-five percent of what they had previously counted as their own—and were moved to reservations. This territorial issue remains an ongoing source of conflict in Chilean society.

With the arrival of Europeans, wine vines became part of Chile's scenery for the first time. These were most probably from Spain although some may also have originated in the Canary Islands (there are conflicting accounts of these first moments of American viticulture). Part of their function was to provide sacramental wine for the Church, whose mission it was to convert indigenous people and maintain a strict religious observance among the settlers. (The variety known as Pais in Chile, also called Mission in California, is thought to have been the chief ingredient of such Communion wine.) The presence of vineyards on the landscape reinforced the permanent nature of the colonizers' settlements.

Among the country's most historic winemaking areas are the north (Copiapó,

La Serena) and central parts (Santiago) as well as southern lands around Conceptión and Maule. In the north, the rumbustious Francisco de Aguirre had set up vineyards by 1550, while Juan Jufré was granted the Macul estate to the southeast of the nascent Santiago in 1564, which he planted to wheat, barley, and vines. Such estates were not only the beginning of wine culture in Chile, they also established a balance of power that has proved enduring—that of a dominant, wealthy minority controlling the country's politics and purse-strings.

By the early nineteenth century, popular revolutions in North America and France together with Napoleon's victory in Spain had sown the seeds of independence in Chilean minds. A Chilean junta was set up in 1810 and formal independence from Spain was finally achieved in 1818. Upheaval in Europe also gave rise to a wave of immigration at this time, one by-product of which was an increased European influence on Chile's vineyards. This trend was compounded by the spread of phylloxera across Europe from the 1860s onward, devastating European wine production and leading to widespread unemployment. Many winemakers headed to more promising pastures in the New World, including Chile.

It was this European and Chilean cross-fertilization, backed up by newfound riches from a booming mining industry in Chile's northern territories, which led to the foundation of Chile's modern wine industry. A new era of international travel among Chile's landowning classes had brought them into contact with European and, specifically, French wines. The result was a concerted program of imports of European noble vine stock, including Cabernet Sauvignon, Malbec, Carmenère, Chardonnay, Sémillon, and Riesling. The first imports are thought to have taken place in the 1830s, and by the latter half of the century the Chilean wine industry was flourishing. It was at this time that what are the historic Chilean wineries of today were founded, including Cousiño Macul, Concha y Toro, Undurraga, Errázuriz, La Rosa, Santa Rita, Carmen, and San Pedro. Exports took off and production rose—this was the Chilean wine industry's first heyday.

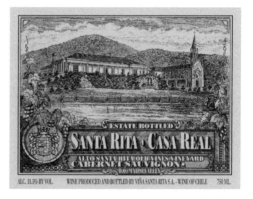

The boom was not to prove enduring, however. By the mid-twentieth century, world wars and economic crises had taken a severe toll on Chile's economy. Alcoholism was rife among Chile's working classes, fueled by cheap and abundant wine that now was struggling to find a market. As a result, Chilean authorities took a hard line, imposing taxes and capping vineyard growth. It led to a period of sustained depression in the Chilean wine industry, which started in earnest in the thirties and lasted until the eighties. It is worth noting that during this period, in the sixties and early seventies, an initiative known as agrarian reform was introduced, aimed at splitting up Chile's large estates and reapportioning land to the country's less affluent citizens. This was, of course, bitterly opposed by the landowners and led to a severe downturn in the wine industry.

The process of land reform ultimately came to a decisive halt after the coup in 1973, when a military junta including army general Augusto Pinochet seized power from the president, Salvador Allende. Chile remained under military rule until 1990. It was a period of history that has proved immensely divisive for Chilean society and

325

remains a source of considerable internal conflict within the country. The transition to democracy in 1990 was, however, surprisingly smooth and successive. Chilean governments have handled these issues with delicacy and responsibility, enabling the country to make significant progress since. One of Chile's main barriers to development, however, remains the steady polarization of its society, though perhaps more in economic than political terms today.

Although the eighties saw the beginnings of a revival in the Chilean wine industry, it was not until the nineties that this process really started to take off. With the return of democracy, foreign markets opened up and investment and expertise from abroad started to flow into Chile. The wine industry bloomed. The national vineyard doubled in size between 1995 and 2002. Total wine production rose from 282 million liters in 1991 to 668 million in 2003. Exports grew from 43 million liters in 1990 to 355 million liters in 2002. Where in 1980 nearly ninety percent of Chilean wine exports went to other Latin American countries, by 2002 over half were being sent to Europe, with North America and Asia also prominent recipients. Although growth is still ongoing, it is at a steadier rate now than before. Nonetheless, this has been Chilean wine's second coming.

THE CONTEXT TODAY

Chile's economy remains export-driven and focused on several key commodities. Mining is by far the country's most domi-

nant economic activity, with copper alone accounting for around thirty-five to forty percent of total exports, with other minerals such as molybdenum (used in the manufacture of stainless steel) and lithium also being big earners. Beyond this there are, in descending order of importance, chemical products, fresh fruit, forestry products, wood pulp, and salmon. Wine ranks around seventh in terms of overall net export value (around two to three percent of the Chilean total) but is a growth sector. Chile's total exports in 2005 were worth nearly forty billion U.S. dollars—in the same year, wine shipments generated US$877 million. (These were both record figures.)

The early twenty-first century has been marked by strong economic growth for Chile. This has been fueled principally by demand from China for raw materials such as copper and has led to economic prosperity and a reduction in unemployment. However, Chile's economy remains vulnerable to shifts in global demand as well as currency fluctuations. In addition, analysts have warned that complacency is a real concern, as is the structure of the economy. As an example, a government report in 2005 revealed that one percent of Chilean firms accounted for eighty percent of income, a polarizing trend that had been accentuated over the previous decade. Government figures also showed that, in 2005, ten percent of firms accounted for nearly half of Chilean exports by value— and of this ten percent, over two-thirds were in the mining business. Strategic planning and diversification have been consistently highlighted as areas for improvement in the Chilean economy.

As one winery owner put it to me, Chile is now looking "to take its second step toward development." A stable and prosperous economy, progressive politics, and improved infrastructure have laid the foundations, but now more underlying issues need addressing, such as the social divide and poverty. In 2005, the annual Human Development Index report by the United Nations Development Programme ranked Chile as the world's thirty-seventh most developed country (out of 177) but also noted the country's poor record in terms of inequality and income distribution. Although the divide between rich and poor is a global problem, it is marked in Chile, where it is estimated that nearly half of total earnings go to the wealthiest ten percent of society while, as of 2003, over twenty percent of the population was living below the poverty line. Within this picture, education remains a high priority for improvement, not only to promote social equality but also to build up the broad skill base necessary to develop a successful and growing economy.

Chile's environment remains under threat from growing industry and development. Pollution is a major issue, not only in Santiago but also in other areas of the country where toxic discharges, improperly managed waste, and other unpalatable industrial contamination provide regular reminders of the need to implement strict environmental regulations on all industries—including wine. Conversely, there also needs to be flexibility and logic built into the system so that regulation does not end up penalizing growth. Fresh water represents a key environmental issue.

Chile's center and north are arid lands that have increasing demand for water for both industrial and agricultural use—their situation needs careful management if it is not to end in disputes, shortages, and lasting environmental damage. To make matters worse, the process of global warming seems to be placing extra pressure on the situation.

A similar balance of regulation and flexibility is required from Chile's wine appellation law, a system drawn up in 1994 that uses the country's administrative regions as the framework for demarcating the various different wine regions, such as Maipo and Maule. (For reference, Chile has thirteen administrative regions, which have both numerical denotations (I–XIII) and names—e.g., Valparaiso for Region V.) Though this system deserves criticism for being too broad-focused and with administrative rather than wine-growing divisions at its heart, it has nonetheless provided a serviceable structure within which Chilean wine has been able to evolve in a relatively progressive manner. However, as there is an ever-greater focus on individual winegrowing sites in Chile and a consequent need to provide a regulatory

327

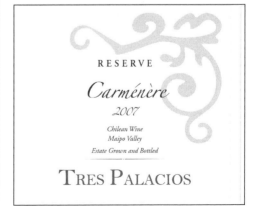

RESERVE

Carménère

2007

Chilean Wine
Maipo Valley
Estate Grown and Bottled

TRES PALACIOS

structure to cater for smaller-scale developments, there will be increasing pressure to reform this system.

Chile's is a young wine industry, still in the throes of development. The same could be said of its fine dining scene. Traditional Chilean gastronomy has consisted either of heavy-handed European imitation or hearty dishes such as corn pie, meat pasties, and sickly-sweet desserts. There have been notable changes since the nineties, however, when chefs started traveling more, experiencing a range of world cuisines and focusing their attention on Chile's natural attributes. The result has been the emergence of an identifiable modern Chilean cuisine based on an exquisite range of seafood and fish (some of which is unique to Chile and the direct result of the Humboldt Current's fertile waters) in combination with the fresh fruits and vegetables that the country excels in producing. New chef and sommelier associations, competitions, culinary concepts, international events, and a newfound sense of confidence are all aiding development in this regard. It is a process still in incipience but, as with its wine, Chile is starting to discover and assert its identity in its food. It is to be hoped that as both Chilean cuisine and wine develop in tandem they can feed off each other's success.

Tourism is becoming an increasingly important part of Chile's economic activities. The wine industry is beginning to capitalize on this and develop its own wine-tourism initiatives and infrastructure. It is a great opportunity for Chile's wineries to develop customer loyalty and promote their wines as well as for smaller producers with less widespread distribution to access a ready market. For those visitors who do make the trip, it is an excellent way to get to know the wines as well as the country.

As a country, Chile is undergoing a profound and exhilarating period of transition and development. This is also true of its wines and wine industry. One winemaker described it to me in evocative terms as *el destape chileno*—a phrase that conveys both shedding of clothes as well as liberalization and revival. (A *tapa* is a lid, so *destapar* is literally to take the lid off something.) It is an exciting time.

AUSTRALIA

AUSTRALIA

Indian Ocean

S. AUSTRALIA
CLARE VALLEY
BAROSSA VALLEY
Adelaide •
ADELAIDE HILLS
McLAREN VALE
YARRA VALLEY
COONAWARRA
Melbourne •

HUNTER VALLEY
Sydney •
NEW SOUTH WALES
RUTHERGLEN
VICTORIA

NORTHERN
TERRITORY

WESTERN
AUSTRALIA

SOUTH AUSTRALIA

TASMANIA

QUEENSLAND

Perth •

MARGARET
RIVER

NEW SOUTH WALES
Adelaide •
Sydney
VICTORIA
Melbourne •
*area of
detail above*

0 Miles   500   1,000

0 Kilometers   500

In 2008 and 2009 I did a world tour of over fifteen countries, one hundred wine regions, four hundred appellations, and tasted over five thousand wines. It was rigorous but I wanted to do it for the rewriting of the twenty-fifth-anniversary edition of *Windows on the World Complete Wine Course*. I had been to Australia before, but only to the vineyards in the states of New South Wales and South Australia.

We all know how long the trip to Australia is—New York to Los Angeles, then Los Angeles to Sydney—and on this trip I continued from Sydney for another six hours to Western Australia and Perth. It had been arranged for me to fly from Perth to the southern wine region of Margaret River. Arriving in Perth twenty-five hours after taking off in New York, having lost my sense of time, day, and body, I was met by a pilot who then took me in his two-seater down the west coast. Flying isn't one of my favorite things to do and I suffer from claustrophobia, but as I boarded his small plane I was so disoriented that I really didn't care!

While Australia is considered a "New World" wine region, they've been making it there since the 1700s. Back then it was mainly fortified wines. Lindemans, Penfolds, Orlando, Henschke, and Seppelt are just a few of the companies that were founded during the nineteenth century. They are now among Australia's largest or most prestigious firms, and continue to produce excellent wines.

Since then, the wine industry has matured. Left behind are the images of kangaroos and Australia rules football. Today there is a new standard of excellence, as Australia is now the sixth-largest producer of wine in the world and is a leader in quality and innovation.

In the 1970s, as in America, there was a shift to making top-quality varietal wines. Along with the increase in quality, as new and more different winemaking techniques were imported or created, there was a tremendous speed in growth: grape acreage increased from 171,782 in 1980 to 322,697 in 2000 (and 429,456 in 2008). With cult status given to many of Australia's top wines; and excellent, inexpensive brands cleverly promoted, wine shipments soared from 1988 to 2008 as exports of Australian wines increased 98.2 percent. In 2008 exports exceeded $3 billion dollars.

One of the main grapes that Australia has based its fame on is Shiraz, known as Syrah in other countries. Australia exported this fantastic dark, deep red with its colorful new name, and the wine industry, and consumers, fell in love with this wine.

—KZ

CLIMATE

James Halliday

As a grapegrower and winemaker, I have come face to face with climate and with weather (the two are quite different, but more or less equally important) for 35 years. As a wine writer and author, I have had to try to come to grips with explaining the means of measuring climate for 25 years. But it is only in the last 15 years that I have come to some understanding of the precise ways that climate impacts on the way vines grow and the way they ripen their grapes.

My first mentor was Dr. Richard Smart, arguably Australia's foremost consultant viticulturist, ironically recognized more internationally than he is domestically. The second was (and is) Dr. John Gladstones, whose peerless work *Viticulture and Environment* should be compulsory reading for anyone contemplating planting a vineyard, or trialing new varieties in an existing vineyard.

As a grapegrower, I quickly came to appreciate the difference between macro-climate (regional climate), meso-climate (site climate), and micro-climate (the climate within a grapevine canopy), the last a much-misused word. I wager that both Smart and Gladstones share the same misgivings as I do in ascribing data to any wine region, small or large, New World or Old World. So much depends on the topography of the region; if it is laser flat, the data may well be accepted at face value. But even there, the French notion of terroir comes into play: this encompasses both terrestrial and aerial factors. Thus Coonawarra has a homogenous climate, but vines growing on the terra rossa (red soil) produce vastly superior Cabernet Sauvignon and Shiraz than those on the sandy gray or (worse still) heavy black soils which, right or wrong, also fall within the official Coonawarra geographic area.

James Halliday is one of the most prolific wine writers in the world and has written or coauthored over forty books on wine. He is the most important writer on Australian wine, and has written about New Zealand and Californian wine as well. As a winemaker he coauthored, with Hugh Johnson, The Art and Science of Wine. He has followed the renaissance of Australian winemaking from its infancy to its world leadership. If you want to know something about Australian wines, you have to read James Halliday to understand this ever-changing and remarkable wine country.

I have also come to appreciate just what an important factor wind is in determining the ability of a region, an individual site and/or a particular vintage to produce grapes of a predictable quality or style. The easiest example to comprehend (if one has visited it) is California's Salinas Valley, followed closely by California's Carneros. Both of these are relatively flat (Salinas particularly) and the winds blow virtually every day through the growing season for a predictable time each day and in an absolutely inevitable direction. They effectively turn what would be warm growing conditions in the absence of wind into cool conditions.

Now take an area like the Yarra Valley in Victoria, with multiple hills and sub-valleys facing variously every point of the compass. South-facing slopes are in principle the coolest, north-facing the warmest. The dominant wind, particularly when wind speed increases, is north or nor' west. In some circumstances a sheltered south-west-facing slope may creep up on an exposed north-east-facing slope in terms of ripening capacity.

Nonetheless, for Australia (exceptions such as Coonawarra to one side) climate is the most significant factor (outside vignerons' control) impinging on grape quality and wine style. As I have observed earlier, for the winemakers of France, terroir is of greater importance.

Indeed, if one looks at Bordeaux and Burgundy, France's two greatest wine districts, and then focuses the microscope on their principal subregions, climatic variation has little relevance and terroir becomes all-important in determining the character of the wines.

For example, the macro-climate of Château Margaux is the same as that at Château Lafite Rothschild, in Pauillac 25 kilometers to the north, and abutting Saint-Estèphe. Similarly, if you consider the Cote de Nuits, the macro-climate of Nuits-St-Georges at the southern end is identical to that of Gevrey-Chambertin at the northern end.

It is true that spring frosts and summer hailstorms may hit one spot and miss another, and no less true that one château or grower may be more successful than his neighbor in one year but not the next. Even more so is it true that climatic swings from one vintage of crucial importance in shaping the quality (and to a lesser degree the character) of the wines of each vintage.

There is a fundamental distinction between climate and weather and by their very nature these swings or changes cannot usefully be individually recorded; one inevitably has to take long-term averages in ascribing temperature, rainfall, humidity, wind, frost, and whatever other data one wishes to use in presenting an overall picture of the macro-climate of a region. So it is understandable that the French tend to take macro-climate for granted, and to look to the effect of terroir to explain and characterize their wines.

All of this in turn proceeds on patterns of classification and constraint which have been built up over many centuries, even if formal French codification did not start until the middle of the nineteenth century and only gained legislative teeth in the twentieth century.

How different the position of the New World. There are effectively no constraints on which grape varieties you can plant, how you prune them or how you use and blend the wine you make from the grapes. Almost every one of the [Australian] regions […] is of much larger scale and of more diverse topography than most of the regions of France: Coonawarra, Padthaway, the Riverland in South Australia, and Riverina in New South Wales are four topographic exceptions on the Australian front.

If this were not enough, the New World's experience in matching terroir, climate, and grape varieties is typically less than a century old, and frequently less than twenty years old. Many classic Australian matches have appeared in this short time—Hunter Valley Semillon, Yarra Valley Pinot Noir, Coonawarra Cabernet Sauvignon, Clare Valley Riesling, Barossa Valley Shiraz, Margaret River Chardonnay—but each of these regions produces a multiplicity of other varieties, and none has an exclusivity on its core variety.

So with an impossibly complex matrix of grape variety, soil, aspect, and topography within each Australasian region (and each subregion) we have had little option but to come back to climate as the most significant factor in determining wine character.

PENFOLDS GRANGE:
Australia's Best Wine?

Campbell Mattinson

It was a meaningless survey until the result came in—and then suddenly it seemed serious. It started because of a conversation, the guts of which centered on Penfolds Grange Shiraz and its heavy use of fresh new American oak. This oak—which gives the wine a sweet, vanilla-like, coffee-cream flavor—was for a long time seen as part of the genius of Grange, and of its creator, Max Schubert. Small oak barrels, concentrated dark fruit flavor, lots of grippy tannin, and, especially after decades in the cellar, so many layers of flavor that a geologist could tell its age by counting the striations on his or her tongue as she or he drank of it. Lustily. This is what Penfolds Grange is all about. It sounds like a simple formula but this is only because it is so familiar: the characters of Grange have been described a zillion times, and just about every Shiraz

wine from McLaren Vale, the Barossa Valley, Padthaway, Langhorne Creek, or even the Clare Valley—all the big red-flavored wine regions of South Australia—have at one time or another, if not still, been imitators of Grange or highly influenced by it, or openly declared mini versions. American oak plus rich South Australian Shiraz; the two go together like Kath and a daughter named Kim.

"I think," this exchange went—and I should point out that I was merely an observer to this talk—"I think Grange should be made with French oak, rather than with American oak."

Which is a statement on the prevailing fashion. Oak grown in France imparts slightly different flavors to a wine than oak grown in America—no matter where that oak is then coopered into oak barrels for the matu-

Australian critic and writer Campbell Mattinson has been writing about wine since 2000. In 2006 he released the book Wine Hunter: The Man Who Changed Australian Wine, *a biography of the Hunter Valley winemaking legend Maurice O'Shea. The book won the NSW Wine Press Club Wine Communicator Award and was described by James Halliday as "one of the most remarkable wine books to ever come my way." Mattinson is currently the SUNDAY Magazine wine columnist and co-editor, along with Gary Walsh, of the website The Wine Front and the annual guide* The Big Red Wine Book. *This piece is from his book* Why the French Hate Us: The Real Story of Australian Wine.

ration and storage of wine. This isn't a snob thing—this is real. French oak and American oak share a lot of similar qualities, but they do smell and taste and behave—as my five-year-old daughter might say—"very lots" different. One difference is that American oak barrels taste sweeter. American oak growers do not feed their trees doughnuts—it's just the way things are.

"But hasn't Penfolds already got that wine, with RWT," comes the obvious retort. A reference to Penfolds Grange's new-ish stablemate, a wine named RWT Shiraz, which is a rich, smooth, blue-fruited wine that is matured entirely in French oak and has a habit of tasting sexier than a silk stocking—not that I've drunk a silk stocking (lately). It's a hell of an expensive way to learn the point—seeing as RWT Shiraz is north of $140 per bottle, and Grange closer to $500—but if you want to know the taste of the best Aussie Shiraz grapes money can buy once they have been matured in French oak, as opposed to American oak, these two top dogs bark the difference to perfection.

"I know all about RWT," continues the discussion. "But Grange is supposed to be the best of the best. And the best of the best should have French oak, not American, because everyone who knows *anything* knows that French oak is the best. It's like buying a Rolls and then finding out they've used plastic fenders."

At which, of course, they laugh. And then laugh again when the other guy adds, "No. I love Grange using American oak—because it emphasizes what a *dinosaur* that wine is."

Grange, of course, knows criticism like Tiger Woods knows how to swing a golf club. From the first time Max Schubert ever let anyone taste it, people have loved to bag it, and in its early days it was even bagged (and famously banned) within the Penfolds company itself. Thank Bacchus young Schubert was a headstrong bugger—and thank Bacchus that Grange seems to have a thick hide. It's needed one. Penfolds in the 1950s, when Schubert was creating the Grange legend and the company was trying to stop him, was an iron-fisted anti-creativity control freak of a corporation, which makes Schubert's courage all the more remarkable. If anyone was caught *smoking* in the cellar at Penfolds back then they were sacked on the spot—and yet Schubert, against a written order of the managing director, went on making Grange, hiding the bottles behind fake walls. If smoking warranted the sack, I hate to think what taking the best grapes out of the commercial mix and using them to make a wine that, in the company's eyes, should not exist would have earned him—but I hope he had a good lawyer in reserve.

The reason Penfolds Grange attracts negative attention—apart from the Tall Poppy target sitting on its forehead—is that it's a concentrated wine that

[. . .] can come across as the wine equivalent of a "wall of sound." In today's Australian wine world there are many wines that are at least as intense, if not more, in their flavor as Grange, but no wine is more famous for having been described as like a "dry port" than Grange; it first copped that tag way back in the 1950s. While this tag is unfair—because Grange is rarely port-like, and is a whole lot more than that besides—if your normal drinking fare is piano sonatas complete with subtle *innuendos*, then Grange might come at you like a wall of *noise*.

Grange might be a magnet for criticism, but it is still, easily, Australia's greatest wine. No Australian wine comes within a bull's roar of it. It was once described as Australia's only "First Growth" wine, a reference to the orderly classification of French Cabernet-based wines, and to the uppermost rank of them. I dare say that Penfolds Grange, barring unimaginable mishap, will always remain so—and never be joined on that pedestal by any other Australian wine.

The trouble Grange has is that each new release is now $500 per bottle. This is still less than "First Growth" French wine, but my accountant doesn't need to speak to your accountant for us both to know that this is an awful lot of money for a red wine.

True, it is possible to buy older vintages for a good deal less than that (it's common misconception that all Grange increases in value over time; in the medium term at least, it most often does not), but you will almost never find a bottle for less than $250, and that means that most everyday red wine drinkers will never pop a cork on one and revel in its reputed beauty. A lot of opinions

are made, then, on the back of its reputation, or on what it's imagined to be, or after a sip of a single vintage of it, or on a personal reaction to "privilege," for and against.

That said, the survey results floored me. I asked a simple question of just over 500 fine wine lovers—people who love wine so much that they subscribe to an "underground" wine newsletter. I expected the results to be overwhelmingly in Grange's favor. The question I asked was: "Penfolds Grange is Australia's most prominent wine, and arguably its most important. Forgetting the label and the story and the prestige, is Penfolds Grange, in general, Australia's best wine?" I then asked for a simple yes or no answer.

Two things: I was surprised that I received over 500 responses so quickly—within thirty-six hours—which just goes to show that love it or hate it, Penfolds Grange stirs a mass of opinion. There was no apathy here: people had a view, and they wanted it heard. For this fact alone Grange can rightly be called a great wine. Indeed, this opinion was so strong that most people who voted couldn't keep their answer to yes or no, and quickly jotted me a few words.

This is where things got interesting—though the statistics themselves were fascinating. Of 516 respondents, 72.8 percent voted NO, Penfolds Grange is *not* Australia's best wine. That mean that 27.2 percent voted YES—there were a handful of "maybes" and "don't knows," but I kept them out of the tally.

I could be entirely wrong, but I suspect that if I had run this same survey in Australia ten years back, the results would have been reversed. Some would argue that I now make a living out of getting things wrong—but that's my hunch. The Australian wine landscape has changed irrevocably in that time, and two factors now work against Penfolds Grange in a survey of this kind: a far greater number of Australian wine lovers now count the lighter Pinot Noir as their more preferred wine type, so that a wine with the inherent heaviness of Penfolds Grange would seem, in the mind if not too in reality, an ugly choice as Australia's best wine—for them. These folks would have jumped on the "no" button faster than Superman could race a speeding bullet.

It has to be remembered, too, that Penfolds Grange has now released more than fifty vintages—a hell of a lot of time for another Australian winemaker to work out the secrets of Grange, and to replicate them. There are a good number of very old Shiraz vines grown in the Barossa Valley and McLaren Vale on land sites as good as those used to grow Grange grapes, and there are a good number of high-talent winemakers capable of turning these grapes into a Grange-like wine. Grange—and this is the interesting, and controversial, thing—is not made from the grapes of the same vineyards each year. It is made from those grapes deemed to be of sufficient quality. This is the strength of Grange—if only one vineyard, or region, does not perform well, there will always be others ready to step into the breach. This is one reason why Penfolds Grange is remarkably consistent—but also why it is remarkably easy to replicate. It is possible to go to a vineyard owner currently selling grapes for Grange, offer him or her more money, and use these grapes yourself—to make a Grange look-alike, at must less cost. This can and does happen every year.

This means that a percentage of the people who voted "no" in this survey would be people who once would have voted "yes," but have found alternative wines made in the same style, from the same wine regions, to similar quality, at lower cost. These folks, too, would have jumped on the "no" button faster than I can burn an egg—that is, faster than I can think. These savvy wine newsletter-subscribing folks have a combination of knowledge and confidence in what their mouth and nose tell them.

I predicted the existence of these folks—I just didn't predict their number. What also surprised me was the tone of their comments.

One voter reasoned that Grange could not be Australia's best wine because you could find "100 other wines in the world that are as good or better. Our best, easy, is Seppelt 100 Year Old Para Port. Find ten other wines in its class in the world—YOU WON'T." Another said, "Grange is a great blended wine, but rarely profound." Another, simply, that it "lacks sophistication." Another, more worryingly, wrote, "It is the best known Australian wine, but we have moved on. There are lots of better wines now." Along the same lines, one voted wrote, "I've always been a bit underwhelmed—it's too big for its elegance—more Loren or Jolie than Blanchett or Hepburn." Another no voter, showing the experience of a lot of those voting, wrote, "I have tasted many Granges, from many different vintages at many different ages. My dad started collecting them in the early 1970s. They are extremely good almost every time I

337

have tried them, and I believe that it does deserve to be regarded as One Of Australia's best wines. But outright The Best? No."

In tune with the dinosaur comments of the conversation I overheard, another voter wrote, "It was Australia's best once, but is now victim of its own time warp. It's now a wine for rich, palate-weak people who need to impress." More positively, another wrote, "I've drunk a few, and it's a great wine, but not our best."

And although I had asked for a simple, and single-worded, yes/no response, one vote couldn't help adding: "There is much global debate currently over what constitutes the soul of fine wine. I think in many ways Australia's greatest wine is Grange, however the flexibility with blending not only regions, but also (grape) varieties, is a luxury NOT afforded to its peers of the old world, by which the creation of Grange was unashamedly inspired.

"This flexibility has been good for Australia (Jacob's Creek, Lindemans, etc.) but has, for a long while, slowed to a glacial pace the development and notion in Australia of regional identity, sub-regional identity, and single vineyard identity (with some exceptions of course)—all cornerstones in the production and marketing of fine wine."

The hornet's nest opened, it was time to peer into it properly.

It's a warm autumn night in March 2005 and I'm about to meet Peter Gago for dinner, the man charged to make Grange—only the fourth to hold this job since 1951. I'm meeting him at the Penfolds Magill Restaurant near Adelaide, but I walk through the back way because I want to see the historic, but working, Magill winery at night. That's when I see Gago, darting from wax-lined vat to wax-lined vat, checking on wines as they ferment. He's wearing his dinner suit, white shirt and all. And against that white shirt the purple mass of bubbling, fermenting Cabernet Sauvignon not only looks rude, but makes me want to put in a call for a case of Napisan. "It's the only vintage I can remember that's been so steady and continuous—normally everything comes in at once, then you have a lull, then it all comes piling in again. This one's just gone straight through," he says of the 2005 vintage.

He fussily rinses his tasting glass and moves back into the guts of the winery, a winery that is not small but is not nearly as large as you might expect. The winemaking area, where the grapes are fermented, is tiny in the context of modern mega wineries. It looks compact, studio-like, a place where a winemaker could get creative—it's easy to see that Grange wasn't created in a factory, it was created in the kind of place a winemaker could love.

There's a moment then when I'm the only one in the Magill winery, a dark night in late March: the bright orange floors, the vats in straight rows, the sound of insects and liquids moving and sluicing and bubbling—all just about exactly as it was when Max Schubert was here, making the first Grange. Earlier in the day Gago walked me down rows, pointing out which vats had created which historic wine. It was a strange experience, the kind that you get at almost no other Australian winery, not just because Penfolds is among Australia's oldest wineries, but

338

because the star wines of its history are more famous than anyone else's. Walking along the vats was like walking down the trenches at Gallipoli, a guide pointing out the terrain and the past's major offensives.

Or something like that.

When I snap out of my pre-dinner reverie, I notice that I'm no longer alone, that standing on the viewing deck is none other than John Bird, who's been part of Penfolds red winemaking team for about fifty years. He's not staring into space, he's up on the deck so that he can stare down a vat, a vat that's full of Cabernet, Cabernet that even at this early stage has been penciled in for the luxurious Bin 707. The look on John Bird's face: intense. Staring into the purple mass. Like he's sitting beside a hospital bed, worried sick at the health of his child.

It makes me think: this is what Grange is all about. Okay, it's about Schubert and Don Ditter and John Duval and Peter Gago, the men famed as the makers of Grange, but as much and more it's about John Bird and those of his ilk—the folks who have worked their arses off for more years than I've lived, who've sat up at night worried about ferments, who've put their heart and soul into making the heart and soul of South Australian red wine.

"Penfolds is part of Australian history," Gago says, and I'm back in Gago-land.

Before we go any further I should note: if you have not seen or heard Peter Gago in action, he is not at all the type you might expect to hold such a position. If you expect stuffy and staid; expect again. He's vibrant, like a circus performer, the willingness to sweep people along with him matched only by his desire to make Grange worthy of its "First Growth" status. Every time I speak with him I get the feeling I could power up half of Adelaide if only there were some way to hook him into the grid. "Adelaide was established in 1836. Penfolds cropped up very, very soon after—in 1844. Penfolds has virtually been here for the entire life of Adelaide.

"Taste this," Gago says. And there's a splashed-purple glass in front of me, dipped straight from a fermenting mass. "Cabernet," he says, "we're very happy with it."

I taste it, it's a few days old, it's like looking at a newborn baby and declaring that it's going to be a doctor or a lawyer, a fashion model or a part-timer in accounts receivable. But it does taste strong, beautiful, and impossibly smooth, and just licking it around your mouth feels like impossible fun—though in the end its tannins are so muscular it's impossible to open its flavors properly. It needs time.

"Wow," I say.

"We could make a special bin wine every year," Gago says, referring to the legendary special bin wines Penfolds has released over the years—a wine called Bin 60A, from the 1962 vintage, the most famous of them. Indeed, many believe the 60A is the best Australian wine ever made, though from the 2004 vintage, Gago has made a mirror-image wine of it, and for a young wine the rapture over it has already been enormous. Gago continues, "But you don't want to take the heat out of 707 or Grange or whatever."

That Peter Gago is here, making Grange, is quite a story. South Australians are fiercely loyal to their fellow croweaters, and even more loyal to the wines of their home state. Gago is not from South Australia (though his wife is now a Minister in the South Australian government), and in wine terms he's something of a blow-in. He didn't start making wine until 1989. The fact that he was head Penfolds winemaking honcho by 2002 is an astonishingly fast ascendancy—and says a lot about the speed at which he impresses people. Before 1989 he was a teacher of maths and chemistry in Melbourne, and before that a student at Melbourne University, where he fell in love with wine. He's a brilliant reference on all things Australian wine—he's been a keen collector and student and drinker of it since the mid-1970s. His own cellar is a treasure trove of where Australian wine has been, and is going—from Macedon Ranges Cabernet to 1955 Grange to Giaconda Chardonnay to most things in between. Peter Gago though has an international sense of wine, and would be as at home in winemaking charge of a great French Champagne house (indeed, he dreams of buying land in the south of England, near-enough to the limestone cliffs of Dover, in an attempt to make great white sparkling wine) as he is at the great Australian red wine head-quarters. It's a point worth remembering.

What characterizes Gago most, though, apart from his palate and his knowledge, is his monumental enthusiasm and energy: know

him for five minutes and you know how he's come so far so quickly. Twelve months ago I asked if I could visit him at Magill, and he said: definitely, though he was booked out for the next ten months. Penfolds folks talk of the fact that you have to tell him to stop working—he'll work twenty-four hours per day, ongoing, every day, month to month, if you don't. The job he holds has become as much the role of a PR spruiker as it is about winemaking—a fact many outside of Penfolds take issue with—though if that's the way it's going to be, no one could do it better than Peter Gago. He is arguably the most talented red winemaker Penfolds, and maybe Australia, has known since Max Schubert.

But we'll come back to that.

First, a duo of anecdotes.

One: Penfolds might be known as one of the homes of big company Australian wine-making, but when Peter Gago makes the Penfolds Sangiovese, he does not add yeast, does not add any acid, does not add any tannin, and does not use any new wood—instead maturing it in big seven-year-old barrels. When it's ready it's then bottled unfined and unfiltered—as a Penfolds wine. Myth-busting doesn't come more dramatic than that.

Two: When Peter Gago was at university, he used to work at a factory in Kororoit Creek Road, Altona, in Melbourne, to pay—among few other things—for the wines he was falling in love with. "They (the managers of the factory) used to offer me twelve-hour shifts, and I used to say, can I do fifteen?"

That's the man pouring his everything into Penfolds now.

SOUTH AFRICA

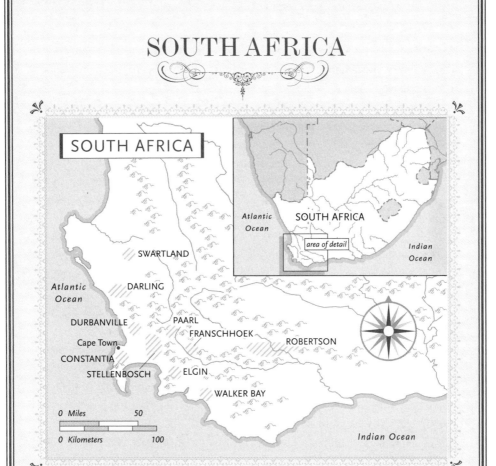

SOUTH AFRICA

Atlantic Ocean

SOUTH AFRICA

area of detail

Indian Ocean

SWARTLAND

DARLING

Atlantic Ocean

DURBANVILLE

PAARL

FRANSCHHOEK

ROBERTSON

Cape Town

CONSTANTIA

STELLENBOSCH

ELGIN

WALKER BAY

0 Miles 50

0 Kilometers 100

Indian Ocean

MANY WINE WRITERS SAY THAT THE VINEYARDS of South Africa are some of the most beautiful in the world (including me!). The Cape wine lands are the only ones in the world influenced by two oceans: the Atlantic and the Indian. While I was traveling through South Africa's ten major wine regions, one thing I found was that you never know what can happen. It's not always about the wines and vineyards. One day we actually could not continue on our road since a family of baboons (at least 50) had decided set up camp in the middle of the road and were disinterested in our needs to be somewhere. On another day we traveled up 1,300 feet right along the Indian Ocean coast to visit one of the best South African wineries. As we were overlooking the Indian Ocean we spotted a family of over 25+ whales putting on a show . . . just for us.

When you visit South Africa, you are immediately struck by the beauty of its wine country. It is among the most beautiful I have ever seen. It is picturesque. Breathtaking.

Originally colonized by the Dutch and by French Huguenots, South Africa has been growing grapes and making wine for some 350 years. With several different soil types, there is a rich, wide diversity of terrain over the country's 250,000 acres of vineyards. Vineyards may be found at altitudes from 300 to 1,300 feet—there are cool vineyards as well as vineyards whose summer days exceed 100 degrees Fahrenheit. With such wide disparity, there is no "recipe viticulture": In South Africa, all wine production is specific to its site.

In the past, most of the wine was sold domestically, with a small amount distributed in Europe. However, in 1994, with the democratic election of Nelson Mandela as president, South Africa's isolation ended and its wines finally became available to world markets.

Before 1994, South African wines were ordinary and production emphasized brandy and fortified wines. Many of these wines were manufactured by large cooperatives that valued output quantity over quality. Few producers made very good quality wine.

But since then, South African wines have improved dramatically. Many now share center stage with some of the world's best wines. And the best is yet to come! More than one-third of all vineyards in the best wine-growing regions have been replanted, and new farming techniques introduced. While the quality of the wines are very good today, as these new vines age and mature, the fruit they produce, and the wines they will help make, should only intensify and get better.

Today South Africa's wine industry calls for quality over quantity. There is a drive and determination to make high-quality wines, using both modern and traditional technologies, as well as the desire to put forth wines that bear a signature style that stays true to the country's terroir.

—KZ

A RECENT OVERVIEW OF THE SOUTH AFRICAN WINE INDUSTRY

Andrew Jefford and Michael Fridjhon

The breathtakingly beautiful Cape Winelands are spread over a relatively small area, but the biodiversity of its winegrowing sites ensures that the area can produce an extensive range of wines to excite wine lovers the world over.

SHAPING THE INDUSTRY

Ironically, South Africa is often labeled as a "New World" wine-producing country; however, winemaking is anything but "new" at the tip of Africa. Vines were originally planted in the Cape of Good Hope in 1655 after the first wine cultivars were imported by the Dutch East India Company. Although the Dutch were responsible for the birth of the local wine industry, their limited wine knowledge proved a definite constraint. Most of these early wines were made from unripe grapes and, together with the lack in hygiene and cellar technology, wines were over-sulfured. The revoking of the Edict of Nantes in 1688 by France's King Louis XIV resulted in Protestant Huguenots fleeing to the Cape. These immigrants were granted land in the secluded Franschhoek Valley, and their wine knowledge greatly improved local grape cultivation. The Vin de Constance, a dessert wine from the Constantia Pocket, became world famous and fueled European demand for South African wines.

The local industry suffered many setbacks despite quality improvements and a newly found market. The dreaded root disease, *phylloxera*, killed many vines during the 1880s. Overproduction followed in the early 20th century, when emphasis was placed on mass production. A ruling cooperative cellar, the Koöperatiewe Wijnbouwers Vereniging (KWV), was formed as a

Andrew Jefford, a Brit, has written more than a dozen books on wine with his most recent being Andrew Jefford's Wine Course. *He also contributes articles for* Decanter *magazine and* World of Fine Wine *magazine.*

Michael Fridjhon was born in South Africa and has been a contributor or coauthor of eight wine books with his expertise on the wines of South Africa. He also is involved in many of the South African wine tasting shows.

343

consequence with full government backing in order to control sales and stabilize pricing. A quota system (1957) limited vine plantings in new areas and the KWV quarantine system strictly dictated which new plant material could be imported.

These regulations limited producers' options and, as payments from the KWV were based on quantity, farmers failed to take into account quality aspects of their grapes and wines. The final blow came in the form of international trade sanctions during the 1980s as widespread protest against the apartheid regime became a reality.

THE TURNING POINT: NELSON MANDELA

Restrictions on international trade during the late 1900s forced producers to turn to the local market. This rather unsophisticated local market, when compared to international markets, did nothing but limit the winemaker's scope for creativity. It was only after Nelson Mandela's release from political imprisonment and the subsequent

democratic elections in 1994 that serious international focus fell on the South African wine industry. Mandela's support for South African wines formed a necessary political stepping stone for the true emergence of Cape wine. Mandela toasted his 1993 Nobel Peace Prize with Cape wine.

CHANGES AND TRENDS

Following the political rebirth, international markets opened up and exports grew significantly, accounting for up to 45 percent of local production. Inexperience and overexcitement resulted in some poor quality wines being exported, which did little to build the South African quality brand. Nor were there any true iconic wines to compete with the best international offerings. The South African wines were focused on price competitiveness. Once consisting of only a few producers and cooperative cellars, the wine industry has grown from just 200 producers to nearly 500 producers during the past few years. Of these producers, 84 percent are privately owned, which indicates a definite trend toward greater hands-on involvement, increased quality, and a definitive development in style. South Africa now competes at the highest level, both at international wine shows and for the wallets of wine enthusiasts.

THE OLD WORLD AND THE NEW WORLD

Mainly a geographical distinction between Europe (Old World) and the Americas,

Australia and South Africa (New World), this distinction takes on a broader meaning in wine language. It differentiates between two philosophies of winemaking. Old World winemaking is defined by tradition; wine is made in the same place, in the same way and style as in the past. Nature is the key factor. Climate variations are expected, and wine is viewed primarily as an expression of terroir rather than individual varieties. Characterized by elegance, complexity, and tightness, Old World wines tend to have lower alcohol levels (alcohol 11–12% by volume). Fruit flavors relating to each variety are less pronounced, and Old World wines have a greater maturation potential that can even run into decades.

New World wines, on the other hand, are defined by progress. New technology, innovative cultivation, and exploration of uncharted areas are the order of the day. Wines are created to be consistent in quality, and the role of the vintage has somewhat diminished. The wines are defined by varietal characteristics and the expression of a wine's fruit characteristics. *Terroir* as a concept is only now being explored. New World wines are more powerful, with higher alcohol levels (as much as 16%) and tend to have a more pronounced upfront fruitiness. Made for earlier consumption, these wines do have maturation potential, but not as much as the Old World wines.

South African wines are often described as lying somewhere between these two worlds, with the structure and restraint of the Old World and the fruit intensity of the New. Set to become a fully competitive world player, South Africa is one of the few New World wine countries which may have the ability to exhibit the fine qualities, elegance, balance,

and restraint comparable to truly great Old World wines. As the many new terroir-focused vineyards mature and winemakers gain an understanding of its interpretation, the sense of place in their wines will certainly deepen.

CHANGING GRAPE VARIETIES AND WINE STYLES

South Africa does not adhere to the strict regulations that govern most Old World wine areas, especially with regard to permissible varieties for certain blends, for example the Bordeaux blend. Since abolishing the quota system in 1992, the search for cooler, quality vineyards has taken entrepreneurs to the tip of Africa and to slopes on higher elevations at the snowline. In recent years, the planted area of five classic varieties (Cabernet Sauvignon, Shiraz, Merlot, Chardonnay, and Sauvignon Blanc) has increased threefold to 36 percent of total plantings, largely at the expense of Chenin Blanc. A local cultivar, Pinotage (a cross between Hermitage or

345

Cinsaut and Pinot Noir), has recently also become a popular drinking varietal. Discussions on a classified "Cape blend," similar to a Bordeaux blend, but including Pinotage, are currently topical. Exchanges between local and foreign winemakers have influenced styles and varietal selections. French, Portuguese, Spanish, and Italian grape varieties are now also being planted and they have attracted serious attention from blenders. This diversification of styles has presented a diverse spectrum from sparkling to fortified and from big, powerful, alcoholic wines to more elegant and delicate wines.

DEVELOPMENT AND TECHNOLOGY

New vinification techniques have also transformed winemaking: cold fermentation and use of specialized yeasts have led to a broader diversification of Sauvignon Blanc styles, while micro-oxygenation and finishing in small oak barrels have improved complexity and refined red wines in particular. In recent years more cellars are using modern technology, but most winemakers are still confident in traditional methods. For example, grapes are still fermented in large, open, wooden vats. Wine is also made without adding cultured yeasts (natural fermentation) and some wines are bottled without lining or filtration. Architecture within the winery has also developed, with the Cape now boasting some of the most impressive production facilities in the world.

BUSINESS AND FOREIGN INVESTMENT

The multimillion-rand wine industry—a great tourism magnet in the Western Cape—is one of South Africa's most dynamic and exciting business sectors. In 2000, Stellenbosch Farmers Winery and Distillers Corporation merged to create Distell Group Limited, South Africa's largest producer and marketer of wines, spirits, and "ready to drinks." The group is listed on the Johannesburg Stock Exchange, employs over 4,000 people, and has an annual turnover in excess of US$800 million. South African Brewers acquired Miller Brewing Company (the second largest brewery by volume in the U.S.) during 2002 and thus became the second largest brewer (by volume) in the world. With interests in Europe, Africa, and the Americas, these companies resemble Foster's in Australia or Mondavi in the United States.

Since the 1990s, many international wine enthusiasts have also become involved in the South African wine industry. Some have set up joint ventures such as the husband-and-wife team of Zelma Long and Phil Freese as well as the French viticulturalist, Michel Rolland. Others have bought wineries, like Anne Cointreau-Huchon, a member of the Cointreau family, who now owns Morgenhof. The Swiss Buhrer family has revitalized Saxenburg. These investors infuse the industry with new ideas and increase exports through their ties to their native countries. Wine consumption in South Africa is much lower than in most other wine-producing nations—just eight liters per capita per annum. In France and Italy consumers imbibe approximately 50 liters per capita per annum. Thus there is great scope for home-market growth as non-traditional consumers develop an interest in wine with rising living standards.

EMPOWERMENT INITIATIVES AND THE INDUSTRY STRATEGIC PLAN

Real success within the South African wine industry is crystallizing as open minds and racial equality have come to the fore. The new democracy has brought about a restructuring of traditional ownership patterns. Significant black-empowered ownership is developing, further instilling a culture of wine among a wider black population in South Africa. While the Black Association of the Wine and Spirit Industry is working toward this objective, the South African wine industry drafted a Wine Black Economic Empowerment charter in 2003. Under this charter, economic equity, enterprise procurement, skills, and social development, as well

as funding mechanisms have been put in place. A scorecard was developed to rate companies on their efforts to empower black and female workers.

Individuals are also making a difference: wine farmers such as Charles Back of Fairview, Beyers Truter of Beyerskloof, and Paul Cluver in Elgin have assisted farm workers to buy their own houses and set up their own winemaking operations. The private sector offers scholarships to young aspirant black winemakers to study viticulture and oenology at the leading University of Stellenbosch Oenology Department.

A second industry document, the South African Wine Industry Strategy Plan, is now accepted as the strategic framework for cooperation and action with specified goals on global competitiveness and profitability, equitable access, sustainable production, and responsible consumption of alcoholic products. The plan aligns the visions and goals of the wine industry to grass-roots action plans managed by several supporting bodies.

BIODIVERSITY

The Cape Floral Kingdom is internationally recognized as a global biodiversity hotspot and World Heritage Site, one of the richest and most threatened reservoirs of animal and plant life on earth. A new partnership between the wine industry and the conservation sector aims to minimize the loss of threatened natural habitat and contribute to sustainable wine production through the adoption of biodiversity guidelines. By promoting cultivation practices that enhance biodiversity in vineyards and increasing the area set aside in contractual protected areas, the initiative will create a unique selling point for Brand South Africa. The world's first biodiversity wine route has recently been established. It includes Elgin, Bot River, and Walker Bay.

348

FLYING, GARAGISTE, AND OTHER WINEMAKERS

"Flying winemakers" made a significant contribution in shifting the international wine industry's focus from "wine is made in the vineyard" to an internally consistent and mutually supportive system integrating viticulture, cellar technology, and grape processing. These trained winemakers (mostly Australian) travel the world and make wine for established as well as up-and-coming cellars in various countries, gathering and exchanging a wealth of knowledge and international winemaking experience.

Another type of winemaker is emerging from the industry—the *garagiste* or garage

winemaker. These are small-scale producers who buy grapes from growers and vinify them themselves. *Garagiste* wines are handmade in very limited volumes and illustrate the individuals' passion and dedication to wine as an art form, while most of them keep day jobs. The wine is usually of outstanding quality; only the best grapes and wood barrels are used.

In South Africa, as in most other wine-producing areas, wine merchants buy grapes or wines from selected areas to blend and bottle wines under their own labels. Some merchants are involved in the actual winemaking process, while others buy the finished wine, which they mature, blend, and bottle. Some outsource their winemaking operations to particular cellars, where they have the wine made according to their prescriptions, dictating vinification and vindication practices. In many instances these wines still represent terroir characteristics and styles. Examples are Stellenbosch Bottling, Douglas Green Bellingham, and Jean Daneel.

There are over 60 cooperative wineries in South Africa focusing on specific grape varieties, blends of varieties, and dessert and distilled wines. Most cooperatives source wines from the vineyards in their immediate proximity. Various cooperatives have adopted a company structure, aligning themselves with current trends. A number have amalgamated and Distell, Rooiberg Winery, and Darling Cellars are good examples.

VISION FOR THE FUTURE

South Africa is still refining its identity and drawing closer to a system where individual regions may better suit specific grape varieties within an area than the marketing department. In new, cool areas like Elgin, Pinot Noir plantings are expanding. Sauvignon Blanc is becoming the grape of choice along the West Coast. In the Stellenbosch area, the Helderberg and Bottelary Pockets are redefining Cabernet Franc and Pinotage production respectively. Many new plantings of Shiraz in Paarl and the Swartland show great promise, and the true potential of old vine Chenin Blanc as a classic wine is gaining recognition. Winemakers are taking a more hands-off approach, allowing wines to express their specific vineyard origins. Single varietal wines remain a consumer favorite, although specific blends are slowly gaining popularity. Recognizing the importance of terroir, cultivation, and winemaking, a blend in Constantia might consist of Sauvignon Blanc/Semillon/Viognier, whereas the Swartland may blend Syrah, Mouvèrdre, and Grenache. The Helderberg producers might find their rhythm with a Cabernet Franc/Merlot/Cabernet Sauvignon/Petit Verdot blend and Robertson might be producing single varietal Chardonnay. Areas showing great potential are Wellington and Tulbagh. Further a field, Napier and the southern coastal areas

look promising with well-known producers developing virgin land. Stylish packaging, innovative and contemporary label design, together with new non-cork closures reflect South Africa's coming of age in the global wine village.

One of the great South African terroir wines is Kanonkop's Paul Sauer. The winery, in Stellenbosch-Simonsberg, has been producing its highly acclaimed flagship wine for over two decades. This is one of the most successful examples in terms of quality and consistency over time. Many new, young producers are following these footsteps to vinous greatness.

❧ ACKNOWLEDGMENTS ❧

Every writer has a long list of people he or she needs to thank for their significant contributions.

I would like to thank all the people at Sterling Publishing, including Marcus Leaver, CEO, for his tremendous support, Jason Prince, Carlo DeVito, Leigh Ann Ambrosi, Caroline Mann, Elizabeth Christiansen, Becky Maines, Pip Tannenbaum, Mary Hern, Rachel Maloney, Elizabeth Mihaltse, Emma Gonzalez and Michael Washburn. I would also like to thank Michelle Woodruff for her help with this collection.

Obviously, I am indebted to the long list of writers who have contributed to this large volume. These are some of the most influential experts in our business, and some of the people whose opinions I most trust. To them I say thank you again.

APPENDICES

THE OFFICIAL 1855 CLASSIFICATION OF
THE GREAT RED WINES OF BORDEAUX

First Growths — Premiers Crus (5)

Vineyard	AOC
Château Lafite-Rothschild	Pauillac
Château Latour	Pauillac
Château Margaux	Margaux
Château Haut-Brion	Pessac-Léognan (Graves)
Château Mouton-Rothschild	Pauillac

Second Growths — Deuxièmes Crus (14)

Vineyard	AOC
Château Rausan-Ségla	Margaux
Château Rausan Gassies	Margaux
Château Léoville–Las-Cases	St-Julien
Château Léoville-Poyferré	St-Julien
Château Léoville-Barton	St-Julien
Château Durfort-Vivens	Margaux
Château Lascombes	Margaux
Château Gruaud-Larose	St-Julien
Château Brane-Cantenac	Margaux
Château Pichon-Longueville-Baron	Pauillac
Château Pichon-Longueville-Lalande	Pauillac
Château Ducru-Beaucaillou	St-Julien
Château Cos d'Estournel	St-Estèphe
Château Montrose	St-Estèphe

Third Growths — Troisièmes Crus (14)

Vineyard	AOC
Château Giscours	Margaux
Château Kirwan	Margaux
Château d'Issan	Margaux
Château Lagrange	St-Julien
Château Langoa-Barton	St-Julien
Château Malescot-St-Exupéry	Margaux
Château Cantenac-Brown	Margaux
Château Palmer	Margaux
Château La Lagune	Haut-Médoc
Château Desmirail	Margaux
Château Calon-Ségur	St-Estèphe
Château Ferrière	Margaux

Château d'Alesme	Margaux
(*formerly Marquis d'Alesme*)	
Château Boyd-Cantenac	Margaux

Fourth Growths — Quatrièmes Crus (10)

Vineyard	AOC
Château St-Pierre	St-Julien
Château Branaire-Ducru	St-Julien
Château Talbot	St-Julien
Château Duhart-Milon-Rothschild	Pauillac
Château Pouget	Margaux
Château La Tour–Carnet	Haut-Médoc
Château Lafon-Rochet	St-Estèphe
Château Beychevelle	St-Julien
Château Prieuré-Lichine	Margaux
Château Marquis de Terme	Margaux

Fifth Growths — Cinquièmes Crus (18)

Vineyard	AOC
Château Pontet-Canet	Pauillac
Château Batailley	Pauillac
Château Grand-Puy-Lacoste	Pauillac
Château Grand-Puy-Ducasse	Pauillac
Château Haut-Batailley	Pauillac
Château Lynch-Bages	Pauillac
Château Lynch-Moussas	Pauillac
Château Dauzac	Haut-Médoc
Château d'Armailhac	Pauillac
(*called Château Mouton-Baronne-Philippe*	
from 1956 to 1988)	
Château du Tertre	Margaux
Château Haut-Bages-Libéral	Pauillac
Château Pédesclaux	Pauillac
Château Belgrave	Haut-Médoc
Château Camensac	Haut-Médoc
Château Cos Labory	St-Estèphe
Château Clerc-Milon-Rothschild	Pauillac
Château Croizet Bages	Pauillac
Château Cantemerle	Haut-Médoc

352

❧ VINTAGE BEST BETS ❧

*Note: * signifies exceptional vintage, **signifies extraordinary vintage*

ARGENTINA
Mendoza: 2005*, 2006**, 2007, 2008**

AUSTRALIA
(Barossa, Mclaren Vale, Coonawarra):
2004**, 2005**, 2006*, 2008*

AUSTRIA
2005, 2006*, 2007

CALIFORNIA

Pinot Noir:

Sonoma (Carneros): 2001*, 2002*, 2003*, 2004*, 2005*, 2006, 2007*, 2008, 2009

Santa Barbara: 2003*, 2004*, 2005, 2007*, 2008, 2009

Monterey: 2002*, 2003*, 2004*, 2005*, 2006, 2007, 2008, 2009

Merlot:

North Coast: 2002*, 2003, 2004*, 2005*, 2006, 2007*, 2008, 2009

Chardonnay:

Carneros: 2002*, 2003, 2004*, 2006, 2007*, 2008, 2009

Napa: 2002*, 2004, 2005, 2006, 2007*, 2008, 2009

Sonoma: 2002**, 2003, 2004**, 2005**, 2006, 2007*, 2008, 2009

Santa Barbara: 2002*, 2004, 2005, 2007*, 2008, 2009

Zinfandel:

North Coast: 1994*, 2001*, 2002, 2003*, 2007, 2009

Cabernet Sauvignon:

Napa Valley: 1994*, 1995*, 1996*, 1997*, 1999*, 2001*, 2002*, 2003, 2004, 2005*, 2006*, 2007**, 2008, 2009

Syrah:

South Central Coast: 2002*, 2003*, 2004*, 2005, 2006*, 2007, 2009

North Coast: 2003, 2004*, 2005, 2006*

CANADA

British Columbia: 2005, 2006   Ontario: 2005, 2006*

CHILE

Maipo: 2005*, 2007*   Colchagua: 2005*, 2007*

Casablanca: 2006, 2007

FRANCE

Bordeaux:
"Left Bank" Médoc/St. Julien/ Margaux/Pauillac/St. Estèphe/ Graves
GREAT VINTAGES: 1990*, 1995, 1996, 2000*, 2003, 2005*, 2009**

GOOD VINTAGES: 1994, 1997, 1998, 1999, 2001, 2002, 2004, 2006, 2007, 2008

OLDER GREAT VINTAGES: 1982*, 1985, 1986, 1989

"Right Bank" St. Émilion/ Pomerol
GREAT VINTAGES: 1990, 1998*, 2000*, 2001, 2005*

GOOD VINTAGES: 1995, 1996, 1997, 1999, 2002, 2003, 2004, 2006, 2007, 2008

OLDER GREAT VINTAGES: 1982, 1989

Chablis: 2002*, 2004, 2005*, 2006*, 2007, 2008, 2009

Alsace: 2001*, 2002*, 2003, 2004, 2005*, 2006, 2007*, 2008

Beaujolais: 2002*, 2003*, 2005*, 2006, 2007, 2008, 2009**

Côte De Beaune (White): 1996*, 2000*, 2002*, 2004*, 2005*, 2006*, 2007, 2008, 2009

Côte d'Or: 1999*, 2000, 2002*, 2003*, 2005**, 2006, 2009*

Mâcon (White): 2005*, 2006*, 2007, 2008, 2009*

Rhône Valley Wines (Red):
NORTH: 1995, 1996, 1997, 1998, 1999*, 2000, 2001, 2003*, 2004, 2005, 2006*, 2007, 2008

SOUTH: 1995, 1998*, 1999, 2000*, 2001*, 2003*, 2004*, 2005*, 2006*, 2007**, 2008

Sauternes: 1986*, 1988*, 1989*, 1990*, 1995, 1996, 1997*, 1998, 2000, 2001*, 2002, 2003*, 2005*, 2006, 2007*, 2008

Loire Valley: 2004, 2005*, 2006, 2007, 2008

White Graves: 2000*, 2005*, 2006, 2007*, 2008, 2009

GERMANY

2001**, 2002*, 2003*, 2004*, 2005**, 2006*, 2007, 2008

GREECE

2005, 2007, 2008*

ITALY

Amarone: 1990*, 1993, 1995*, 1996, 1997*, 1998, 2000*, 2001, 2002*, 2003*, 2005*

Piedmont: 1990*, 1996**, 1997*, 1998*, 1999*, 2000**, 2001**, 2003, 2004**, 2005*, 2006*, 2007

Tuscany: 1997**, 1999**, 2001*, 2003*, 2004**, 2005*, 2006**, 2007

NEW ZEALAND

North Island (Hawke's Bay and Martinborough): 2005, 2006*, 2007*, 2008

South Island (Central Otago and Marlborough): 2006*, 2007*, 2008

OREGON

2002*, 2004*, 2005*, 2006*, 2007, 2008

PORT

1963*, 1970*, 1977*, 1983*, 1985, 1991*, 1992, 1994*, 1997*, 2000*, 2003*

SOUTH AFRICA (WESTERN CAPE WINES)

2005*, 2006, 2007, 2008

SPAIN

Penedés: 2002*, 2003*, 2004*, 2005*, 2006, 2007
Priorat: 2004*, 2005**, 2007*

Ribera del Duero: 1996*, 2001*, 2004**, 2005*, 2006, 2007*

Rioja: 1994*, 1995*, 2001**, 2003, 2004**, 2005*, 2006, 2007

TOKAY ASZÚ

2000*, 2002, 2003, 2005*, 2006*

WASHINGTON STATE

2001*, 2002*, 2003, 2004*, 2005*, 2006*, 2007*, 2008

⚜ GLOSSARY ⚜

Acid: One of the four *components* of wine. It is sometimes described as sour or tart and can be found on the sides of the tongue and mouth.

Acidification: The process of adding acid, usually tartaric or citric, to grape *must* before fermentation in order to boost low levels of acidity, creating a more balanced wine.

Aftertaste: The sensation in the mouth that persists after the wine has been swallowed.

Alcohol: The result of *fermentation* whereby yeast converts the natural sugar in grapes to alcohol.

AOC: Abbreviation for Appellation d'Origine Contrôlée; the French government agency that controls wine production.

Aroma: The smell of the grapes in a wine.

Astringent: The *mouthfeel* created by tannins in wine.

AVA: Abbreviation for American Viticultural Area. AVAs are designated wine-producing areas in the United States.

Balance: The integration of the various components of wine such as acid, alcohol, fruit, and tannin. To be balanced, no one component should dominate the wine's taste.

Barrel-fermented: Describes wine that has been fermented in small oak barrels rather than stainless steel. The oak from a barrel will add complexity to a wine's flavor and texture.

Biodynamics: A type of farming based on the principles of organic farming— for example, compost, manure, and intercropping are used instead of chemical fertilizers or pesticides.

Bitter: One of the four tastes of wine, found at the back of the tongue and throat.

Blend: A combination of two or more wines or grapes, to enhance flavor, balance, and complexity.

Body: The sensation of weight of a wine in the mouth. A wine high in alcohol feels heavier than a wine with low alcohol.

Botrytis cinerea (bo-TRY-tis sin-AIR-e-a): Also called "noble rot," *Botrytis cinerea* is a mold that punctures the skin of a grape allowing the water to dissipate, leaving a higher than normal concentration of sugar and acid. *Botrytis cinerea* is necessary in making Sauternes and the rich German wines Beerenauslese and Trockenbeerenauslese.

Bouquet: The smell of a wine, influenced by winemaking processes and barrel aging.

Brix (bricks): A scale that measures the sugar level of the a liquid.

Brut: A French term used for the driest style of Champagne and/or sparkling wine.

Chaptalization: The addition of sugar to the must before fermentation to increase the alcohol level of the finished wine.

Character: Refers to the aspects of the wine typical of its grape varieties, or the overall characteristics of the wine.

Classified châteaux: The châteaux in the Bordeaux region of France that are known to produce the best wine.

Colheita (coal-AY-ta): Means "vintage" in Portuguese.

Components: The components of a wine make up its character, style, and taste. Some components are: acidity, alcohol, fruit, tannin, and residual sugar.

Cru: Certain vineyards in France are designated *grand cru* and *premier cru*, the classification indicating level of quality.

Cuvée: From the French *cuve* (vat); may refer to a particular blend of grapes or, in Champagne, to the select portion of the juice from the pressing of the grapes.

Decanting: The process of pouring wine from its bottle into a carafe to separate the sediment from the wine and/or to aerate it.

Demi-sec (deh-mee SECK): A Champagne containing a higher level of residual sugar than a brut.

DOC: Abbreviation for Denominazione di Origine Controllata, the Italian government agency that controls wine production. Spain also uses this abbreviation for Denominación de Origen Condado.

DOCG: Abbreviation for Denominazione di Origine Controllata e Garantita; the Italian government allows this marking to appear only on the finest Italian wines. The G stands for "guaranteed."

Dosage (doh-SAHZH): The addition of sugar, often mixed with wine or brandy, in the final step in the production of Champagne or sparkling wine.

Drip irrigation: System for watering vines that applies water directly to the roots through a network of emitters or microsprayers; drip irrigation conserves water and nutrients and minimizes erosion.

Dry: Wine containing very little residual sugar. It is the opposite of sweet, in wine terms.

Estate-bottled: Wine that is made, produced, and bottled on the estate where the grapes were grown.

Extra dry: Less dry than brut Champagne.

Fermentation: The process of transforming sugar into alcohol in the presence of yeast, turning grape juice into wine.

Filtration: Removal of yeasts and other solids from a wine before bottling, to clarify and stabilize the wine.

Fino (FEE-noh): A type of Sherry.

357

Finish: The taste and feel that wine leaves in the mouth after swallowing. Some wines disappear immediately while others can linger for some time.

First growth: The five highest-quality Bordeaux châteaux wines from the Médoc Classification of 1855.

Fortified wine: A wine such as Port or Sherry that has additional grape spirits (brandy, for example) added to raise the alcohol content.

Fruit: One of the components of wine that derives from the grape itself.

Grand Cru (grawn crew): The highest classification for wines in Burgundy.

Grand Cru Classé (grawn crew clas-SAY): The highest level of the Bordeaux classification.

Gran Reserva: A Spanish wine that has had extra aging.

Harvester: A machine used on flat vineyards. It shakes the vines to harvest the grapes.

Hectare: A metric measure of area that equals 2.471 acres.

Hectoliter: A metric measure of volume that equals 26.42 U.S. gallons.

Halbtrocken: The German term meaning "semidry."

Kabinett (kah-bee-NETT): A light, semidry German wine.

Maceration: The chemical process by which tannin, color, and flavor are extracted from the grape skins into the juice. Temperature and alcohol content influence the speed at which maceration occurs.

Malolactic fermentation: A secondary fermentation process wherein malic acid is converted into lactic acid and carbon dioxide. This process reduces the wine's acidity and adds complexity.

Meritage: Trademark designation for specific high-quality American wines containing the same blend of varieties that are used in the making of Bordeaux wines in France.

Méthode Champenoise (may-TUD shahm-pen-WAHZ): The method by which Champagne is made. This method is also used in other parts of the world to produce sparkling wines.

Mouthfeel: Sensation of texture in the mouth when tasting wine, e.g., smooth or tannic.

Must: Unfermented grape juice extracted during the crushing process.

"Noble Rot": See *Botrytis cinerea.*

Nose: The term used to describe the bouquet and aroma of wine.

Phenolics: Chemical compounds derived especially but not only from the skins, stems, and seeds of grapes that affect the color and flavor of wine. Tannin is one example. *Maceration* can increase their presence in wines.

Oenology: The science and scientific study of winemaking.

Phylloxera (fill-LOCK-she-rah): A root louse that kills grapevines.

Praedikatswein (pray-dee-KAHTS-vine): The highest level of quality in German wines.

Premier Cru: A wine that has special characteristics that comes from a specific designated vineyard in Burgundy, France, or is blended from several such vineyards.

Proprietary wine: A wine that's given a brand name like any other product and is marketed as such, e.g., Riunite, Mouton-Cadet.

Qualitätswein (kval-ee-TATES-vine): A German term meaning "quality wine."

Residual sugar: Any unfermented sugar that remains in a finished wine. Residual sugar determines how dry or sweet a wine is.

Sediment: Particulate matter that accumulates in wine as it ages.

Sommelier (so-mel-YAY): The French term for cellarmaster or wine steward.

Sulfur dioxide: A substance used in winemaking and grape growing as a preservative, an antioxidant, and also as a sterilizing agent.

Tannin: One of the components of wine, tannin is a natural compound and preservative that comes from the skins, stems, and pips of the grapes and also from the wood barrel in which wine is aged.

Terroir: A French term for all the elements that contribute to the distinctive characteristics of a particular vineyard site that include its soil, subsoil, slope, drainage, elevation, and climate, including exposure to the sun, temperature, and precipitation.

Varietal: A wine that is labeled with the predominant grape used to produce the wine. For example, a wine made from Chardonnay grapes would be labeled "Chardonnay."

Vintage: The year the grapes are harvested.

Vinification: Winemaking.

Vitis labrusca (VEE-tiss la-BREW-skah): A native grape species in America.

Vitis vinifera (VEE-tiss vih-NIFF-er-ah): The grape species that is used in most countries for winemaking.

359

❧ CONTRIBUTOR BIOGRAPHIES ❧

Gerald Asher held the post of wine editor at *Gourmet* magazine for thirty years. He has been recognized for his writing on wine and the international wine trade by the New York Wine and Food Society and the James Beard Foundation, among others. The French government awarded him the Ordre du Mérite Agricole in 1974, and in 2009 he was inducted into the California Vintner's Hall of Fame. His books include *On Wine, Wine Journal, The Pleasures of Wine,* and *Vineyard Tales.*

Eric Asimov is the chief wine critic for the *New York Times.* He has held the post since 2004. He has written about wine for other publications including *Food & Wine* magazine, *Martha Stewart Living,* and *Sommelier Journal.*

Tony Aspler is an author, educator, and wine expert. He has written fifteen books on wine and food and was the wine columnist at the *Toronto Star* for twenty-one years. He now writes for a variety of publications on wine, among them *Wine Spectator, Decanter.com,* and *AppellationAmerica. com*, and is also the author of nine novels.

Joseph Bastianich is a restaurateur, chef, vintner, and author. He is coauthor, along with journalist and wine expert David Lynch, of *Vino Italiano.* Bastianich and business partner chef Mario Batali are responsible for numerous celebrated restaurants. In 2008, the James Beard Foundation awarded Bastianich and Batali with the Outstanding Restaurateur Award. Bastianich owns vineyards in Argentina and Italy.

Alexis Bespaloff's wine column ran in *New York* magazine from 1972 until 1996. His first book, *The Signet Book of Wine*, published in 1971, has sold more than a million copies. His other books include *Alexis Bespaloff's Guide to Inexpensive Wines* and *The Fireside Book of Wine.* He died in 2006.

Michael Broadbent is a British wine critic and author. He has written many books on wine, including *The Great Vintage Wine Book,* a reference book featuring tasting notes on more than 6,000 wines. He has been a regular contributor to *Vinum, Falstaff,* and *Decanter* magazines. He earned his Master of Wine title in 1960.

Molly Chappellet is the cofounder of Chappellet Winery located in St. Helena, Napa Valley, California. She is the author of three books: *The Romance of California Vineyards, Gardens of the Wine Country,* and *A Vineyard Garden* for which she was awarded a James Beard Foundation award.

Oz Clarke is the author of *The Essential Wine Book, Oz Clarke's New Classic Wines, Oz Clarke's Pocket Wine Book,* and, most recently, *Let Me Tell You About Wine,* among others. He has been the wine correspondent for the *London Daily Telegraph* newspaper and has appeared on several BBC wine programs.

Clive Coates is the author of *The Wines of France, Grands Vins: The Finest Chateaux of Bordeaux and their Wines,* and *Cote D'or: A Cele-bration of Great Wines of Burgundy,* among others. *Cote D'or* won the Veuve Clicquot Prize and the James Beard Foundation Award for Best Wine Book of the Year. Coates published his own fine wine magazine, *The Vine,* from 1984 to 2005.

Francis Ford Coppola is a film director, producer, and screenwriter. His most famous works include *The Godfather* films and *Apocalypse Now.* An accomplished vintner, Coppola owns Rubicon Estate Winery in Napa Valley and the Francis Ford Coppola Winery in Alexander Valley, California.

Joseph DeLissio has had over thirty years of experience as wine director at New York City's River Café. In 2000, he decided to share his wine knowledge and expertise with the public and wrote *The River Cafe Wine Primer.*

Mike DeSimone and Jeff Jenssen, also known as the World Wine Guys, are wine, spirits, food,

and travel writers. When not traversing the globe, they divide their time between their homes in New York City and southern Spain. Their articles and photographs have appeared in *Wine Enthusiast, Wine Spectator,* Saveur.com, *Sherman's Travel, International Living,* and *The European.* The duo regularly host wine tastings, including a recent one for the Washington, DC, diplomatic community at the Spanish Ambassador's Residence. In June of 2010, they were inducted into Les Piliers Chablisiens. Hobbies include chasing the harvest, stomping grapes, and dinner parties with winemakers and cellar masters.

Mary Ewing-Mulligan and Ed McCarthy are two wine lovers who met at an Italian wine tasting in New York City's Chinatown and subsequently merged their wine cellars and wine libraries when they married. They have since coauthored six wine books in the *Wine For Dummies* series (including two of their favorites, *French Wine For Dummies* and *Italian Wine For Dummies*) as well as their latest book, *Wine Style* (Wiley); taught hundreds of wine classes together; visited nearly every wine region in the world; run five marathons; and raised eleven cats. Along the way, they have amassed more than half a century of professional wine experience between them.

Christopher Fielden is the author of eleven wine-related books, including *The Wines of Chile, Argentina, and Latin America.* He was trustee of the Wine & Spirit Education Trust and is a past president of the Wine & Spirit Association. He boasts over forty-five years in the wine trade.

Michael Fridjhon, a leading expert and wine writer on South African wines, is the author of

The Penguin Book of South African Wines and a contributor to *The Complete Book of South African Wine* and *The Oxford Companion to Wine*. He is a regular contributor to *Wine & Spirit, Decanter,* and *Wine* magazines, among others.

Evan Goldstein is the author of *Perfect Pairings: A Master Sommelier's Practical Advice for Partnering Wine with Food* and coauthor of *Wine and Food Pairing*. His latest work is entitled *Daring Pairings: A Master Sommelier Matches Distinctive Wines with Recipes from His Favorite Chefs*. He passed the Master Sommelier exam in 1987. At the time, he was the youngest person to do so.

James Halliday is an Australian wine expert, author, and critic. He has written and coauthored more than forty books on wine including *James Halliday's Wine Atlas of Australia* and the annual *James Halliday Australian Wine Companion*. He is the co-founder of Brokenwood Winery in Hunter Valley and the owner of Coldstream Hills Winery in the Yarra Valley wine region of Australia. He has received many awards for his writing on wine including the James Beard Foundation Award in 1993 and 1994 and the Julia Child Award for Best Wine, Spirits or Beer book in 1994.

Andrew Jefford is the author of *The New France: A Complete Guide to Contemporary French Wine, One Hundred and One Things You Need to Know About Wine,* and *Andrew Jefford's Wine Course,* among others. He has won dozens of awards for his writing on wine, including eight Glenfiddich awards. He is a regular contributor to *Decanter* magazine.

Hugh Johnson is one of the greatest British wine experts, and has written numerous books on wine. His first, *Wine,* was published in 1966. He has since published volumes more, including *The World Atlas of Wine,* the first serious attempt to map out the world's wine regions. *Decanter* dubbed him 1995's Man of the Year and in 2007 he was made an Officer of the British Empire.

Steven Kolpan is the author of *A Sense of Place: An Intimate Portrait of Niebaum-Coppola Winery and the Napa Valley,* which was awarded the Versailles Award for Best American Wine Book in 2000. Kolpan is Professor and Chair of Wine Studies at the Culinary Institute of America and a contributing editor for *The Valley Table* and *Salon.com.*

Matt Kramer is a wine critic, author, and columnist whose work has appeared in the the *Portland Oregonian,* the *New York Sun,* and the *Los Angeles Times.* He is a regular contributor to *Wine Spectator.* Kramer is the author of six books, including: *Making Sense of Wine, Making Sense of Burgundy, Making Sense of California Wine,* and *Making Sense of Italian Wine.*

Alexis Lichine is the author of *Wines of France, Guide to the Wines and Vineyards of France,* and *Alexis Lichine's Encyclopedia of Wines and Spirits.* He was the founder and owner of Lichine & Cie, a leading exporter of fine wines. He owned several wineries, among them Château Prieure-Lichine, where he was the first winery owner to introduce wine tasting rooms for the public. In 1987, he was named Man of the Year by *Decanter* magazine. He died in 1989.

David Lynch is a writer and wine expert who served as senior editor of *Wine & Spirits* magazine. He is coauthor of *Vino Italiano: The Regional Wines of Italy*. Lynch served as wine director and, later, general manager for Mario Batali's and Joseph Bastianich's acclaimed New York restaurant Babbo. He is currently the wine director at Quince restaurant in San Francisco.

Kermit Lynch is the owner of Kermit Lynch Wine Merchant, a successful importing and retail outlet based in Berkeley, California. His book *Adventures on the Wine Route* garnered the distinction of the Veuve Clicquot Wine Book of the Year Award. He was named Wine Professional of the Year by the James Beard Foundation in 2000.

Karen MacNeil is a wine educator, author, television personality, and consultant. She is Chair of the Culinary Institute of America's Professional Wine Studies Program in Napa Valley, California, and is host of the televison program *Wine, Food & Friends with Karen Mac-Neil*. She is the author of *The Wine Bible* and in 2004 was recipient of the James Beard Foundation's Outstanding Wine and Spirits Professional Award. MacNeil is co-owner of Fife Vineyards located in Mendocino County, California.

Campbell Mattinson is an Australian writer and wine critic. His books include *Wine Hunter: The Man who Changed Australian Wine* and *Why the French Hate Us: The Fight to Save Australian Wine*. He has written for *SUNDAY* magazine and *Gourmet Traveller Wine* in Australia, and writes for and edits

The Wine Front, an independent, online wine review website.

Jay McInerney is an author and screenwriter whose first novel, *Bright Lights, Big City*, was published in 1984 to great acclaim. Other novels include *Ransom, Story of My Life, Brightness Falls,* and *Model Behavior*. McInerney has written about wine for *House & Garden* magazine. His essays on wine have been collected in *Bacchus and Me* and *A Hedonist in the Cellar*. He was awarded the James Beard Award for Distinguished Writing in 2006, and now writes for the *Wall Street Journal*.

Robert Mondavi founded the Robert Mondavi Winery in Oakville, California, in 1966. He was one of the most influential people in the industry, and was the mentor to many California winemakers. He was named *Decanter* magazine's Man of the Year in 1989. His autobiography, entitled *Harvests of Joy* was published in 1998. He died in 2008 at the age of 94.

Robert M. Parker Jr. is the founder of *The Wine Advocate,* for which he also writes. He is a contributing editor for *Food and Wine* magazine and writes a weekly column for *Businessweek*. He has been profiled in many American and European magazines and newspapers including *Time, Newsweek, Esquire, GQ,* the *Economist,* and the *New York Times*. He has written fourteen books on wine.

Frank J. Prial was wine columnist for the *New York Times* for twenty-five years, writing a weekly column until 2005. He is the author of several books on wine including *Wine Talk* and *Companion to Wine. Decantations*, published in

2001, is a collection of articles from his *Times* "Wine Talk" column.

John Radford is an award winning author on the subject of wine. His books include *The New Spain, The Wines of Rioja.* and *Cook Espana, Drink Espana.* He has won the Glenfiddich Award for Drinks Book of the Year and the Livre Gourmand Award for Best European Wine Book awards, among others. He writes about wine for a number of publications including *Harper's, Drinks International, Decanter,* and *Spain* magazines.

Peter Richards is an English writer, wine expert, and TV personality. He is the author of two wine books: *Wineries with Style* and *The Wines of Chile.* He is an international wine judge and a frequent contributor to the *Times Online* and *The Wine Report.* He holds regular TV and radio spots on the BBC.

Alan Richman is an author, journalist, and food correspondent for *GQ* magazine. Richman has won fourteen James Beard Foundation Awards for his wine and food writing. A collection of Richman's culinary essays were collected in his book, *Fork It Over: The Intrepid Adventures of a Professional Eater,* published in 2004.

Andrea Robinson is one of only sixteen women to have been appointed Master Sommelier. She was also the first woman to achieve the distinction in the United States. She is the author of *Great Wine Made Simple, Andrea Immer's Wine Buying Guide for Everyone, Great Tastes Made Simple,* and *Everyday Dining with Wine.* She is the host of her own television show *Pairings with Andrea* on the Fine Living TV Network.

Jancis Robinson is a British wine expert, author, and journalist. She began her wine writing career in 1975 when she worked as assistant editor of *Wine & Spirit* magazine. Since then, she has written and edited over a dozen books on wine. She edited *The Oxford Companion to Wine* and coauthored *The World Atlas of Wine.* In 1984, she became the first non-trade person to earn the Master of Wine title. She has won multiple Glenfiddich awards and a James Beard Foundation Award, among many others.

David Rosengarten is a journalist, TV personality, and author. He has written articles and recipes for publications such as *Gourmet,* the *New York Times,* and *Wine Spectator,* among others. He is editor of the Rosengarten Report, a newsletter that won the 2003 James Beard Award as America's Best Food and Wine Newsletter.

Neal Rosenthal is the cofounder and owner of Rosenthal Wine Merchant, a retail, importer, and distributor of fine wine and food products. He is the author of *Reflections of a Wine Merchant,* an autobiography of his life, explaining how he made is way up in the wine industry.

Baron Philippe de Rothschild, member of the Rothschild banking family, was also a successful vintner. He was head of his family's winery, Château Mouton Rothschild in Pauillac, France, and his business expanded with his purchase of the Château Clerc Milon in 1973 and the formation of the Opus One Winery in Oakville, California, with fellow vintner Robert Mondavi. Rothschild remained active in the wine business until his death in 1988.

Frank Schoonmaker is the author of *The Complete Wine Book* and *Frank Schoonmaker's Encyclopedia of Wine*. As an importer, Schoonmaker was influential in finding American markets for wines from small scale vineyards in Burgundy and helped to create a market for wines bottled by the winery as opposed to a separate merchant. Schoonmaker, along with fellow wine writer Alexis Lichine, introduced the practice of labeling wines according to their varietal names instead of varieties named after European regions.

Peter Sichel is a fourth generation wine grower and wine merchant, and an authority on German wine, often editing Frank Schoonmaker's writing on the subject. He ran the Blue Nun winery in Germany until selling it in 1995.

Joy Sterling is the CEO of Iron Horse Winery and the author of four books: *A Cultivated Life, Vintage Feasting, Vineyard: A Year in the Life of California Wine Country,* and *A Vintner's Guide to Red Wine*. Sterling gave up her post as Deputy Bureau Chief for ABC Network News in Los Angeles in 1985 to join her family's business at Iron Horse. She became CEO of the winery in 2006.

Tom Stevenson is a British author and wine expert. He is the author of twenty-three books, among them *The Sotheby's Wine Encyclopedia, Christie's World Encyclopedia of Champagne and Sparkling Wine,* and *The Wines of Alsace* which won the Veuve Clicquot Book of the Year Award in 1994. Stevenson has won the Wine Writer of the Year award three times and was a recipient of the distinguished Wine Literary Award.

Lettie Teague is a wine columnist for the *Wall Street Journal*, and former columnist for *Food & Wine* magazine where she also served as wine editor for twelve years. Teague won the M.F.K. Fisher Distinguished Writing Award from the James Beard Foundation in 2003, and is the author of *Educating Peter*, published in 2007.

Calvin Trillin, journalist, author, and raconteur has written for the *New Yorker* magazine since 1963. He has also written a column for *The Nation* magazine. He frequently writes about food and travel for his *New Yorker* articles, and his books include *Travels with Alice, Too Soon to Tell,* and *Family Man*.

Gary Vaynerchuk is the author of *Gary Vaynerchuk's 101 Wines: Guaranteed to Inspire, Delight, and Bring Thunder to Your World* and *Crush It!: Why Now Is the Time to Cash In on Your Passion*. He is co-owner and Director of Operations of The Wine Library, a wine store located in Springfield, New Jersey. Vaynerchuk is also the host of *Wine Library TV*, a video podcast on wine related topics.

Joshua Wesson is cofounder of the popular wine retail shop Best Cellars which opened its first store in New York City in 1996. Wesson was named Best Sommelier by French *Wine & Spirit* in 1984. He is a regular contributor to Public Radio's program *The Splendid Table* and has made numerous television appearances. He is coauthor of *Red Wine with Fish: The New Art of Matching Food with Wine*.

❧ CREDITS ❧

"The Power to Banish Care" extracted from THE STORY OF WINE written by Hugh Johnson, first published in 1998 by Mitchell Beazley, an imprint of Octopus Publishing Group Limited. Copyright © Octopus Publishing Group Ltd 1998 Text copyright © Hugh Johnson 1998.

"What Constitutes a Great Wine?" reprinted with the permission of Simon & Schuster, Inc., from PARKER'S WINE BUYER'S GUIDE, Seventh Edition, by Robert M. Parker, Jr. Copyright © 1995, 1999, 2002, 2008 by Robert M. Parker, Jr. All rights reserved.

Excerpt from *How to Taste: A Guide to Enjoying Wine* by Jancis Robinson reprinted with the permission of Simon & Schuster, Inc. Copyright © 2000 by Jancis Robinson. All rights reserved.

"American Names for American Wines," by Frank Schoonmaker, used with permission of Whitney I. Gerard, Executor, Estate of Frank Schoonmaker.

"Discover Grape Varieties" excerpt from *"Let Me Tell You About Wine"* Copyright © 2009 Anova Books, Text copyright © 2009 Oz Clarke.

Pages 23-26, 32-26 from *Crush It!* by Gary Vaynerchuk copyright © 2009 by Gary Vaynerchuk. Reprinted by permission of HarperCollins Publishers.

"Terroir" from *Reflections of a Wine Merchant* by Neal I. Rosenthal. Copyright © 2008 by Neal I. Rosenthal. Reprinted by permission of Farrar, Straus and Giroux, LLC.

"Silent Revolution" by Gerald Asher originally appeared in *The Pleasures of Wine* (Chronicle Books, 2002). Reprinted with permission.

Excerpt from *The River Café Wine Primer* by Joseph DeLissio copyright © 2000 by Joseph DeLissio. Reprinted with permission.

Excerpt from *Educating Peter: How Anybody Can Become An (Almost) Instant Wine Expert* by Lettie

Teague reprinted with the permission of Scribner, a Division of Simon & Schuster, Inc. Copyright © 2007 by Lettie Teague. All rights reserved.

"$25,000 Wine Week" by Alan Richman originally appeared in *Food & Wine*. Reprinted with permission.

"The Pour: Ancient Messages, Hidden In a Dusty Bottle From Long Ago" from the *New York Times*, © January 3, 2007, The *New York Times*. All rights reserved. Used by permission and protected by the Copyright Laws of the United States. The printing, copying, redistribution, or retransmission of the Material without express written permission is prohibited.

"The Red and the White"—Copyright © 2002 by Calvin Trillin. Originally appeared in *The New Yorker*. Included in *FEEDING A YEN* by Calvin Trillin. Published by Random House. Reprinted by permission of Lescher & Lescher, Ltd. All rights reserved.

"A Corking New Wine Theory" by Alexis Bespaloff originally appeared in *New York* Magazine, May 23, 1977. Reprinted with permission.

Excerpt from *Great Tastes Made Simple: Extraordinary Food and Wine Pairing For Every Palate* by Andrea Immer, copyright © 2002 by Andrea Immer. Used by permission of Broadway Books, a division of Random House, Inc.

Excerpt from *Daring Pairings: A Master Sommelier Matches Distinctive Wines With Recipes From His Favorite Chefs* by Evan Goldstein used by permission of University of California Press.

"The Great, the Bad, and the Average" from RED WINE WITH FISH by David Rosengarten and Joshua Wesson published by Simon & Schuster. Permission granted by David Rosengarten & Joshua Wesson copyright © 1989.

"What to Drink with Chocolate" reprinted by permission of International Creative Management, Inc. Copyright © 2007 by Jay McInerney.

Excerpt from *A Vineyard Garden* by Molly Chappellet reprinted with permission of the author.

"Taste" from HARVEST OF JOY, MY PASSION, MY LIFE, copyright © 1998 by Robert Mondavi, reproduced by permission of Houghton Mifflin Harcourt Publishing Company.

Excerpts from *Sense of Place: An Intimate Portrait of the Niebaum-Coppola Winery and the Napa Valley* by Steve Kolpan reprinted with permission of Routledge Publishing Inc., a division of Taylor & Francis Group LLC.

Excerpt from *Baron Philippe: The Very Candid Autobiography of Baron Philippe de Rothschild* by Joan Littlewood copyright © 1985 by Joan Littlewood. Used by permission of Crown Publishers, a division of Random House, Inc.

Excerpt from *A Cultivated Life* by Joy Sterling, copyright © 1993 by Joy Sterling. Used by permission of Villard Books, a division of Random House, Inc.

"Bordeaux" written by and published with the permission of Michael Broadbent.

Excerpt from Alexis Lichine's *Guide to the Wines and Vineyards of France* by Alexis Lichine, Copyright ©1979, 1982 by Alexis Lichine. Used by permission of Alfred A. Knopf, a division of Random House, Inc.

Excerpt from *The Wines of Burgundy* by Clive Coates used by permission of University of California Press.

Excerpt from "Southern Rhône" from *Adventures on the Wine Route* by Kermit Lynch. Copyright © 1988 by Kermit Lynch. Reprinted by permission of North Point Press, a division of Farrar, Straus and Giroux, LLC.

"Putting on the Style," excerpted from *World Encyclopedia of Champagne & Sparkling Wine*, copyright © Tom Stevenson, published by Absolute Press, 2003.

Excerpt from *Vino Italiano: The Regional Wines of Italy* by Joseph Bastianich and David Lynch, copyright © 2002, 2005 by Joseph Bastianich and David Lynch, Photographs copyright © 2002 by Alessandro Puccinelli. Used by permission of Clarkson Potter/Publishers, an imprint of the Crown Publishing Group, a division of Random House, Inc.

"Piedmont: A Land, a Grape, a People," written by and published with the permission of Mary Ewing-Mulligan and Ed McCarthy.

Excerpt from *Wines of Germany* by Frank Schoonmaker/Peter Sichel used by permission of Hastings House/Daytrips Publishers.

Extract from *The New Spain* written by John Radford, first published in 1998 by Mitchell Beazley, an imprint of Octopus Publishing Group Limited. Copyright © Octopus Publishing Group Ltd 1998. Text copyright © John Radford 1998.

"Postcard from Porto" written by and published with the permission of Mike DeSimone and Jeff Jenssen.

"The Day California Shook the World," by Frank Prial, used with permission of the *New York Times*, copyright © 2001.

"Napa Valley" excerpt from *The Wine Bible* copyright © 2001 by Karen MacNeil. Used by permission of Workman Publishing Co., Inc., New York. All Rights Reserved.

"Sonoma County" excerpt from *Matt Kramer's New California Wine* copyright © 2004 Matt Kramer. Reprinted by permission of Running Press, a member of the Perseus Books Group.

"Icewine" excerpt from *Vintage Canada: The Complete Reference to Canadian Wines* by Tony Aspler © 1999 McGraw-Hill Ryerson Ltd. Reprinted with permission of McGraw-Hill Ryerson Ltd.

"Argentina" excerpt from *The Wines of Argentina, Chile and Latin America* copyright © 2006, MITCH. Reprinted with permission.

Extract from *The Wines of Chile* written by Peter Richards, first published in 2006 by Mitchell Beazley, an imprint of Octopus Publishing Group Limited. Copyright © Octopus Publishing Group Ltd 2006. Text copyright © Peter Richards 2006.

Excerpt from *The Wine Atlas of Australia* by James Halliday used by permission of University of California Press.

"Penfolds: Australia's Greatest Wine?" excerpt from *Why the French Hate Us* published by Hardie Grant Books, Copyright © 2007 by Campbell Mattinson.

"A Recent Overview of the South African Wine Industry" reproduced with kind permission of Cheviot Publishing, from *The Essential Guide to South African Wines*.

⚜ INDEX ⚜

373